BLACK REVOLUTIONARY

Black Revolutionary

William Patterson and the Globalization of the African American Freedom Struggle

GERALD HORNE

UNIVERSITY OF ILLINOIS PRESS
URBANA, CHICAGO, AND SPRINGFIELD

© 2013 by the Board of Trustees
of the University of Illinois
All rights reserved

∞ This book is printed on acid-free paper.

Library of Congress Cataloging-in-Publication Data
Horne, Gerald.
Black revolutionary : William Patterson and the globalization of the
African American freedom struggle / Gerald Horne.
pages cm
Includes bibliographical references and index.
ISBN 978-0-252-03792-4 (hardcover : alk. paper) —
ISBN 978-0-252-07943-6 (pbk. : alk. paper) —
ISBN 978-0-252-09518-4 (e-book)
1. Patterson, William L. (William Lorenzo), 1890–1980.
2. Civil rights workers—United States—Biography.
3. Communists—United States—Biography.
4. African American lawyers—Biography.
5. African Americans—Civil rights—History—20th century.
6. African Americans—Segregation—History—20th century.
7. Civil rights movements—United States—History—20th century.
8. Scottsboro Trial, Scottsboro, Ala., 1931. I. Title.
E185.97.P32H67   2013
323.092—dc23   2013003510
[B]

CONTENTS

Introduction 1

1 The Road to Revolution 15
2 Moscow Bound 29
3 The World Confronts Jim Crow 41
4 Scottsboro—and Collapse 55
5 Back in the USSR 67
6 Black Chicago 79
7 Turning Point 93
8 Prison Looms 109
9 "We Charge Genocide" 125
10 "I Am a Political Prisoner" 141
11 The CP's "FBI Faction" Rises 157
12 Fighting Back 173
13 Patterson and Black Power 189
14 Death of a Revolutionary 207

Notes 219

Index 285

Illustrations follow page 92

BLACK REVOLUTIONARY

INTRODUCTION

William L. Patterson was determined.

It was December 17, 1951, and the bespectacled, balding, and somewhat burly black lawyer—and Communist—was in Paris on a historic mission. Following in the footsteps of Frederick Douglass, who repeatedly had taken the plight of the enslaved African to an international audience—particularly to London, Washington's prime antagonist and the citadel of abolitionism—Patterson was in Paris making a similar appeal, but this time to all nations organized within the United Nations: he was targeting his country's hateful Jim Crow system. Snow was falling softly, and the temperature was frigid, so he buttoned his coat as he strode hurriedly a few blocks to the Palais de Chaillot, stopping briefly for fortification at a restaurant on the East Bank of the Seine, where he had often eaten over the years. He had coordinated this campaign with Jacques Duclos of the French Communist party, who remembered Patterson's yeoman service in Western Europe in the anti-Nazi underground in the 1930s. With Duclos's assistance, he secured a hotel room near L'Opéra and conveniently near the American Express office.

At the eatery he espied and embraced Clarina Michelson, whom he had known in Boston in 1927, where he had arrived from his home in Manhattan in a vain attempt to halt the slated executions of the renowned political prisoners—and anarchists—Sacco and Vanzetti. They chatted briefly about his mission, which involved seeking global support for an indictment of U.S. authorities for "genocide" against African Americans. His relationship with her had deepened further when Patterson became the chief organizer to save the lives of the Scottsboro Nine—young black men falsely accused, then convicted of the rape of two white women and scheduled to be executed. There too a massive global crusade had stayed the hand of the executioners, providing the powerful lesson that global solidarity was the key to compelling a retreat of the U.S. authorities.

Finally he arrived at his destination, and it was there that an epochal divide was solidified in black America. At the Palais de Chaillot he encountered Channing Tobias, a fellow U.S. Negro who had been associated with the premier civil-rights organization, the National Association for the Advancement of Colored People (NAACP). Tobias was mightily displeased with Patterson's bold demarche. As Patterson recalled him, Tobias was a "handsome man more than six feet tall and with a beautiful head of grey hair and a light complexion." The irritated leader beckoned to Patterson and "without offering his hand or even so much as a how-do-you-do," Tobias said beseechingly, "'Why did you do this thing?'" As they engaged in a bitter philippic, they attracted the attention of a photographer who captured this historic moment when, symbolically, centrist and leftist Negroes divided and departed on separate paths.[1]

For as Tobias's presence in Paris well demonstrated, Washington was in the process of an agonized retreat from the more egregious aspects of Jim Crow, which would lead to the promotion to the highest levels of those like himself—but, like a seesaw, the price paid for this emolument was a fierce attack upon and imprisonment of those like Patterson, who had refused to accept the bargain offered (civil-rights concessions in return for backing away from militant internationalism). The decline of this militant left also involved a marginalizing of progressive trade unions,[2] which left an overwhelmingly working-class black community barely protected in an increasingly globalized economy, as middle-class elements like Tobias rose on the class ladder, even to the stratospheric climes of the official U.S. delegation in Paris.

But in December 1951, this outcome was not foreseen by most. Surely, it was not simple to predict that Patterson himself—theretofore viewed widely as a preeminent leader despite his Communist affiliation—would be subjected to a concerted campaign of ostracism that, by the time of his death in 1980, left a deep imprint on his public image. A few months before his fateful rendezvous with Tobias in Paris, his close friend and comrade Paul Robeson had announced what seemed obvious when he proclaimed, "I think that most of the people in the United States know the name of William Patterson."[3] Upping the ante, the *Baltimore Afro-American* referred to Patterson as "internationally famed."[4] The *Black Dispatch* of Oklahoma City concurred, adding that "like Robeson, he represents the unqualified thinking of black men, without reservations," embodying the "courage of William Monroe Trotter or Frederick Douglass."[5] At one juncture in his circuitous career, the celebrated novelist Ralph Ellison wrote of a continuum of Negro leadership that featured "Douglas/[Denmark] Vesey/[Booker T.] Washington/[W. E. B.] Du Bois"—and Patterson.[6] Yet what distinguished Patterson from these other leaders was not only his training—and skill—as an attorney, which gave him an opportunity to confront his opponents in the courtroom. He was also trained politically abroad (in Moscow) to confront his opponents. Such ties have virtually obliterated Patterson's contributions from the historical record, as historians have tended to impose contemporary views of radicalism upon the desperate plight of U.S. Negroes who decades ago could not afford to ignore Patterson's brand of leadership.[7]

Thus, when the centrists and leftists in black America split, it was not solely a function of pressure from on high upon the former. It was also a function of the NAACP in particular being able to gain a decisive advantage over those to their left, not least the organization headed by Patterson, the Civil Rights Congress (CRC). When the CRC was being formed in 1946, the NAACP's leader, Roy Wilkins, pointed out worriedly that "a number of our NAACP branches were represented"; thus, he warned, "we should watch very carefully" the CRC's activities," since it "carries a distinct threat to the Association's activities as a civil rights organization."[8] Strikingly, the top NAACP leader, Walter White, was informed that of the "resolutions adopted," there were "none of which one can particularly quarrel."[9] Tellingly, this did not bar the association from shunning and then battering what could have been a useful ally.

Ostensibly this was attributable in no small part to Patterson's and the CRC's ineffable ties to Communists, including those in Moscow. But it was also part of a process to redraw the boundaries of the political landscape to exclude those on the left. Otherwise, it would be hard to explain why the NAACP also chose to shun the Workers' Defense League—not very friendly to Moscow either but, as Wilkins pointed out, "closely identified with the Socialist Party,"[10] which too was not a fan of the Soviets (though the point was that it was disfavored in Washington, too). The NAACP even chose to boycott the popular congressman Vito Marcantonio of East Harlem,[11] though he was not a Communist—but he was decidedly of the left.

This centrist capitulation only won limited concessions, however. For even Negro anticommunists, such as the labor leader A. Philip Randolph, were treated roughly abroad—not unlike how Patterson was mishandled. In the pivotal year of 1951, Randolph limited his stay in London to seven days, as one black journalist put it, after being submitted to "rigid questioning" and being "treated little better than William Patterson."[12] Mutual anticommunism was insufficient to transcend racism, and anticommunism alone was insufficient to explain why Patterson and his CRC were hounded by those with which it held numerous principles in common.

The centrist NAACP leadership did not seem to realize, however, that their participation in the isolation of those to their left not only weakened the overall struggle for equality—Patterson would have been overjoyed if his CRC had aid from the NAACP in Paris—but also left Wilkins's organization itself exposed as the target of choice on the left, after Patterson was jailed in 1954.

This split dramatized in Paris was not foreordained. Still, a fatal point was reached just before this French encounter when the NAACP's most dynamic and intellectually gifted leader, Charles Hamilton Houston—a Harvard-trained attorney and mentor of the future Supreme Court justice Thurgood Marshall—died prematurely. Houston's admiring biographer concedes that he rejected the NAACP's proliferating anticommunism and "saw himself closer to some of the positions espoused" by those like Patterson.[13] Houston, who was quite friendly with Patterson,[14] acknowledged that his friend's contribution to the cause of freedom was immense, notably in the Scottsboro case, where the Communist-led

International Labor Defense "made this oppression of the Negro a world-wide issue" while "exposing the weakness of the NAACP approach [in] that its active fighting is confined to a few top leaders." Thus, the ILD "set a new standard for agitation for equality"—a standard that deeply influenced this paragon of NAACP jurisprudence.[15]

And even for those like Patterson, presumed recipients of the fabled "Moscow gold," the issues were not so clear, particularly given that nineteenth-century abolitionists were said to be recipients of "London gold."[16] The situation in the United States was so unforgiving and hostile to the Negro that external aid of various sorts was a veritable prerequisite for progress. It was shortly after the liquidation of the CRC that Patterson gravely pronounced that "the Negro people have no white allies in the USA in the sense to which this term is used," though optimistically he said that such a partnership had "existed" in the "Reconstruction Era." Instead, he opined that "what is of the greatest political significance is the moral condemnation of the racist practices of the rulers of America by the Asian, African, and Eastern European peoples."[17] But it was these to which Patterson with his Communist ties had organic connections and which the NAACP had shunned purposely, though it was precisely this force that proved decisive in the struggle to erode Jim Crow.

In November 1950, while seeking—futilely—to save the lives of Negro prisoners in Martinsville, Virginia, Patterson sought, per usual, to leverage the substantial global support that anti–Jim Crow advocates received abroad: the international community, he asserted, "cannot understand why the progressive white people of the U.S. permit the persecution by government to continue."[18]

As we bask in the glow of the postapartheid era, it is easy to forget how horrid things were in the United States and how steep the climb from the nadir was. It was in 1960 that the Cuban Communist leader Blas Roca remarked in words that were hard to contradict that "twenty million North American Negroes are in a situation that is in many respects worse than that suffered by millions in Latin America."[19] The year before, *Dissent,* a journal that styled itself as being on the left in the United States, published a piece that actually backed legal restrictions on interracial marriage, and six years later polls revealed that 90 percent of Euro-Americans—and 97 percent of this group in Dixie—were opposed to anyone in their family marrying across the color line.[20] Given such encrusted attitudes, it was almost mandatory that an external force was needed to explode the inured innards of Jim Crow.

Besides, this grave concern for material aid from abroad to the beleaguered of the United States was, unsurprisingly, not viewed as negatively by the beleaguered themselves. The renowned Negro economist Abram Harris in 1926 was remarkably complacent about the notion that black Communists might be getting Moscow gold. "If the servant is worthy of his hire, he expects remuneration for his labor whether performed in behalf of the Rotary Club or directed toward organizing Negroes for the class struggle. It is of little concern to me," he concluded dismissively, that Negroes' "radical proclivities led [them] to barter with the Communists instead of seeking possibly more lucrative hire with the Rotarians." Anyway, this issue of Moscow gold was "irrelevant," since it was "evident" that Negro radicalism "could [not] have come to pass merely because Soviet Russia or some of its missionaries bade it." No, he insisted, "not Soviet gold but social facts furnish the explanation" for this leftward turn.[21] Decades later, as Patterson was about to decamp to Paris, the similarly renowned journalist J. A. Rogers, after observing that the Communist leader and those of a similar outlook such as Robeson and Du Bois "have seemingly come to see Russia's attack on injustice to American Negroes as the most effective solution," added sagely that "peoples for long have been helping others from the outside," as when "France jumped in here during the Revolutionary War."[22]

Although there was much gnashing of teeth about Patterson's ties to Moscow—including his extended stay in the city—Washington sought a similar alliance during the Second World War when it found itself under threat. Certainly, before the rise of the Scottsboro case in 1931—the turning point for the erosion of Jim Crow[23]—black America was writhing in a unique agony that required ever more desperate remedies. In November 1930, the NAACP leader Walter White sent to President Herbert Hoover a detailed list of twenty-five lynchings from previous months—and a like number barely prevented.[24] This was a follow-up to a letter White had sent days earlier, requesting a "brief interview for discussion of a plan" to halt the "recent alarming increase in lynching." In those baneful days, White lamented disconsolately that "to date we have had neither a reply nor an acknowledgment."[25] Hardly attracting attention was the fatal beating of S. S. Mincey, a Negro leader in Georgia of Hoover's own GOP, brought to the White House's attention by another Negro leader—Benjamin Davis Sr., the father of the soon-to-be Communist leader Ben Davis Jr.[26]

Then Scottsboro hit the nation—and, more importantly, the world—with a crushing left hook. In March 1932 alone, "in the names of three hundred thousand workers in Germany," came a stinging protest of this frame-up.[27] From Washington's listening post in Riga, Latvia, Felix Cole informed the secretary of state days earlier that "the campaign carried on in Soviet Russia for the liberation of the Negro defendants at Scottsboro is being conducted on a very large scale"—which, if anything, was an understatement.[28] Weeks later, in volatile Beirut, the U.S. consulate was attacked, windows were broken, and, said the consul, a note was attached "to the door [that] protested the execution of the Negroes involved in the Scottsboro affair."[29] One of the earliest protests emerged in Johannesburg.[30] This fierce protest gave succor to African Americans, who realized they were not alone,[31] while it helped to convince U.S. rulers that an atrocious Jim Crow was complicating the effective execution of foreign policy, thus jeopardizing national security. As a U.S. consul in Germany put it, "[T]he attention being focused on the Scottsboro case is due to the desire of the Soviet regime to get itself into favor in the United States with the Negroes," since "prominent Soviet leaders [feel] that the Negro is their most sure and their most easy approach" to the neighborhoods of the budding superpower.[32] Even in the midst of denouncing his Communist antagonists, Roy Wilkins conceded that "through their international connections they made Scottsboro a household word throughout the world," which was a renewed trend in the centuries-long struggle of black America.[33]

It was during Patterson's leadership of the Scottsboro campaign that the globalization effort reached its apex. It was also a time when the defendants scored some of their most significant victories, in the face of constant bickering with the NAACP. Yet the sentiment of the defendants themselves was captured in 1932 when they were heard singing in their cells: "I looked over yonder and what did I see [/] Comin' for to carry me home? Mr. William Patterson and the ILD [/] Comin' for to carry me home."[34]

Patterson and the Communist-backed International Labor Defense had the global connections that besieged African Americans needed so desperately—and which could have benefited the NAACP. More to the point—and quite unusually—Patterson had been trained in Moscow, arriving shortly after his vanguard role in Sacco-Vanzetti protests in Boston and residing there for a few years to the point where his fluency in the language was such that he informed inquiring U.S. adjudicators, "I wouldn't starve in a . . . country where Russian is spoken." It was in 1929—"to the best of my recollection," he added—that he married a Soviet woman of Jewish descent in Moscow. "I had two children"—both daughters—"and the marriage was terminated by divorce . . . to the best of my recollection it was 1937," after she initiated a divorce.[35] "She thought it would be harmful to my work," said Patterson, "if in the face of racism in the USA, she came to live with me here."[36]

Patterson's training in Moscow was even more significant, as it reflected a Pan-African initiative. Benjamin Gitlow, a founder of the U.S. Communist party who then denounced this organization, was not far wrong when he acknowledged that the Communist International, based in Moscow, "hoped through a Negro minorities movement in the United States to give leadership to a colored nationalist movement of world proportions in the countries of South and Central America, Africa, Asia, and the Antipodes. The American Nationalist Negro movement, Moscow believed, would provide the leadership for such a world movement."[37] Thus, Patterson spent a considerable amount of time in Cuba in the 1930s,[38] while his work in Europe was heavily in Hamburg with seafarers, many of them of African descent. Patterson's rapid rise in radical circles was spectacular—but it also bespoke a kind of affirmative action, whereby Communists were keen to promote leadership emerging from the most degraded sector of the proletariat. Gitlow argued that "Negro Communists were actually accorded special privileges."[39]

Patterson was born—probably—in August 1891 in San Francisco. His grandmother was born on the Galt (or Gault) plantation near Norfolk, Virginia (presumably connected to Edith Bolling Galt, the spouse of President Woodrow Wilson). Her white slave-owner was also a rapist "husband" to her. Through dint of hard work—and exhibiting a flair for sports, notably the pugilistic arts—Patterson made it through the University of California, including the law school, becoming one of a few Negro attorneys. By the early 1920s he was earning a princely salary of eight thousand dollars per year in Manhattan. It was then that the Sacco-Vanzetti case captured his attention, and he made it to Boston in 1927, which, he recalled later, was "inflamed into a state of hysteria," as "none of us knew when the mob might fall on us. It was a tense and dangerous week." He was impacted profoundly by this experience in the trenches, and upon returning to Manhattan he resigned from his law practice. "I joined the Communist Party and went down to the International Labor Defense," an allied grouping, "and offered them my life."[40]

Soon he was off to Moscow, where he communed with the son of a Chinese leader, whom he called "General Chiang kai Shek," and a niece of the Indian leader Pandit Nehru. "I formed a habit," said the physically fit Patterson, "of getting up early and walking," as "time and time again I walked around the Kremlin."[41] Patterson received a political education in Moscow before returning to his homeland just in time to take over the Scottsboro campaign. But—at least according to the FBI—by 1934 he was back in Europe, where he served as "a member of the Communist Underground in Germany" until 1937,[42] as the Nazis surged to power. He was in and out of Hamburg and Paris frequently and confessed primly to government interrogators that during his years abroad, "I took some classes at the Sorbonne but I didn't attend school regularly"—"just to enhance my knowledge," he added modestly. And, yes, "[I] spent several days at the University of Berlin, I lectured before a group of English-speaking Africans and Americans," and, yes, he made it to Halle for a "meeting." He earlier attended the Second Congress of the Anti-Imperialist League in Frankfurt; he was there "four or five days"—but only as "an observer," mind you. Yes, "I may have spoken," he conceded.[43]

Thus, Patterson had a depth of experience—including spine-tingling moments that brought an uncommon maturity—that soared beyond that of his contemporaries. An acquaintance of his, Mollie Moon (who was married to Henry Moon, who later served as an NAACP leader), was in Berlin in 1933, just before Patterson was thought to have arrived there. She was there on Wednesday May 10, the "great day," she said with bizarre brio, "for burning of all books on communism and sex." These "included all the Negro books such [as] James Weldon Johnson, [Countee] Cullen, [and Langston] Hughes," as "Hitler says they didn't want to encourage the Negro problem." Wildly unlike Patterson, her fellow U.S. Negro, she added, "I admire their nationalism, we need more of it."[44] Though often overlooked, a yawning chasm often separated the center and left in black America on potent foreign-policy matters beyond Moscow.

Returning from Europe, Patterson moved to Chicago, which at the time had one of the more significant Negro memberships in the Communist party, including the novelist Richard Wright, whom he befriended—a relationship that survived the writer's rocky relations with the Reds.[45] It was there that he married Louise Thompson, an activist and Communist in her own right who, like her spouse, was an indelible part of the fabric of black America. As early as 1934, the NAACP journal announced that "Miss Thompson is the leading colored woman in the Communist movement in this country."[46] In 1989, their close friend, the eminent actor and playwright Ossie Davis, recalled that "Louise had the opportunity to work with some of the foremost Black artists, including: Langston Hughes, Zora Neale Hurston, Arna Bontemps, Alice Childress, Aaron Douglas, Beah Richardson, Theodore Ward and Augusta Savage,"[47] all of which was useful to her and her various campaigns. Davis could have added that Beah Richards, who received an Oscar nomination for her role in the paradigmatic film *Guess Who's Coming to Dinner* (costarring Sidney Poitier) and for years was a Hollywood luminary, resided for a number of years in the Pattersons' Harlem abode—and was fingered as a Red herself by a stool pigeon.[48] Part of Patterson's influence with artists stemmed from his deep and ramified friendship with Robeson, who in turn impacted numerous artists. When asked in the 1970s if he were the "principal influence in the development of Paul's thinking," Patterson responded accurately, "I believe I was. Paul said that more than once."[49]

This circle of artists included the eminent writer and expatriate Julian Mayfield. By his own admission, he was in "awe" of Patterson. Once, in the early 1950s, Patterson hopped into the taxi Mayfield was driving to supplement his income, headed toward the East Side of Manhattan to the residence of his fellow CP leader Henry Winston. When they arrived, Patterson inquired about the fare. "He must have thought I was an idiot," said Mayfield, "because when we got there I couldn't answer. Like any normal young man I was already planning to tell my friends about the 'conversation' I had just had with William L. Patterson."[50]

Patterson and Thompson were also a significant influence on Langston Hughes, as his biographer noted that this justly popular writer "repeatedly . . . solicited their opinions [and] obviously valued them."[51] The larger point was that black Communists continued to wield influence even during the valleys of the Red Scare.

In Chicago, Patterson solidified an essential characteristic of his organizing: forging an alliance with black business and the black affluent more generally, a tie that was animated by his own ability to forge commonalities when none were apparent. October 1939 found him at a banquet in celebration of the first anniversary of the Golden State Mutual Life Insurance Company, where, he observed, "a cross-section of Negro life was present. There were insurance men, newspaper men, doctors, lawyers, and businessmen." He stressed that "economically, politically, culturally, we are forcibly and tyrannically held back whether we be businessmen, professionals, politicians, or what not. We are bound by common ties of persecution"—and thus they had a basis for uniting.⁵² But by December 1951 this united front had been disrupted, as those with whom he had connected in Chicago twelve years earlier were induced to break relations with him.

This break did not include a man widely regarded as the most prominent Negro businessman in Chicago of that era, Earl Dickerson.⁵³ Dickerson continued to ally with Patterson even after the destruction of the center-left alliance, and through him Patterson met the man who came to symbolize the black affluent—John H. Johnson of the Ebony-Jet publishing empire, whose initial ventures were staffed heavily by talented Communist writers, a number of whom were close to Patterson.⁵⁴ It was in 1939 that Johnson made one of his first ventures into print when he took to the pages of a local Communist publication edited by Patterson to assert that "public ownership means [the] nickel fare"—and to praise Dickerson.⁵⁵ In mid-1944, the *Chicago Defender*—a major press organ among African Americans—reported an astonishing spurt in national CP membership:"[O]f the 24,000 new members recruited, one third, 8,000, were Negroes," while in their corner of Illinois, a "Chicago businessman, L. C. Fox, had brought in 55 members, most of them Negro professional people."⁵⁶ Some of this crew accompanied Patterson when he and Dickerson met for an hour with the chewing-gum magnate and leader of the Chicago Cubs baseball franchise, William Wrigley, about the desegregation of the sport, which followed shortly thereafter.⁵⁷

Patterson's Communist party soared to new heights during the antifascist war of the 1940s, which engendered a fierce counterreaction when the conflict ended. Even before August 1945, omens had appeared. Claude McKay, the Jamaican writer, too had spent time in Moscow, but by 1940 he was in full retreat from his earlier stances and warned brusquely about what he saw as a strategy of some Negroes—like Patterson—to "rally to the Communists," as "they imagine that they can use the threat of Communism among Negroes to wring concessions from major political parties." Yet he saw this approach as a "grave internal danger to the Negro minority," since "other minority groups and weak and subject nations have invited disaster by pursuing such a policy," pointing to the "Armenians in Turkey" as evidence: genocide had been their cruel fate.⁵⁸

Blissfully dismissive of McKay's admonition, by 1948 Patterson had returned to Manhattan to assume the helm of the Civil Rights Congress—which was to forcefully charge Washington with genocide in Paris a few years later. The CRC was a successor of sorts to the ILD, but in a more challenging environment. In 1950, a familiar scene unfolded in Washington, D.C.: Patterson was hauled before Congress to be badgered by Dixiecrats about his Communist ties and aggressiveness toward Jim Crow. But this episode deteriorated dangerously, as one notably boisterous lawmaker deployed racist epithets. The epithets were nothing unusual, but Patterson's response was: as a nearby officer nervously fingered his weapon, Congressman Henderson Lanham of Georgia lunged at the startled witness with mayhem in mind. "I would have killed him had he hit me!" Patterson asserted. A heavy water pitcher was within reach, and the former boxer declared that he would not "have hesitated to use it." A Negro journalist was not far wrong when he proclaimed that "blood barely missed staining the halls of Congress."[59] When the white Communist leader Junius Scales spoke of his trial—from the Forsyth County jail in his native North Carolina—he termed it "the most legal, well-mannered lynching bee in recent history." Patterson was not as lucky in his confrontation with the authorities, perhaps suggesting a racist difference in how Communists were treated.[60]

Given such intimations of violence, it was fortunate that Patterson exercised regularly. He once told an FBI informant who offered him a drink as a prelude to a discussion after a laboriously cloistered meeting, "Drink? Well, I drink milk and other things. I don't touch any of the other stuff. I would be very glad to take a walk around the block with you and we can talk. That way we can get a little fresh air and a little exercise after these many hours in here." He was unusually well prepared for confrontation.[61]

This bruising congressional encounter was a facet of the effectiveness of the Civil Rights Congress under Patterson's leadership, a so-called Communist front[62] that was spearheading numerous campaigns against racist and political repression at a moment when the cold war had grown scorching hot in Korea. Many were having a hard time understanding why the nation should shed blood and treasure profusely abroad to crush Communists, while allowing the likes of Patterson to broadcast what was coming to be seen as a subversive message at home. Yet because of his fearlessness in defending the Scottsboro Nine and networking adroitly across class lines in black America, he had established a firm foothold that could only be disrupted by accompanying the smashing of the radical left that he symbolized with an assortment of civil-rights concessions garlanded on his erstwhile centrist allies. It was more than coincidence that by 1954 he was wasting away in federal prison as the high court chose to find Jim Crow unconstitutional.[63]

Yet the seeds he had planted continued to sprout. When the centrist Negro writer Saunders Redding visited India in the 1950s, he was confronted repeatedly by angry students waving Patterson's "Genocide" petition like a truncheon.[64] Though behind bars in 1954, Patterson sensed that the epochal changes erupting all about—the step away from Jim Crow in the United States, for example—was driven by such global pressure.[65] More than virtually any other analyst—even others on the left—Patterson interpreted the retreat from Jim Crow in 1954 as a result, in the first place, of global forces.[66]

Patterson's reflections about global support were not empty theorizing; they were drawn from his own experience. When in 1950 he was seeking to save the lives of young Negroes known as the Martinsville Seven, he found "widespread indignation in every country of the world" over their proposed execution; there were "1,024 resolutions adopted by trade unions, collective farms, city councils and all kinds of organizations" from Europe alone.[67] When yet another Negro, Willie McGee, was being threatened with execution in Mississippi during the same time, protest in France particularly was intense; the story was in the news on a virtual daily basis,[68] largely thanks to Patterson. When Jim Crow abuse retreated, it was in large part a capitulation in the face of global pressure.

The centrists and their patrons in Washington may have had a decisive advantage at home, but abroad such was not the case. The problem for black America was that these domestic concessions were easier to grant to those who aspired to be Ivy League professors, like Redding, or Supreme Court justices, like Thurgood Marshall, but ever harder to allocate to the broader black working class, whiplashed by racism at home and cheap-labor competition abroad.

As for Patterson, after the compelled liquidation of the CRC in 1956, he performed various leadership functions for the CP, while continuing to retain a broad array of contacts in black America, thereby foiling his foes who assumed that this more open Red affiliation would make him radioactive. For 1956 was also the year of destiny, when revelations about the past crimes of the Soviet leadership were unveiled, causing disarray in the United States. Membership plummeted. The talented poet Bob Kaufman, a well-known activist, reputedly averred that when he joined the CP in the aftermath of the 1956 bombshells, he could hardly get in the door past the crowd of people rushing to exit.[69] But this rush of humanity decidedly did not include Patterson—not to mention other Negro comrades, such as Ben Davis.[70] Not only did they have fewer options, though both were skilled lawyers and orators; they also had fewer illusions about the beneficence of the country of their birth and realized that the radical sword should not be sheathed. Surely, Patterson knew more than most that—not unlike the halcyon days of the Scottsboro case—Moscow continued to place pulsating pressure on Washington's Achilles heel, Jim Crow, which was useful to the erosion of this atrocious system.[71]

The fateful year of 1956 also witnessed the triumph of the Montgomery bus boycott and a new stage in the struggle against Jim Crow. But examining this tumult after its apparent success, Ralph Matthews—a columnist for a popular Negro newspaper—had his doubts: "With all its dramatic import, the historic bus boycott . . . never reached the proportions or gained the support of world opinion as the Scottsboro case. . . . [B]ecause present day leadership has rejected either aid or comfort from the international radical elements, their movement [has] been reduced to purely domestic agitation. All the rest of the world knows of these struggles is fed to them through the accepted and orthodox news gathering media which seldom arouse the emotions or militancy in lands—[like] the Red network was able to do." He wondered if the trade-off—the bludgeoning of the left in return for civil-rights concessions—was worth it. "History now in the making," he mused, "will determine whether this renunciation of international support was a gain or loss." Implicit in his farsighted remarks was the notion that white supremacy was so ingrained in the United States that weighty global forces were necessary to erode it. Domestic forces were insufficient—and, at that juncture, only the organized left had the necessary global network.[72]

Moreover, despite its weakened condition, the CP was far from being nugatory. The Federal Bureau of Investigation concurred, particularly in early 1959, when their ubiquitous bloodhounds captured Ben Davis recounting that the "grandfather" of Dr. Martin Luther King Jr. and Davis's "father were close friends politically in Georgia." When King visited Manhattan recently, Davis saw him and "talked to him," and the cleric was "very friendly" and knew of his record—including his imprisonment on thought-control charges. After King had been stabbed by a deranged woman in New York, barely escaping death, it was Davis and another Communist leader who "each contributed a pint of blood for King and started others contributing"—confirming the bureau's assessment that the pastor's lifeblood was red in every sense.[73]

Patterson's and Davis's relationships with a strategically important African American community did not magically disappear simply because U.S. elites decreed in the 1950s that some of the more awful aspects of Jim Crow should be deep-sixed—at least formally. Howard Fast, the prolific writer, once shared a trench with Patterson—"I joined the Communist Party in 1943," he said—before shedding this affiliation in February 1957, shattered by the news about Josef Stalin. Yet he still allowed that though "numerically the Communist Party of the United States was insignificant," it remained the "Communist Party of the most powerful nation on earth and therefore it had importance beyond its size or effectiveness."[74] This was sufficient reason for Patterson not to desert his battle station, but the perceptive Fast also acknowledged that "one of [the] fine glories of the Communist Party of the United States was that we fought and often died for black freedom, and the truth that nobody much remembers is that in the very early years of the struggle for civil rights, we were at the side of the blacks and precious few others who were not black were there with us. There is enough to be said against the party, but it's wrong to wipe out all the brave and wonderful things we did." Continuing in this vein, the man who revived the legend of Spartacus as a leader of slave rebellion referred to Patterson as an "extraordinary man, a close friend" who "could have been a millionaire token black but chose his own road, to be a civil rights leader in the days when the civil rights struggle had just begun, led—indeed, undertaken from scratch—by the Communists, in particular the black Communists."[75]

Of course, working in the highest reaches of the CP in the 1950s was no crystal stair, not least for one like Patterson. As is now well known, the party had been penetrated at the highest levels by Washington's agents, and they were adroit in blocking his ambitious plans, particularly those that spelled black freedom. Thus, in 1957 he met with the CP's leading international representative, Morris Childs,[76] who also happened to be the authorities' main agent within the ranks—and who spent an inordinate amount of time kneading Patterson's capacious plans into curlicue knots. They were in the basement of CP headquarters in Lower Manhattan on a summer day when Patterson indicated that—assuming he could get a passport (not a given)—he would like to tour Latin America to rally support for U.S. Negroes. With bureaucratic deftness, Childs replied that such a journey would require discussions with and permission from the "entire leadership" of the CP and that, besides, it might be dangerous. Childs took careful note of Patterson's idea of obtaining funds from Eastern Europe for such a venture, as the plan was suffocated in embryo.[77] Nevertheless, Patterson continued to push aggressively for global support for the unfolding civil-rights movement in the face of Childs's bureaucratic jujitsu and FBI interference.[78]

In any case, during the tumultuous 1960s, when the Communists were thought to be sidelined, the U.S. authorities had reason to question whether this perception applied to Patterson: he played a critical role in a radicalizing process that was symbolized by the rise of the Black Panther party and the campaign to free the young Communist Angela Davis. It was in 1967, just after their founding, that he confessed to "meetings and talks with the Panthers which for me fall into priority category politically, ideologically, organizationally, and programmatically."[79] In 1969 he dusted off his legal credentials and joined the legal-defense team of the BPP founder Huey P. Newton.[80] The BPP returned the favor when its journal referred to Patterson glowingly as a "crack warrior, strategist, and organizer of Black liberation and working class movements."[81] And when Professor Davis was arrested by the FBI shortly thereafter in Manhattan, it was Patterson—then about eighty years old—who called his comrade, the longtime CP attorney John Abt. Abt and Patterson hurried to the Women's House of Detention—a "high-rise sooty brick [building resembling] nothing so much as a medieval fortress," as Abt recalled. "I went with [Patterson] in the middle of the night to try to meet with Angela," but "the authorities would not allow our visit." Undeterred and reviving the technique he had honed in the 1930s in the Scottsboro case, Patterson charged back into yet another winning campaign, involving impassioned advocacy inside the courtroom and spirited organizing beyond this narrow confinement—particularly overseas, where black allies were to be found in profusion. Many of these allies had their own scores to settle with Washington—a potent point that the centrists did not seem to comprehend.

And what of Patterson's ultimate vision, his socialist project? After all, he was a self-proclaimed revolutionary who sought to abolish capitalism and install socialism in a step-by-step process that involved the continuous struggle for expansion of democratic rights. As he saw things, capitalism as it evolved in the United States had been grounded in a racist slavery and Jim Crow and in order for justice—not only economically but also politically and culturally—to arrive for the beleaguered Negro, this system had to be extirpated root and branch. Was this project invalid insofar as it involved an alliance with a Soviet Union that now has disappeared? I think not—unless one argues that Washington's own alliance with Moscow during the 1941–45 era, which was instrumental in defeating a larger foe, is similarly invalid. In any case, a key element in the downfall of the Soviet Union was a U.S. alliance with China, whose human-rights record was comparable to Moscow's during its bleakest days—yet that successful alliance stirred little concern during the time and hardly does now. Instead, "Nixon to China" has become a catch phrase for a diplomatic masterstroke across the U.S. political spectrum[82]—though the payoff to Beijing was massive foreign direct investment that bids fair to allow this Communist-ruled nation to surpass its erstwhile ally, an ironic conclusion to the cold war.[83] Arguably, the nation might be better off today if Patterson's path of amity toward Moscow had been followed. And though Patterson—unlike some Reds—was never accused of espionage, U.S. patriots need to acknowledge that just as Nelson Mandela's African National Congress owed no allegiance to an illegitimate apartheid state and was justified in collaborating with Moscow, Jim Crow was similarly illegitimate and certainly required a like amount of obeisance.

As the United States endures what might very well be a Great Recession, featuring skyrocketing unemployment, new forms of racism and sexism, and repetitive military conflict, it is well past time to revisit the road not taken—the road advocated by William L. Patterson.

1

The Road to Revolution

"The story of [William Lorenzo Patterson]," said the writer, Mike Gold, was "like a tale told by some American Gorky."[1] No, said another analyst, "his full-life story reads like an epic tale told by a Dreiser or a Tolstoy."[2]

This man of legend was born in San Francisco on August 29, 1891 (or thereabouts—his birth records perished during the 1906 earthquake). His mother was born a slave in Virginia, and his father was born in St. Vincent, a small Caribbean island. He graduated from Mt. Tamalpais High School in Marin County in 1911 and the Hastings College of Law in San Francisco in 1919.

Yet this bare outline of his early biography fails to capture the characteristics that defined him. "My great grandfather had undoubtedly full knowledge of the uprising led by Gabriel Prosser" in 1800, he said, a revolt that "contemplated" the "capture of Richmond," headquarters of the slaveholding class.[3] His father had been born on an island that early on established a heroic reputation in its fierce confrontation with European colonizers.[4] James Patterson was born in St. Vincent on August 5, 1872. James's father, Jacob Patterson, was a "labourer," while his mother—Eliza Laurent Patterson—had no listed occupation.[5] Jacob Patterson's mother was said to be an indigenous Carib, and his father, said William Patterson, was a "full-blooded African"; it was this combination that fought the colonizers so heroically. Like his son, James Patterson "seemed to know little about his mother and even less about his father." James Patterson was a sailor and cook who "made a fortune," reportedly "smuggling Chinese coolies," which allowed him to settle in San Francisco at 717 Mason Street, near the "Chinese quarter" and what was called the Barbary Coast, a "notorious red-light district." But the merchant marine did not long hold the elder Patterson's fancy, for once he was swept overboard in the Indian Ocean and attributed his survival to "God's mercy." This "loner," as his son described him, chose to devote his remaining years to missionary work, giving away his wealth to the Seventh-Day Adventist church. James Patterson had little formal education, though his Spanish was better than his English (and he spoke French and German as well). Described by his son as a "mystic," he eventually left his family and the United States for good and established a dental practice in the Panama Canal Zone. He died in 1922.

"I never learned to love my father," said Patterson. "I never hated him either," though "the passion with which he beat us children when he believed we had failed properly to observe some religious tenet was frightening." These "punishments made an indelible impression upon my thinking and especially my attitude toward religion." Thus, strikingly, "I found nothing in his life's work or family relations with which I could identify." "To me, he was a lost soul," and thus, "I condemned the society in which he lived and not him." William Patterson was forced to adopt an objective view of the nation, as opposed to a subjective view of individuals.[6]

Similarly, Patterson belatedly recognized that "not until quite late in my youth did I come to realize that in a spiritual sense I had never known my mother." This "lack of close contact," he confessed, "retard[ed] me in my long struggle to find identity with those of my own people." Nevertheless, she "talked to us about her childhood on the Virginia plantation where she was born," not far from Norfolk. She knew little of her father, an enslaved African on an adjacent plantation toiling as a coachman for his master—who was also his father. It was while driving his father back and forth on visits to the Turner plantation that William Galt came to meet Elizabeth Mary Turner, the enslaved woman who was to become his spouse and Patterson's maternal grandmother; she was a personal maid to the white wife of her father and mother. "Her mother," said Patterson "was head of the house slaves and her owner's slave woman," while "my mother's grandmother lived among the field slaves" and cooked. "She was an attractive woman," he continued, "and as the story goes the master found more than her cooking to his taste. She became the mother of his three slave children"—though, typically, his wife knew of this illicit relationship with the family cook.

Patterson's mother, Mary, was ten years old when her grandfather sent his black children westward to the Golden State. Patterson's grandfather, along with the legendary Mammy Pleasant, organized anti-Confederate forces during the Civil War (the "California Zouaves") who were honored subsequently for their heroism. By 1865, five U.S. Negroes were appointed as porters to the state senate, and Patterson's grandfather was among them.[7]

This uneasy relationship with his parents inexorably colored Patterson's adulthood. His role as "Communist guru" mirrors, in a sense, his father's missionary work. In 1968 he conceded that—not unlike his father—"I am ... not a family man. Family for me has always been an accident over which those produced and gathered into the clan had nothing to say. Perhaps that sentiment emerged from my father's devotion to his god rather than family."[8] This vexed relationship with religion, which contributed to a turning away from family in favor of fierce political engagement—a path prepared by his emergence from a family bred in a militant anticolonial and antislavery context—all led Patterson on a road of revolutionary struggle. His father's wanderlust was inherited by his son, who too sailed the seas—except that his mission was the search for meaning, particularly of the political variety. San Francisco was an appropriate launching pad for both in that by 1880 it had the largest percentage of foreign-born residents in the United States. Correspondingly, from 1860 to 1910, one in seven of its residents of African descent was born abroad.[9]

After Patterson's father became a missionary and gave away his wealth, the family moved to Myrtle Street in Oakland. He attended school on Market Street near Twenty-first, then Durant School on Grove near Twenty-eighth—and it was there that he first heard the slur "nigger," an emblem of the degraded status he had inherited. Such experiences "developed in me a distrust of whites," he recalled. "What kind of people were these? A deep resentment arose in me." Then his peripatetic father returned from Tahiti and moved his brood to Napa County, northwest of Oakland; it was a small house in which they resided, with only four rooms, though the locale was isolated and beautiful. Perhaps this isolation enhanced the resentment of his brother, Walter, toward their father, whom he came to "hate." The unstable family moved back to Oakland when the father departed once more, this time to Grove near Twenty-second, near a "large and beautiful Catholic church"—though, Patterson confessed, "I never dared to go in. It was a 'white' church. White churches of nearly all denominations were then Jim Crow, which fact set me to wondering how God would divide his heaven. I concluded that if this were the manner in which God instructed his children on earth, I wanted no part of his eternal abode." His father may have argued in response that this was why the family was evicted from the small home in which they lived—divine retribution—where "excessive" rent was extracted by an unlikable landlord. Thus, the landlord was not disconsolate when the sheriff arrived to place the furniture of the Pattersons on the street—though Patterson himself was confused by the apparent class-based sympathy of their white neighbors, given his gathering antiwhite posture. They moved into yet another home; this one had been a stable for horses and was infested by rats. All this sent him to Oakland High School at Twelfth and Grove with a souring attitude.[10]

Ultimately, his zigzagging across San Francisco Bay led to Patterson graduating from Mt. Tamalpais High School, after having excelled as a sprinter and boxer—along with playing football in the fall and baseball in the spring.[11] Based in Larkspur, it was a relatively small school, containing a mere sixty-three students near the time of his graduation.[12]

He then attended the University of California at Berkeley,[13] intending to become a mining engineer and then escape to Mexico or South America. But the entrance fees and costs of the engineering college required more money than he had, so instead he entered law school in 1915. At Hastings College of Law he wandered into a progressive bookstore, where he was introduced to Marxism. A turning point occurred there when he met the legendary Marxist and suffragette Anita

Whitney. "I half expected her to do the usual thing," said Patterson retrospectively, "start asking me how it felt to be a Negro or tell [me] her Negro maid was like a sister to her." Instead, she engaged him politically, discussing the travails of the fabled activist Tom Mooney. Patterson rushed to inform the editor of a local Negro newspaper, John Derrick—along with other colleagues—about his freshly minted friendship, and they all became agitated when they learned that he was going to join the crusade to free Mooney, who had been unjustly imprisoned for supposedly dynamiting a pro-war rally.

Patterson was at an ideological crossroads. "At this period in my life, I was growing increasingly subjective; I was more Negro than American or even human." When Derrick claimed falsely that Mooney was a racist, Patterson abruptly quit the campaign. Yet his tie to Whitney grew in importance nonetheless. Patterson was exposed to what he termed "a peculiar view of the racist mind-in-uniform through a friendship I had developed with Colonel Charles Young, then the highest ranking black officer in the [U.S.] army." Despite his years of service to the stars and stripes, he was repeatedly flayed with this banner, and by World War I he had been exiled to the Presidio in San Francisco. Patterson traveled to this lovely fort that hugged the bay, where the stiff-necked officer was hospitalized. They became "fast friends," as he recalled; yet Patterson was "puzzled" by Young's "attitude toward the Indian wars. How could he, a black man," participate in such racist slaughter? "He explained lamely that he did it out of love for government," but for Patterson that rationale did not resonate. "Although he was a brilliant, well-read man, he was completely devoid of any understanding of the structure of society."

Interestingly, his relationship with a white woman of the left (Whitney) and a firm believer in U.S. imperialism who happened to be black (Young) was transforming Patterson's consciousness. "These talks with Young and others," he observed, "along with my reading in law, brought me to the realization that something was wrong with the government." In particular, "The hours of discussion with the downcast soldier led me to reject completely his social views." This realization was unfolding as the war proceeded bloodily and, along with "the mistreatment my friend received, strengthened my conviction that the war was a white man's war." In Shellmound Park in Emeryville—a wedge abutting Oakland and Berkeley—on a Saturday at a picnic, Patterson became embroiled in a heated public debate. Energized, he leapt onto a table and spoke his mind, declaring the war to be a "white man's war." Two young Negro sailors nearby took umbrage and reported his remarks to the authorities. Patterson was arrested and held incommunicado for five days. Fortunately, Whitney and the newly organized NAACP chapter intervened and arranged to free him. It was then that he met an Irish revolutionary, Rose Murphy, who fortified his antiestablishment views when she denounced monarchy. Gradually he was coming to see that—contrary to his previous belief—all those of European descent were not hopelessly supportive of the status quo.

At his trial, Patterson was charged, inter alia, with seditious association with Irish and Indian revolutionaries (Murphy was a liaison with dissidents from South Asia), though he managed to elude severe punishment. His once bright future apparently disrupted, Patterson—quickly assuming quasi-celebrity status because of the rarity of being both a budding attorney and a germinating radical—was asked to chair a meeting where the NAACP leader James Weldon Johnson was invited to speak at an auditorium near Lake Merritt in Oakland. By this juncture, Patterson was designated as chair of the association's "legal advisory committee." At this scenic locale, Patterson, rapidly developing the inciting speaking style that became his signature, provided a rousing introduction for the main speaker—then Johnson repaid the favor by praising the war, as Oakland's mayor beamed nearby. A stunned Patterson was driven to reread Mark Twain, which reinforced what became the neophyte attorney's bedrock stance: that a sharp distinction had to be made between the country and the government that purported to represent it, with unremitting hostility to the latter. Independently, Patterson developed the idea that there were three kinds of Negroes: those who think they can "outsmart the white man," the "Uncle Tom," and those who choose the path of struggle—the category in which he counted himself.[14]

Patterson was evolving. He recalled subsequently that theretofore he had been enmeshed "in the realm of nationalism, nationalism of a separatist character." He was a self-confessed "emotionalist"; "for me at that time all whites were savages."[15]

To be sure, these recent years had provided Patterson with a wealth of experience. He had sold newspapers, and the excessive sampling of his wares provided him with an eye ailment that dogged him for the rest of his life. He had sought to read Karl Marx as well, with mixed results. In 1914, to earn enough money to subsidize his education, he was working on a ship that visited Panama, occasionally playing billiards to earn a few extra dollars. While at Hastings, he worked the night shift in a hotel in San Francisco, sleeping from 3:00 to 8:00 A.M., and then attending classes. It seemed that his encounters with other Negro men of note—such as Colonel Young and the NAACP's Johnson—were decisive in providing potent examples of a road he did not want to travel. Thus, Patterson found it "unsatisfactory" when the illustrious James Weldon Johnson counseled him: "He advised me to stay in the West and 'grow up with the country,'" make money, live a good life, avoid radical entanglements. A bludgeoning blow was inflicted when Patterson met with Senator Samuel Shortridge in anticipation of a legal post, along the lines suggested by Johnson, but was stunned when the politician informed him abruptly, "Well, it is my opinion that they would find it difficult to adjust themselves to talking business and personal matters with a Negro." This, Patterson wrote, "made a tremendous impact on me."[16]

Instead, Patterson chose to tread a path to the left of the NAACP. First, he had to pass the bar examination—but he flunked at first, which he attributed to the examiners' negative reaction to his notorious political stances, while fellow Negro jurists told him that even had he passed, he would have been rejected on the nebulous ground of having questionable "character." By the summer of 1919, Negro communities nationally were being pillaged by marauding racist mobs seeking to establish the consensus that Negro militancy, buoyed by the war, would not pay; contrarily, inspired by the Bolshevik Revolution, a new political party—the Communist party—was coming into being. It was unlike other political entities in a nation immersed in white chauvinism in that it made a conscious attempt to recruit and promote the usually battered Negro.

A frustrated Patterson decided that he should abandon North America and move to Africa. By August he was on a ship headed in that direction with his mother, sisters, and friends bidding him a fond adieu—while stuffing a then-handsome $120 in his pocket. "Mother cried as we kissed goodbye," he recalled affectingly. "I never saw her again. I did not see California again until 1941." Now, like his father, a laborer on a vessel, he made his first stop in Acapulco. "When I set foot on the soil of Mexico," said this wayward son ecstatic about abandoning his homeland, "I knelt and kissed the ground." Passing through the Canal Zone, then under U.S. administration, his anti-Washington revulsion was reinforced when he espied the horrid Jim Crow then in force. He did have a chance to confer with his father, a dentist in Panama City at the time. "I was glad to see him," said Patterson; "he was terribly emaciated . . . dying from tuberculosis of the stomach." Wasting away, the elder Patterson soon returned to St. Vincent, where he died a few years later, "alone, forgotten by the church" he had served—a bitter lesson for his son. But at that meeting in the vital chokepoint that was Panama, they talked for an hour. "[He] knelt down to pray for my welfare," said Patterson.

Heading northward, Patterson arrived in Norfolk, Virginia, where his mother had once resided, then headed eastward to the Azores, where a fellow worker requested that he accompany him to a brothel. Aghast, Patterson, replied, "I had never been in a house of prostitution and I was not ready to take any such stop." As fall approached in 1919, he arrived in Grimsby, England—but when he sought to rent a flat in nearby London, the landlady insulted him, assuming he was of South Asian ancestry. "I was flabbergasted," said a wounded Patterson. Absorbing a difficult lesson, not unlike what he had learned from Rose Murphy and Colonel Young, the rapidly evolving Patterson concluded, "I had come across a form of prejudice not based precisely on color." He began poring over the newspaper of the Labour party, met the editor, and submitted articles. He spoke at length with George Lansbury of this party; "His remarks had a sharp awakening impact," said Patterson. Then he met with McCants Stewart, the father of a man alongside whom he had worked in the legal field. He was a small man, about five and a half feet tall, brown-skinned, and balding. Again, Patterson was taken aback.

"His voice was brusque and showed no sign of welcome. He did not smile [and] his manner was cold." Above all, Stewart discouraged Patterson from moving to Liberia. A thought then crystallized in Patterson's churning mind: "The trip already had done wonders for me. I felt I saw my homeland more clearly from that newspaper office in London than I had ever been able to see it from a San Francisco classroom."[17]

It was not only the view from the Labour party office that proved so clarifying but those he encountered there—particularly his extended conversations with Lansbury. Patterson had imbibed the militant messages from A. Philip Randolph's then-radical journal and the Negro press more generally and felt at ease discussing the plight of his people. But then he was asked what he thought of the Bolshevik Revolution, and he was compelled to "confess ignorance." He was briefed but acknowledged that it "meant nothing to me." When Stewart dashed his African dream, he was a "beaten young man." He crossed the Atlantic Ocean back to a homeland he had spurned, deep in thought, his mind swirling with ideas, arriving in Harlem virtually penniless.[18]

Appropriately, he was residing in the upscale Harlem neighborhood known as Strivers' Row—139th Street between Seventh and Eighth Avenue—and was seeking work on the docks. He had arrived home with his worldly possessions in a small bundle, which conflicted sharply with his surroundings, ultimately eliciting a request from his landlady that he might feel more comfortable in different surroundings. Fatefully, he found a home in which resided Eslanda Goode—soon to be the spouse of his lifelong friend, Paul Robeson—and her roommate, Minnie Sumner, who quickly captured his attention. The slender, always stylishly dressed young woman was completely dedicated to her middle-class aspirations. She had a "languid tone," Patterson wrote of this enchanting woman: "As she spoke her hands moved in graceful gestures." Patterson was smitten with both: "I had never before met women like them." So taken was he that he reversed field, becoming an expert writer of legal briefs with accompanying financial success and with entrée into the rarified realm of the Negro middle class.

It was 1920 when the thirty-one-year-old attorney met Paul Robeson, a relationship that was to shape the lives of both men. He had departed Strivers' Row for a small apartment a few blocks away, near 132nd Street. Harlem was then saturated with gambling joints, and Patterson, no slouch when it came to games of chance, had gone to several of them. At a poker game on the southeast corner of 134th Street and Seventh Avenue, he noticed a man who resembled him. "I heard him called 'Pat,'" he recalled, a sobriquet with which he was addressed quite frequently. A startled Patterson encountered yet another man with whom he shared a close tie—his brother, Walter. He wore an eye shade, indicative of his expertness in the field. They embraced and bantered, with Patterson learning that his brother resided a half block away. Walter Patterson had departed San Francisco in 1906, in the aftermath of the dislocation brought by the earthquake, and wound up in Montreal before heading southward. Patterson moved in with his brother, which provided further stability. He had more money in his pocket, making a wage of thirty-five dollars monthly as a downtown lawyer—buttressed by occasional poker winnings.

Still, reminders of discordant experiences akin to those in Grimsby and Emeryville continued to stalk him. Once, in Westchester County, due north of New York City, he and a colleague stopped for refreshments but were refused service on racist grounds. Nonplussed, the man with him pulled a pistol in order to compel a reversal, which quickly followed. Subsequently, Patterson met an up-and-coming lawyer with similar Caribbean roots—Thomas Dyett—and by 1923 he was a named partner in what became the city's leading Negro law firm, Dyett, Hall, and Patterson. This momentous move came after consultation with three who had become his closest friends and allies: Eslanda Goode, Paul Robeson, and Minnie Sumner. Patterson's law office—at 2303 Seventh Avenue—had become a beehive of activity, attracting those rising on the economic and political ladders alike. On the same floor was the dental office of Dr. "Hap" Delaney and his sister, Bessie, ardent nationalists both, with whom he shared more than a scintilla of philosophy.

Finally, he passed the written portion of the bar examination, though the oral part eluded him still. Thus, he was tasked to meet with the future secretary of state Henry Stimson, who was appointed to be his mentor. This was yet another eye-opener, not unlike those with Stewart and Lansbury and Senator Shortridge, providing further insight into a ruling elite that he would come to challenge. He passed the second part of the bar and began what was to become one of the more significant legal careers yet to commence in North America. This was followed by his marrying Minnie Sumner at City Hall; Eslanda Goode accompanied the delighted couple.

The two moved to a three-room second-floor flat near Walter's residence, which must have been a relief for Patterson, since he rapidly found that he shared little in common with his new wife. She was "apolitical," he said bluntly. "I was a radical." The counterpart couple, Robeson and Goode, with "deep concern watched us grappling with our problem which in truth [was] more social than individual," in that Patterson "was rapidly coming to the conclusion that the reign of the dollar over men's lives would come to a close before I died," and she thought otherwise. "Nasty quarrels" did not engulf them—"I was not one for a drag-out fight in any of human relations save politics," he pointed out. A graduate of Howard University, she had emerged from the sophisticated—and sophistical—middle-class life of Washington, D.C.

Then, as so often happens in a crisis, a deus ex machina intervened. His mother died—"her body was found on the doorstep, the key inserted in the lock"—and his beloved sister, now bereft, wished to move eastward. He put the question to his spouse, which turned out to light a fuse, as she took strong exception. That was the final act of this drama. "I packed my belongings and moved out," Patterson declared.

"Some say if one looks deeply enough into a drop of water, the universe can be seen," said a newly liberated Patterson of his resultant intense political discussions in Harlem. "I saw a great deal of Paul Robeson," and "we became close friends," though they "argued over the nature of the present struggle." Recalling his conversation with Lansbury, Patterson began a study of the Bolshevik Revolution. "I was avidly trying to get Paul to see what was happening in the former Tsarist regime"; "it was during this period that I met a number of professional theater people, mostly Afro-Americans"—Robeson's milieu—and the "discussions we had were sharp."

Now sharply focused, Patterson resumed his relationship with the NAACP, frequently visiting their downtown office at Twenty-third Street and Fifth Avenue. Nearby he met Nora Holt, who caught him on the rebound. This Negro woman was "vivacious, her conversation sparkled. She was scintillating. She had a fascinating figure, about five feet four with copper-colored skin and golden hair," and a fabulous wit. She was part of the cultural world that included Robeson, being an entertainer herself. "It was the beginning of a delightful friendship," though it did not distract Patterson from his developing political goals. He also bonded with the pianist Lawrence Brown—who was to become Robeson's accompanist—and along with Holt, "We took in fights, concerts, and the theater and often dined together." Holt introduced Patterson to rising entertainment stars, including Florence Mills, Freddie Washington, and Rose McClendon. Patterson "came to know [Mills] best," and he described her as "a woman of taste and delicacy"—though again a bracing political message was transmitted when "racism sent her to an early death."

Patterson was living large, accumulating a sizable bank account. In Albany, he encountered the fabled Ferdinand S. Morton, a "leading Negro spokesman and fixer.... As we shook hands, I left two five-hundred-dollar bills in his palm," which is suggestive of Patterson's income, his influence, and his reach. All the while, the radical Richard B. Moore was continuing to troop regularly to his office, proselytizing about Marxism at a time when Patterson was studying same. Moore was sometimes accompanied by Cyril Briggs, who was well known because of his association with the profoundly radical African Blood Brotherhood. Moore and Briggs handed Patterson Karl Marx and Friedrich Engels's *The Communist Manifesto* and hovered nearby as he absorbed the transforming words. They brought him the writings of V. I. Lenin. "I had come to a great crossroads," said Patterson portentously of this moment in the mid-1920s.

Patterson was changing before their very eyes. "A Negro's attitude toward the State is of the utmost importance if he wants clearly to see and to understand his status in his native land," he concluded—and he had turned decisively against the state apparatus. At that moment, the case of Sacco and Vanzetti, anarchists accused of crimes in Massachusetts, had assumed the importance in his life that Tom Mooney once had. "I called meetings in the office" about this charged matter, which did not endear his law partners to him. Arriving were the leading Marxists of the era: Moore, Briggs, Otto Huiswood, Lovett Fort-Whiteman, and Grace Campbell—"a magnificent Negro woman," he averred.[19] Moore should not be discounted either, for his fellow Communist, Nemmy Sparks, deemed him to be to "the finest speaker I have *ever* heard in my life."[20] They "strengthened my morale," Patterson concluded later, "with plenty of facts" and steered him to the Communist-affiliated Worker's School. Yet even with the arrival on the scene of these militants mostly of West Indian origin, Patterson observed another pervasive influence: "During this really formative period of my life when I was working, courting, marrying, [divorcing,] and discussing the day's challenging issues, I saw a great deal of Paul Robeson. We became lifelong friends." It was also then that he "had begun a study of the Soviet Union."[21]

Perhaps understandably, what Patterson did not mention in his account of the sweeping changes that transformed his life in the 1920s was the precise nature of his divorce, which may have influenced his decision to abandon Manhattan for Moscow. The *New York Amsterdam News* provided the messy details. Early in 1926 the paper reported breathlessly that a certain "Harlem attorney" was "trapped with Nora Holt-Ray." A detective "accompanied by several witnesses" and Patterson's erstwhile spouse found him and Ms. Holt-Ray "undressed" and "in bed." This "beautiful wife of Joseph Ray" was found at 4:30 in the morning by these witnesses, accompanied by a "uniformed policeman" whose presence proved helpful when a "fist fight" erupted "between the [Harlem] attorney and one of the detectives" in this abode that Patterson had rented for a then hefty eight dollars per week. Nora Holt had married Joseph Ray in July 1923; he was the "confidential secretary of Charles Schwab," a noted investor and president of Bethlehem Steel. She was also an affluent widow, as her previous spouse had "left her a considerable sum of money." Patterson's spouse was described as an "expert dressmaker," and it was observed that they had been "separated for some time." The alert journalist who gathered this material also pointed out that "two divorce actions and possibly two alienation suits" were "expected."[22]

Clearly, one divorce did follow—that of the Pattersons—which may shed light on what appears to be a sordid drama. New York had draconian divorce laws, with adultery being one of the few bases for an official marital rupture, and it was not unknown during this era for calculated scenes—such as the one that enveloped Patterson in early 1926—to be staged expertly. The fisticuffs that marred this early morning scene, however, do seem to suggest that things were not unfolding according to a prearranged script. In any case, for a man like Patterson—who was to garner a well-deserved reputation for abstemiousness and decorum (the Communist Monsignor, as some termed him)—it may not have been easy to absorb the awkwardness of having one's personal life splattered in newspaper headlines.

Indeed, his Spartan reputation may have accelerated inexorably as a corrective reaction to this untoward incident—though decades later, Patterson confided to his good friend Langston Hughes, "I am not a prude."[23] This episode may have been a tipping point—perhaps not in driving him to the left, but in making the idea of spending time abroad in Moscow seem ever more attractive.

Thus, while Patterson was being recruited intensely by Marxists and Communists, the ground beneath his feet was shifting; for this radical ideological trend was taking hold in black America as it had attained state power in Moscow, seeming to represent the wave of the future. Patterson's law practice reflected this increased militancy, moving away from greasing the palms of the corrupt in Albany. In early 1925 he was reacquainted with James Weldon Johnson as they united in demanding a stiff penalty for a New York judge who told a Negro defendant that if he had been in the South he would "have been burned at the stake" for a routine robbery,[24] as his reputation as an attorney allied with the NAACP grew.[25]

Yet Patterson was a link between this NAACP militancy and the rising Communist trend, for it was in 1926, as he was wrestling with diverse ideological (and personal) tendencies, that the *New York Times* noticed that "Communists" were "boring into Negro labor."[26] There was a fear in elite circles—as one *Times* journalist put it—that "Negroes of [the] world" were the "prey of agitators,"[27] not least because of the abysmal treatment to which they were subjected globally. This dynamic—an aggressive push from the left fomenting nervousness on the right—was to transform the conditions of Africans worldwide, and at this fraught moment, Patterson proved to be essential to this gathering trend.

A focus of his attention then was the International Labor Defense (ILD),[28] which Patterson was to serve during the Scottsboro case, and the American Negro Labor Congress (ANLC), where he was listed as president by 1927,[29] a vertiginous rise and a reflection of the esteem in which we was held on the left. In 1926, the leading Negro intellectual Abram Harris informed readers of the NAACP journal that "Soviet Russia's avowal to organize American Negroes into a revolutionary working class movement has come to partial fruition in the American Negro Labor Congress." He was not exaggerating when he averred that, in response, "the national press suffered paroxysms of fear." When Harris was asked, "After Garvey-what?" he responded bluntly: "Had I known what I think I know today I would have answered, 'Communism.'"[30] The journal's editor, W. E. B. Du Bois, found the Soviet "experiment" to be "astonishing" and dismissed with a wave the "question merely of 'dictatorship,'" since "we are all subjects to this form of government"[31]—notably racist dictatorships, in the case of the Negro. As for Patterson, he stressed the need for unionization of workers, for "as long as the masses of Negroes are unorganized, there will be lynching and race riots."[32] In 1926 he made official what some assumed was the case—he joined the Communist party—though an epochal event the following year led to his making this political decision, a career choice to become a professional revolutionary.[33]

Ironically, the event that pushed Patterson toward a half-century commitment to the Communist party involved two embattled and persecuted anarchists of Italian descent. Ferdinando Sacco and Bartolomeo Vanzetti were convicted of murdering two men during a 1920 armed robbery in South Braintree, Massachusetts. They were executed on August 23, 1927,[34] despite the strenuous objection of the ILD. "I followed the Sacco-Vanzetti case with all my soul," said Patterson.[35] It was at this moment that a weighty realization dawned: "I came to the conclusion then," he said on the occasion of his seventieth birthday, "that through the channels of the law and of more legal action [alone] the Negro would never win equality," for "if a white worker like [Tom] Mooney and white foreigners like Sacco and Vanzetti could be so victimized, what chance was there for Negroes at the very bottom?"[36]

On or about August 10, 1927, at 7:30 A.M., Patterson boarded a bus at 80 East Eleventh Street in Manhattan and headed to Boston to protest the impending execution.[37] For days he was present, raising his voice in a protest that included the writers John Howard Lawson, Edna St. Vincent Millay,[38] Mike Gold, Dorothy Parker, and other activists, including Mother Bloor and Clarina Michelson. They picketed for days, and Patterson was arrested three times. As his comrade Gold put it, "As a Negro, the press and police concentrated on him, naturally. A Negro needs twice the courage of a white in any such struggle," and this Patterson possessed. They threatened to "have him put in an asylum," assuming that a Negro attorney seeking to save the lives of Italians in the 1920s must be daft.[39] He was derided as a "nigger anarchist" and worse. "Cheers mingled with boos, curses with words of sympathy, hand claps with catcalls," he noted at the time.[40]

Looking back thirty years later, he recalled speaking at a "mass meeting" alongside John Dos Passos and Edna St. Vincent Millay and remembered that "some of the meetings at which I spoke were broken up by police action," notably "one in which I spoke with Ella Reeve [Mother] Bloor, [where] the firemen turned the fire hose on her. I was standing alongside of her [and] also got wet." This occurred at Boston Common and "was broken up by police on horseback." Detained, "I was forced to ride on the outside" of the police wagon, since he was told, "We won't let the nigger ride inside with the white woman." After he was bailed out, they returned to demonstrating and were arrested again, and then again after being bailed out. Each time, he was "Jim Crowed in prison," and the third time this occurred, the judge told Patterson and his eminent attorney, Arthur Garfield Hayes, that if he appeared in his court again, "I would be thrown into an insane asylum," a fate that befell his fellow protester, Hapgood Powers.[41]

He was nervous about going to Boston in the first place, sensing that the ILD might not want him to join the delegation. Of course, he was mistaken, not least because they needed all the help they could muster. When they arrived in Boston and raised their placards and voices, Patterson recalled that "the mounted police let us have it. One of them seemed particularly anxious to get me. I ducked behind a tree and evaded him for a few seconds but another cop got me. As he grabbed me by the collar, he said, 'Well, this is the first time I ever see[n] a nigger bastard that was a Communist,'" a not-infrequent epithet at the time. Then the officers refused to place him in their vehicle because—said an aghast Patterson—"there was a white woman inside! So we walked to the police station." Countervailing this typical response was what greeted him behind bars: "When I was brought in to be locked up, the other prisoners sent up a big cheer. It was the first time such a thing had happened to me. White people, workers, writers, cheering me, the first solidarity cheer I had ever heard. I shall never forget." Above all, Patterson acknowledged, "the more I thought and read about this case, the more I began to see that terror was not reserved for the Negro people alone."[42]

This was not the only example of interracial fraternity that left an impression upon him. "Do you remember the first night at headquarters?" Patterson queried Mike Gold. "We were all asked if I had a place to sleep that night. I hadn't, and you took me to the home of the comrade where you were staying." This made a "deep impression" on him, as he had—as Gold put it—"not yet got over his suspicion of whites, probably not even of white radicals."[43]

As he stared at the visage of Crispus Attucks,[44] heralded as a martyr for his willingness to give his life so that colonizers could be liberated, Patterson acknowledged that his presence in Boston was an indication of his decision to abandon a promising career as an attorney and commit himself to a life of struggle, where law would be merely one tool in his kit. His commitment was an acknowledgment that a multiracial alliance grounded within an empowered working class was the preferred strategic option, the road to revolution. As Patterson viewed his life retrospectively, he conceived his own development in three stages: the "nationalism" exemplified by his antiwar protest in Emeryville, which evolved into a kind of "humanism" that followed in the wake of his sojourn in Manhattan, and then "Communism," which was coterminous with his experience in Boston. As Patterson saw himself, he "had not simply exchanged one for the next but had retained the essential and useful content of each stage."[45]

As Patterson stood outside the Charlestown prison, the moments to execution ticking relentlessly, his eyes espied hundreds of armed guards—the external symbol of what was about to transpire inside the death chamber. Then the lights in the prison dimmed three times. As he put it, "For me the world had changed. . . . I could not practice law again. . . . I had come back to New York as from a university."

He left his law firm, instead devoting his life to the Communist party and its idea of a step-by-step drive to socialist revolution, paved all the way by one democratic advance after another—as demonstrated in the first major instance by the Scottsboro case. Soon he could be found at the subway entrance at 135th Street and Lenox Avenue, selling the CP newspaper, which he would later serve as its top official. He began participating in street-corner meetings and distribution of leaflets, and he attended classes at the party school. Redolent of the catch that he was, Jay Lovestone—then a top-level official of the CP with extensive contacts in Moscow—"condescended," in Patterson's words, "to come to Harlem to visit me." Lovestone objected to the notion emphasized by Reds like Jack Stachel and William Weinstone that this rarity of rarities—a radical black attorney—be dispatched to Moscow for further polishing and revolutionary training.[46] But Lovestone was overruled, and, once again, Patterson was headed across the Atlantic—this time with more conviction and less fuzziness.[47]

2

Moscow Bound

On November 14, 1927, William Patterson—then residing at 181 West 135th Street in Harlem—was issued a U.S. passport (another was issued on April 7, 1930, in Warsaw) and journeyed across the Atlantic for Moscow. He was to reside there until late December 1929, and from that point until April 1931 he lived in Britain, France, and Germany.[1] His mission, as he put it, was to matriculate at the "University of Toiling People of the Far East," whose student body was peppered with Chinese and Indians but also included Africans from throughout the world. "I was determined to have a complete house cleaning as regards capitalist thought and ideas," said Patterson, and in this he succeeded.[2]

This initial journey found him sailing aboard the *Ile de France* and docking in Le Havre, France, where he was met by friends and comrades. Then it was on to London for a ship to Leningrad, with a stop in Copenhagen. His stay in Leningrad, he said, "was one of the most pleasurable and peaceful moments in my life," though his final stop in Moscow was hard to top, as he was embraced there by officials of International Red Aid, of which his International Labor Defense was a constituent element. He then was "immediately installed in one of the best hotels in Moscow," befitting a radical Negro attorney of whom much was expected.[3]

At least since August 1814, when Negroes participated joyfully in the pillaging of Washington at the hands of invading British troops, major powers with unresolved grievances against the United States had viewed the Negro as the aching Achilles heel of the regime.[4] Visiting the Soviet Union near the same time, Claude McKay, the Jamaican-born poet who had attained renown in the United States, said as much to the readers of the NAACP journal: "The Negro, as the most suppressed and persecuted minority, should use this period of ferment in international affairs to lift his cause out of national obscurity and force it forward as a prime international issue," since "not the least of oppressed that fill the thoughts of new Russia are the Negroes of America and Africa."

"Liberated Russia [feels] toward the Negroes of America" in ways akin to how Washington approached "Czarist persecution of Russian Jews." After all, "Lenin himself grappled with the question of the American Negroes." Thus, during his sojourn in Moscow, McKay "was in demand everywhere—at the lectures of poets and journalists, the meetings of soldiers and factory workers."[5]

Though McKay spent "most of [his] leisure time in non-partisan and anti-Bolshevist circles" and "among the young anarchists and Mensheviks [sic]," this pro-Negro attitude was similarly evident. "Officers and commissars were unanimous in wishing that a group of young American Negroes would take up [military] training," and McKay himself was "elected" to "honorary membership in the Moscow Soviet." Yes, he concluded, "Russia is prepared and waiting to receive couriers and heralds of goodwill and inter-racial understanding from the Negro race."[6]

McKay's opinion was not his alone, for the usually staid *New York Amsterdam News*, which appealed to a growing population of African descent in Harlem, reported that "Russia welcomes trained Negroes": "Perhaps no land offers just now a better opportunity of the young educated Negro," and the exemplar of this was "William Patterson, formerly an attorney of Harlem," who "is there" supposedly "as one of [the] under secretaries in the Soviet government" and "is making himself felt."[7]

As one recent scholar put it, "[T]he Soviet Union simply lacked the complex legacy of racism which existed in the United States," and, consequently, "blacks experienced a greater level of freedom in the Soviet Union which produced an enormous sense of liberation," all of which "provided a critical antecedent for the burgeoning Modern Civil Rights Movement."[8] Thus, after residing in Moscow, Patterson enthused, "It is as if one had suffered with a painful affliction for many years and had suddenly awakened to discover that the pain was gone."[9] This trend was not wholly a product of happenstance, for at the Second Congress of the Communist International (Comintern) in 1920 in Soviet Russia, the U.S. journalist John Reed passed a note to the rostrum asking Lenin, "Should I say something about the Negroes in America?" Without hesitating, Lenin scribbled a response that translated as "absolutely necessary." There ensued an engaged discussion of the desperate plight of African Americans in the context of national and colonial matters, which led inevitably to the idea that conflated their situation with that of Africans globally. This led to the recruiting of young African Americans like Patterson to study in Soviet Russia, where the curriculum included training in the principles of conspiratorial and underground work, including espionage, small-arms training, guerrilla warfare, rules of conduct while under surveillance, arrest and interrogation, and the like.[10] Ultimately, the conflation of the plights of Africans and African Americans was to become one of the more significant aspects of Moscow's Pan-African intervention.[11]

Unsurprisingly, when McKay, Patterson, and other Negroes began trickling across the Atlantic and decamping in Moscow, it was not greeted with equanimity. "Negroes said to be tools of Reds to plant Bolshevism on Yank Soil," screamed one typical article deemed sufficiently instructive to be retained by the NAACP. Patterson's American Negro Labor Congress was singled out.[12] A consensus emerged that Negroes were to be the vector through which socialism was to arrive in the United States.[13]

That Lenin and his successor, Josef Stalin, took such a direct interest in what came to be called the Negro Question insured that Patterson would receive a warm embrace in Moscow and that he would be placed on the fast track to leadership within the ranks of the CP.[14] This also meant, as one analyst put it, that "black recruits" in the United States "joined less to enter the ranks of American Communism than to affiliate with the party of the Communist International and world revolution.... [T]heir loyalties were to Moscow," and "in later years, some black recruits extended this process to direct (and long-standing) loyalty to Stalin, whom they perceived as the leading Comintern figure responsible for pressing the [U.S.] revolutionary Left to address the 'Negro Question.'"[15] This reliance on global forces to crack the calcified prejudices obtaining in the United States stretched back to the founding of the republic,[16] and it also meant that Negro comrades like Patterson were more reluctant to break with Moscow when so many did in the wake of the 1956 revelations about Stalin. But it also meant that the Negro comrades were more sensitive to the global aspects of U.S. imperialism—the source of super-profits—which made them more dangerous, as they already embodied in their very person the nation's major weakness.

Still, all was not roseate for these African Americans—including Patterson—often thousands of miles away from home. One British Communist who was there contemporaneously recalled seemingly interminable meetings punctuated by lengthy speeches, where one's Bolshevik mettle was measured by the ability to stay awake. In her section, the routine involved the reading of various periodicals in English, whose intriguing portions were collated for wider distribution; this provided all with a panoramic view of global trends—though not the pulsating excitement some craved.[17] Then there were the horrid conditions. This vast land had barely recovered from war and famine. Signs of poverty were everywhere—in the ill-clad people, the numerous beggars, the bands of unkempt orphans, the sparsely stocked stores, the dilapidated buildings, and the overall heritage of czarist backwardness.[18]

Harry Haywood, an African American in Moscow at the same time as Patterson,[19] referred to a "party cleansing" session that ensnared this Harlem attorney. Designed to root out presumed vestiges of bourgeois mentality, Haywood recalled a "series of violent and false charges at Patterson" and a fellow African American, Maude White. "They were kept on the stand for hours attempting to refute them. In Patterson's case, his cleansing had taken up one whole evening and was extended to the next." Patterson's sponsor, William Weinstone, a U.S. Communist of Jewish origin, "finally interceded to get Pat off the hook," rescuing him from this "process of purification"—a "scrutiny of both conduct and conviction"—which was "designed to purge from our ranks all noxious elements, factional troublemakers, and self-seeking careerists," a harrowing trial in which Patterson was acquitted.[20]

Patterson may have been an African American, but he was also a lawyer,[21] and despite Lenin himself having received a law degree, there remained a sectarian suspicion of one who soared to untold heights on the class ladder and chose to throw in his lot with the dispossessed. Fortunately, all were not so suspicious, and this included the fellow refugee Endre Sik, a recognized scholar in the study of Africa who served as his native Hungary's foreign minister decades later and whose warmth helped to further thaw Patterson's rapidly melting belief that every person of European descent was hopelessly racist: "I never met a man for whom I had greater respect," he said of Sik. "Sik was very fond of Afro-Americans he met in Moscow. He talked with them, hours on end," and thus, "as often as possible I met at Sik's home."[22] Further solidifying Patterson's new outlook was another relationship he developed during that time. He met Vera Gorohovskaya, who had worked in China previously and was not a party member. Her home was Leningrad, but she spent her summers in Moscow, and it was in that city that he embarked on his second marriage.[23] She was a "most attractive and cultured woman" who "spoke several languages," Patterson said. "We were to have two daughters"; they resided in Leningrad at the time of his passing in 1980, with the oldest, Lola, being an engineer and the mother of six children, while the younger, Anna, was a correspondent for the Soviet news agency Tass.[24]

Having survived ideological hazing, the trial by ordeal that was "cleansing," Patterson was now progressively climbing ever higher in the ranks of these revolutionaries. In 1928, he was to be found at an important gathering of the Communist International where cogitation on the critical Negro Question was a preoccupation and emerging was a logical corollary of the conflation of the problems of Africans, be they in North America or Africa itself—the so-called Black Belt thesis, or the idea that U.S. Negroes were entitled to self-determination, up to and including construction of a Negro republic in Dixie (though day-to-day fighting of Jim Crow was the immediate prescription). Terming U.S. Negroes an oppressed group that merited not only self-determination in the Black Belt South (areas of black majority) but equal social and political rights throughout the nation elevated this struggle to a level of global prominence and gravitas hardly seen previously. In short, the plight of U.S. Negroes was not simply a matter of "race" (an imprecise term in any case). This thesis mandated a relentless struggle against "white chauvinism" and for racial equality nationally, which prepared the battlefield for the titanic battles of the 1960s. This thesis was implemented practically with the emergence of the Scottsboro case. This thesis also was to cause Patterson and his party some grief; but as the Scottsboro campaign exemplified, it was hardly fatal to their attempt to build a mass movement against Jim Crow.

When the Soviet stalwart Nikolai Bukharin delivered his report to the Communist International, the Negro Communists Harry Haywood and James Ford were dissatisfied, as Patterson later put it, "with the way in which Bukharin handled the relationship of the Black man in the United States to the colonial movement." Thus, he continued, "we discussed the matter with Otto Kuusinen, Dmitri Manuilsky, and a number of other comrades," and as a result, "a meeting was arranged with Bukharin."[25] Like Ford, Patterson was also upset with how the U.S. party had handled the Negro Question in recent years, which led to a sharpened focus on this matter.[26]

Before Bukharin spoke, the leadership of Patterson's party framed the Negro Question in Pan-African terms that conflated the plight of African Americans with that of Africans worldwide. This conflation, by adding to the strength of the beleaguered minority that had been slaves only recently, contributed force to the African American struggle—though this conflating may have augmented the idea that this was a grouping deserving of nationhood.[27]

Moreover, just as Stalin had pressed Haywood as to why more Negroes were not part of the U.S. party—"we have no more than fifty Negroes" as members, Ford announced in 1928—it was patently obvious that any revolutionary party worthy of the description should be flooded with applications from the most degraded sector of the body politic. Thus, it was precisely during the discussion of Bukharin's report that a Negro comrade from the United States declared that "there is more chauvinism in the American Party than in any other Party of the Comintern," which is unsurprising, given its emergence from a nation founded on unwavering principles of white supremacy.[28] The Comintern responded by instructing the U.S. party to be more ferocious in attacking "white chauvinism," adding that "the Party must seriously strive for the preparation of cadres of Negro comrades, fit to lead the Negro movement"—the kind of "interference" from Moscow in U.S. internal affairs that would have been appreciated by many Negroes.[29] This intervention in turn compelled U.S. Reds to become more vigorous in fighting mossback conservatism, which was combating antiracism furiously.[30]

Of course, this may have been unfair to white comrades who were the best of an otherwise putrid Euro-American lot when it came to combating chauvinism. In April 1928, months before Bukharin spoke, as party leaders like William Z. Foster sat in attendance, a motion was carried unanimously that mandated that "the Party should begin a campaign to increase the Negro membership." Later it was urged that "as many Negro comrades as possible should be among the delegates to the Sixth World Congress of CI [Communist International]," a mandate that was executed,[31] then implemented decisively three years later as the Scottsboro campaign was taking flight, when what was described as "the third group from the States to attend" a Communist International congress was studded with Negro delegates.[32]

Similarly, when the executive leadership of the Comintern met in late October 1928, a body that included both Bukharin and Kuusinen, there was a sharp focus on "white chauvinism," and the U.S. Communists were instructed sternly to "strive for the preparation of cadres of Negro comrades, fit to lead the movement"— comrades like Patterson, in other words.[33] As should be evident, all influence of the Comintern on the United States was far from malignant, particularly when it came to an inured and encrusted white supremacy. An ironic confirmation of this idea can be deduced from Patterson's staunchest foes, such as the former Communist Manning Johnson ("the highest position I attained was candidate for the Political Bureau . . . of the Communist Party"), who complained of the "Red Plot to use Negroes"; this "plot to use Negroes as the spearhead," he said, "was concocted by Stalin [in]1928" at the aforementioned Comintern meeting. Patterson was singled out as being among the "treacherous Negro Red leaders who serve faithfully their masters in the Kremlin." Writing in 1958, Johnson also assailed the "harmful and deadening effect of Communist inter-racialism (integration)"—that is, unlike subsequent analysts, he did not argue that the Black Belt thesis meant segregation, but the opposite. That Archibald Roosevelt, son of Theodore, endorsed his words provided added heft.[34]

In other words, the Comintern resolution on the Negro Question in the United States, adopted in 1928, which called for self-determination for African Americans,[35] caused great consternation. Though the emphasis was placed on day-to-day struggles against Jim Crow, as Scottsboro was to exemplify, what captured the attention of many was the idea that—in line with conflating the plight of Africans and African Americans—a Negro republic would be constructed in Dixie and, contrary to Manning Johnson, this would mean segregation. Given that Jim Crow was the bane of Negro existence, it was easy to suggest that Patterson's party was complicit with the worst the republic had to offer—Scottsboro notwithstanding. Harry Haywood took credit for this resolution—though, per usual, Stalin was viewed widely as the author. Often lost sight of were notable precursors, such as Cyril Briggs's African Blood Brotherhood[36] or even Marcus Garvey,[37] not to mention the preexisting attempts to establish a "Forty-ninth state" for Negroes—just as Oklahoma had been intended to be the land of indigenes.[38]

Patterson was not an early supporter of the idea of a "Negro nation" in the Black Belt. At the Moscow congress, he coauthored a position paper with James Ford that said as much. Calling U.S. Negroes an "oppressed racial minority" whose plight stemmed not from economic or class oppression alone, Patterson and Ford advocated the establishment of a "mass race organization for Negro workers"—something akin to the ANLC, which was in the process of decomposing.[39] Often neglected is the fact that it was precisely after the proclamation of this thesis that the CP made some of its most significant breakthroughs among Negroes and more generally.[40] Surely this new thesis was a correction of the preceding lack of sharpness on this all-important Negro Question.[41] The wider point is that when Moscow did not enjoy diplomatic relations with Washington, it was easier for their U.S. allies to unleash blistering and clarifying attacks in a manner that crystallized understanding for ever wider audiences.[42] Certainly, the Negro press made some of its more glowing assessments of Marxism-Leninism precisely during this period.[43]

Patterson made some of his most stringent critiques of Negro centrists during this period. From Moscow in 1928 he launched what was to be a long and involved career as a cultural critic. "Yesterday Langston Hughes sang of revolt," he said of a poet who was to become a close ally, but "today that note is lamentably missing." "What is Claude McKay today?" he asked querulously of a former fellow sojourner in Moscow. "There is little in recent Negro poetry," he lamented, "that would lead one to believe that the poets are conscious of the existence of the Negro masses. There is no challenge in their poetry, no revolt," while "millions of blacks are suffering from poverty and cruelty"—"and black poets shut their eyes," as "they voice the aspirations of a rising petty bourgeoisie." They were "cowards," he charged, "whimpering in the parlors of white and black idlers and decadents." Well, concluded Patterson, there was a new cultural sheriff in town, and the poets should expect no more "mawkish and sentimental" critique: "[L]et us sound the call for militancy," he insisted. "Let us have strong vital criticism. . . . Marxian criticism," in other words.[44] This stinging rebuke, drafted in Moscow while the Black Belt thesis was being debated, was the kind of assault from the left that had not been mounted consistently—though, naturally, assaults from the right were a matter of course and, thus, were more likely to have effect. The new line of the CP, weaknesses notwithstanding, provided more clarity and guidance to all-important cultural workers—and ultimately many others.

Patterson did not stop there in his effort to push his fellow Negro intellectuals to the left. "The voice of a Roland Hayes, a Paul Robeson, a Lawrence Brown, the songs of Cullen, Hughes, Toomer, Johnson, and McKay may wake to ecstasy the cultured bourgeoisie of the North, the absentee Southern landlords, the exploiters of black labor," but "tens of millions of the most ignoble creatures, the most debased and dehumanized of mankind, ten millions of blacks in the savage South are unaware of their existence. The economic position of these lowly blacks does not change because these New Negroes thrill high heaven with the beauty of their songs." "Actually," Patterson charged, "the new Negro is still in the offing. He will come! But he will not be an aesthete," he said with confidence. Like himself, "He will be a revolutionist!" For, he asserted, "only through the travail of revolution will he realize his full expression as a man, not through poetry and aesthetics."[45] Hughes responded by celebrating the publication of his book—*Not without Laughter*—in the Soviet Union and included appropriately revolutionary words in that edition.[46]

Though a relative neophyte in Communist circles, Patterson found himself enmeshed at the highest levels of the movement[47] and recognized as an authoritative voice.[48] His viewpoints did not always prevail, but he was generally at the table when decisions were forged.[49] By July 1929, he was in Germany at the congress of the League against Imperialism, where he encountered the NAACP's William Pickens, though—like Ralph Bunche in Paris years later—he avoided Patterson and wrong-footed the Communist's attempt to critique his address by speaking in German.[50] This congress was in Frankfurt, and he was there about five days as an observer. "I may have spoken," Patterson told U.S. government inquisitors much later. He also informed them that he "spent several days at the University of Berlin. I lectured before a group of English-speaking Africans and Americans" before departing for Halle, then back to Moscow.[51]

Shortly thereafter, Patterson was arranging a meeting of workers of African descent from across the planet that had been slated for London, but the authorities balked, which led to a convening in Hamburg.[52] Among those present were George Padmore, a Trinidadian national with whom Patterson worked profitably before a bitter split, and Jomo Kenyatta, the founding father of modern Kenya. They returned via the Baltic Sea to the Gulf of Finland to Leningrad. "The beauty of the scene," Patterson mused, led to intensely heady political discussion: "We talk[ed] about linking the liberation of black men with the struggle for the liberation of mankind."[53] In 1930, Patterson was back in Germany, though he was disappointed with the response of antifascist forces to the looming threat he espied. He then departed for Britain and France but was forced to borrow funds from comrades and friends to survive and continue his organizing, which concentrated on those of African descent in these nations. His comrade James Ford apparently sought to learn Kiswahili in order to organize more effectively while in Hamburg, suggestive of how seriously black Communists were approaching their weighty duty of Pan-African revolution.[54]

Ford and Patterson had become quite close. Subsequently, the former leader recalled how "Patterson and I walked across Moscow in the funeral of the late Bill Haywood," and how in 1930 they had "worked together at Hamburg" in the ranks of the First International Trade Union Conference of Negro Workers. Before that, in 1927, they had both attended the World Congress of the Anti-Imperialist League at Cologne as "bona fide American delegates."[55]

Instead of avoiding Patterson, as Pickens had done, other Negroes were seeking to follow in his footsteps. The growing list included John Sutton, a scion of one of the more prominent Negro families in San Antonio, who arrived in the USSR at the behest of the famed Negro scientist Dr. George Washington Carver. "The Soviet Russian Government has asked me," said Carver, "to select twenty-five or thirty colored specialists in cotton growing to go over there."[56] Like Patterson, Sutton married a Russian woman, spoke Russian, and fathered children there as Moscow began to take advantage of the persecution of Negroes in the United States, just as Washington was taking advantage of the persecution of Germans in Berlin.[57] Years later, the elderly Patterson congratulated the equally aging Sutton and his mentor, Dr. Carver, since his "sending of you to the Soviet Union was a far-, far-reaching potential step and gave evidence of the vision of the man."[58]

Thus, by 1931—the year of Sutton's arrival in the Soviet Union—Patterson had reason to be pleased with his transformation from a callow lawyer placing greenbacks in the hands of the corrupted to a Communist determined to participate in a revolution. Earlier, he had traveled to Warsaw to renew his passport in preparation for a return home and thus had a glimpse of the turmoil that was soon to descend on the troubled continent.[59]

While abroad, he recounted, "I had met leaders [and] liberation fighters of almost every country in the world," an invaluable experience that gave him a depth of understanding beyond the ken of most of his peers—left, right, and center. "I reported to my party," said this soldier, and "asked to go to Pittsburgh," the grimy industrial center where exploited proletarians abounded. Upon arrival, he secured a tiny room in the "Jim Crow YMCA," as he put it, in the Negro neighborhood known as "the Hill," and quickly became involved in labor struggles. His education in political economy in Moscow proved handy in instructing mine and metal workers, as he took a leading administrative role in a workers' school. He was also recruited to serve as an attorney in one of their cases, handling adeptly a five-day trial: "It was to be the last case that I was to participate in, as a lawyer, for many years." While there, he had a nasty encounter with police officers. "Suddenly the car was braked to a stop at a lonely stop where the road ran through a wooded area," he recalled. "They told me to get out," with "hardened" faces. "My muscles constricted" at the thought of the "revolver shot I *knew* was coming. I climbed out of the car and felt the impact of a boot on the seat of my pants," which "caused me to stumble." "When I recovered my balance I heard a voice speaking in Russian," barking, "Get lost, nigger, and never come back!" This epithet was hurled after Patterson surprised him by addressing him in return in Russian, after they stumbled into a colloquy in what was becoming a stigmatized language.

It was unclear if this is the reason that Patterson soon decamped for Manhattan to lead the ILD, which had just become embroiled in the case of the Scottsboro Nine, which would transform the Negro and the nation. For it was in western Pennsylvania that Patterson led a huge antihunger march—in the appropriately named city of Uniontown—that ruffled feathers regionally. This demonstration got quick results, as the mayor immediately allotted several thousands of dollars for relief of the distressed. Then Patterson was arrested for assisting in returning the furniture of a Negro woman who had been evicted, which led to the trial in which he acted as counsel that persuaded a jury to return a not-guilty verdict. Patterson then moved on to organizing in Ohio, where he was duly arrested and faced the threat of lynching, which caused his comrades to maintain an all-night vigil to foil vigilantes—until a magistrate chose to release him.[60]

Being in this economically depressed area was an education in itself for Patterson. "I found that many of the miners, adults from Kentucky, Tennessee, and southern Ohio," he recalled later, "both Negro and white, couldn't read and write, some of them couldn't sign their names. It was for that purpose" that he helped to organize a school, a task he took on with equal success in Chicago in the following decade. It was "after the great 1930 strike of the miners, to give the miners an understanding of the economics of that strike," that the school was organized.[61]

As the Great Depression began to place its death grip on a Negro community already writhing in agony, Patterson's radical message began to be heard. The authorities had begun to monitor him,[62] and the Negro press had begun to feature what appeared to be a "believe it or not" narrative: the Negro attorney who turned his back on potential riches in favor of an uncertain path in behalf of the downtrodden. Patterson told readers of the *Baltimore Afro-American* that Moscow "holds open wide the door of opportunity to skilled workers in the United States, who will be admitted on the same basis as other racial groups"—a concept that seemed bizarre to many. Patterson, it was said, "has become an uncompromising Communist"—"'the ruling class,' 'imperialism' and 'capitalism' are terms frequently used by Patterson," it was said almost wondrously.[63] In gushing over Patterson, the *Chicago Defender* noted that a Negro mechanic who had arrived to work in the Soviet Union "had been discriminated against by two southern whites" there—instead of the Negro being rebuffed in his complaint, as would have occurred in Dixie, "word went out to all workers in Russia and they demanded that these white men be punished"—"and they were made to apologize."[64]

Patterson leapt on this case with relish, wiring the *Afro-American* in August 1930 that this was an exemplar of "the spirit of international solidarity" that stood in "direct contrast to the bourgeois American anti-Negro spirit" that characterized his homeland, which was "adding fuel to [the] new wave of lynching sweeping" the nation. That these men were sentenced to two years of imprisonment, commuted to ten years' banishment from the Soviet Union, buttressed Patterson's claim.[65] *Time* magazine, an arbiter of public opinion, featured Patterson—fresh from Moscow, nattily attired in a soberly dark double-breasted suit: "In Russia, according to Communist Patterson, he made his living by writing and lecturing on capitalist countries. He now plans to make it in the U.S. by writing, lecturing on Red Russia."[66]

Because of the presence of leading personalities such as Patterson—combined with the depths of economic and social misery—the press, particularly the Negro press, began to pay more careful attention to the Communist party. It was not long after he had returned from Moscow that the NAACP journal featured an eye-catching forum, "Negro Editors on Communism." Carl Murphy of the *Afro-American* argued that the "Communist Party appears to be the only party going our way. They are as radical as the NAACP were twenty years ago." William M. Kelley of the *New York Amsterdam News* opined that "since America's twelve million Negro population is so largely identified" with the working class, "the wonder is not that the Negro is beginning, at least, to think along Communistic lines but that he did not embrace that doctrine en masse long ago." E. Washington Rhodes of the *Philadelphia Tribune* thought that there were more "dark-skinned than white Communists" in his town and that the CP was "becoming a black party."[67] Under Du Bois's leadership, the NAACP journal went a step further in 1930 when it solicited a missive from a leading Moscow publication—"a sort of Message to the American Negro," was requested. "We would be very glad to publish it."[68]

Writing for the journal of the usually moderate National Urban League, T. Arnold Hill exposed why Patterson joined the Communist party and why others were emulating him: "If Communism [was] making headway with Negroes," he determined, "it was due to the severe exploitation" they were compelled to endure. He foresaw the "probability of the growing sentiment of Communism among Negroes."[69] Like the NAACP journal, that of the Urban League gave extended coverage to the surge of interest in socialism that was plainly evident in black America. Asbury Smith, a Baltimore pastor, acknowledged that "undoubtedly this sudden interest in Communism has in large measure grown out of the Scottsboro case," a campaign that Patterson led after departing Pittsburgh. But, like others, he worried about the danger involved of Negroes moving to the left among a white majority not moving similarly: would that leave the minority isolated and more susceptible to elimination?[70] In contrast, a prominent jurist from Los Angeles, Loren Miller, argued that there was "one way out—Communism."[71]

The founder of the American Civil Liberties Union, Roger Baldwin, instructed readers of the Urban League journal that class struggle was a useful remedy for besieged Negroes and added, while referencing Scottsboro, "The Communists know it. They face it with courage."[72] That was not necessarily the consensus opinion among Euro-Americans concerning the apparent shift to the left among Negroes, as Reverend Smith's foreboding supposition seemed to be closer to the reality.[73]

Though Patterson was the prized Communist recruit, as the rapt attention in NAACP and Urban League circles suggested, he was far from alone, which lent credence to the idea that he was riding an inexorable wave. A report from early 1930 showed that of the 954 new recruits in New York, 114 were Negroes.[74] The Scottsboro campaign—which Patterson spearheaded in its all important early stages—was the breakthrough that led to even more Negroes flooding into radical ranks, which effectively informed U.S. rulers that the status quo on Jim Crow was no longer sustainable. This set the table for the rising of a bountiful civil-rights movement.

3

The World Confronts Jim Crow

When nine African American young men and boys were arrested and tried in Alabama in the spring of 1931 for allegedly molesting sexually two white women, few could envision that this would become a paradigmatic case that would transform the unfortunate plight of the Negro, while catapulting William Patterson into the front ranks of Communist and Negro leadership. In 1969, well after the full measure of this trailblazing case could be taken, Patterson said quite accurately, "Perhaps no living American knows better than I the history of the Scottsboro Case, for I lived with it sixteen of its seventeen years' duration."[1] "I knew something about the case of the nine lads," he continued. "I had debated with Robert Vann," the affluent Negro publisher of the *Pittsburgh Courier,* at a local university while this self-proclaimed revolutionist was still residing in the Keystone State. "Vann turned against the Negro militants, especially the Communists"; Patterson, the Moscow-trained radical, turned in the opposing direction.[2]

The Scottsboro case was profoundly important not least because it was seized upon by the Communist party and its global network of activists to highlight Jim Crow. This placed tremendous pressure on the nation's rulers at a time when national security was being challenged frontally, it was thought, in leading capitals—Moscow particularly—which had decided to focus on Jim Crow, while training talented Negroes like Patterson to subvert this hateful system. Late in life, one of the Scottsboro defendants, Clarence Norris, admitted the obvious: "I believe," he said in 1979, "the spotlight the 'Reds' put on Alabama saved all our lives. The ILD was working everywhere on all levels." Patterson, as a result, "is a good friend today," he said appreciatively, recalling that the Communist barrister "led a march for us to the White House, five thousand strong"[3]—which was quite unusual (perhaps even today) for an antiracist cause.

Norris was not mistaken, for only months after the Scottsboro campaign had been launched, the CP was crowing about the gigantic steps that had been taken on the anti–Jim Crow front.[4] Scottsboro, for example, occasioned a massive counterattack by the radical left not only on the antiracist front but with regard to the lineaments of Negro history generally—which was seen as similarly crucial.[5]

Ultimately, however, a delicate pas de deux was performed whereby those like Patterson, who had helped to place Jim Crow in the global spotlight, were sidelined, and in compensation, Jim Crow was eroded. This tendency was evident early on, for even in 1933 the government had begun to investigate the Scottsboro campaign, which was viewed contemptuously—but not falsely—as "an opening wedge for a Communist campaign that will probably outdo the Sacco Vanzetti case in publicity." This was all done, it was said, at the behest of "Moscow's orders"[6]—a hypothesis that was bolstered, it was thought, by the prominent presence in both cases of the Moscow-trained Communist William L. Patterson. As for Patterson, citing Dr. Mordecai Johnson of Howard University, he sniffed that, on balance, "the policy of godless Russia would be a boon to the Negro masses of Christian America."[7]

State Department representatives were probably too busy ducking picketers, nasty imprecations, and (literal) brickbats to tease out the larger implications of what they were experiencing in the early 1930s. It was with exasperation that the NAACP in late 1934 editorialized that "the whole thing has been dramatized from Moscow to Manchukuo"—apparently unaware that this was the key to eroding Jim Crow and saving the defendants' lives.[8] The protests poured in: Sydney,[9] Madrid,[10] and particularly Riga[11] were among the vectors of these anti–Jim Crow reports. Indeed, emerging from the "cotton fields of Central Asia," said a U.S. official in Riga, were "eleven American Negroes working" there, who handed over brusquely a protest about Scottsboro.[12] Other protests shook France, Scandinavia, and Melbourne, Australia.[13]

The case "re-echoes over the world," it was said in early 1934.[14] Romania militantly joined the fray.[15] Rotterdam escaped merely with the "defacement of front door and coat of arms of [the] American consulate."[16] Oslo deemed itself lucky when "mass demonstrations" did not occur—only intensely spirited ones.[17] The Communist press in London trumpeted the "world wide campaign" on behalf of the defendants.[18] A mother of the defendants was embraced in the British House of Commons.[19]

In Panama, workers demanded "clemency" for the defendants.[20] Confirming the Comintern's Pan-African intervention, Scottsboro was characterized as an "African issue," while a "concerted effort [was] being made on the part of the British government to keep from the Crown Colonies the knowledge" of the case—notably in West Africa and Trinidad, where a decree barred mention of this matter in this prime source of petroleum for the empire. Congressman Oscar De Priest of Chicago, a lone Negro sitting in this body, transmitted to President Hoover a plea and protest on this case from U.S. nationals then residing in Paris.[21] In Dresden, angry protesters smashed windows of the U.S. consulate in mid-1931.[22] "A delegation of Communists," said the U.S. consul in Munich, "from the Neuhausen section" had been protesting the case.[23]

By August 1931, the Berlin legation of the United States was under tight police guard because of frequent Scottsboro protests.[24] In Hamburg, the Communist leader Ernst Thaelmann addressed a massive rally of one hundred thousand that focused on Scottsboro.[25] Cuba too featured confrontational Scottsboro protests.[26]

Scottsboro marked the point when a tsunami of global opposition mounted against Jim Crow, sounding the death knell for this atrocious system. This became clear when the well-known began joining the clamor. H. G. Wells was among the celebrities jumping aboard the bandwagon.[27] A more genteel group from Berlin that included Thomas Mann and Albert Einstein—part of the Committee for the Deliverance of the Victims of Scottsboro—shared with the White House their grave concern.[28] George Bernard Shaw, Charles Chaplin, and Rabindranath Tagore were among the millions worldwide who took a public stance against an essential element of U.S. society.[29]

From Selma, Alabama—soon to be a byword of antiracism—the secretary of state heard directly from the local Chamber of Commerce, which was worried because in "this [affected] County there are some 30,000 negroes and about 3,500 white people."[30] Decades later, a still stung FBI was continuing to recount in painful detail that "during 1933 Scottsboro demonstrations were rampant in foreign countries," which was inextricably linked with another bitter reality: "It was the first big battle conducted by the Communist Party USA among Negroes and was used by them as a steppingstone to penetrate broad masses of the Negro people and to extend Communist influence among them."[31]

The ILD was at the tip of the spear, forcing the Scottsboro crusade into global consciousness, and it was led by J. Louis Engdahl, who in the pivotal year of 1931 warned Secretary of State Henry Stimson that his organization "and its affiliate[s], totaling more than 250,000 members," had more in store.[32] When Engdahl died suddenly, Patterson took his place and delivered on the vow made to Stimson.[33] Given the prodding from the Comintern—and Negroes themselves—about elevating African Americans to high-level posts, it was virtually inevitable that Patterson would be asked to take his place. Even the State Department, as if it were sizing up an adversary, took note that "this is the highest office in the Communist Party's subsidiary organizations yet attained by a member of that race."[34]

Engdahl's passing was even more telling in that he worked himself so relentlessly, he suffered a collapse—something that was to befall Patterson by 1934. Engdahl was "worn down by a half a year of most intense struggle on behalf of the Scottsboro" defendants, said Patterson; he was "harried from land to land by the police" and "weakened by his untiring activities." Why, sputtered Patterson, "even the Socialist police chiefs of German cities prevented Scottsboro meetings; the Belgian and Czecho-Slovakian governments deported" him; yet, despite this harassment, Patterson concluded triumphantly, "the question of the enslaved

CHAPTER THREE

Negroes of America gained recognition as a phase of the struggle of the oppressed of the world."[35]

Carl Hacker, a charter member of the CP, subsequently told federal investigators that "during the [ILD] national convention in Cleveland in 1932 I remember distinctly during that convention, that Earl Browder [the party leader] himself proposed that William L. Patterson become the national secretary" of the ILD "at the earliest possible moment."[36] Browder was prodded by the Negro Department of the CP, which included Patterson and had recommended him similarly[37] (and strongly).[38] Thus, when the ILD convention "unanimously recommended" Patterson as their new leader—while terming him a "Negro militant and able revolutionary leader"—few were surprised.[39]

Harry Haywood, who called Patterson affectionately "my friend," was among the many pleased with his 1932 selection as top ILD leader,[40] not least since he provided the global experience that the organization relied upon.[41] Given his tours of duty in Hamburg and Moscow, Patterson was not engaged in idle boasting when he said, "I had met leaders and liberation figures of almost every country in the world," which meant that he was well positioned to take advantage of worldwide disgust at the reality of U.S. apartheid.[42] Of similar import was the reality reported by one observer: Patterson "had enormous prestige among the members of the Comintern."[43] Since Engdahl had served on the Executive Committee of the Comintern—one of two U.S. nationals to do so, the other being William Z. Foster—Patterson's elevation was suggestive of his rising prominence.[44]

Patterson's ever-increasing frontline duty was also suggestive of his growing prestige. While in Pennsylvania, he had worked closely with insurgent trade unionists, and when notified of the decision to make him ILD leader, he was in Washington acting as an attorney for Negro army veterans arrested following the expulsion of the Bonus Expeditionary Force from Anacostia Flats.[45]

Fortunately, Patterson did not inherit a shell, for the ILD—unlike the ANLC—was a force on the U.S. scene. In early 1930 it was reported that a "large percentage of Negro workers" had joined the ILD; in fact, "thousands of workers, hundreds of Negroes, have joined the ILD in all parts of the country. In the South, where no ILD existed a year ago, the membership is increasing."[46] The ILD had grown out of a 1925 Moscow conversation between "Big Bill" Haywood and James P. Cannon about the need for a comprehensive defense organization for political prisoners in the United States, and later that year, one hundred persons met in Chicago to execute their idea. Initially, antiracism was not their forte—of the three hundred cases handled before the 1929 convention in Pittsburgh, only six involved Negro defendants—but this changed decisively after the 1928 Comintern congress.[47] Thus, reporting in late 1929 on the "ILD after four years," Engdahl boasted proudly that the organization had "handled nearly 6,000 arrests within the recent period" and admitted that its recent energy had been driven by its emphasis on antiracism: "The long-delayed recognition of the fact that it must wage unrelenting struggle against lynching, that it must take up seriously the fight against race discrimination, broke with full force."[48]

Patterson accelerated this trend when he took hold of the leadership baton. "A bloody holiday is being 'legally' prepared," he said of Scottsboro weeks after the case had gained renown. "They used to call such things 'Roman holidays,'" he said scornfully. On the facing page of his missive was a letter from the Ku Klux Klan of April 10, 1931, blaring, "You Negroes are invited to Alabama. We want your scalp—along with the Nine we already have."[49] Still simmering when speaking of the case in 1969, he declared that Scottsboro "exceeded in its program of terror and murderous viciousness the cases of Mooney and Billings. . . . Sacco and Vanzetti and the most infamous legal murder of all, that of Ethel and Julius Rosenberg." And he remained critical of the NAACP's role after all these years.[50]

Having been posted abroad, Patterson had a more developed and ramified network of international contacts than any of his counterparts—before or since—and rather quickly contacted the influential Nancy Cunard in London, instructing her to "draft the sharpest kind of a letter to *L'Humanite*," the journal of the French Communist party, "and to the British *Daily Worker*, bringing their attention to the use they can make of the Scottsboro campaign to develop their own colonial struggles." This strategy was of a piece with the philosophy that conflated the conditions of Africans globally. That the U.S. authorities were able to grab this letter did not blunt its impact,[51] for Cunard was already thinking along parallel lines.[52] Surveillance aside, Patterson's strategic emphasis was clear. In his 1932 "Manifesto" directed "to the Negro People," he proclaimed, "These struggles must be carried to a higher level, this unity must be made international. There is no other way out for us."[53]

There was, in short, good reason for the State Department to pay so much attention to a seemingly domestic case centered in the backwater that was rural Alabama. For Patterson and his comrades had decided that a primary pressure point determining the fate of this case—and the Jim Crow of which it was a part—was overseas. This became clear when the noted Soviet writer Maxim Gorky—whose leadership of the Comintern committee on the case indicated the importance in which it was held—wrote the riveting "Terror against the Negro Workers in America" during the summer of 1931.[54] Its initial publication run was a whopping three million copies, perhaps the most concentrated barrage against a U.S. domestic issue to that point.

It was apparent that Moscow seized upon the diplomatic advantage provided by Jim Crow, which contrasted nicely with the land of Pushkin's relative dearth of bigotry targeting Africans and placed Washington on the defensive and allowed for antiracist advances led by the likes of Patterson. As one scholar put it, Moscow made an "effort to base the Soviet Union's identity on a rejection of American racism" and simultaneously discredited its foe by "equating the United States with horrific racial violence," as demonstrated by frequent lynchings. Contrary to today's Washington consensus, all emulation of Moscow was not automatically regressive—as Meredith L. Roman has pointed out, "Just as Soviet leaders sought to define the country through a rejection of American racism and the inclusion of black workers, U.S. Communist leaders attempted to define the Party in similar terms." Raymond Price, a non-Communist Euro-American from Jim Crow Washington, D.C., was stunned when visiting Russia in 1931, since "one hears and sees—for posters everywhere are graphic even to the illiterate and foreigner—more of the American Negro problems than in our southern states." Three African American laborers who arrived near the same time corroborated his observation, explaining, "everywhere the Russian workers inquired about the Scottsboro Boys. Pictures of the Scottsboro Boys and of Tom Mooney are to be seen everywhere—on street corners, in factories, in hotels and clubs." When the famed African American writer Dorothy West visited Russia in 1932, she attended rallies for the Scottsboro defendants and found that some of the locals were more knowledgeable than her fellow U.S. Negroes about the case. Euro-Americans there, unaccustomed to seeing African Americans having equal access to education and public facilities—not to mention consorting with and marrying Russian women—were discombobulated. Some felt that this liberality was dangerous, causing these Negroes to adopt "extremely offensive" attitudes toward all Euro-Americans that would be exported to the United States. It seemed that miscegenation was the aspect of Soviet life that many Euro-Americans found most disconcerting.[55]

Ironically, it was Germany—Hamburg specifically—that became the headquarters of Comintern antiracism targeting Africans globally.[56] The journal for which Patterson wrote, the *Negro Worker,* was based there and, consonant with the Black Belt thesis, took a Pan-African approach to the difficult situations of Africans in the Americas and Africa.[57] The groundwork for the global push on Scottsboro was laid at the First International Conference on Negro Workers in Hamburg in 1930, in which Patterson played a key role.[58] This approach bore fruit when a report emerged from South Africa in 1932 that the ILD affiliate was "also leading the struggle on behalf of four million Negroes."[59]

Langston Hughes, taking seriously Patterson's admonition that he should write like a "revolutionist" and not an "aesthete," responded accordingly in their pages, conflating the conjoined fates of Africans, be they in the Americas or Africa itself.[60] When the Kenyan Jomo Kenyatta joined Patterson, Cyril Briggs, and Padmore as contributors to this radical periodical, it seemed that this Pan-African project of a new type had accelerated. When Patterson announced in early 1933 that "this is the first time that I think such a large Negro delegation has come directly from the colonies to Moscow," it was suggestive of the new reality that the adrenalin provided to the movement for antiracism and socialism by Scottsboro had leaped the borders of the United States and begun to spread.[61]

In other words, though the conflating of the separate catastrophic spheres faced by Africans and African Americans alike had the obvious downside of eliding critical particularities, it had the advantage of creating synergy and consolidating forces and often sparse resources among those that—after all—were hardly hegemonic. This held a particular benefit for African Americans in that it was their cause and parlous situation—as embodied by Scottsboro—that became the major concern globally. As things turned out, this was an effective strategy insofar as newly empowered African Americans could then press the government in Washington on anticolonial grounds, aiding in the empowering of Africans, which in turn could aid African Americans, thus creating a virtuous circle of solidarity. This was reflected when Patterson, joined by Ada Wright—the mother of a Scottsboro defendant—spoke in Harlem at a rally honoring Nat Turner and the heroic Zulu leader Dingaan under the banner of honoring the "Glorious Revolutionary Traditions of the Negro People."[62] Yet even before Patterson had ascended to this high rung of ILD leadership, he was exemplifying this trend. When he heard that two boys from Uganda were being housed at the Central Park Zoo accompanying animals that had been captured in Africa, he sprang into angry action.

By the fall of 1931, Patterson was leading a delegation to Albany, New York, that opposed four pending jobless bills, as he demanded substitution of the Communist program. Speaking as both a Negro and a Communist, the dual identity that had been honed in Moscow, he attacked the legislators for their seeming inability to deal with growing unemployment and a shrinking workforce—spurred by automation and declining markets. Patterson presciently demanded unemployment insurance—soon to be a commonplace—and projected a two-layered "affirmative action" program for the working class in general and the black masses in particular.[63] When ten thousand protested in August 1931 in Union Square in Manhattan on an antiwar and antihunger platform, the *New York Times* recorded the presence of Patterson, who was listed as the "Negro Director of the Communist Party."[64]

Thus, in addition to handling the ILD portfolio, Patterson was vice president of the organization that had supplanted the American Negro Labor Congress, the League of Struggle for Negro Rights (LSNR), which Langston Hughes served as president.[65] It was Patterson (and James Ford) who had decided that the ANLC was too narrow and proposed that it be replaced with what became the LSNR in November 1930.[66]

In the turbulent conditions of the Great Depression, Patterson's radical message—and evident global backing—was reaching a more receptive audience. When the *Afro-American* reported that he declared "Long Live Revolution," it was not seen as far-fetched or beyond the pale.⁶⁷ When Patterson encountered what was routinely mundane—the sharp edge of Jim Crow—this journal took up his cause as if it were their own.⁶⁸

The massive offensive on Scottsboro by Patterson and the radicals seemed to suggest that the NAACP—accustomed to being in the vanguard of anti–Jim Crow protest—was being eclipsed. While Patterson approached this case with a global army of solidarity at his back, the NAACP—as even their chief lawyer, Charles Hamilton Houston, acknowledged—approached this complex matter with a corps of talented attorneys determined to sway the pro–Jim Crow opinions of a Euro-American elite, as reflected in the judiciary. This was a mismatch that greased the skids for lynching and state-sponsored execution, victims of which the Scottsboro defendants were on their way to becoming, before the ILD's intervention. Early on in this case, Patterson laid down the critical differences between the contrasting approaches. While a traditional lawyer, he said, "has to concern himself only with the judicial aspects of the case," the mass legal defense pioneered by the ILD covered that aspect—but made sure that "the legal defense of the accused" was "political" by campaigning beyond the narrow confines of the courtroom. "The courtrooms of the working class are the streets," Patterson bellowed, and "the determining factor in the class struggle in the capitalist courts, as elsewhere, is the relation of class forces," not the wizardry of legal magicians. Certainly "the legal defense must be of most expert character," he conceded, and "every legal technicality must be used," since "the more far-reaching the knowledge of the lawyer retained by the ILD, the more easily and effectively can the worker be shown that the guarantee of justice extended him by the ruling class [is] meaningless."⁶⁹ It was the "lesson in internationalism that must be learned," he emphasized. "Legal defense"—standing alone—"has won no victories for Negro rights or for the working class generally in America. Legal defense linked up with mass pressure has won many victories."⁷⁰

In short, Patterson and the ILD were able to overcome the pro–Jim Crow bias against the Scottsboro defendants and others like them by mobilizing an intimidating public opinion—particularly global public opinion. Later, Patterson stressed that those he defended "can be guilty for all I care. I'm concerned with *rights*."⁷¹ Did the Scottsboro defendants receive a fair trial? Did racist bias infect the selection of the jury? When Patterson and the ILD won on these grounds, these *rights* were then extended across the board—not only to Negroes but to anyone being charged with such serious crimes.

Patterson was not alone in this viewpoint as, ironically, Charles Hamilton Houston—who had a surfeit of experience in Jim Crow courtrooms—agreed with him, once going so far as to rebuke publicly the NAACP leader William Pickens for taking a different posture. According to Houston, Pickens thought that justice for the Scottsboro defendants could arrive "without outside pressure. Personally I do not believe it. What sort of justice did they obtain in Alabama before the

[ILD] entered the picture?" he asked of these youth who were on the verge of execution. It was "absolutely immaterial to me," he added, if the case was "being supported by the" radicals. To think otherwise would be to accept the terms of reference of one's foes.[72]

Houston and Patterson's opinions were hardly greeted with unanimity within the higher councils of the NAACP. At this hinge moment, marking the transition to a new epoch of struggle, the left and the center were not necessarily united. The problem for the NAACP—and particularly their paramount leader, Walter White, the former insurance-industry executive from Atlanta—was that their early approach to what became a defining case was torn with contradiction. "The NAACP as a whole was slow to respond" to the defendants, concludes one in-depth analysis; actually, emphasizes the historian Kenneth Robert Janken, "*dithered* might be a more apt descriptor." There was a class dynamic at play, says Janken, since White "handicapped himself from the beginning by betraying prejudices against blacks who were not from the middle class": "He tried not to conceal his contempt for the defendants and their parents," all from desperately poor backgrounds. By way of contrast, the ILD, led by Patterson, and the CP, of which he was now a leader, "had demonstrated admirable commitment—it was practically alone among white liberals, progressives, and radicals in its practice of militant inter-racialism and its demand for racial equality." Moreover, "Communists offered the black freedom struggle unprecedented world exposure and an alternative to the NAACP."[73]

In short, the ILD and the NAACP were competitors, and it was not preordained that the NAACP would emerge triumphant, as it did in the 1950s when Patterson was jailed and Jim Crow was eroded in return. This raises the potent point as to whether an alternative route was possible for what came to be called the civil-rights movement, wherein there would not have been a capitulation to the Red Scare—and evisceration of civil liberties—as civil rights were expanded tentatively.

Part of the problem with the NAACP approach was their seeming initial readiness to accede to ILD leadership in what became a historic case, then backpedaling furiously once it became evident that the case had become paradigmatic. Oakley Todd of Chattanooga sought to remind one and all that the when the ILD entered the case in April 1931—"before the trials were even over"—William Pickens of the NAACP "had written to the *Daily Worker* congratulating the ILD on 'moving faster' than any other agency to save the boys. Pickens sent the ILD a check for the defense of the boys!" As for White, he was "caught napping by the Scottsboro case."[74]

White begged to disagree. He admitted that "many Negroes looked upon the Communist as a new Messiah, a new Moses sent to lead them from . . . bondage," as with "Jesuitical zeal and cleverness the American Communist agitator sought to fan this flame of discontent." His fundamental point was that the ILD and CP were somehow illegitimate—but if Negroes did not receive justice, they would turn to the Reds en masse, which meant that support for his NAACP should be hiked by an order of magnitude to block a radical advance (not that the two should work in unison on behalf of Negro advance).[75] It was with worry instead of guarded elation that White averred that it was "increasingly clear that the Communists are determined to make a Sacco-Vanzetti case out of the Scottsboro cases."[76] "Even handed justice," according to White, was "the only antidote to the spread among Negroes of revolutionary doctrines." His reflections on this case received mass attention nationally, an indication of the profound import of that which he conveyed.[77] His idea that anticommunism required concessions to the besieged Negro in order to bar his or her shift leftward was to become holy writ by the 1950s.

White's appeal struck a chord among those who seemed to be more concerned with Red advance than with the defendants receiving justice—which did redound to the benefit of the Scottsboro Nine (though it suggested, ironically, that if the Reds were subdued, similarly positioned defendants would not necessarily receive justice). The contestation between the ILD and the NAACP—or Patterson and White—did, however, create a competitive dynamic that moved some white centrists away from indifference toward racism or (worse) to fear that otherwise radicals would gain traction and their vaunted way of life might be jeopardized. Others were of the view of the Negro leader J. Finley Wilson, who told White that Scottsboro was "enough to try men's souls and if someone does not protest the black man in America will be as his brother in South Africa."[78]

Wilson was not the only person contemplating the global implications of this case. Writing from Paris, one friend of the NAACP queried White about what his organization was doing on this front in light of French-left and Communist activity involving such eminences as Romain Rolland, Henri Barbusse, and Rene Maran—a sheaf of clippings showing as much was attached.[79] Others were forwarding items from Germany concerning all manner of ILD activity, suggestive of the weight of Patterson's organization and what the NAACP was up against.[80]

It was in August 1931 that Patterson, recently returned from Moscow serendipitously as the Scottsboro case was taking off, appeared at the annual meeting of the nation's premier organization of black lawyers, the National Bar Association (NBA), then convening in Cleveland. The NAACP was briefed as if this were a matter of counterintelligence, with reference made to the cordial relations between the ILD delegation led by Patterson and the NBA leader, Raymond Pace Alexander—perhaps Houston's only real competitor for the title of leading Negro attorney in the nation. Alexander too was a graduate of Harvard Law School, and in addition he was the first Negro to graduate from the prestigious Wharton School at the University of Pennsylvania.[81] According to his biographer, Alexander was "not afraid to work with radical and left wing organizations," and he had raised eyebrows by inviting Patterson to this gathering.[82] Alexander had returned recently from Moscow himself—accompanied by his equally accomplished spouse, Sadie Mosell (the first Negro woman to receive a doctorate and to receive a law degree from the University of Pennsylvania)—where he emphasized that "the Soviet Union.... *is the only country that offers liberty and equality to all people black and white.* When I go home to America," he declared forcefully, "I will tell my people, the Negroes, that their salvation lies in Communism."[83] After Alexander was rebuked by the NAACP for this apparent warmth directed toward radicals, this learned Philadelphia lawyer responded in kind, noting his attempt to get a NAACP representative to speak[84] and pointing out how he had offered his eminent services to the NAACP on behalf of the Scottsboro defendants as early as April 1931.[85]

The Negro press noticed this kerfuffle, underscoring the "unexpected visit and addresses" from Patterson and how the "talks by the Communist representatives brought about a heated discussion as to the relative merits" of the NAACP "as compared with" the ILD—a comparison bound to sharpen ideological clarity. "The question was finally settled by having the Bar Association endorse the efforts of both groups"—a de facto victory for the ILD.[86]

The NAACP chose to accept the perceived challenge from Patterson's ILD. Pickens, who had flummoxed Patterson by speaking German in Frankfurt during their most recent encounter, was unequivocal: "The issue is clear: war has been declared by the Communist crowd. They shall have it."[87]

As for Patterson, he was bogged down in a war of another sort, embarked on a dangerous mission to the heart of darkness that was Alabama in 1932. Traveling in spartan Jim Crow accommodations all the way, his initial stop was a Negro church, where he spoke vociferously against racism. Preceding him was a letter he had published in a local newspaper, which provoked outraged peals of protest. As a direct result, said Patterson, "I was thereby enabled to organize considerable mass sentiments against the outrageous attempts on the part of the authorities to segregate" more extensively—no easy task. In Chattanooga he visited the mother of the defendant Eugene Williams and the families of his codefendants and arranged to take a trip to Kilby Prison where they were warehoused. The poverty-stricken Mrs. Williams, he recalled, resided in a two-room cabin—"the front room served as bedroom, parlor, and dining room combined"—yet threw caution to the wind when she chose to accompany him on his dangerous journey. Thus, with the sisters of one defendant and father of another, the unlikely team set out by car for Atlanta, where they picked up other relatives of the defendants before embarking for the prison. The "families," Patterson said at the time, "express great faith" in the ILD.

They must have, for it did not require an advanced degree to recognize that in Dixie few things were more dangerous than consorting with a "black Red"—the prospect of which sent dreams of necktie parties coursing through the more febrile imaginations in this benighted region.

Arriving at Kilby, they found—predictably—that the "prison guards were hostile and insulting." They refused entrance to a white member of the ILD delegation on the premise that "it was 'Nigger Day.'" Finally, the delegation marched through an iron gate that led into a corridor and then past a series of iron gates to the stairway leading to the death cells. There they were stopped. A guard approached. "Have you searched these niggers?" he inquired. They were searched thoroughly. Finally they were admitted to the inner sanctum, where the defendants were sited. They conferred there in the presence of "surly and hostile guards" who, after twenty minutes, interrupted and ordered an end to the meeting, though they were scheduled for forty-five minutes. They complied.

Back in Atlanta, they organized Scottsboro defense meetings, as a Negro owner of a theater donated his facility free of charge for a fund-raising concert. From Atlanta, Patterson departed for Birmingham and took three of defendant Roy Wright's sisters to visit him in jail. They found that their lobbying had paid off when one of the defendants was transferred from death row at Kilby. Birmingham was as trying as Kilby, as the delegation stood exposed in a thunderstorm and waited interminably while the police examined and searched each visitor. Again, the white member of the delegation was refused admittance, as apartheid barriers were maintained strictly. Patterson confronted a guard as a result and was confronted with vociferation in turn. "You get out of town," he was instructed, "and don't you ever come back here." The guard rose as if he was going to execute his mandate unilaterally. "Git," he said, with venomous finality. Patterson departed and soon found that he was followed by a "Negro stool pigeon." The Negro Communist then proceeded to organize more defense meetings in Birmingham and Chattanooga, all while he was shadowed by a plainclothes officer. Patterson managed to elude him and ducked into a local shrouded ILD office.

There he found that Mrs. Williams had been told by the chief of the Red Squad that he knew that this "Nigger Red" was in town and that if he were not careful, his dead body would soon be found in the streets. Undeterred, Patterson began a search for the two white women—Ruby Bates and Victoria Price—said to be molested by the defendants and was told that they were "on the 'Island.' This island stands in the river, some distance from town, and is a refuge for escaped criminals, a haven for bootleggers and an assignation place for whites and Negroes of both sexes who mingle there without prejudice and without being molested." His search proved unfruitful—but in another sense, his detailed report, published in the Negro press, was a fruitful announcement that a new kind of fearless leadership had emerged that did not seek justice solely through biased courts and did not shrink from confrontation, if need be.[88]

Patterson's comrade Nat Ross later recalled this dangerous mission. He had warned Patterson how perilous it was to prowl around Paint Rock, Alabama, particularly for one with his accent and politics. All he could prevail upon Patterson to do was to exchange his New York homburg for a proletarian cap. In his narrative to the Negro press, Patterson neglected to note how two gunmen had grabbed him and forcibly ejected him from Birmingham.[89] But later he did tell government investigators that he "had been run out of Birmingham and the feeling was that there was a likelihood of my being lynched," as "there were threats" to the effect that "I would be lynched if I was caught there again." While visiting Birmingham jail, "Threats were made to me from guards with hands on their pistols." Thus, he chose to take "an assumed name in Birmingham"—though the "Pray Sundays" held for Scottsboro in Negro churches in Birmingham apparently did not require a cloaking of identity.[90]

Remarkably, Patterson had chosen to make a habit of journeys into Jim Crow bastions. Near this same time he had traveled to Maryland's eastern shore—where Frederick Douglass had been enslaved—to visit another unjustly imprisoned Negro, Euel Lee, this time fifteen minutes before his slated execution. It was a "Dantesque region," said the Communist writer Mike Gold—though, apparently, Patterson had not abandoned all hope when he entered there. Lee was illiterate, caught up in a typical frame-up, accused of murdering his white employer and family. "He had a noble fortitude," said Gold, and "would have been a Chapayev under other conditions, the leader of a slave revolt"—and that is how Patterson treated him. "I'm not afraid to die, Mr. Patterson," he said. "Don't worry about me none, but keep right on, defending our poor people." Lee was quite religious and thought Patterson had been sent by God, which was understandable given the indefatigable labor expended by the Communist on his behalf, including leading a delegation to the governor, whom Patterson addressed angrily. "Timid and conservative members of our delegation were shocked by my manner," said Patterson later. "But sometimes it is necessary to present the issue sharply."[91]

His brusqueness proved unavailing—but not without consequence. Paul Robeson later admitted that "as a young man, I was tremendously inspired by [Patterson] going into the South and fighting in that area." Thus, before he headed to war-torn Spain, "Pat and I had long conversations" that compelled the artist-activist to deepen his own political commitments. Still, it was unmistakable that Scottsboro—not least because of the expression of global solidarity it engendered, accompanied by Patterson's personal fearlessness—indicated that a new day had arrived and that Jim Crow had entered a downward spiral of crisis that could be only resolved with its liquidation.[92]

4

Scottsboro—and Collapse

Buoyed by massive global support, the Scottsboro campaign took black America and then the nation by storm. Patterson asserted accurately in early 1934 that Scottsboro "has raised the question of international working class solidarity to its highest level. It is linking Tom Mooney and the oppressed Negro masses inseparably together."[1] Thus, he said beamingly, "Every Negro worker and toiling slave on the land breathes freer because of the activities of the ILD," while the "southern landlord lynchers have learned to curse its name and to dread the presence of its organizations." The main point, he stressed, was "a new understanding of the term—international working class solidarity."[2] Patterson later argued that as a result of this case, "the right of Negroes to sit on juries in the South was won again." "Never before had there been so vigorous a defense of the Negro victims of terror since the Reconstruction era," he said with satisfaction in 1945. "The case was made a world cause because it was symbolic of Negro persecution." Most importantly, "The world began to act on the [mal]treatment of [the] Negro."[3] This was particularly true in the aftermath of 1945, when the United States found it necessary to more effectively charge Moscow with human-rights violations—in part to counter Moscow's charges about Washington's deficiencies in this crucial realm.

Scrambling to not be overtaken by events, Walter White recognized that—at least in the short term—he would have to work out an entente with Patterson and the ILD. White was blunt in acknowledging "what the Communists have done in making [the Scottsboro] case one of world-wide interest—and we must admit that they certainly [have] done this."[4] The ILD at this point was comparable to the NAACP in membership—and since the former stressed mass action, they appeared even larger—with Patterson overseeing a group that contained many branches in New York City: as of the spring of 1933, there were 1,092 members on the Upper West Side of Manhattan alone.[5] The ILD had "two hundred thousand members and affiliates," announced Patterson in mid-1933.[6] By early 1935, James Ford announced that in Harlem alone, there were "11 branches," a

CHAPTER FOUR

"total membership of 1,090," and a "solid membership of 850. The composition of our membership is 650 Negro, 440 white," with a "core of about 300 active comrades"—though "Party comrades number less than one-third of these," and most of the latter were "new Party members."[7]

Like a well-oiled machine, the ILD maintained a strict checkup on tasks proposed and executed,[8] while their close ally, the League of Struggle for Negro Rights, pressed ahead vigorously on numerous fronts as it sought to incorporate the splintered remnants of Garvey's followers into the ranks.[9]

Thus, by early 1933, White's deputy, Roy Wilkins, reported that he had had a "conference" with "Mr. William Patterson" and "came to an understanding whereby the Association is to have presented to it by the ILD certain bills in connection with the strictly legal work of the case and the NAACP will pay these bills out of a segregated Scottsboro defense [account]"[10]—an accord that was broadcast far and wide,[11] as the NAACP hastened to seem relevant to this new stage of a movement they thought they headed.[12]

The ILD-NAACP pact required delicate negotiations. White knew that the man he called "Dear Pat" was "rushed" but hurried to insert himself into his schedule.[13] "Dear Pat" was pleased with the "splendid offer of financial cooperation" that ensued, a case study in building the "united front."[14] When the bargain was struck, it took place at the neutral venue of the ACLU—with Roger Baldwin acting as a kind of referee.[15]

This Negro line of Tordesillas, demarcating the diverging jurisdictions of left and center, was a mighty concession by the NAACP. But did they have a choice, given the association's weaknesses?[16] Leading a mass movement that galvanized the international community was not their forte—but this scorned option was precisely the route to Negro liberation, with jockeying in biased courtrooms (their specialty) being at best an accoutrement. In a sense, Martin Luther King Jr. filled the vacuum left by the NAACP in the 1950s when they were not able to meet the obligation to propel a mass movement, just as Patterson did beginning in the 1930s. By adding their legal firepower to the ILD's, which too was considerable, the NAACP served to propel Patterson into the front ranks of Negro leadership. Perhaps gritting his teeth, in late April 1933 White found himself sitting alongside the two Communist leaders—Patterson and the recently recruited Ben Davis—at a rally of 2,500 for the Scottsboro defendants at Harlem's Abyssinian church.[17]

The recruitment to the CP of Davis, a Harvard Law graduate and scion of a leading Atlanta family that was in the same circle as King's, was emblematic of the ripples driven by Scottsboro. While in Atlanta, Patterson had arranged to hire a "prominent white firm," as he put it, to handle the similarly important case of Angelo Herndon, a young Communist charged with a major offense after leading demonstrations against economic misery. Patterson handed over eight hundred dollars to the firm, but then he met Davis. "I asked if he would like to participate in the legal defense. He was agreeable. I returned to the offices of the white firm and informed it that I would like to see Ben Davis as co-counsel. 'No dice' was the reply." Peremptorily, Patterson "released" this obdurate lawyer, though—slyly—he refused to return the retainer.[18]

Thus, moving swiftly and adroitly, Patterson was bolstering steadily the ranks of the ILD. Yet rather than Tordesillas, the ILD-NAACP pact was more like the Treaty of Ghent of 1815 in that it served as a rest stop before more squabbling erupted, as the weight of conservatism—notably in Dixie—was too formidable to allow Reds like Patterson to gain a consistent advantage. Thus, only months after Wilkins's entreaties, White addressed Patterson in highly combative terms.[19] Derisively, he referred to Patterson's "14 page letter," which was "written for publicity purposes and was dictated by your political philosophy," studded with "misstatements" and "lack of information." Actually, given the general rancorous tenor of their relationship, this response could be deemed conciliatory.[20] For his part, Patterson demanded that White transfer to ILD coffers certain funds collected by the NAACP on behalf of the defense. Chillily, Patterson reminded White of a "conversation . . . in your office" and the larger point that "it was the combined mass and legal defense which raised Scottsboro to so high a political level and chiefly distinguished it from the many cases otherwise similar that preceded it"—i.e. cases handled by the NAACP that failed to gain as much support as this one. "Because of this," Patterson continued confidently, "Scottsboro has become unique in the annals of defense struggle for Negroes in this country," and "it was this mass influence which penetrated deeply into the ranks of the membership of your own organization which forced you to offer a proposal to raise funds for the . . . defense. For two years, we had been requesting a united front of all organizations sincerely desiring to cooperate in the defense of these innocent boys. During those two years," he said with contempt, "you had not only held yourself aloof from this united front, but had continually assailed our leadership and defense policies." Yet when the ILD presented "legal" bills by prior arrangement, the NAACP balked.[21] After ritualistically lambasting their "refusal to involve the masses" in the case, Patterson declared that this was "the most unprincipled case of robbery known in the history of the struggle of the Negro masses."[22]

Patterson said that his ILD had "one hundred seventy thousand American workers, members, and affiliates" and thus was not to be trifled with.[23] It was partly due to the strength of the Communist-oriented left that even the NAACP—contrary to their views in the 1950s, when this situation changed drastically—could not always refuse the hand of cooperation from the ILD. Before this turning point, it was more widely acknowledged that anticommunist practices often quickly became anti-Negro practices.[24]

This contestation over Scottsboro was to be reinterpreted after Patterson and the radicals had been eclipsed and the NAACP emerged triumphant. The allegation was propagated that the ILD had misappropriated funds meant for the defense and diverted them elsewhere—perhaps to Moscow, in a reverse of the usual trope about the ILD being funded by "Moscow gold." But Earl Browder—after he had been ousted from Communist leadership and had turned against the party he once headed—disagreed sharply, asserting strongly that the ILD was the wronged party in this case.[25]

Internecine disputes aside, the thunderous footsteps of marching Negroes—and their allies globally—could not be ignored by the NAACP or Dixie. Thus, it was Patterson—accompanied by the mother of Tom Mooney—who marched to the U.S. Supreme Court in the fall of 1932[26] and who—accompanied by James Ford and Louise Thompson—was marching in Manhattan for the Scottsboro defendants.[27] Patterson took the lead in the recently formed League of Struggle for Negro Rights, Langston Hughes's nominal presidency notwithstanding.[28] In May 1933, Patterson escorted Ruby Bates—now on board with the defense—to the steps of the White House[29] and on Mother's Day 1934 led a delegation that included the mothers of Scottsboro defendants again to the White House in search of a meeting with President Franklin D. Roosevelt. The delegation included representatives from South Africa and the doyenne of the Negro movement, Mary Church Terrell, along with Patterson's old comrade Richard B. Moore. From abroad, mothers of political prisoners—including that of the famed Bulgarian Georgi Dimitrov, who had faced down the Nazis in a courtroom in Germany—made pointed appeals. Theodore Dreiser, the well-known novelist, was enlisted to write the appeal carried by Patterson.[30]

Patterson had intended that the "suffering" Scottsboro mothers would interview Roosevelt,[31] and he lamented that the "failure of the President to meet with these grief-stricken mothers" was "objectively giving moral support to the lynchers," which was not accidental. "Undoubtedly his position as leader of the political party which has to its credit—or shame, as one may view it—a record of five thousand lynchings" was at issue. This "leads the Southern oligarchy to regard the present administration as its spokesman; which belief is of course far from incorrect."[32] Ultimately, Roosevelt's party would be forced to surrender—in part—on Jim Crow, with the sacrifice of Patterson's leadership and the simultaneous defection of white voters from Democratic ranks in Dixie for generations becoming part of the ill-advised bargain.

Still, the 1933 march on Washington, where he was accompanied by Thompson and Ford, then his closest comrade, was also suggestive of why White could not afford to ignore Patterson. As a new president took office in a nation wracked with economic pain, thousands marched within hailing distance of his residence. Thompson, the "provisional secretary" for this effort,[33] recalled that upon departing from Harlem that morning, "the streets were roped off between 7th [and] Lenox" near their office on 135th Street. "The whole block was just a mass of people who had turned out," she said, still in awe. "We didn't have enough buses," as the delegation from New York alone "was 3,500, mainly blacks." Speaking in 1981, she remained caustic, charging that "the ILD was doing the kind of mass action which was protested very vehemently by organizations like the NAACP, who felt that what was being done was an exploitation of blacks" instead of their salvation.[34] As for FDR, he may have become accustomed to overtures from Patterson, since in late 1932, while he was still governor of New York and president-elect, the Communist barrister arrived at his doorstep in Albany to lobby for freedom for Tom Mooney. A "prolonged argument" erupted, it was reported, between Patterson and the president-elect's retinue, with Patterson asserting that his delegation "would return tomorrow and remain outside the governor's office until they got in."[35]

Patterson later recalled how he accompanied Mooney's mother to Albany. He had joined this campaign as early as 1916, adding, "I . . . had many occasions to take Mooney's mother to the White House." But this encounter was just before FDR moved southward: "There was a delegation of five, which I headed, and we discussed the matter with the President[-elect] in the Executive Mansion in Albany and [he] on that occasion telephoned."[36]

The Mother's Day mobilization, which may have been the apex of the entire Scottsboro campaign, found Patterson heading a delegation of twenty-five that was ushered into the office of Louise Howe, FDR's chief of staff. As Patterson spoke, a grimace graced Howe's face—particularly when Patterson used the word "demands," which he did frequently. At that precise moment, said a reporter, the president was meeting with representatives of "Fascist Italy and Fascist Germany" and did not have time to discuss Scottsboro. Patterson insisted that Howe reach FDR by phone so that his delegation could have a "showdown with him," and Howe sought to comply. "No," was the word FDR uttered, which emerged audibly from Howe's telephone, "loud and emphatic enough to be heard by everyone in the room"—this in response to a "demand" for a face-to-face meeting. They left Howe with a copy of their Bill of Civil Rights for the Negro People and proceeded to the office of Congressman Oscar De Priest of Chicago, where he received the same presciently far-sighted document that "demanded" "full social, political and economic rights for the Negroes."[37]

As Patterson's prestige grew, the Harlem pastor Adam Clayton Powell Jr. invited him to address a gathering, which drew a considerable 1,500 people; this, said one scholar, "demonstrated both the respect Patterson commanded for his individual talents and the Party's newfound credibility as an exponent of practical reform."[38] This was the embryonic stage of an alliance between Powell and radicals that culminated with his election to Congress and his backing of Patterson's comrade, Ben Davis, to succeed him on the New York City Council. There the two radical lawyers joined the leading journalist and intellectual Heywood Broun in protests about hospital cutbacks,[39] one more indication of Patterson's growing presence—and Scottsboro's—in Harlem (particularly in the pews of Negro churches).[40]

But Patterson did not obtain this popularity in exchange for softening his radical message. During this same period he was to be found at the newly opened Harlem

Workers' School lecturing on something he knew well—"The American Negro as Revolutionist." A reporter described the meeting as "fairly well attended by an informed and enthusiastic audience."[41] Likewise, when he spoke in Philadelphia before what was described as a "huge throng at Girard Manor Hall, 911 West Girard," and spoke dramatically of the U.S. Negro "as the most persecuted group in the world today," it was indicated that collaborating with him were the premier black leaders of that metropolis: Raymond Pace Alexander and Robert Nix, like Powell, a future congressman.[42] Remarkably, also present was the man who was to become Delaware's premier Negro attorney, Louis Redding, then described as a "recent professional convert to Communism"[43] A few months later, Patterson scored an even larger coup when the man who may have been Hollywood's brightest black star in its firmament—William "Bojangles" Robinson—gave Patterson a check for fifty dollars for the Scottsboro defendants.[44]

At the end of the day, what gave Patterson and the ILD the strength to compete with the NAACP and make a mark on an otherwise recalcitrant United States were the global connections that he had made while abroad. Almost to the day that Wilkins announced the ILD-NAACP accord, speaking from what was becoming his second home—Chattanooga—Patterson declared that at his behest, the ILD had "cabled all its international affiliates to demonstrate before American embassies and consulates abroad."[45] Patterson even crossed the border to Canada—"illegally," said the authorities—to address a May Day celebration with Scottsboro on the agenda.[46] Internationalism was not a one-way street, as Patterson sought to link repression in Alabama and Germany.[47] This ability to link the local and global provided radical synergy that redounded to the benefit of the antiracist struggle and laid the groundwork for the final retreat of Jim Crow,[48] again under international pressure, during the cold war.[49]

When Patterson was linked (supposedly) in mid-1934 with Eleanor Roosevelt and the anthropologist Melville Herskovits as a member of a so-called Red Network, it was an indication that not only had he arrived in prominence but that the radicalism he represented was a force to be reckoned with.[50] It was also an indication of his effectiveness, since this "honor" had been preceded by the announcement that for the first time in a half-century, a retired Negro postal worker in Chattanooga served on a jury—the precise issue at play in nearby Scottsboro.[51] Still dissatisfied, Patterson demanded that all criminal cases involving Negroes be transferred to federal court—a blatant contravention of the "states' rights doctrine" so cherished in Dixie—and then infuriated white chauvinists further by insisting on the "right of self-defense,"[52] decades before this basic demand had been thought to have gained momentum. The Scottsboro initiative was a recognition of the fact that breaking the back of reaction meant in the first place a fierce confrontation in Dixie.[53] Thus, Patterson was increasingly to be found in Virginia[54] and the Alabama-Tennessee border region, as the NAACP observed nervously.[55]

Patterson's ever bolder interventions were a reflection of his own growing profile—and that of the radical left, of which he was becoming an important symbol. But he was not alone, for not only were figures like Pace Alexander, "Bojangles," and Redding hovering within his orbit, but he was surrounded by a growing circle of Communists and fellow travelers in his adopted home in New York, including Ben Davis, Louise Thompson, Loren Miller (another talented Negro lawyer), Langston Hughes, James Ford, Harry Haywood, Cyril Briggs, Richard B. Moore, and many others, all of whom conferred regularly, particularly at meetings of the League of Struggle for Negro Rights, routinely held at their Harlem office at 131st Street and Lenox Avenue.[56] Hughes—who, according to one astute analyst, was "deeply influenced by the Scottsboro trials"[57]—also seemed to be noticeably moved by Patterson's challenge to act as a "revolutionist" and not an "aesthete." Paul Robeson was moved similarly.[58]

Robeson may have had in mind how Patterson had helped to recruit Ben Davis to the ranks of radicals early in his tenure with the ILD. Patterson visited the client, Angelo Herndon, in Fulton Tower Prison and on his behalf "sent letters to defense organizations in Europe, in South America and in Cuba, to Latin American countries," which—like Scottsboro—led to "demonstrations . . . before American embassies."[59]

But Patterson's reputation had not seduced everyone. His oratorical skills were highly persuasive to those he addressed regularly in Negro churches, but many liberals, often on the receiving end of his biting critiques, were not as moved. Broadus Mitchell of Johns Hopkins University, for example, found him to be "fanatical, unyielding, and suffering from acute egomania."[60] The first two adjectives had been deployed previously by others to describe Patterson's highly religious father.

Nevertheless, at this juncture, anti–Jim Crow momentum was galvanized—particularly in New York City—by Patterson and his ILD and LSNR, as suggested by the luminaries flocking to their banner. One of Patterson's closest relationships at this juncture was with the leading NAACP attorney Charles Hamilton Houston,[61] whom he familiarly referred to as "Charlie" (and, like so many others, Houston referred to his colleague as "Pat").[62] "I hope to be able to spend some time with you," Charlie told Pat in the midst of Scottsboro organizing,[63] as he offered his own home as a place for the embattled Communist to rest, rather than confront substandard Jim Crow lodging.[64] Patterson was "too tied up with other matters," including serving as "Marshal of the March" on the White House on Scottsboro, to find time to speak at Howard but pledged to correct this oversight.[65] Afterwards, Patterson was effusive in seeking to "appreciate every courtesy you extended both to Comrade Haywood and myself while in Washington and, as well, to the other comrades who found your advice and assistance of an extremely welcome character."[66] Their warm and personal tie was emblematic of a larger political reality: the uniting of Communist and non-Communist on a common platform of unremitting hostility to Jim Crow. On the legal front, Patterson coordinated approaches with Houston. As the latter noted, his NAACP was proceeding from "a racial point of view" while knocking on an open door by urging that Patterson proceed "from a class point of view."[67] Houston tried to serve as a bridge between the often clashing Patterson and White,[68] though Patterson did not mince words in referring to the "utter bankruptcy of the leadership of the NAACP."[69] Houston went further by freely extending to the ILD what Patterson termed "material assistance."[70]

But what united Patterson with his NAACP counterpart was agreement on politics, particularly concerning the trailblazing Scottsboro case. Houston knew that in "making Negro oppression [a] world-wide issue," the ILD had changed the calculus of Negro resistance, having "introduced [the] Negro to [the] effect of mass pressure." This incited the "Negro masses" and "gave them a sense of power," as this was "struggle by the masses instead of a struggle for the masses"— the latter being the NAACP's approach, while the former was the ILD's. The ILD did a service as it "fought the case not as an isolated incident but as one phase of the struggle." This "marked a new kind of struggle in the South." It also "showed the Negro bourgeoisie the insecurity of his position"—no small item.[71] The ILD "exposed American hypocrisy which plays missionary to the heathen but supinely tolerates the exploitation of the American Negro right in its own front yard"; "whatever the defects of its philosophy [it] is on the right track when it identifies all its members actively in its activities." Thankfully, Patterson's organization "has put the so-called Negro leaders on the spot," compelling them act to emulate the ILD.[72]

The two had met in the 1920s, when Patterson was residing in Harlem and not fully committed to radicalism. Though part of the NAACP hierarchy, Houston thought "it was very important that the ILD did win" out over the NAACP in the intense bickering over the case, "because it marked an historic departure in the struggle for Negro rights in the South." The ILD brought a "new day," a "new approach," in the "absolute insistence without any apology whatsoever that Negro witnesses and Negroes be given the same rights in the Southern courts as anybody else." Yet "even more fundamental," he emphasized more than once, was the "identification of the masses of the people in the struggle for liberation," since "in the Scottsboro case for the first time, the masses of Negroes were identified with the struggle itself, were made to feel it was their struggle." For "the first time," he said, Negroes and their allies "were taught" that "the whole set up of the Southern government was an instrumentality which was not designed to give them justice, but to keep them in their places"; that is, "the courts were instrumentalities of the status quo and [black people] must ultimately depend for their liberation upon their own power and the solidarity of the white and black masses of the South."[73]

Part of what distinguished Patterson and his ILD from groups like Houston's NAACP was the former's attempt to shape electoral politics directly, so as to alter the atmospherics and landscape for democratic advance. As his developing relationship with Powell suggested, Patterson was not immune to the call of electoral politics, a call he answered in 1932 when he ran for mayor of New York on a CP ticket, stressing the attack on unemployment and including the demand that Negroes be hired as "conductors, motormen, electricians" in the subway system. As with the NAACP, Patterson took a bare-knuckles approach in handling those who could be deemed to be on his side of the barricades, assailing his Socialist party counterpart, since "right here in Harlem," the Socialist party "Jim-Crowed Negro workers in their halls and kicked them out when they protested."[74] He was heartened by the fact that—perhaps due to Scottsboro—Negro registration in Gotham had doubled in the runup to the election.[75]

Mainstream politicians were not heartened by Patterson's growing presence. The *New York Times* reported that four thousand filled Arcadia Hall in Brooklyn—most of them Negroes—at a rally where the mayor pleaded with them to continue to have faith in the United States. The mayor—who, it was said, "refused to speak at meetings with Patterson" and "apparently had been oblivious to his presence" until the Communist rose to speak—"left the hall at once," but Negroes were more concerned with Jim Crow than ideological litmus tests.[76]

Patterson had been billed to speak, but "Tammany politicians"—as the ILD put it sourly—stalled until "only half of the fifteen thousand [*sic*] who had jammed the hall to hear about Scottsboro were present." When he finally rose to speak, "the Tammany demagogues who had already spoken and who were on the platform with him, rose and left the hall." Unruffled, Patterson reminded those remaining that though the ILD was "not a Communist organization," it was the CP "which first of all brought the Scottsboro infamy before the workers of the world, rousing them to protest. Where were the Democratic, Republican, and Socialist parties at the time?"[77]

What is often lost sight of in the debate concerning squabbling between and among progressive forces as the reality of fascism rose in the 1930s is that there were principled differences between erstwhile allies that were difficult to paper over. For example, should Patterson have remained silent on SP failures on the antiracist front? Might that have eroded his own credibility, if he had done so? In any case, Patterson chose to challenge his SP counterpart, Morris Hillquit, to a debate "specifically on the Negro Question."[78] Hillquit responded harshly, denouncing Patterson's "purely nationalistic" approach, which "strikes me as neither Socialistic nor Communistic"; however, his response and that of other Socialists tended to suggest that Patterson and his comrades had placed radical pressure on the SP as with the NAACP, compelling change.[79]

Predictably, sparks were emitted in profusion when the candidates met in debate. The *Baltimore Afro-American*, which seemed to cover Patterson's activities as avidly as the *Daily Worker*,[80] was struck that the candidates chose to "lock horns," as "wise cracks and feathers" flew. Their man—Patterson—"carrie[d] off

[the] toga in applause," they reported. He "rode roughshod over his opponents and received the widest and most prolonged applause from an audience made up mainly of Republicans and Democrats." Thus, when "Patterson took his seat there was prolonged applause. Some of the outstanding men and women in the audience declared that their eyes had been opened."[81]

Hillquit notwithstanding, Patterson's leadership of the Scottsboro defense virtually guaranteed that his run for mayor would garner attention,[82] though a poll at the City College of New York showed him trailing his Socialist counterpart badly (though he was ahead of both the Democrat and Republican candidates). Patterson's twenty-four thousand votes in this race was not paltry—though Hillquit received about ten times as many,[83] indicating that despite the Communists' inroads in the wake of Scottsboro, there was considerable room for improvement. On the other hand, 260,000 votes for Socialists and Communists in the nation's leading city indicated a solid base for left-wing advance.

Patterson's ascension was also part of an affirmative-action plan,[84] whereby those emerging from the most degraded sector of the international proletariat were boosted—which immediately placed the headquarters of Jim Crow on the defensive, adding national security to Dixie's lengthening list of woes. Another aspect of this sprawling initiative was Moscow's decision to produce a cinematic epic highlighting Jim Crow that would feature in various phases of production a long list of African Americans, including Patterson's future spouse, Louise Thompson.[85] Her profile was burnished, since she headed the project,[86] hastening the day when she and Patterson would be partnered: she too left Moscow with a positive assessment of Soviet antiracism—particularly compared to Dixie.[87] This logistically challenging enterprise faced immense difficulties from the start, then collapsed in recriminations, with the future NAACP leader Henry Moon asserting forcefully that the project was canceled for political reasons having to do with Moscow seeking better relations with Washington.[88]

Though Patterson was not part of this project directly, his reputation as the embodiment of rising radicalism drew him inexorably into the vortex. So, at the tail end of his race for mayor, Patterson was dragged into the fierce debate about this failed film. "Technical difficulties alone led to its postponement," he countered, before donning the experiential mantle. "I spent three years in the Soviet Union. I saw with my own eyes every effort to smash race and national barriers." Thus, to Henry Moon, the journalist Ted Poston, and other naysayers, he made the same declaration with which he had greeted Hillquit: "I therefore challenge you to meet me in debate."[89] Like so much that combined Negroes and Moscow, onlookers were seemingly as riveted as the participants by these events. Writing from Berlin in 1932, Poston observed accurately that "the whole matter has created quite a stir in the European press." Whenever outsiders scrutinized the U.S. Negro, the left seemed to emerge victorious, as the horrific Jim Crow hardly placed Washington in the best light.[90]

After journeying to the dankest precincts in Dixie, leading delegations to the White House, running for mayor, managing James Ford's 1932 vice-presidential race,[91] running in a local Manhattan district in 1933,[92] and administering a major mass organization (in addition to debating), Patterson took on yet another difficult assignment when he opted to travel to Cuba, then in the midst of a rapidly deteriorating political situation. Yet, like South Africa—and as part of the Comintern's then-reigning perspective—Cuba also had an affiliate of the ILD, which had organized clandestinely in 1930 and then emerged gradually from the shadows by 1933, with Patterson arriving soon after.[93]

He spent two suspense-filled weeks there in 1934, "helping the Cuban workers organize their legal defense apparatus," as he told his comrade, Mike Gold. He only changed his clothes twice during that period, indicating his around-the-clock activity and furtive scurrying from site to site. He met his Cuban counterparts clandestinely while dodging hit squads organized by right-wing politicos and gangsters alike.[94] There was "little sleep" and "tremendous tension," he confessed later.[95] This kind of "underground work," as he put it, was nothing new to him, given his experience in Europe. There was a tense meeting in a "sugar field" in what turned out to be a massive learning experience for him. "I learn[ed] something about the export of racism," he confessed later. "American occupation increases and deepens racism on the Cuban isle," for "black Cubans as well as black citizens of USA [are] not allowed in Havana's plush suburb of Miramar," while "gambling joints run by American gangsters [are] all Jim Crow."[96]

Patterson was no stranger to Cuba or Cubans, having broken bread earlier with Juan Gomez, whom the *Chicago Defender* termed the "Frederick Douglass" of the island.[97] Patterson was also a figure of repute in the region generally, with the State Department reporting nervously in early 1933 that "Communist activities in Haiti" had "close connections with radicals in the United States, notably New York," with Patterson singled out.[98]

Skulking perils aside, this was a trip worth making, for Cuba—in the U.S. sphere at least since 1898—had become a fortress of ILD support. In July 1931, the Tobacco Workers Union of heavily African Santiago protested vigorously the "proposed electrocution" by "imperialistic murderers,"[99] referring to Scottsboro: this case struck a chord in this nation with a sizable population of African descent. By early 1934, there had occurred a militant demonstration before the Havana office of a U.S. steamer: windows and doors were smashed. At another demonstration before a British consulate, the Scottsboro case was linked with London's backing for U.S. imperialism.[100] Scottsboro was seized upon by Cuban radicals as a tool with which to batter the growing military dictatorship, seen as closely allied with Washington, their nemesis. Five hundred amassed at one protest, leaving many injured, thirty arrested and one murdered. Following in this murderous wake was a declaration of martial law, placing five of six Cuban provinces in this difficult strait.[101]

The ILD's work in Cuba reverberated in New York when the NAACP was informed of major newspapers in Havana publishing lengthy articles on Scottsboro with a repetitive theme, as one member was told: "Your organization did not participate in the defense." As a result, "[NAACP] leaders Walter White and William Pickens have been denounced to the public opinion as a couple of renegades at the service of great industries."[102] Finally, the pressure and tension and tireless labor reached a deafening crescendo. Upon returning from Cuba, Patterson suffered a physical collapse—and barely escaped with his life intact.

5

Back in the USSR

Patterson returned from Havana to Harlem, and as he talked with his sister in her apartment, he found that one of his lungs had collapsed. He fainted dead away, as if this were a scene from a bad movie. He had been working too hard for years, with Cuba being the capstone of this ill-advised course. Harry Haywood and other friends and comrades insisted that he travel forthwith to the Soviet Union for treatment, as it was the only place where a Negro without money—a category that now included the once relatively affluent attorney—could get adequate medical care. He spent a year on his back at a sanitarium on the Black Sea, it was said—then two more years, according to his comrade Mike Gold, "studying the life of the former oppressed nationalities who were the Negroes and Jews under czarist racism and now are free."[1]

A collapsed lung was not the only problem that resulted from his nervy journey to Havana. "Uncle Sam made me prove my citizenship when he found my protests to racism annoying," said Patterson, for upon his return, it seemed as if his entire status in the land of his birth had collapsed likewise. The authorities—as he put it later—"saw fit to allege that I was an undesirable alien," and his cousin was compelled to submit an "affidavit which prevented the Immigration Service from declaring me to be a West Indian"—one from a region thought to be a general carrier of a radical virus.[2]

The FBI maintained that it was during this star-crossed era—the mid-1930s—that Patterson was ensconced in the anti-Nazi underground in Europe, darting furtively in and out of Hamburg and Paris particularly. The authorities had reason to know, as they kept track of his movements as the ailing Communist—then listed as residing at 181 West 135th Street in Harlem—departed from New York for Europe on July 21, 1934, after spending a tumultuous two weeks in Cuba in May.[3] Patterson was not the only U.S. Negro who had served time in the Soviet Union, for his comrade James Ford had spent more than two years there as well,[4] as Moscow, along with Hamburg, had become a fortress of anti–Jim Crow and anticolonial resistance.

The FBI had reason to believe that as early as 1930, Patterson was toiling in Paris, "making contact with American Negroes in France" as well as "French colonial troops" on which the regime was heavily dependent. His mission in Cuba, it was believed, was also prompted by Moscow-based authorities—International Red Aid (IRA), in this case. By 1935, it was thought, Patterson had ascended to lead the "Anglo-American section" of the IRA and in this capacity had spoken publicly in Paris and Copenhagen, among other sites. While in France, it was said, Patterson organized a number of protests at the U.S. embassy in Paris, denouncing Washington's stance on the Civil War in Spain—all this before returning to his homeland in the winter of 1937.[5] (Louis Budenz, the infamous stool pigeon who once worked alongside Patterson in Chicago, contended that during this period Patterson was actually "representative of the Anglo-American Communist Party of the Communist International." Patterson, he maintained, was a "Super Communist."[6]) The FBI may have noticed that after Patterson decamped to Europe, all of a sudden the *Negro Worker*, the Pan-African publication produced theretofore in Hamburg, could now be found more readily in Harlem but also in Johannesburg, Cape Town, and Port Elizabeth—not to mention London and Paris.[7] Though Patterson claimed that it was James Ford who "was the moving force behind the First International Trade Union Congress of Negro Workers Hamburg, Germany," the FBI may well have deemed this to be classic misdirection on Patterson's part, seeking to deflect attention from his own sizable role.[8]

It was Patterson who provided detailed instructions for activists in West Africa,[9] while continuing to provide updates about Scottsboro.[10] In Germany near the same time as Patterson's visit, the prominent Negro socialite Molly Moon—also the spouse of an NAACP leader—effused about the rise of Hitler to her friends: the "situation in Germany is really thrilling," she asserted gushingly. Patterson would have agreed, but not in the sense that she intended,[11] indicative of the ideological split in black America that was to crest in the 1950s.

Actually, both Patterson and the FBI were correct—the only question is precisely when during his three-year absence from North America was he recovered sufficiently to resume political duties: the FBI placed this much earlier than Patterson did. Patterson said that his job title at the time was "secretary" of the "Anglo-American Section of International Red Aid," not seconded to the Comintern. He admitted that he made it to Leningrad, where he saw family, including his daughter Lola. He acknowledged conferring with Max Yergan in Moscow—this African American Communist had moved to South Africa, and the placement of the *Negro Worker* in the beleaguered continent probably had something to do with his presence. Yes, said Patterson, he conferred with James Ford in Paris—Ford may have been as critical to revolutionary activity among Negroes globally as Patterson. In Paris they met with Ralph Bunche, the Howard University professor, then of the left but on a fast track to the center. He also met with Alain Locke, yet another Howard teacher with international aspirations. Thyra Edwards, the

Texas-born African American activist, was also on his itinerary—they met in Paris, while she was on her way to Spain. And, yes, he met with high-ranking Ethiopian officials there too in the wake of the Italian invasion. Patterson could rightfully claim partial responsibility when this latter war became a sacred cause in the Pan-African world, a part of his still-shrouded mid-1930s legacy.[12]

Patterson could also look back with satisfaction at his handiwork in the United States. During his tenure, the ILD transformed Scottsboro into a global cause célèbre with gargantuan consequences for Jim Crow. As a result of this case, Negroes were to be included on juries in hundreds of counties in Dixie, where they had been barred previously, which led to thousands of men and women walking the streets who might have been otherwise incarcerated—or executed—and manifold ripples leading to a retreat of Jim Crow. With pressure lifted somewhat on the most degraded portion of the proletariat, they were more able to contribute to the massive union-organizing drive that broke out simultaneously—and not coincidentally, the overall environment for civil-liberties expansion was improved decisively. As one ILD staffer put it, "Our work of solidarity extends beyond the borders of the United States, into Spain [and] into Germany, for the victims of Hitler's fascism; Italy, Finland, Bulgaria, Cuba," and elsewhere. "This is not idle boasting," it was said with punctuation. One hand washed the other, for these lands also contributed mightily to the Scottsboro defense and U.S. victories.[13]

This had redounded to the benefit of the radicals. George Charney, who ultimately turned on the CP, acknowledged that by the mid-1930s, "the party in Harlem was already well established as a result of the Scottsboro movement," as "it had several thousand members," with a headquarters on Lenox Avenue that "was a beehive of activity, day and night."[14] Ironically, as the CP and ILD pushed back aggressively against Jim Crow, thus serving to incorporate Negroes more firmly into the body politic, in a sense they were undermining this base of support, as blacks may have felt less of a need to become radicals. As one scholar notes, "Plainly put, by 1936 Communism was helping blacks to become twentieth-century Americans." For it was during this conflicted era that "there were some 3,895 blacks making up nearly 10 percent of the total Communist membership; in 1938 black membership reached a peak of 6,900"[15]—though these figures may understate the reality, since the growth of CP membership in the mid-1930s was nothing short of spectacular, with Patterson's New York district leading the parade.[16]

Although Patterson's health problems were not fictitious, the FBI had a point in thinking that he was not bedridden for three years and that his physical collapse provided an opportunity to utilize his evident talents on the global—not the national—level. As early as May 1935, a reporter found him at the massive May Day parade of 1.8 million marching in Moscow—not Sochi. His ebony hue made him easy to spot in a crowd.[17] Subsequently, he was found not on the Black Sea but "recuperating" and residing at the "Savoy Hotel, the second largest hostelry in Moscow."[18] Weeks later, he was present at a gala international theater festival in Moscow, consorting with the likes of the talented and lovely Sylvia Chen.[19] When the Negro activist Thyra Edwards[20] arrived in Moscow, she had the opportunity to be lectured by an upright Patterson.[21] Nancy Cunard, the bohemian heiress, also found that Patterson appeared healthy when she conferred with him in Moscow in July 1935.[22] In fact, by mid-1935, even the Negro press was lampooning the notion that Patterson was bedridden.[23]

Others too found an energetic Patterson in Moscow, including Paul Robeson, who had reached a turning point in his life. He and Patterson had bonded in Manhattan in the early 1920s, and since then Robeson had followed his friend's trajectory with clear interest. In the mid-1930s in Moscow they had intense discussions—about Jim Crow, global politics, and the like—which evidently convinced Robeson to deepen his own commitment to justice.[24] At times the two friends were joined by Robeson's brothers-in-law and his accompanist, Lawrence Brown (also well known to Patterson). Thus it was on New Year's Eve, December 31, 1935, that the companions had a high old time to the point where three days later, Eslanda Robeson—also present—remained "still full of vodka, caviar, champagne, and Russian cigarette smoke." Though there were still internecine struggles among the black expatriates and the black leadership of the CPUSA—embodied by Patterson—there was little (public) comment on the bitter battles enveloping the leadership in Moscow that surpassed in intensity those of the expatriates by several orders of magnitude.[25] Indicative of Patterson's reach was the fact that when a brother of Ms. Robeson got into trouble in the Soviet Union, they enlisted Patterson to rescue him.[26]

Patterson and Robeson met repeatedly in London, Paris, and Moscow during this period, and upon returning to Chicago in 1937, the performer kept his Communist friend up to date about global developments, leading the usually buttoned-down Patterson to conclude effusively, "for me he is the truest friend I ever had, except my sister."[27]

Likewise, it was Patterson who made connections for the non-Communist Negro journalist Homer Smith, then reporting from Moscow for the Negro press.[28] When Nancy Cunard arrived in Moscow in July 1935, she took this journey not least because Langston Hughes and Patterson had assured her that her innovative book on the Negro would be translated into Russian. While there, she conferred with Patterson—representing the State Publications Bureau—who assured her that the Soviets "adored" her work and that he was authorized to present her with three intriguing possibilities: a translation of her book into Russian, a contract to write a book on African colonies, and the possibility of organizing a traveling exhibit of African and Asian art. Patterson was in a position to see that all three were executed,[29] just as his frequent jaunts to Hamburg facilitated his pioneering role in utilizing African seafarers as couriers, delivering revolutionary instructions globally.[30]

Just as Washington a few years later chose to look the other way as severe internal problems percolated in Moscow when it desperately needed to forge an antifascist alliance, Patterson and his comrades chose to do likewise. So did the Negro press, to a degree, which did not inform its readers instructively about political repression in Moscow but instead, in mid-1934, as Patterson was just arriving, effused about the imposing statue of Pushkin in Moscow: "Only in four countries of the world can be found official monuments honoring black citizens and Russia is one of these."[31] In their emphasis on Pushkin in divining Soviet attitudes toward the Negro, they mirrored Patterson.[32] Indeed, the prominent role played by Pushkin in Russia—which contrasted sharply with the degradation of Jim Crow—provided Moscow with an automatic advantage among Negroes,[33] a reality that infuriated many U.S. patriots.[34]

Even the NAACP, soon to be ensnared in a purge of real and imagined pro-Moscow advocates, was at this juncture carrying advertisements promoting travel to Soviet Russia.[35] This may have been attributable to the pro-Soviet bias of Du Bois—but even after he resigned in 1934 and evidence of repression in Moscow had become widespread, the journal he formerly edited continued to carry articles revealing what anticommunists could well have characterized as pro-Moscow themes.[36] Even the *Pittsburgh Courier*, not necessarily a friend of Patterson, seemed impressed by what their reporter witnessed in Moscow when "a class of 52 white American children, sons and daughters of American engineers and specialists here, began their first school work in an English-speaking Russian school with a Negro professor," a "member of the Russian Communist Party" who was "teaching mathematics and chemistry." This favorable opinion reflected on Patterson, as he was "recognized as a leading force among Communists here."[37]

Instead, Negroes (and others) in search of the promised land kept pouring into Moscow and Leningrad. It was reported that George Kennan, soon to be renowned as an intellectual godfather of the cold war, had "given this matter" of the deluge of U.S. nationals arriving in Russia "careful study."[38]

Still, it would be one-sided—and incorrect—to suggest a unanimous pro-Soviet opinion among Negroes (though it was true that there was less reservation about this nation among this beset community than among most whites). For such a view would hardly shed light on other pivotal events, which catapulted Patterson once more into the headlines of the Negro press. Soon after arriving in the Soviet Union, Patterson found himself at the receiving end of prickly barbs launched by his erstwhile comrade from Hamburg, the Trinidadian George Padmore.[39] The story was reported that Padmore had broken with the Comintern because Stalin—in pursuit of friendlier relations with colonial powers in order to corner fascism in Germany—had wanted to reduce support for anticolonial agitation, to which Padmore took sharp exception. Though this story fits the prevailing anticommunist zeitgeist, recent scholarship has called it into question,[40] for at the time, the issue seemed to be Padmore's ever closer ties with Liberian elites.[41]

Patterson struck back fiercely in mid-1935, assailing Padmore's "cowardly traitorous face" and his "lie that white workers will not fight side by side with the black for the liberation of black masses."⁴² Using Padmore as a punching bag, Patterson charged that his analysis was replete with "startling contradictions,"⁴³ and the Trinidadian was among those rebuffed for daring to group Stalin with Hitler and Mussolini. He was a "renegade," said Patterson of Padmore, who engages in "infantile analysis," since "the Negro people alone, scattered and unorganized, are undeniably in no wise a serious force against world imperialism." Thus, "Padmore's position objectively aids Mussolini," who was then ravaging Ethiopia.⁴⁴ When Patterson's close friend Nancy Cunard complained about his battering of Padmore, Patterson just looked at her pitifully and said, with a sigh and without repentance, "Oh, Nancy. . . ."⁴⁵

The godfather of Negro conservatism, George Schuyler, rushed to Padmore's defense. Patterson and Ford were his principal targets, though the CP itself was termed "one of America's most unnecessary organizations," replete with "shameless opportunists."⁴⁶ Earlier, Patterson was said to deploy a "gatling gun of invective and bizarre class-war verbiage" against the NAACP, as ideological cleavages deepened.⁴⁷

Patterson being at the tip of the spear when Padmore was assaulted represents a turnabout of sorts. They had met in Moscow upon Patterson's arrival there in 1927. "That was our first meeting," Patterson recalled years later. "We came west together to set up the First International Negro Workers' Congress which was convened in Hamburg."⁴⁸ Still, it should not be deemed surprising that Patterson was front and center as this assault was launched, as more responsibility had been thrust upon him in Moscow, a function of his skill as an administrator; his Bolshevik ideological rectitude; his competence as an attorney, which provided a useful mode of thinking through problems; and his manner, which though direct, was not confrontational nor threatening. Fundamentally, during his second tour of duty in Moscow, he had become an exceedingly influential figure coordinating revolutionary activity globally—but principally in Europe, Africa and the Americas. After Padmore's departure from higher councils, Patterson's role was enhanced further.

The conflict with Padmore was part of a wrenching series of events, including a diplomatic thaw between Moscow and Washington, which in turn was driven by the grave apprehensions that accompanied the rise of fascism in Europe. This was the backdrop to the change of political line by the Communist International, stressing the "popular front" or broad antifascist unity with those who may have been denounced only recently. Patterson was in Moscow as this new approach unfolded. This 1935 alteration helped to give rise to the opinion that shifts in Moscow were dictating changes in North America; the pressure that had been placed upon an expansionist Berlin by coordination across borders, not least from Hamburg and Moscow, was overlooked. This antifascist pressure had not succeeded in checking the rise of fascism, propelling a mandate for change. Surely, if the political temperature changes, the thermometer should adjust.

Even before this 1935 demarche, evidence was mounting that despite the remarkable advance of radicals, as evidenced by the unparalleled success of the Scottsboro campaign, the sight of Patterson working himself into a tizzy of collapse was suggestive that something was awry. Patterson had worked himself into a near-death experience because of the immensity of the task at hand and the relative weakness of his forces. In mid-1934, just before sailing eastward, Patterson informed his troops that "despite its mass influence," the ILD "is today after nine years of growth still organizationally small and not fully equipped to cope with the growing terror and the developing fascist tendencies" spreading globally and nationally.[49] This was not the first time that Patterson had uttered a pessimistic note about the group he headed. In the fall of 1932 he had referred disconsolately to the "weakened state of our organizational structure," which was "paralyzing," not to mention the national office's "hand-to-mouth existence."[50] All the while, a Great Depression was biting deeply, leaving few unscathed. Patterson detected the "worsening of the conditions of the working class all around," with "speed-up, stretch-out, wages below the starvation level," all of which strained the resources of his ILD, the self-proclaimed "defense arm of the working class."[51]

Patterson had a point. For an organization with such an ambitious agenda, the ILD had a conspicuously modest budget.[52] And despite the growth of the Communist party in Harlem, this organization too faced deep difficulties[53]—difficulties that had not ceased by 1937, when Adam Clayton Powell announced that "our community does not possess an active Scottsboro Defense Committee."[54]

In mid-1935, as Patterson looked on anxiously thousands of miles away, Harlem exploded in a paroxysm of violence, pushed to the brink by what had become mundane: an expression of white supremacy. That his future spouse, Louise Thompson, was in the eye of the hurricane as the tumult unfolded made it all the more poignant.[55] Undeterred, from afar Patterson hailed the new reality—"Negro Harlem Awakes" was his conclusion, as he seized the opportunity once more to castigate Negro leaders deemed to be not sufficiently leftist.[56]

In this context, Patterson's jousting with the NAACP seemed misguided, as police brutality spiraled and the fascist danger rose[57]—even as his antagonist, Padmore, aligned with the association.[58] For even if the NAACP was bogged down in "bourgeois reformism," did this note have to be sounded by Patterson? Should not he have sought to deepen an alliance with these forces? Of course, it was not foreordained that the left would be driven downward and the NAACP would be uplifted. Would not this "leftist" approach backfire when—as occurred two decades later—the ruling elite turned its full fire on Patterson, leaving him desperately in search of allies himself? Certainly, the NAACP had weaknesses, as non-Communist observers of the left were quick to point out—but was it not more important to join hands with the association as the fascist peril rose?[59]

This was precisely what one of Patterson's closest friends and colleagues—Charles Hamilton Houston—had been saying for some time, even before 1935. In mid-1933, he warned Patterson and the ILD not to "waste their effort" by "fighting" with the NAACP but to seek common ground instead.[60] An unconvinced Patterson continued to refer to the "utter bankruptcy of the leadership of the NAACP."[61] After engaging in the usual rapping of Du Bois, Patterson predictably chortled that "the impact of Scottsboro is shattering the ranks of the NAACP leadership."[62] Houston found Patterson's hostility to the association "very disappointing"; though the two "have very definitely disagreed on many matters," the law dean accused the Communist of spreading tales about the NAACP that were "unequivocally untrue."[63] He assailed the Black Belt thesis as "race suicide" and further charged—like Padmore—that the ILD had dialed back on Scottsboro as the Moscow-Washington thaw tantalizingly arose.[64]

Ben Davis symbolized the often condescending approach taken by comrades to sturdy allies like Houston.[65] Roy Wilkins rebuked Patterson after finding ILD literature that assailed the NAACP and advised that "some sort of entente cordiale must be maintained on the surface at least for the time being."[66] Adam Clayton Powell, much influenced by Communists at this juncture, was criticized likewise by Wilkins after having reportedly told Harlemites that "our own NAACP has sold us out."[67]

By the same token, John H. Holmes of the NAACP, who stood second to none in his passionate anticommunism, still reproachfully told Wilkins that "before burying the hatchet in the earth, you buried it in the flesh of the Communists."[68] Patterson was not the only one that could be accused of sectarianism, for, as the ILD saw things, it was the "Trotskyite and Lovestoneite agents who harangued . . . against asking a united front with ministers," men who had become a fortress of ILD support. "Religion is not an issue in the Scottsboro defense," said Patterson, adding ominously, "Anyone who makes an attack on this defense on anti-religious grounds will also be attacked by us."[69]

Louise Thompson joined in the fracas, rebuking the NAACP, though she focused on the disbursement of funds.[70] The ILD, the main generator of the case and attendant funds, had the whip hand, as Wilkins acknowledged.[71] Ideological conflicts aside, this ILD-NAACP rift was driven in no small measure by money and the funds flooding into Manhattan as a result of the ILD's global initiative.[72] Financial and ideological conflicts were worsened by gossip, not least about Thompson, the rare woman in an arena heavily populated by men.[73]

The conflict came to a head at the NAACP convention in Chicago in July 1933, which ILD representatives took by storm as journalists watched, bewildered. "Despite the repeated attempts of the NAACP leadership to stifle the growing rank-and-file opposition from the floor," said one, "the delegates forced discussion on the Scottsboro movement." James Ford "was enabled to speak because of the overwhelming sentiment in his favor. The success of the ILD in the defense of the boys was repeatedly pointed out," as "Communism together with Scottsboro was the most important issue at the convention" in the face of "autocratic control of the [NAACP] leadership."[74] Unsurprisingly, the next year, when Patterson requested participation of mothers of the Scottsboro defendants and other allies in the NAACP convention,[75] Walter White promptly rebuffed him.[76]

But with the shift in political line globally, Patterson and the ILD pulled back from their repetitive reproach, as the erstwhile "bourgeois reformists" of the NAACP became allies to be courted. No line is all upside, and neither was this new one, for lost was the ability to point out to the wavering or the uninformed that white supremacy could not be subdued by legal wizards alone, as the NAACP seemed to suggest—a point that might have carried weight two decades later, when the ruling elite began the process of jailing Patterson, leaving the lingering impression that the NAACP approach should be the only game in town. The turn toward the popular front also served to blur distinctions between the center and the left—to the detriment of the latter. In some ways, this turn brought mixed results, as previously the ILD seemed to be motoring ahead and getting the best of the NAACP in their repeated tiffs. Kelly Miller, one of the more articulate Negro centrists, was thinking this thought in the mid-1930s.[77] However, the rise of fascism dictated—in a sense, literally—that business as usual was unsustainable.

The shift to the popular front, driven by fear of right-wing recrudescence, probably played a role in the redeployment of Patterson back to his homeland. That he was dispatched to Chicago—an industrial center with a sizable Negro working class and middle class, and thus a basis for building decisive radical strength—was not coincidental.[78] The CP had established a stronghold this city well before Patterson's arrival.[79] By the spring of 1938, the party in Illinois had 5,800 members, "twice as large as at the time of the previous state convention two years ago," it was said with pride; in the two weeks prior to this report, "more than 300 members" were "recruited in Illinois."[80]

Thus, by October 1937 Patterson's allies at the *Baltimore Afro-American* found him in hale spirits, "back after 3 years in Russia" and detailing how "colored technical men are making good in the Communist republics." Further, he said, "colored technicians who were unable to find opportunity for using their training in the U.S." should follow the path trod by John Sutton—and many more.[81] He continued to omit mention of what the FBI had detailed—his political deployment in Western Europe. Instead, before arriving, he chose to "deplore illness," which supposedly prevented him from being "personally" at the side of his ILD comrades.[82]

The popular front was well under way, embodied in the National Negro Congress (NNC)—spearheaded by Reds, though membership stretched across the ideological and organizational spectrum—which came into being months before Patterson's arrival in the big-shouldered metropolis. Lester Granger of the Urban

League seemed displeased by the NNC's explosive early growth, observing that it "has stirred up more bitter controversy than any gathering of Negroes since the days of Marcus Garvey's 'provisional presidential incumbency.'" It was "idle to attempt its dismissal as 'a Communist gathering,'" as some were invidiously doing, since "as a matter of fact, delegates were plentiful from the states where radical parties are weakest."[83]

Kelly Miller, a tribune of the centrists, seemed alarmed by the "leftward drift" of the NNC, as he too invoked the nationalist comparison in pointing to an organization already "unequaled by any undertaking since the heyday of the Garvey movement." He seemed displeased that "James Ford, famous Negro Communist, exerted the dominant influence" on their deliberations—though Patterson and his comrades seemed pleased that NAACP members and Reds alike had united on a common anti–Jim Crow platform that struck a chord of popularity in the Midwest most notably.[84] Patterson revealed early on why he was sent to Chicago—and not New York—when he informed Charles Hamilton Houston that "we in Chicago have a sense of responsibility to the country as a whole, since we alone have the power to elect a Negro Congressman." That he wanted Houston to endorse his good friend Earl Dickerson for this seat over the incumbent, Arthur Mitchell—"the guy is of no earthly good. We do not [need] a rubber stamp in Congress"—was an example of how the popular front was being executed.[85]

It is unclear how NAACP leaders greeted this unilateral ceasefire on the part of Patterson and his comrades, though it appears to have been accepted with equanimity on all sides—notably in the early stages. It required little prompting for Patterson to push Houston as a candidate for the U.S. Supreme Court—"I sent a telegram to Roosevelt recommending your name," he confided.[86] Such favors no doubt encouraged Houston to respond by endorsing Dickerson.[87] Walter White joined Patterson in endorsing Houston in this example of amiable coalition building.[88] The bilateral amity was revealed when William Pickens exhibited his formidable writing skills in the left-led publication *New Masses*—and Patterson praised him for same.[89]

This pattern continued when Patterson joined progressive trade unionists in pressing the American Federation of Labor to drop racist barriers against Negro plumbers.[90] Similarly, Patterson became a passionate defender of the New Deal, something of a turnabout from the time when he was leading militant delegations to FDR's doorstep.[91] Roosevelt, he said, was "the first President since Lincoln to attempt to smash barbarism in the South."[92] He defended the New Deal from "renegades" like the publisher Robert Vann and reminded one and all, "Let us not forget that the New Deal is not the same as the Democratic Party,"[93] which still contained a potent Dixiecrat wing. Instead of reprimanding the emerging performer Marian Anderson for her political transgressions—as he did with Negro poets in 1928—he sought to show sympathy and understanding for her dilemma of seeking to be popular in a Jim Crow society. Though he contrasted her invidiously with Paul Robeson—who by that point had committed firmly to the left—he displayed remarkable understanding for her situation, though she may have benefited more from a relentless dissection.[94]

Thus, by the time of Patterson's arrival in Chicago, the CP was informing the Comintern about advances in "Negro work" since the Seventh World Congress. Still, they warned, "sectarianism and isolation has not been eradicated." There was more work to do in terms of involving the NAACP and Urban League in the work of the NNC, it was reported.[95] The shift in line apparently had not aided the ILD, for it came in for reproach because of its "narrow character."[96]

For his part, Patterson seemed pleased with the results of the change in line. By June 1938 he was back in Manhattan, marveling at the twenty-two thousand that filled Madison Square Garden to the rafters for a CP rally. "It is said that only the Bolsheviks can pack the Garden," he boasted, adding with pride, "reaction has sneeringly labeled the Communist Party" the "Party of the Negro."[97] Like many Harlemites away from home, he seemed homesick at times,[98] which suggested that it would not be long before he returned.[99] As it turned out, he would remain in Chicago for more than a decade before returning to Manhattan as the popular front was crumbling and the Red Scare was rising.

6

Black Chicago

After operating semiclandestinely in Europe and coordinating the Scottsboro campaign, being deployed to Chicago almost seemed like a demotion for Patterson. Surely, the Second City was no backwater, and given its steel mills teeming with proletarians, it was more eye-catching for a self-respecting Marxist-Leninist than a relatively less-endowed Manhattan. The simple presence of those like the well-regarded writers Richard Wright and Frank Marshall Davis (who was later to make his mark in Honolulu) was sufficient to show that Chicago was a vanguard city.[1] Still, the abjectly horrible conditions faced by the Negro working class—including many abodes bereft of water or even toilets—were suggestive of the fact that there was much work to do.[2] Patterson was dumbfounded by what he found in black Chicago: 60 percent of Negroes were unemployed, which was "reflected in the terribly dilapidated houses, the crowded kitchenettes, the gambling and vice." Thus, he said, "We need scores of housing projects that exceed the Ida B. Wells project in scope and in provision" since "the Negro ghetto is an eyesore to democracy."[3]

Patterson was serving as an editor at the *Midwest Daily Record*. It could be found on 360 newsstands in Chicago, including scores of distribution points in the Loop alone, more on the North Side, and also on the mostly Negro South Side (though, tellingly, fewer than in the first two).[4] When funds needed to be raised for the paper in 1938, five hundred "house parties and money-raising affairs" were announced "to be held by branches and individuals," suggestive of the reach of the journal and their Communist sponsors.[5] It was an impressive periodical with full coverage of sports and films, news from all over the Midwest, and lavish illustrations.[6] "With his experience of living in Moscow," said the Euro-American journalist Ben Burns of the *Record*, Patterson "became our political 'commissar' in interpreting political right and wrong." Though Burns says that Patterson was placed in his post in part to keep an eye on Louis Budenz (soon to emerge as a notorious stool pigeon), the reverse might have been the case,[7] since in Chicago Patterson also worked alongside Morris Childs—who would emerge as the most valuable asset of U.S. authorities in the ranks of the Communist party and Patterson's frequent foil.[8] The presence of Budenz and Childs guaranteed that sooner or later, Patterson would come under close surveillance.[9] And that did occur, as he was monitored relentlessly, including his very appearance. In 1941 he was listed as five feet, ten inches tall and two hundred pounds, "stout and heavyset," with a "high forehead" and "partially gray-curly hair,"[10] much of which was to depart in years to come, leaving a veritably bald and shiny dome. More ominous than surveillance was the prospect—said the FBI—that he should be "considered for custodial detention in the event of a national emergency."[11] There was microphone surveillance of the CP office in Chicago, and, reflective of the tense atmosphere, when Patterson ventured to Peoria, reportedly he "saw more guns down there . . . among our people" than he had ever seen before, which suggested that "violence" was nigh. Strikingly, J. Edgar Hoover was unsure if "our people" meant Reds or blacks.[12] Whatever the case, Patterson conceded that he had to "to leave that city without speaking," as "there were mobs parading the streets."[13]

No longer a student, he was now an educator, providing pedagogical points regularly in his weekly column and leading a discussion on world affairs every Sunday night at the CP's Workers' School at 431 South Dearborn.[14] Reportedly, Patterson told an informant from the FBI that he—Patterson—"has quite an influence as a teacher" and pointed to the crowds attending his lectures as evidence.[15] "Many people are impatiently looking forward," said one of his many fans, to the time when he "will resume his regular Sunday evening forum on current events."[16] He had become a regular spokesman for the CP and the popular front and a regular presence at Negro churches, which he knew well from the Scottsboro campaign.[17] Thus, he was a moving force when the CP's South Side Section held a "festival of Negro Culture" at the Savoy Ballroom at Forty-seventh and South Parkway on the twentieth anniversary of the party's founding and the seventy-fifth anniversary of the Emancipation Proclamation.[18] When 1,400 were expected at a Communist rally in October 1939, Patterson could rightfully claim a large share of the credit.[19] The same could be said when eight thousand materialized to greet a recently freed Tom Mooney.[20] Patterson was equally prominent when the NNC began organizing regionally from Chicago, with the experienced lawyer briefing the assembled on the nuts and bolts of "social legislation."[21]

Of course, he was part of the leadership of the NNC.[22] Similarly, he was still part of the leadership of the ILD, working alongside the future East Harlem congressman Vito Marcantonio.[23] In 1941, at the Hotel Piccadilly in Manhattan, he was again elected vice president of the ILD—by acclamation.[24] In the wake of Scottsboro had emerged a number of court decisions advancing civil rights to the point where Patterson was moved to proclaim in 1939 that "Negroes felt the ILD was sent by God," while their anticommunist opponents endured "a spasm of fear and hatred" at the mere mention of the group. Seeking to write the first draft of history, Patterson said, "No federal government gave the black South the right to sit on juries"—the ILD did.[25]

Even before Patterson's arrival, Communists had in large measure attained leadership positions in a number of Congress of Industrial Organizations (CIO) unions, not only in the industrial sector but also in the Newspaper Guild, of which staff at the Negro organ the *Chicago Defender,* where Patterson was featured regularly, were prominent members. It was not long before Patterson was in the forefront of a strike against the *Chicago Herald Examiner,* viewed widely as insensitive to Negro aspirations. The *Defender* and *Herald Examiner* clashed sharply when the former charged the latter with a "frame up" for bringing criminal contempt charges against Patterson for his role in labor unrest. Throughout his tenure in Chicago, Patterson played a pivotal role in shaping the editorial politics of this influential Negro periodical. It was Patterson who recommended the Euro-American writer Ben Burns to the *Defender* and to Earl Dickerson's staff, then to the staff of what became the Ebony-Jet enterprise led by the eventual multimillionaire John H. Johnson.[26] One Chicagoan queried if the *Defender* felt that "Mr. Patterson is so well known that you did not need to identify him."[27]

It is not clear whether this correspondent was joking or serious—but Patterson's role within this organ was more than friendly and fraternal. This became evident when Patterson complained to the State Department during the war after the government of Haiti objected when reportedly Washington demanded that no personnel be posted in Washington "unless they pass for 'white.'" This was after Haiti was pressured not to have diplomatic relations with the then-ally in Moscow. "Patterson was very much upset over this situation," said the FBI in a "highly confidential" report, and as a result, "articles will appear in the *Chicago Defender* concerning this matter which will actually be written by Patterson but attributed to the anonymous source."[28] As the FBI saw things, in addition to his many other duties, Patterson was dabbling in running one of the top Negro newspapers in the nation. Supposedly, he was complaining bitterly in the summer of 1943 about their personnel practices. "They fired this boy who wrote articles on [the labor leader] Randolph.... [T]hey wanted to fire Langston [Hughes]," an irate Patterson was cited as saying. In response, he was on the offensive: "Now I would like to get as many as I could, a bunch of letters, in there calling for ... saying this is a disgrace.... [F]rom what I understand, word came from Washington to fire them," which was alarming to him.[29] The FBI well knew that he used pseudonyms—"Dean Victor" and "Dr. Baker Patterson"—to write for this periodical.[30]

These close ties with the *Defender* came in handy when Patterson chose to run for Congress in 1940, challenging the incumbent, Arthur Mitchell. From his busy campaign office at 3517 Indiana Avenue, he savaged the six years of meager results delivered by his opponent. Jobs were the main issue, though he also raised high the slogans, "Keep America out of the imperialist war!" and "Protection and equal opportunity for women."[31]

From his position in Chicago, Patterson boosted into existence the Southern Negro Youth Congress—a sister of the NNC—which was instrumental in militant challenges to Jim Crow, particularly in Birmingham.[32] It was Patterson who set in motion demonstrations that drove the racist film *The Birth of a Nation* out of Chicago,[33] before tackling its counterpart, *Gone with the Wind*. Patterson successfully collaborated in obtaining an injunction compelling the local plumbers' union to stop harassing Negro workers.[34] Patterson's busyness on behalf of workers was so conspicuous that during his stay in Chicago, J. Edgar Hoover himself provided material from a "confidential informant" to the White House aide Harry Hopkins about his initiative.[35] Patterson, said the FBI, was "vitally interested in trade union activities" and was "frequently consulted by top officials of several unions and particularly by officials of the United Electrical, Radio, and Machine Workers" and the "United Farm Equipment and Metal Workers," both of which were thought to have Communists within the leadership. He also "met frequently with prominent union officials regarding resolutions for presentation at the CIO National Convention held in November 1944."[36] "Technical surveillance" of Patterson was duly authorized by the FBI—a maneuver that Hoover thought would prove to be "enlightening."[37] FBI surveillance was a reflection of the growing paranoia about Patterson to the point that when he visited Casspolis, Michigan, because of his "hay fever," it was noted worriedly that "the place where he is going used to be a station of the Underground Railroad."[38] When in 1944 Patterson considered hiring a Japanese American secretary, alarm bells seemed to blast loudly at the local FBI office.[39]

Naturally, Patterson greeted the rise of the CIO with enthusiasm[40]—though, thought the FBI, the "largest Communist representation occurred in Local 351 of the Dining Car Workers union with twenty-eight comrades," which included the rising Red Ishmael Flory.[41] Flory, said the FBI, was also the "regional organizer" of the National Negro Congress and "has consulted Patterson concerning every step that has been taken by the Congress."[42] According to the FBI, Patterson was trying to place "sympathetic Educational Directors" in midwestern unions[43] and was "vitally interested in trade union activities."[44] Of course, Patterson had plenty of help for the Communist party, and its tens of thousands of members were engaged nationally and locally in a dizzying array of activities that was altering the political landscape decisively.[45]

Yet, beyond the daily drama of political organizing in an industrial center, there was another reason for Patterson to wind up in Chicago, for this town provided a venue for a heightened engagement with a comrade of whom he had become quite fond: Louise Thompson.[46] In 1933 she had become the first Negro employee of the International Workers Order (IWO), a noble experiment in providing insurance for those traditionally underserved—particularly

Negroes. She organized a multiracial lodge, and her adept managerial skills eventuated in her election in 1940 as vice president of the IWO. She was deeply involved in organizing black members in Chicago, including two thousand in 1940 alone. At her behest, a community center was established with fundraising assistance from Paul Robeson and Lena Horne.[47] Though often ignored, the IWO was an important link in a radical chain, suggesting her importance to the movement.[48]

Patterson's betrothal to Thompson was greeted as a kind of breakthrough by many heterosexual Negro women comrades, who—for various reasons—felt that they were routinely ignored and neglected by men of various stripes: Negro men like Patterson not least. Just before his marriage to Thompson, a number of these women reportedly had written to the Comintern and to Stalin himself beseeching them to do something about this matter. Thompson did not disagree, noting that "as far as black women were concerned, . . . if we had just had limited ourselves to the Communist circles, we would have been very lonely. . . . [There were] too many black men who became interested in white women and the reverse never took place." This was "resented," she said, "but it never bothered me much," since "joining the Communist Party does not make people whiter than sin." Thus, said the diminutive woman whose lighter skin contrasted with her spouse's dark hue, "when Pat and I married, there was a real celebration on the part of many black women to see that one of the leaders of the Communist Party had married a black woman."[49]

Patterson and Thompson had much in common, as their fondness for the NNC and rendezvous in Paris[50] at an important 1937 antiracist conference exemplified.[51] She was actually born in Chicago in 1901, though—like her spouse—she spent much of her youth in the West, including Oakland. She too had formative experiences with racism that were burned into her consciousness. Just as he had been shaped by an early encounter with Col. Charles Young, her encounter with the boxing champion Jack Johnson left an indelible impression upon her. Patterson came from an ultra-religious background, and Thompson's mother put her in a convent for a year. "I became very enthralled with Catholicism," said Thompson. "It captured my imagination," though "we attended the Christian Science Church" for a decade. She too attended the University of California at Berkeley and was not monolingual (she was elected to the Spanish Honor Society at her alma mater). A turning point for her arrived when Du Bois spoke in Berkeley, leaving her bedazzled and enthralled. She had encountered Patterson as early as 1919 in Oakland; apparently, he had invited her to the Soviet Union with him in 1927—"but I wasn't ready for that," she said. She taught at what is now Hampton University in Virginia, where she confronted the Ku Klux Klan. "I felt that if I stayed there any longer, I would become a kind of psychopath," she recalled. She moved to New York and worked closely with Langston Hughes and Zora Neale Hurston, and when Patterson returned from the Soviet Union in 1931, she and Augusta Savage—the renowned sculptor—arranged a forum for him to discuss his experience there. So inspired, she began an intensive study of Marxism—particularly Engels and Lenin, which were "eye openers," though it was "William Patterson [who] had introduced me to the subject of Marxism."

She spent three suspenseful weeks in Spain in 1937 during the height of the conflict. "The defeat of the Republic," she averred subsequently, "was something that touched me in a way that, until the devastation of Hitler, I had never felt before."[52] (This fondness for Spain was shared by Patterson.)[53] Spain aside, she was celebrated for her presciently feminist remarks upon her return from Madrid on "the place of women in a changing world," just as—like her spouse—she was praised for her courage when she was arrested in Birmingham while organizing IWO chapters.[54] Yet, also like Patterson, she had a decided interest in literary matters as an acknowledged leading figure in what came to be called the Harlem Renaissance. She "was the woman Hughes' mother had hoped Langston himself would marry," says the bard's biographer. Along with the attorney Loren Miller, the Communist leaning comrades were regarded as the "L'Raising Trio" during the ill-fated Moscow film project.[55]

Patterson recalled rhapsodically the moment he met his future spouse—it was in 1919 in Oakland at an event featuring the NAACP leader James Weldon Johnson. "I loved to dance," he recollected, "and I took Louise on her first visit to the Savoy Ballroom."[56] This was in 1927, when she passed through New York.[57] And so began a whirlwind (though elongated) relationship that culminated in a marriage in 1940, presided over by the influential Archibald Carey.[58]

Patterson and his spouse moved into a two-family house at 5341 South Maryland Avenue, with the Communist couple on the top floor and—reflective of the Jim Crow that thrust radical and nonradical alike into close quarters with obvious political implications—the leading Negro attorney Sidney Jones on the bottom floor. This particular block happened to be racially integrated—but this was far from the norm in this city (then as now).[59] It was an upgrade from his earlier residence at the not-so Grand Hotel at 5046 South Parkway.[60]

In many ways, Patterson had good reason to be pleased with the arc of his life thus far. Now approaching fifty years of age, he had finally found a life partner with whom he held much in common—not least ideological compatibility—and had under his belt years of practical organizing on the burning issues of the day. He was the rare Communist who could fairly be considered a Negro leader simultaneously, while his legal training placed him in the occupational stratosphere at a time when most people of his ancestry were consigned to be hewers of wood and drawers of water. Now he was in Chicago, whose brutally cold winters and unforgiving summers could not obscure the reality that if radicalism were to take root in the United States, it was more likely to occur here than most sites. But having spent considerable time overseas and having been deeply affected by the turn to the popular front driven by the rise of fascism, he knew better than most that profound changes could be in the offing that could easily bend drastically the rising arc of his life.

Patterson also knew better than most that the local and the global were unavoidably entangled—how else to explain his shifting approach to the NAACP? His arrival in Chicago was congruent with dramatic shifts in the global climate. Part of Patterson's dilemma was to continue to support progressive aspects of the New Deal—particularly the Wagner Act, the Magna Carta of labor organizing—while remaining critical about the same Democratic party's alliance with Dixiecrats, which inevitably meant backsliding on civil rights. Thus, when FDR came to Chicago—just as Patterson was settling there in 1937—to announce that Washington would seek to "quarantine the international aggressor," the Communist attorney insisted that the president should seek similar action in Dixie against the "aggressor." The "Negro Problem," said Patterson "[is] an inseparable part of world problems," just as the rise of fascism meant ill for antiracism, and the persistence of Jim Crow made it harder for the White House to confront its close cousin, fascism.[61] Patterson, who was in a position to know, compared the plight of U.S. Negroes to that of "national minorities" in Eastern Europe, such as the "Jewish people" in Poland (he had been in Warsaw years earlier) and the "abysmally oppressed Ukrainians" in that same nation.[62] "Black America, look at Germany!" he cried, since "that is the direction in which the feudal landlords of Dixie want to go."[63] "I have the greatest concern for the fate of Czechoslovakia," he said, "because I am desperately concerned about black men, about America, about humanity."[64]

Complicating matters further, said Patterson, was the nagging problem in Chicago of police brutality, targeting Negroes with a combination "of viciousness, of connivance with the underworld, and with the political overlords."[65] Shortly after arriving in this midwestern metropolis, Patterson found that "anti-Semitism is being very subtly promoted, very systematically and persistently fostered among the Negro people" via the circulation of various specialized newspapers.[66] There was an "underground fascist organization known as the American Rangers" in his new hometown that was engaged in military drills and seeking to build a Negro auxiliary.[67] Thus, Patterson seized upon the wildly popular boxing match between the "Brown Bomber" Joe Louis[68] and his German opponent, Max Schmeling, whom Patterson characterized as a "Nazi agent,"[69] leading to his joy when the German was bested.[70] "The cause of Jewish Germany," said Patterson, "is the cause of progressive and democratic humanity everywhere. But this cause of stricken people is particularly the cause of the Negro in America."[71] Contradictions emerged when rallies were held on this important matter—Negroes were excluded, as if some Chicagoans wanted to maintain white supremacy at home while fighting anti-Semitism abroad.[72]

The Democratic party with which Patterson and his party were allied was also a major part of the problem they were fighting. The exigencies of fighting fascism made this alliance understandable, but no less difficult. Repeatedly, while in

Chicago, Patterson raised a banner of opposition against FDR's frequent silences about lynching,[73] once telling him bluntly, "Get the Negro peon in the picture, Mr. President."[74] He also launched broadsides against Roosevelt's Dixiecrat comrades and their promotion by the *Chicago Tribune,* seeking to undermine both.[75] Yet in the pivotal election year of 1938, Patterson announced unabashedly, "I shall go to the polls and vote a straight progressive ticket"—meaning mostly Democrats, except for the Negro Congressman William Dawson."[76]

But there was another aspect of the problem that made Patterson's challenge even more difficult: Tokyo's decades-long appeal to Negroes on the basis of joint opposition to white supremacy. Combined with Japan's "anti-Comintern" alliance with Berlin—and the continuing Jim Crow policies of the Democrats—Patterson and his comrades were placed in a viselike position.[77] The ill-famed Negro conservative George Schuyler played upon this complication, to Patterson's dismay, when he declared that "so far as the colored peoples of the earth are concerned, it is a tossup between the 'democracies' and the dictatorships. Neither care anything about the darker folks except to exploit them."[78] Frequently, Patterson found it necessary to rebuff a growing pro-Tokyo sentiment among Negroes, which was buttressed by a complementary black nationalism.[79]

It was in this context that the religious grouping that became the Nation of Islam began to take root—initially, on an explicit pro-Nippon platform—first slowly, then enjoying explosive growth a couple decades later as the left-wing alternative symbolized by Patterson began to crumble. Patterson faced an exceedingly complex matrix: battered Negroes being catered to by Tokyo; some white Americans willing to combat fascism abroad but not necessarily Jim Crow at home; and unsteady Democratic allies in the same boat. Thus, when Berlin and Moscow negotiated a nonaggression pact in 1939, many were left disoriented, feeling that the nation they had thought to be the beacon of antifascist unity—the Soviet Union—had sold out.

"Confusion is rife," Patterson moaned, as "lies are being manufactured by the minute"; "all condemn the Soviet Union for protecting the lives of its own people after its proffered protection for Poland was brazenly rejected by [Neville] Chamberlain and his Polish puppets."[80] Patterson would have none of this. The nonaggression pact "does not mean that the Soviets endorse fascism," he thundered, "any more than the signing of such a pact with the United States would mean that the Soviets suddenly endorsed lynching [and] Jim Crowism." Assuming the mantle of authority, he concluded, "I have been in the Soviet Union," and "I know whereof I speak."[81]

Complicating an already complex scenario, in black Chicago Patterson encountered the contention that it was all a "white man's war."[82] This sour opinion made it difficult for him to provide unqualified support for London in its conflict with Berlin, particularly given Britain's continuing role as a colonial pariah in the Caribbean, Africa, and Asia.[83] "The war is not a white man's war," as so many

Negroes charged, but it was the "second imperialist war . . . for the purpose of keeping the Negro enslaved the world over."[84]

Inevitably, the European war and the bitter attitude of many Negroes toward it introduced further strain into the popular front. When in early 1940 Patterson's topic of choice was "Roosevelt Speaks for War," this was considered hardly unusual.[85] "Stop this imperialist war!" became his repeated cry—which was not much appreciated by those allies who thought (as Patterson was to think soon) that the battle against fascism should take precedence over all else.[86] These strains were revealed further when Richard Wright, the writer and prized Communist recruit, left the party in a huff, which was a major blow—though Patterson blamed his comrade, Harry Haywood.[87]

It was not long before the *Midwest Daily Record*, which had done so much to galvanize the popular front, began to wobble. Only weeks after the Berlin-Moscow pact was revealed, Patterson bemoaned how "financially weak" the paper had become.[88] The daily soon retreated to a weekly, and the reproach was added that "we had relied upon the support of certain outstanding New Dealers but now we find them intent upon pushing forward the present imperialist war."[89] A few months after this, the weekly had expired,[90] victimized in no small part by difficulties inherent in forging center and left in the face of a perilous threat presented by fascism.

A similar backlash enveloped the National Negro Congress, the embodiment of the popular front. By the spring of 1940, the *Chicago Defender*—now viewed as something of a house organ for Patterson, akin to the *Baltimore Afro-American*—reported how the NNC's top leader, A. Philip Randolph, had bolted from the ranks. "We disagree on the question of the Soviet Union," he said. "There have been some sentiments that in the event there is a war between Russia and the United States, the Negroes will not fight in a war against Russia"—anticipating by a decade a controversy that undermined Paul Robeson. The pointed remarks of the leading labor figure were greeted with stunned silence at the NNC confab in which he spoke. Perplexity reigned, since earlier in the evening Patterson, serving as chairman of the Resolutions Committee, had submitted his report in which it was stated that ninety-five resolutions had been heard by the committee, and seventy-three were accepted, an apparent display of unity. There were three thousand delegates present, but Randolph's exit marked the beginning of a sharp erosion of NNC influence, culminating in 1946, when it was folded into the Civil Rights Congress—which Patterson was to head by 1948.[91]

Randolph had broken Negro unity, based in part on a hypothetical foreign-policy concern—which was like radicals shunning him based on his evidently naïve faith in the beneficence of U.S. elites. That it was not long before Moscow and Washington were actually allied in a death match against fascism—a prospect that could have been anticipated even as Randolph spoke—was also suggestive of his dearth of perspicacity and his importing a crisis into a sphere where Negro interests should have been paramount: for whose record was better on the Negro Question anyway?[92]

To say that Patterson was disappointed with Randolph would be gross understatement. "He denounced collaboration with whites in the Negro Congress," said Patterson irascibly. "He called [for] the very isolation of Negro labor [that] Frederick Douglass had condemned. All white support to the NNC was slanderously labeled Communist"—which was false, but did suggest accurately that those Euro-Americans who were courageous enough to challenge Jim Crow frontally were either Reds or within their orbit. Patterson condemned the "collapse of this man," the "complete debacle," and was outraged that he had "resorted to worn out canards concerning Moscow gold"; this "Negro Judas" had "never permitted democracy to prevail in his own Brotherhood." Finally, Patterson declared that "Negro America is against this war." But the break with the NNC and what it portended seemed to inflame Patterson's ire.[93] Patterson requested that Langston Hughes take him on—"maybe," said the now literary counselor, "this could be in the form of that conversation between you and [your] friend," a reference to Hughes's "Simple" series.[94]

Hence, by the early 1940s, the simple truth was that the once-affluent attorney not only was unemployed, as his newspaper job had disappeared; he was embedded in a radical movement that had reached a fork in the road. "I reported to the Chicago [Communist] Party office ready to go to work," he recalled, and "was assigned to public relations work," which also became his fallback position after the Civil Rights Congress went out of business in 1956. He downsized and became a more frequent orator at Washington Park, polishing a skill that had served him well during the Scottsboro campaign. It was there, he recounted, that Richard Wright "first encountered professional revolutionaries"—those like himself, in other words.

Seeking to build upon his tenure at the paper, Patterson thought it might be wise to establish a school for labor education, and to that end, he met with Marshall Field, heir to a major fortune, who was also not unfriendly to radicalism. Soon the Abraham Lincoln School was under way in the Loop; Patterson served as an administrator and provided instruction in Negro history with others providing courses in music, art, film, Spanish, Russian, French, German, and "rapid reading."[95] Hughes made contributions to this venture,[96] and his fellow writer, Frank Marshall Davis, served on the board.[97]

By this time, the United States had entered the war, and the popular front had stabilized, as Patterson and his comrades no longer felt the need to assail purported "warmongers" in Washington, though it was not easy for centrist allies to forget the scorn that had been heaped upon them only recently. By early 1943, one newspaper was "expect[ing] 1,000 war workers to enroll in new school here,"[98] speaking of Patterson's enterprise. "Four freedoms will be taught at new school," said another,[99] indicating that the left had acceded to a major slogan of the White House.

It did not take long for the FBI to start paying even closer attention, reporting that Patterson was "very much concerned over the fact that [a] 'Chicago Reporter' had attended the Abraham Lincoln School and then ran a series of articles about the Communist influence of the school." There was concern that Communist influence would seep into the marrow of the working class via this school, an idea that did not abate when Patterson penned a pro-Soviet article in the *Chicago Defender*. He was meeting with the progressive artist Orson Welles about support for the school and was "instrumental" in "getting the United Electrical, Radio, and Machine Workers" to "pledge money for the support" of the school. That Patterson was earning only $41.24 weekly for this job seemed to stoke further suspicion.[100] He was tracked by FBI bloodhounds as he arrived in Manhattan on November 12, 1943, to confer with the charismatic Welles, who then agreed to visit Chicago.[101]

Forming this school—with the failure of the newspaper fresh in mind—was an uphill climb. "It has been a herculean task," he said in early 1943, addressing his old comrade from the League of Struggle for Negro Rights, Langston Hughes. "I hope you don't think I am without modesty," Patterson continued, as he analogized his laboring to the "activities of the Negroes that helped to create Wilberforce University" in Ohio decades previously; but this initiative was "on a political level of the educational institutions that came out of that other great struggle for human freedom," abolitionism.[102] It was not a "worker's school," though it targeted labor.[103] It was more akin to the construction of a popular front—including non-working-class elements—within a school. It was mandated, he told Hughes, since "if we make changes economically and politically while the idea of racial superiority is not fought on the cultural front, no stable base for economic and political change is realized." This task was all the more important given "the domination over our cultural-educational life assumed by the South after 1876 and maintained up to the present time."[104]

Another kind of education also captured the rapt attention of the FBI. In 1943, one of their "confidential informants" reported that "in the Chicago 'Black Belt,' South Side Party members were writing letters to Negro soldiers, as a service," and "the goodwill has resulted in increased friendliness in Negroes [in] this district to the Communist Party. At this time there are reputed to be 300 Negro members in the Party and four YCL [Young Communist League] branches." Worthy of mention was the fact that "Patterson was successfully distributing through Negro churches the Dean of Canterbury's booklet, 'Soviet Power.'"

Patterson had not improved his image with the FBI when he vocally objected to the detention of "Negro followers of the Temple of Islam"—soon to be known as the Nation of Islam—and "the Peace Movement of Ethiopia"; instead, said the outspoken Communist, "Father Coughlin," the right-wing cleric, and those of his ilk "are the ones who should be locked up." As the FBI indicated, Patterson and his comrades "were meeting opposition in some quarters by Negroes who maintain that if Japan were to win the war, it would not make any difference to them. To eradicate this belief," said Patterson, "race discrimination must be eliminated"—which was his constant cry during the war, an irony since afterward he was accused repeatedly of abandoning the anti–Jim Crow front and somehow allowing the war to take precedence (setting aside the inextricable links between these two).[105]

As the flowering of black nationalism in Chicago suggested, the self-proclaimed Land of Lincoln at times seemed to be below the Mason-Dixon Line, as the White House was informed in mid-1943. "The black market in pistol and ammunition buying in the Negro area has boomed. Although revolver shells are selling in the Negro district for twelve cents instead of two cents, their usual price, there are plenty of customers for them. Occasionally one can see a colored man carrying a rifle or a shotgun wrapped up in a newspaper or a gunny sack on the street." There had been "hate" crimes not only there but nationally, and "if trouble does start, the Negroes do not want to be unprepared." It was confessed that left-wing forces, including the CIO, "ha[ve] done a very creditable job in combating [racial] tension. Considering how strong they are in the fields of steel and meat packing," it was concluded, "it is particularly fortunate that they are considering the problem as their own."[106] Patterson was outraged by the strike by Euro-American students at the presence of Negro students at Froebel High School in neighboring Gary, Indiana.[107] Even the mayor of Chicago found that "hate groups" were deeply involved in these high-school battles.[108]

Patterson's school was a prophylactic intervention against this pestilence, but growing rifts within the popular front made it harder for his efforts to prevail. On the one hand, Patterson's influence was evident in his increasingly close relationship with the prominent and popular attorney Earl Dickerson, who was also a prominent businessman and mentor to John H. Johnson, soon to be recognized as the leading Negro businessman of all. This reality had not escaped the attention of the ever-prying FBI.[109] Patterson worked with the well-connected Dickerson in lobbying the White House about antiracist and antidiscrimination measures.[110] That Dickerson served simultaneously on the board of Patterson's Lincoln School and FDR's Fair Employment Practices Committee, and that this was noted by both the *Daily Worker* and the FBI, was noteworthy.[111] Dickerson was seen by the FBI as both an ally of Patterson and a "friend" of the other Communist attorney, Ben Davis—a possible indicator of deep Communist penetration in black Chicago.[112] The dynamic duo of Patterson and Dickerson also launched a vigorous lobbying effort targeting the Chicago Cubs baseball team on the ticklish matter of racial desegregation of this popular pastime.[113]

The fight to desegregate baseball became like a holy crusade to Patterson. "I myself had pushed the campaign vigorously," he said of this sports campaign that culminated in grand success. "Leaflets were distributed in white and Black neighborhoods. Communists everywhere were active," all of which forced a meeting with high-level executives who ultimately had to surrender.[114] After this pressure was exerted, the lords of baseball chose to meet with a delegation led by Patterson and which included Robeson and Flory.[115] This was one of several meetings these baseball executives—including William Wrigley and Kenesaw Mountain Landis—were compelled to endure. Patterson insisted later that "it was the consistency of the Communist leadership in this struggle that enabled all forces in this battle to achieve victory. The mass media has concealed this fact."[116]

The seeds for this victory—like so many others—had been planted in the rich and fertile loam of an antifascist war that had driven Moscow and Washington into a shotgun marriage and had created favorable conditions for progressive advance by undermining illiberal anticommunism. Communists were now on the side of the angels—not perceived as embodying what was to be termed later the Evil Empire—and hard-nosed conservatives were backpedaling furiously. How could Washington rationalize Jim Crow effectively when supposedly race hatred was driving their foes, Berlin not least? Herein were laid the foundations of what was to emerge full-blown a few scant years later as the heralded "civil-rights movement"—and, again, as with Scottsboro, only the unobservant could fail to notice that progress for the persecuted Negro was driven largely by a concatenation of a domestic situation infused with a powerful global dynamic.

Put crudely, as the cold war supplanted the antifascist war, Negroes were faced with the moral equivalent of Sophie's choice: after centuries of wandering in the wilderness of North America, they were asked to accept a bargain that promised a share of what was to be a growing pie (as the major global rivals of the United States were prostrate). There was, however, one major condition: throw overboard those leaders like Patterson—and Robeson—who had led them to that fateful juncture. A path for Patterson that had begun in Boston and then wound its way through Moscow, Pittsburgh, New York, the Black Sea, Hamburg, and Paris, reached a dramatic turning point in Chicago.

Patterson, fourth from left, prepares to depart Lower Manhattan for Boston in 1927 to campaign for the freedom of two celebrated anarchists. This campaign drew him closer to the left and, ultimately, to the Communist party. (Daily Worker/Daily World Photographs Collection, Tamiment Library, New York University)

As the Great Depression deepened in the 1930s, Communist-led protests proliferated, buoying Patterson's rise. (Daily Worker/Daily World Photographs Collection, Tamiment Library, New York University)

The Scottsboro Nine pose while detained in 1931. Their case, which Patterson spearheaded in its important early phase, was a turning point in the struggle against Jim Crow, insofar as the plight of the U.S. Negro was internationalized via Communist and left-wing networks. (Daily Worker/Daily World Photographs Collection, Tamiment Library, New York University)

Rally to free the Scottsboro defendants. The protest generated by this case led to the establishment of important legal rulings for criminal defendants that continue to stand. (Daily Worker/Daily World Photographs Collection, Tamiment Library, New York University)

Patterson marches in Washington on behalf of the Martinsville Seven, African American defendants executed by the Virginia authorities in 1951. This was one of many cases of injustice that the Civil Rights Congress—an unheralded crusader against Jim Crow terror—fought during Patterson's tenure as its leader. (Daily Worker/Daily World Photographs Collection, Tamiment Library, New York University)

Louise Thompson Patterson, Patterson's spouse for decades, was also a leader of the left in her own right and was similarly close to Paul Robeson, one of her husband's dearest comrades. (Daily Worker/Daily World Photographs Collection, Tamiment Library, New York University)

Willie McGee—an African American executed unjustly by the authorities in Mississippi in 1951—was defended vigorously by Patterson, bringing global attention to Dixie at a time when the United States was competing vigorously for "hearts and minds" in Africa, Asia, and Latin America. (Daily Worker/Daily World Photographs Collection, Tamiment Library, New York University)

Patterson rallies support for the jailed CP leader Henry Winston. (Daily Worker/Daily World Photographs Collection, Tamiment Library, New York University)

Patterson rallies support for Angela Davis in the early 1970s, alongside her mother. Like in the Scottsboro case, Patterson played a leading role in devising an international campaign that led to freedom for this intellectual and activist. (Daily Worker/Daily World Photographs Collection, Tamiment Library, New York University)

7

Turning Point

The war against Hitler was entering its terminal phase, which should have been an occasion for joy, but as Patterson surveyed things in the summer of 1945 from a steamy Chicago room—30 West Washington Street—he did not seem ecstatic. "Nationally we have no program for Negro work," he moaned, addressing his comrades, Revels Cayton—the scion of a Negro family that had soared to prominence in Seattle—and Matt Crawford, one of his closest allies, a resident of Berkeley. "We have no collective Negro leadership" either, he said of his Communist party—which would have come as a surprise to those who viewed from the outside his collaboration with James Ford, Ben Davis, and others. But Patterson would have none of this. "I shall make the most vigorous attack upon our present organizational setup in Negro work," he continued. "I do not think that [Ford] is capable of giving the necessary organizational and political lift to Negro work." Doxey Wilkerson, who had stunned many by leaving a faculty post at Howard University for the uncertain life of a professional revolutionary, or Ben Davis "could give this leadership," he mused, "and I believe that I could. But under all circumstances a change is necessary."

But it was not only a change in personnel that was mandated, he said. A change in policy was also needed. "Land tenure, the utilization of water power, development of [a] multi-crop system, development of educational facilities, perhaps the nationalization of railroads in the South to defeat Jim Crow practices, end of the child labor practices"—all and more must be pressed, he insisted, notably in Dixie. In the North and West, "the Negro legislators have got to introduce legislation that extends beyond the needs of the Negro people," as they must become tribunes for the working class as a whole. Would this call for reconsideration of the much debated Black Belt thesis and self-determination for the Negro? "Today the oppressed Negro people is seeking integration," he offered; nonetheless, "the Negro people are an oppressed nation."

These remarks reflect a bitter internal party struggle that stretched from mid-1944 to mid-1945, leaving in its wake a momentous shift on the much discussed

Negro Question, involving a retreat from the Black Belt line of self-determination, presumably since the Negroes were "seeking integration."[1] Patterson was viewed as the high priest on these matters, and he was struck by continuing "land hunger" in the Black Belt: the "slogan of equal rights, used alone, obscures the revolutionary character of the Negro liberation movement. It becomes a tool of liberalism"—and, actually, this did occur. "It has been said that there has been no expression of nationalism from the Negro people. I answer: analyze the Garvey movement, analyze the movement for a 49th state," which sunk roots in his Chicago.[2]

This complex and painful debate in mid-1945 was to result in the reinstatement of the old line—then another shift in 1956 in the aftermath of the conniptions caused by the invasion of Hungary and the revelations about Stalin's crimes. All the while, Patterson and his comrades continued grinding away against Jim Crow, though it was understandable that some thought their efforts had been sidetracked by abstruse polemics.

Patterson's anguished remarks came in the bitter aftermath of a cyclonic series of changes that pounded the CP, as the war was climaxing. Ostensibly the conflict centered around the leadership of party leader, Earl Browder, who, it was said, executed the popular front to the detriment of militancy and to the benefit of the presumed class foe on Wall Street. Yet, such "class collaboration" in a sense inhered in the idea of the popular front, as it privileged the construction of the broadest possible front against the plague that was fascism; in such a desperate context, it was not difficult to tip toward that of which Browder was accused.

In any case, he had plenty of help. It was Patterson—not Browder—who praised repeatedly the former slave trader who became a U.S. president, Andrew Jackson,[3] an outgrowth of this policy of class conciliation.[4] Patterson praised Jackson on more than one occasion, suggesting that it was not a temporary lapse in thinking.[5] It was Patterson who objected when the *Chicago Defender* railed against FDR substituting Henry A. Wallace as his vice president with Harry S. Truman—perhaps the most disastrous personnel shift that radicalism had to endure in the entire twentieth century.[6] It was Patterson who spoke at a February 1944 symposium at the Grand Ballroom of the Hamilton Hotel, where he was reported to have provided a wildly optimistic view of the Tehran line, suggesting that it meant gradual elimination of the capitalist class in the United States. It was Patterson who deflected the thrust of black nationalists who asked why they should oppose Tokyo when what was being foisted on many occupied territories in Asia was hardly worse than what they faced daily in North America. Patterson felt compelled to argue that Negroes did not face fascism but quasi-fascism. The black nationalists thought he was downplaying their plight.[7] And it was during this same period that Patterson referred to the now-reviled Ford as one who "has taken up the mantle of Frederick Douglass."[8] In short, as it became apparent that the CP lamb would not be allowed to recline in repose with the Wall Street lion, the decision was made to adjust the prevailing line—and Browder was insufficiently nimble to make this adjustment. That Patterson was undergoing simultaneously the misery of not knowing what had befallen his daughters—Lola, thirteen, and Vera, seven—as the Nazis rampaged through the Soviet Union only added to his angst and, perhaps, affected his usually shrewd judgment.[9]

By at least mid-1944 Browder had become captivated with the idea that the Moscow-Washington alliance as reflected at their summit in Tehran was not just a temporary phenomenon but was of transnational permanence.[10] This was followed by the liquidation of the CP as a political party and its reconstitution as a political association, a kind of loosely organized lobbying arm within elite circles. The comrades had not taken total flight of their senses—there was internal objection to this shift, but there was also substantiation for it, in that there had been conspicuous growth in party ranks during the antifascist war, and the reduction of anticommunism propelled by the war had something to do with this. It was also in mid-1944 that it was said of the CP that "of the 24,000 new members recruited" of late, "one-third, 8,000, were Negroes."[11]

Thus, when the CP leadership, of which Patterson was an essential part, met in June 1945 to assess domestic and global matters, it was not preordained that the Tehran line would be swiftly dispatched. But that is precisely what happened, with Patterson voting enthusiastically with the majority as he waxed at length on what he saw as the noxious impact of this line on work among Negroes, an elaboration of what he was to tell Crawford and Cayton. It was noticeably disheartening that Patterson felt that he had to speak expansively "because few if any of our white comrades will deal at length with the ramifications of our mistakes in this region." He took sharp exception to "Comrade Browder's statement of yesterday [about] me. I felt the arrogance," he said; "to look for modesty was to look for the needle in the haystack." Unlike the CP, said Patterson, "the bourgeoisie regarded the affinity of their interests and our national interests as a momentary affair." He confessed that "we Negro comrades have contributed to these mistakes," since "for years we have made no serious attempt to enrich our theoretical understanding of the Negro Question." Thus, he insisted, "The right of self-determination cannot be decided by the oppressed nation alone and the Negro remains an oppressed nation despite our dropping of this issue." He was miffed that International Publishers, the party's firm, "has never seen fit to utilize a Negro," which was compounded by the omission of having "contributed" little "to the solution of the Caribbean problem, even in the Virgin Islands, America's colony."[12]

An hour or two after Browder's impassioned defense of Tehran—which had preceded Patterson's remarks—there was a recess, and Patterson's old comrade from the *Midwest Daily Record*, Louis Budenz, materialized. "Patterson," said Burdenz, "had a fine case of anger against his former chief. Shaking his head, [Patterson] declared, 'Earl has made no case at all.'" "It has been a bankrupt performance," said Patterson,[13] as the Negro Communist reentered the meeting room—and the fray. Like others before him, Patterson may have been thrown by Browder's manner. He was a quiet person, unusual for a supposedly fire-breathing Red, and had the distracting habit of concentrating on the matter at hand so that for long moments he remained expressionless, giving the impression that he was providing inattention to his interlocutor or even not listening to those speaking. In such a combustible and racist atmosphere as existed in the United States at the time, this may have been enough to drive even allies over the edge.[14]

Patterson's disgust was a reflection of bitter recriminations that had exploded—with the fuse lit by Negro comrades in particular. This set the stage for a postwar crusade against "white chauvinism," which had multiple effects. It infuriated many Euro-American comrades—Howard Fast termed it the approach of a"lunatic"—easing the way for their departing the ranks;[15] but it also represented the abject difficulty of seeking to build multiracial unity in a nation constructed on principles of white supremacy. Joseph Starobin, a Communist at one time, later reported that during this intense gathering, "for the first time important Negro leaders voiced views" heretofore deemed to be heretical. "It was now suggested" by Patterson "that Browder had been cool to [him and Ford] as individuals, and *ipso facto* had been guilty of profoundly underestimating the Negro Question and its importance as a revolutionary factor in the postwar period." According to this observer, Ben Davis then flipped from his previous "affirmation early in May of Browder's staunchness on the Negro Question," as he did "not repeat his defense of Browder but joined the attack."[16] Inexorably, as Jim Crow came under attack in the United States, it emboldened Negro comrades simultaneously.

Bella V. Dodd, a Communist turned fervent anticommunist who was present at this pivotal 1945 meeting, recalled being attacked by Ben Davis. He "promptly turned his violence on me," she cried. "I was guilty of chauvinism, he insinuated." Patterson and Pettis Perry, another Negro comrade, took her to lunch and tried to soothe her brittle feelings. She "liked" them both—even though they "tried to justify Ben Davis' intemperate attacks and said I did not understand the national minority question well. All I could think as I listened was, 'Has everyone gone mad?'" When Anna Damon, who once worked closely with Patterson at the ILD, committed suicide, Dodd suggested that it was an outgrowth of the tensions generated by the 1945 tumult.[17] As for Dodd, she was subsequently expelled from the CP—"they said I was anti–Puerto Rican, anti-Negro, anti-Semitic, anti–working class," she said with lingering rancor.[18]

The contretemps surrounding Browder was simply the beginning of a prolonged agony for Patterson and his remaining comrades.[19] His ouster was followed quickly by a Red Scare that frightened thousands from the ranks, reducing a party that once was groping toward a six-figure membership to a bottom-scraping low four-figure membership, with a concomitant reduction in influence. That this occurred as Jim Crow was in retreat did not assuage the pain—in fact, it was connected to it, since this retreat undermined lingering support among Negroes.

Yet for Patterson the most profound of the profundities that befell him was in a related sphere. For despite gargantuan struggles around Scottsboro, baseball, and more, the CP had to fight the repeated charge that they had downplayed Jim Crow during the war, that it was subordinated to the struggle against fascism, all of which was a kind of non-sequitur: first, because their day-to-day activity on this front did not necessarily shrink to the extent critics imagined; and second, because this formulation was like saying that the struggle against male chauvinism was subordinated to the struggle against male supremacy, given the importance of subduing fascism to the struggle against racism. Patterson's fellow Chicagoan Horace Cayton would have none of this, concurring with the idea of the Negro conservative George Schuyler that the Reds "quit the struggle for Negro rights." Patterson termed it "slander," and in any case, the war had transformed for all time the antiracist battle. "The war has changed America. It has changed the world"; "Negro boys died in the jungles of India [so] that lynching may be ended in the jungles of Mississippi."[20]

This view of Patterson was not Cayton's alone—which suggests that it reflects a radically altered landscape that inexorably led to different understandings, including revised histories. For if the war's conclusion meant anything, it meant that the Negro—as in 1919, when their dreams were drowned in blood—was unwilling to accept the prewar Jim Crow dispensation, which meant that this rancid status quo could very well be compromised. It was the decidedly non-Communist Negro journalist Roi Ottley—not Patterson—who concluded that the "Nuernberg [sic] trials should have tremendous meaning to Negroes in the U.S. because the establishment of the principle of collective guilt can now be applied to the American scene." In words that were to be repeated in essence by Patterson in Paris in 1951, Ottley said accusingly, "The President of the United States cannot take a hands-off position in crimes against innocent minorities. Nor can public officials. The principle indeed extends to each white person in the U.S."[21]

Far-reaching alteration of the political climate was ignited when world war almost inevitably bled into cold war, and as the ground beneath the feet of activists shifted, severe ructions appeared almost effortlessly. This scenario seemed to envelop Ben Burns, the Euro-American writer who had served at Patterson's side during the heyday of the *Midwest Daily Record,* then migrated to the *Chicago Defender,* but was now being driven into the waiting arms of John H. Johnson and his growing Ebony-Jet enterprise. He complained that "Pat and some other responsible people in the party were quite dissatisfied with my work on the 'Defender,'" and, as a result, "I took about the worst beating I've ever taken in years in the party. Both Pat and [Ishmael] Flory ganged up on me." In turn, said Burns, "I got pretty hot the night of the meeting with Pat." Licking his wounds, Burns countered, "I thought I had done a fair job with *Defender* circulation going from 80,000 to over 200,000" in a brief period "and its influence extending all over the country," undermining the "reactionary [Pittsburgh] *Courier*," headed by Patterson's frequent opponent, Robert Vann. Burns acknowledged, "I made mistakes, lots of them"—but he thought that the reaction by Patterson and Flory was much too severe, helping to chase away a competent comrade.[22]

"Why not go down and have a man-to-man talk with Pat," said John Pittman, a leading Negro comrade—and fellow journalist—in whom Burns had confided. "He's one of the best guys I know, with a keen sense of fair play."[23] But it was too late. Yet another comrade fled—one among many thousands to come.[24]

The end of the war meant—almost simultaneously—the end of the antifascist alliance, which had provided such favorable conditions for Red advance and racial desegregation at the same time. The end of the war also meant that the anticommunists and Jim Crow advocates were eager to claw back what they had relinquished. The internal party wrangling, the ouster of Browder, and the confusion around the Black Belt thesis all contributed to this feverish atmosphere. Framing the febrile postwar environment was also an explosion of strikes and labor unrest that was similarly—if not more—unsettling. Patterson, said the FBI, "kept in close touch with recent strike activities in the Chicago area with particular reference to the part played by Negroes in such activities." By 1946, Robeson was firmly in the camp of the organized left and thus was frequently seen at Patterson's side in the midst of these titanic battles. When striking Packinghouse Workers, a bastion of left-wing influence, held a mass rally at Du Sable High School in Chicago, Patterson and Robeson were side by side—but also there was Robeson's fellow entertainer, Cab Calloway, suggestive of how the forces of the left had yet to be pushed back effectively. "As a member of the Communist Party and known as such by the public," said the FBI nervously, Patterson had a "tremendous advantage. In addition to this advantage [Patterson] was noted as having a large following among the non-Communist party groups."[25]

The FBI in late 1945 believed that Patterson had reduced his role in the Abraham Lincoln School and instead was crusading against restrictive covenants that sought to delimit housing options for Negroes by pressuring the "the Oakland-Kenwood Property Owners Association."[26] The relentless flyspecking of his every move by the local and national authorities was an indication that despite his democratic and antiracist patina, there were those who thought Patterson had another agenda.[27] These concerns were not allayed when he was forcibly ejected from a legislative hearing in Springfield—as lawmakers deliberated over anticommunist legislation designed to defenestrate him and his comrades.[28] The legislature was actually split as to what to do, but not sufficiently divided to stop Patterson's ejection after he admitted openly to those assembled that, yes, he was a Communist.[29]

From the outside, it may have seemed as if the Chicago Communists and Patterson were on the ascent, given the stronghold they had established among Negroes and unions. But anticommunist insiders knew better. "Commies are worried out this way and for good reason," said one in 1947, since "the anticommunist feeling is very strong."[30] Apparently, Gil Green, the influential Red leader, was in touch with this man—"he is a New York Jew so [I] was able to talk turkey with him because of many mutual acquaintances," he confided. "He informed me that due to [the] situation in the Midwest recruiting had been stopped except in [the] Chicago area, that things were under way and that party activity was almost underground. I believe it."[31]

As Negroes and their leadership, symbolized by Patterson, were tugging furiously to the left, the nation in which they resided was moving aggressively to the right. But why should African Americans tail after Jim Crow rulers—unless concessions were granted that would provide a rationale to toss to the wolves those like Patterson, a Moscow-trained Negro who was the embodiment of what was now feared and despised? And that is what happened effectively, though the terms of this bargain were rarely put so explicitly.[32]

Charles Hamilton Houston, who was present at the creation of the new order brought by Scottsboro, bucked the NAACP leadership overall, which was more than willing to accept this new bargain. He was part of the legal team in Washington, D.C., that tried to allow the dissident Henry A. Wallace—now in full flight from the Democratic party—to hold a rally for the nascent Progressive party in mid-1947.[33] But Houston's voice was increasingly ignored in the higher councils of the NAACP, leaving Patterson further isolated at a moment when internal party battles were providing a portrait of instability. For how could the NAACP buck President Truman, who was promising so much? The Republican senator from Kansas, Arthur Capper, chose to do so, arguing that his "Truman Doctrine to combat Communism will cost the nation more than $10,000,000,000 in the next two or three years"[34]—tax dollars that could have been devoted to eroding the miserable effects of centuries of slavery and Jim Crow. But his too was a voice that was not heeded.

Thus, just before this Washington lawsuit, Patterson was embroiled in a retreat that was billed as an advance. Two organizations with which he had been closely identified—the NNC and ILD—liquidated and merged with a third to form the Civil Rights Congress.[35] This merger allowed for the concentration of progressive forces in one trench, yet it could not obscure the reality that the NNC and ILD had two different mandates, and no amount of rationalization could obscure the reality that this merger was also a setback. Patterson, who had played a prominent role in both of the dearly departed groupings, was a logical choice to head their successor—which occurred in 1948.

The CRC could have overcome this obstacle if it had received more cooperation from the NAACP—but, still smarting from the squabbling over Scottsboro and intoxicated with the idea that Jim Crow would retreat if only the pesky Reds were tossed into the gutter, they were hardly in a mood to cooperate. Reporting from Detroit, where the merger was effectuated in a ceremony pronouncing the birth of the CRC, the NAACP operative and fierce anticommunist Gloster Current was singularly unimpressed.[36]

What seemed to preoccupy Current was the prospect that numerous NAACP branches would find the forceful CRC program attractive and that this could bollix the bargain brokered with U.S. elites, which was designed to forestall such an eventuality. "There were many representatives from the NAACP [present] throughout the nation," Current reported worriedly. Speaking in code and referring to the Reds as if they were a benign fraternity, he told Walter White, "It might be well for you to investigate and appraise the branches in order that they do not become tools of the 'Elks.'"[37] Lulu White, a leader from the branch in Houston who was present in Detroit, disagreed with Current and White with regard to their staunch opposition to the CRC, but her view did not prevail.[38] Dr. Carlton Goodlett, perhaps the leading figure in black San Francisco—Patterson's initial training ground—for more than a generation, sought to emulate White, but he too was slapped down.[39] Setting aside anticommunism and the emoluments promised if Moscow-trained Communists were shunned, the NAACP had reason to be intimidated by the fierce reaction of the ever-potent Jim Crow advocates, who seemed to think the rise of the CRC was akin to the coming of the antichrist.[40] "The Negro people represent the balance of power—the ultimate balance of power in any liberal movement in the United States," said Charles Hamilton Houston, speaking to the ILD in 1939.[41] So when the fulcrum of political gravity among Negroes was pushed to the center and away from the left, it was inevitable that the nation as a whole would be moved to the right from the center.

Undaunted—and perhaps tactlessly—Patterson continued to hammer erstwhile allies in the NAACP and the American Civil Liberties Union. "Who else but we," he proclaimed of the CRC, "are batting our heads against Truman's and [Attorney General Tom] Clark's plan for a 100 percent Jim Crow police state?" As he saw it, these would-be allies would not "go beyond the courts" and were "willing to let freedom die a slow death in the courts"; unlike the CRC, they would not implicate "imperialism" in their indictment of Jim Crow.[42]

Thus, as black America remained suspended between the present promise of a full-scale retreat of Jim Crow, driven by the courts and the White House, and the past promise of Scottsboro and its premise that domestic mobilization was simply insufficient to guarantee rights, Patterson returned to Harlem to assume the helm at the CRC. "Louise and the family will again be residents of your fair and unfair city," he told Langston Hughes in the summer of 1948, as they moved to 409 Edgecombe Avenue,[43] overlooking the Bronx and Yankee Stadium.

Len Goldsmith was at the CRC when Patterson arrived. Later, he told government inquisitors that the hiring of Patterson was a CP—not a CRC—decision. He recalled particularly a meeting with an up and coming Negro comrade, Henry Winston, where he was simply instructed that Patterson would be arriving soon to take the reins of leadership. "I didn't know Patterson, had never met him," said Goldsmith. He did know that Patterson was "Vice-Chairman of the Communist Party of Illinois." Though he had joined the CP in 1937 and had departed in 1942, Goldsmith objected to his presence, though Winston and the CP leader Eugene Dennis insisted. This was the beginning of a ruffled relationship, as he found that Patterson was "in strong disagreement with some of my ideas. I was in strong disagreement with some of his"—"the differences revolved around the structure of the organization, the failure to permit the organization to have a really functioning Executive Board, the centralization of all policy decisions out of the hands of the elected leadership of the organization, where every decision was subject to review by the Communist Party, through Patterson."

In short, this former Communist found himself ensnared in what he thought to be a "Communist front," which he deemed to be illegitimate. Goldsmith recalled once when there was "an urgent need for $3,000 in a hurry. The Civil Rights Congress didn't have it, and Patterson went down to the Party headquarters at 12th Street and came back with it"—at least, that is what he was told. Yet, at a time when the CP leadership—including Winston—was fighting long prison terms, Goldsmith maintained that this same Winston diverted CRC energy from CP defense into that of the Trenton Six, a "northern Scottsboro" involving an evident frame-up of young Negroes. One would think that a true "Communist front" would not have acted thusly. Goldsmith, an apparently contentious sort, who after the CRC had a dispute with his next employer—"Yes, there was a dispute involving the spending of union funds"—did not agree.[44]

Neither did Bella Dodd, who joined Goldsmith in testifying against the CRC. She was no neophyte, having once met with Eugene Dennis, William Z. Foster, and other CP leaders on a regular basis. According to Dodd, "In preparation for the launching of the Civil Rights Congress there was practically a year's work done in preparing for it" by these higher-ups. They found, she said, that the ILD was reluctant to relinquish its mission and that Patterson's predecessor at the helm of the CRC, William Lawrence, was not put there by the organization itself: "He told me that Gene Dennis had intervened to place him in a job with the [CRC]."[45]

Whatever the case, it did seem that the most fervent anticommunists—perhaps recalling the halcyon days of the ILD under his leadership—were gravely concerned with Patterson's CRC. It was "one of the best illustrations that could be presented" of a "Communist front," said his now sworn foe, Louis Budenz: "It has had a powerful influence in confusing American thinking on the Communist issue,"[46] perhaps because it focused so intently on Jim Crow. Subsequently, it was asserted that the CRC's "tactics were harbingers of the Civil Rights Movement that was on the verge of happening. The CRC became a textbook example of an organization decimated by repression"—though, possibly not coincidentally, the movement symbolized by Dr. King gained acclaim in 1956, the same year that the CRC was driven into desuetude.[47]

As Goldsmith's words indicate, Patterson's tenure at the CRC got off to a rocky start. Goldsmith became a turncoat, denouncing former comrades and allies in a highly ritualized performance. However, he was not alone, for suggestive of the polecat status it was forced to endure as the Red Scare dawned, the CRC—in some ways, the most effective and publicized group led by a Communist—was riddled with informants from its inception, who were determined to rout an organization pressing hard against the nation's Achilles heel that was Jim Crow, thus providing a coup to Moscow (or, as others would have it, providing a blow against Jim Crow). Apparently, some of these informants were ex-Reds, still fuming about charges of "white chauvinism" that led to their hasty departure—or expulsion—from the ranks.[48] Others profited handsomely from providing detailed reports to the FBI, with one stool pigeon receiving about fifteen thousand dollars over a ten-year period.[49] Mary Stalcup Markward of Silver Spring, Maryland, received twenty-four thousand dollars from the FBI between 1943 and 1950. She was both a CRC and CP leader who hustled subscriptions to party publications and then turned over the names of subscribers to the FBI, after going door to door in an increasingly black Washington, D.C., making the pitch that the left stood for full citizenship for Negroes.[50] Barbara Hartle, a graduate of Washington State University, was a leader of the CP in Spokane who recruited fresh new comrades, then turned their names over to the FBI.[51] Clark Harper of Maple Valley, Washington—this state was a juicy target for infiltration because of its justifiable reputation for progressivism[52]—was a poultry rancher who joined the CP in 1944 and stayed until 1953. He began informing in 1944, receiving eighteen thousand dollars for his troubles.[53] Rev. Obidiah Jones of St. Louis, a Negro pastor, joined the CP in March 1946 at the behest of the FBI, then chaired the CRC chapter until 1954—when he turned up to testify against them. He got about ten thousand dollars as a result of this association and recruited for the CRC in his church—then turned over the names to the FBI.[54]

Suggestive of the intractable problems that Patterson faced was the erstwhile CRC member John Glatis of Boston. He too became an informer for the FBI. Why? He asserted that members of his family were "murdered by members of the Communist Party in Greece," and "included among them was a favorite uncle." He photographed the CRC membership list and turned it over to the authorities.[55]

Matt Cvetic may have made out better than any of them. Born in Pittsburgh in 1909, he joined the CP in 1943 at the FBI's behest, though he had worked on the bureau's behalf as early as 1941. He testified later against Patterson, alleging that he asserted, "We must learn how to hate our enemies enough to want to kill them." For his troubles, he wound up with a movie deal from Warner Bros., along with a radio series and massive publicity in general.[56] This occurred despite the fact that he was described as a "degenerate barfly." Over a seven-year period, he filed twenty thousand typewritten pages at the rate of fifty-nine pages a week and further supplied his FBI overseers with thirty thousand pages of exhibits, letters, press releases, and the like from his erstwhile comrades, not to mention a thousand of their names; he wired meeting places and secretly filmed those attending. Before these escapades, he ran afoul of the law when he assaulted his sister-in-law and broke her wrist.[57] Patterson recalled meeting Cvetic at a CRC gathering in mid-1949, though he suggested that this informant was not as informed as his riveting testimony suggested.[58]

It was Timothy Evans who captured best some of the tensions and conflicts that compromised irrevocably the missions of the CP and CRC. Born in Arkansas in 1917, he resided in Oakland and joined the CP in 1948, and then the CRC, before departing in 1952. All the leaders of the CRC were Red, he said, including Decca Truehaft, a member of a prominent British family who later attained a measure of fame as the writer Jessica Mitford. What Evans told the authorities was indicative of why Patterson and his radical band were whipsawed so vigorously during the Red Scare. He recalled a meeting where the highly articulate Truehaft was accused of a "superiority" complex, which became the subject of internal "discipline" within the CP. "Being an eloquent speaker," he recalled, "Decca wormed out of it pretty well." Increasingly, he testified, CP meetings were "more secretive, and they were held under more security" than had been the case previously. He recounted one meeting where "we weren't supposed to tell anyone that we were going to have such a meeting. We were first supposed to meet at a place and then from this first place we were taken by another car to the meeting of the second convention." He too was the recipient of lush payoffs from the FBI—but the larger point is that neither internal backbiting nor external pressure were conducive to left-wing growth, thereby eroding Patterson's base. The much-persecuted Negro was put through the wringer as Jim Crow began its agonized retreat.[59] Evans's view that allegations of "white chauvinism" fueled angry revenge on the part of those so charged was corroborated by others.[60]

Though it was to be claimed later that this campaign against "white chauvinism" in the land of Jim Crow was misguided, it was hard to dispute the anger of Pettis Perry when he pointed to the assertion that at least forty-six comrades had signed leases containing restrictive covenants barring Negroes, while others resisted adjustments to seniority to allow Negro workers to make gains. Yet he did note astutely that such a campaign presented the "danger that agents" and "provocateur[s]" could "manipulate" this initiative, buoyed by the influx of new members during the war—and that is what happened.[61]

Yet as damaging as these infiltrators were to the fortunes of Patterson's fledgling CRC, the beating—literally and figuratively—that they absorbed in Peekskill, New York, in the summer of 1949 was a warning to one and all that allying with a left that was said to be close to Moscow was akin to playing with a raging fire. There were two concerts planned—the first on August 27, and the second on September 4, the latter supposedly being a statement that the left would not be intimidated after being routed at the former by an infuriated mob. The cruel violence unleashed in Peekskill left the impression with Patterson and his comrades that fascism was nigh, a judgment that led to a number of comrades going underground and into exile and assuming a posture that isolated the radicals just as the opposite of fascism—the slow but steady retreat of Jim Crow—was occurring. The error in judgment was understandable, but no less damaging. For as one analyst put it, Communists and their allies—not least because of the punishment absorbed in Peekskill—had a "very real, almost paranoid belief and fear at this time that fascism was about to take over in the United States in 1949–50 the way it did in Germany in the early 1930s," a subject with which Patterson was all too familiar. "People really *believed* this was going to happen," it was stressed.[62]

Patterson, like others, was caught by surprise by Peekskill. His spouse routinely toured with Robeson as an advance organizer for his concerts, but on this August evening, Patterson's birthday was being marked, so she invited some folks to their home before the concert for cake and beverages. Not expecting anything major, she stayed home as her spouse headed north.[63]

Tens of miles north of the Bronx, the site selected was seen as pleasant and bucolic with Communists like Robert Minor and his artist spouse, Lydia, the talented cartoonist William Gropper, the prolific novelist Howard Fast, and the Communist theorist Alexander Bittelman all living in nearby Croton. Peekskill was thought to be a nonthreatening place for a summer outing for Reds and fellow travelers.[64] Yet this analysis may have ignored the ugly side of this area, where the Ku Klux Klan had established a lengthy tradition of anti-Catholicism, galvanized most notably when Governor Al Smith ran for President in 1928. The American Labor Party, a left-wing ally of the CRC, did quite well in Gotham, but not so well due north.[65] The former view of this region prevailed—how else to explain why organizers would choose a site that had only one road leading in an out of the grounds, creating sitting ducks for the violence-prone? Pete Seeger, the popular folk singer, tried to reassure by crooning what was to become the anthem of popular resistance a few years later—"We Shall Overcome"—but these inspiring verses could hardly compensate for the fact that those being beaten were being overcome by a much stronger force.[66]

According to the playwright Arthur Miller, who was quite friendly to the organized left, 1949 was a turning point: "It was the year it came apart," the "last postwar year to me. An era can be said to end when its basic illusions are exhausted."[67] By 1949—as Peekskill reflected—it was evident that the left would be on the defensive for some time to come, just as (paradoxically) Negroes would emerge partially from the wasteland to which they had been consigned. Older illusions were exhausted as newer ones emerged: The road to Negro redemption rested with reliance on powerful elites and routing Reds, or so it was thought.

It began innocently with Paul Robeson slated to perform in a benefit concert for the CRC. He had given three concerts in the region in the three preceding summers without incident, and therefore Patterson was blindsided by the tornado of protest that enveloped the concert grounds. Things had moved rapidly in preceding months, with hysteria about Communists on the march worldwide and the festering idea that, as it was said, Robeson aspired to become the "black Stalin."[68]

Patterson was present in late August, along with twenty thousand concertgoers. "I was on my way to the concert grounds," he said later, "when I was prevented from coming there by state police and legionnaires and citizens." "As we drove up to the entrance of the concert grounds which was a little off the main highway, we noted that a large truck had been turned over in front of the entrance blocking it, and the police and legionnaires and citizens were hurling things at the automobile. They prevented our going down, even attempting to enter the concert grounds. We attempted to turn back and were stopped by the legionnaires and police," as "they prevented us from going back and made us go forward. As we approached the entrance to the concert grounds, I saw one melee going on, and there was Mr. Lawrence Brown," Robeson's accompanist. "I grabbed him in my arms," he continued, "and pulled him out and helped to put him in our automobile. And then we went forward. After driving a mile past the concert grounds, I directed the driver to return and as we came back we saw that the fight was at its height, automobiles were being overturned. You could hear the cry, 'Kill the niggers, kill the kikes, kill the Communists' and stones were thrown at our automobile." Patterson and company fled helter-skelter, as if from a breath of the apocalypse.

They made it to the amphitheater and espied a "sort of cordon of concert people," all with "arms linked to each other, with the women and children in the center"—"this was around 3 o'clock in the afternoon. The concert was slated to begin at 3:30." The CRC supporters were barely able to escape, and many of them decamped to Harlem, where an angry protest ensued. "I said here was a mobilization of storm troopers," said Patterson, that there was a "danger of fascism in America," that "elements of the State Troopers [were] remnants of the Bund," that there was an "attempt to murder Paul Robeson," that "gunmen were up in the trees prepared to shoot Paul Robeson."[69]

The second concert in early September, meant as a rebuff to the disrupters, faced similarly severe reproach. Patterson would lead a delegation to Albany, demanding that Governor Thomas Dewey address their grievances; instead, they were repudiated once more.[70] Undeterred, Patterson charged hotly that the battering the CRC received "was planned and carried out by Klansmen and a mob of fascist hoodlums hiding behind a so-called 'veterans' front." How else to explain that "people were brutally beaten, cars overturned, and KKK crosses burned in a night of violence" while "not a single arrest was made"?[71]

Patterson's fury was comprehensible. One writer in the *Baltimore Afro-American* was aghast when seeing "Jean [sic] Bullard, first colored aviator in World War I and holder of the French Croix de Guerre, knocked down at my feet and brutally kicked and beaten by State Troopers as he lay on the ground because he spat back at an anti-Robeson veteran who had spit on his face. I saw a colored man," said this correspondent, "who was in his car on the way home, dragged from his car, hit over the head . . . beat on the ground by the troopers as he attempted to crawl under his car for protection. He was then dragged from underneath the car and beat on by four troopers as he crawled helplessly down the narrow road leading to the concert area."[72] He was among the many victims, which included the future congresswoman Bella Abzug. She worked with the CRC as an attorney and remained proud to the end of her days of the little scar above her eyebrow where a rock struck her during this bloody revolt.[73]

It was unnerving when—despite the blatant anti-Semitism expressed—a popular Jewish newspaper, as one writer put it, "exhibited the same glee over this hoodlum attack as did Goebbels in his hey-day." Of course, a good deal of the Jewish press unequivocally condemned this assault—though not a peep was heard from the American Jewish Committee or the Anti-Defamation League for, like the NAACP, they may have sensed that overall the walls of anti-Semitic bigotry were collapsing and, it was thought, only the Reds and their acolytes were scheduled for bludgeoning.[74] It was remarkable that in Peekskill, even Jewish war veterans who were there were jeered and insulted by anti-Semites. The onetime Socialist A. Philip Randolph denounced the comrades when they were most vulnerable, causing Patterson to rebuke him for suggesting that the concertgoers had been "aggravating the situation. . . . Mr. Randolph would have us believe that the fascist-like attack 'was not racial.'"[75] This stunning reality could only deepen the actual and imaginary isolation of Patterson and his comrades.[76]

Patterson's anger may have been exceeded by that of Robeson. Surely the idea was in the air that—similar to the idea that beating one amply muscled and powerful slave keeps the entire plantation in line—battering Robeson to his knees would serve as a signal that even the famous could not escape wrath, while concessions would flow as a salve to those who acquiesced. Thus, as CRC supporters retreated pell-mell to the citadel that was Harlem, Robeson stood shoulder to shoulder with Patterson outside the Hotel Theresa at 125th Street and Seventh Avenue. As the dusk gathered in the warm summer air, the former Rutgers football star watched in silent horror, tears streaming down his stunned visage, as dozens of shattered buses arrived with bleeding people—men, women, and children alike.

What had helped to spark the venomous Peekskill assault were remarks attributed to Robeson where—in Paris—he seemed to call into question whether Negroes could be relied upon to fight against Moscow if war erupted. After those inflammatory remarks were reported, Walter White met with him at a Harlem church, where it was proposed that Robeson stick with performing and steer clear of political activism. As Robeson's son recalled this meeting, White told them, "The guys who run intelligence will be given license to kill you if you don't take this deal. The mix of the race issue, the Communist issue, and the war issue is just too much for them.'"[77] It was not too much for Patterson. "He is my friend," he said of Robeson. "I know him well and love him dearly."[78]

But matters had spun far beyond Patterson's evident affection for his old friend. The brutal events in Peekskill were denounced unreservedly, said one close analysis, "in the capitals of Europe, Asia, [Africa,] and South America as reactionary and fascist-minded."[79] Even this rainbow of good news carried a dark cloud, for this could encourage the reactionaries to double down in their beating of those who had brought obloquy upon their beloved homeland.

Pockmarked with agents of subversion, perennially desperate for funds, confronting an unforgivably hostile atmosphere where opponents did not flinch at the prospect of unremitting violence, it remains astonishing that Patterson and the CRC were able to accomplish as much as they did—capped by a whirlwind trip to Paris, where he again brought the global spotlight on Jim Crow, fortifying the idea that it required global pressure to force this calcified system of bigotry to retreat.

8

Prison Looms

William Patterson had earned his spurs in the burning crucible that was Scottsboro, and in that environment he was able to drag the NAACP, albeit reluctantly, into a division of labor where he focused on mass organizing and they on legal wizardry. But with the rise of the Red Scare, which demonized Communists like himself as subversive agents of a foreign power, such a de facto alliance was no longer feasible. Yet there were some in the U.S. ruling elite who recognized that Jim Crow was a massive burden on national security—how could Washington credibly charge Moscow with human-rights violations as long as domestic apartheid reigned?

"Race bias termed assistance to Reds," charged a bold headline in 1951, reporting how John D. Rockefeller himself was pouring more funds hastily into the United Negro College Fund, which he called "investments," not donations.[1] "Soviet[s] for inquiry on Negroes in U.S.," charged an earlier headline, almost prompting Rockefeller's demarche, with Moscow demanding "immediate investigation of the Negro problem."[2] Objective forces were compelling a retreat of Jim Crow. It was almost as if the U.S. ruling elite felt that unless radicals were crushed, acceding to desegregation would have tipped the balance uncomfortably against them. Yet, with the labor movement being purged of Communists and fear stalking the land, the roughly 12 percent of the nation who were African American—and their chief tribune, the NAACP—felt that they had little choice, not to mention that eroding the base of what had proven to be a formidable competitor—the predecessor of the CRC, the ILD—could provide White and Wilkins with more of the spotlight (and funds). Nonetheless, what the radicals—even Patterson—did not seem to grasp was that in the 1930s, Washington felt the need to recognize the Soviet Union, then ally with it in the 1940s, in no small part as a hedge against the rise of fascism in Europe and militarism in Japan. But with Moscow having served its role in helping to squash this threat by 1945, the U.S. elite felt that it could now happily crush Moscow's domestic allies, while undercutting its base—and occupation of the moral high ground—by eroding the more egregious aspects of

Jim Crow (which had the added benefit of undermining simultaneously Tokyo's Negro allies, who had gained no small traction before 1941).[3]

The NAACP leadership knew well the fundamental perils involved in not only illegalizing the CP in a real sense but placing its leadership in prison; nonetheless, Wilkins counseled his branches to stay away from any defense of those leaders when they were placed on trial in 1949,[4] the First Amendment notwithstanding.[5] Instead of collaborating with Patterson, it may have been during this time that Thurgood Marshall—according to an admirer—began collaborating with the FBI against the likes of Patterson.[6] For Marshall recognized what a scholar acknowledged years later: "Not only the Congressional committees but also the Justice Department clearly adopted the view that to defend the constitutional or legal rights of a subversive was in itself a subversive action."[7]

Still, the refusal of the NAACP to make the smallest gesture in favor of these defendants outraged the attorney George Crockett—a future member of the Congressional Black Caucus, representing Detroit—and many others.[8] Extraordinary pressure had to be placed on Negroes, still languishing in the parched desert of Jim Crow, to compel them to shun the Communists (whose Scottsboro activism demonstrated that they could deliver gains) in exchange for the still distant promise of eroding Jim Crow. A vignette from Patterson's days at the helm of the CRC captures neatly Washington's dilemma. One day, a man who identified himself as a post office inspector showed up at the Manhattan office of the CRC. Speaking directly to Patterson, he leaned forward and confided in a whispery though conversational tone, "We have been instructed to open all mail addressed to you. Be careful." This was counsel that Patterson already had ingested, but what followed is even more notable. The man placed ten dollars on Patterson's desk and remarked, "Just a present from Uncle Sam," then smiled and strolled away. "He was a Negro," said Patterson, indicating that this factor virtually by itself suggested why he acted thusly—which was not altogether inaccurate.[9]

In other words, Patterson and the CRC were not without ammunition, provided on a gold-encrusted platter by Jim Crow. According to the historian Mark Naison, "between 50,000 and 100,000 people went *through* the [Communist] Party in Harlem between 1930 and 1950, although the stable membership was never more than 2,500 at any one time."[10] Multiply that by other urban areas—including Dixie, where admittedly the numbers were less—and one glimpses the still extraordinary sway held by radicalism as the dam broke and the Red Scare tide surged.

Thus, there was extraordinary force placed upon the NAACP, illustrating why they chose to surrender to the right wing. They were under tremendous pressure—pressure that seemed to signal their own impending liquidation.[11] This pressure, which ordained turning a cold shoulder to Patterson, also impacted membership. By late 1949, when the Red Scare was well under way, Franklin Williams, soon to be promoted by U.S. elites, akin to Marshall—U.S. ambassador to Ghana at the time of the overthrow of Kwame Nkrumah less than two decades later—confided that despite the population growth in Florida, "membership over the past several years in the state has fallen off tremendously."[12] Pressure plus membership stagnation created a spiral of decline that fed upon itself, replicating this dire result.

When Patterson sought a replay of Scottsboro in defending the seven young Negro men charged similarly in Martinsville, Virginia, Marshall—one of Charles Hamilton Houston's most promising students—treated him as if he were a political leper.[13] An evidently dismayed Patterson countered, reminding the future high-court judge about his—Patterson's—journey to Richmond and his conferences with the NAACP leadership there, "with some 25 members of your organization and my own." He further reminded Marshall of the "late and brilliant Charles H. Houston," who stood for center-left unity, and added in Olympian fashion, "this is not time for petty bickering or name-calling," nor the "hush-hush policy" of the NAACP,[14] which had yet to master the mass-defense approach that had led to the Scottsboro breakthrough.[15] Patterson did not seem to realize that with Houston's death, the popular-front alliance that he represented, which had led to the opening in the 1930s that was to be realized in the 1950s, died with him.

The CRC could cooperate with the NAACP at the local level, even when relations at the highest level in Manhattan were decidedly frosty. But when Patterson reached out simultaneously to the NAACP leadership in Philadelphia about the case of the Trenton Six—yet another case of maltreatment of young Negroes—it was as if the days of yore, when the likes of Raymond Pace Alexander and Robert Nix collaborated fruitfully with Patterson, never existed. In fact, Patterson was upbraided by a local NAACP leader, who went as far as calling into question the essence of the CRC's approach to such cases, observing that in "your letter, you pointed up that mass pressure caused the New Jersey Supreme Court to reverse the case of the Trenton Six." Patterson was told—bluntly and briskly—that he was sure this court "would resent this statement by you" and made explicit what this portended: "I repeat that joint action between the Civil Rights Congress and the Philadelphia branch of the NAACP is impossible."[16]

The denouement of the Scottsboro case was also telling, still shooting off sparks decades after the initial arrest.[17] When Haywood Patterson, one of the remaining defendants, escaped to Detroit, Gloster Current, an adroit anticommunist knife fighter, wondered—perhaps unduly—"whether or not CRC could . . . be prosecuted for aiding a fugitive. Of course," he added, seemingly dropping a hint, "that would depend on whether Patterson would testify against them."[18] Current was on to something; near that time, the self-described "black Bolshevik" Harry Haywood got a call from Patterson, telling him, "There's somebody I'd like you to meet," and "sitting there was Haywood Patterson," who had just escaped from prison.[19]

But the more sophisticated Walter White chose to use this case in a way that captured the spirit of the era when Jim Crow and the cold war collided. Rather than follow the hint left hanging by Current and collaborating with the state to prosecute the CRC, he opted to raise the ominous specter of Communist advance at the expense of Jim Crow. Thus, he chose to emphasize "the far reaching and possibly disastrous result of again giving the Communists a drum to beat all over the world in attacking race prejudice [that] coincides with the charge made by the present Chinese government that the Korean situation is the beginning of a world wide war between white and colored peoples. Unless the Haywood Patterson [case] is handled justly and wisely," he warned, "we can be sure that Moscow radio and every Communist agent in Asia will use the case to attack again the United States because of its actions so far as colored people are concerned."[20]

With such a perspective, the NAACP leadership was hardly disposed to cooperate with Patterson and the CRC as an important civil-rights mobilization approached in 1950. Fresh in the memories of some NAACP leaders were the sharp attacks on their positions launched by Patterson and his comrades—before the proclamation of the popular front.

Thus, when Patterson offered an olive branch to the NAACP leadership in late 1949, Marshall and Wilkins huddled and pored over his peacemaking proposal skeptically. "Your offer of cooperation is not made in good faith" was among the "suggestions for reply" to Patterson's letter drafted by Marshall, as he recounted what in his view disqualified the CRC from a NAACP-led front: "You and your associates were conspicuous by your absence in the fight against segregation and discrimination during the period of our last World War and especially after Russia's intervention in the war. During that period we were unable to get the support of any of your associates."[21] Talking points in tow, Wilkins then turned to Patterson, under siege after Peekskill, and curtly berated him and all that he thought he represented.[22] Patterson, seeking to invoke the popular front, told Wilkins that it was "necessary to stress that which unites us, and not that which sets us apart," while complaining of the "distortions" he perceived of his and ILD views: "The past must not be allowed to control the present," he cried, adding, "we seek to avoid repeating yesterday's mistakes."[23] But with President Truman sending a signal about desegregation of the armed forces, a possible harbinger that would spread to society as a whole, Wilkins felt that this was no time to be friendly with one of the Missourian's staunchest foes. (All Patterson could offer, it was thought, was a "mock trial on Military Jim Crow," exhibited in Los Angeles to much fanfare.[24]) And to make sure that the White House and its backers knew about his stern rejection of the CRC, what was termed the "Patterson-Wilkins Correspondence" was disseminated widely to the press.[25]

As so often happened during this conflicted epoch, rank-and-file NAACP members objected strenuously to Wilkins's maneuver—it was not "worthy of a democratic organization"—but opposition was hardly hegemonic within the organization as a whole.[26] Wilkins could have countered deftly that it was not only Communists—and their reputed "fronts"—that he was barring, for also excluded was the Workers' Defense League (whose anti-Stalinist credentials probably exceeded Wilkins's), though it had attracted to its banner a number of the fabled "New York intellectuals," who were to be so influential in coming years.[27]

Wilkins went on to boast to an inquiring Pentagon official that "our anticommunist record . . . goes back to the very beginning of our organization"; he dismissed the participation of Socialists then and maintained that—as the cold war turned hot in Korea—"the number of Communist Party members is probably nil."[28] Thus, when the NAACP's crucial civil-rights mobilization took place in 1950 in Washington, standing sentry at the door were such anticommunist stalwarts as A. Philip Randolph, Willard Townsend, and Herbert Hill—battle-toughened veterans of labor wars and, consequently, as an ally put it, "conversant with CP tactics and personnel, [they] spotted and barred all but a few of the Communists, regardless of the guise in which they appeared"—which often meant simple left-liberals who had cooperated with the Reds during the war (which conceivably could have included FDR himself).[29]

Undoubtedly, this ban excluded progressive trade unions with admirable antiracist records, while including unions with ignoble records. Dr. Carlton Goodlett, a leader of the NAACP branch in San Francisco, pointed this out. He noted accurately that barring those unions "accused of Communist infiltration" would serve to "tremendously reduce the effectiveness of the [NAACP] in its work on the Pacific Coast," referring to the antiracist labors of such champions as the International Longshoremen and Warehousemen's Union (ILWU), a primary victim of the Red Scare. The zeal with which anticommunism was pursued was exposed when it was reported that barred from the NAACP gathering were about "800 persons," including University of Chicago students and professors, the entire membership of the Howard University chapter, and several hundred members of the New York City chapter. They, along with Patterson, were not among the five thousand present at this historic gathering, and it was considerably weaker as a result.[30]

Thus, the NAACP refused to join Patterson in objecting to the high-court appointment of Truman's attorney general, Tom Clark of Jim Crow Texas; in fact, when Patterson testified at the hearing, he was confronted with a supportive letter from Marshall wielded like a baton by a gleeful senator, Pat McCarran, an avatar of anticommunism.[31].

Of course, the NAACP was not isolated.[32] This was revealed when in mid-1949, Lester Granger of the National Urban League and the baseball star Jackie Robinson—a direct beneficiary of Patterson's activism—appeared at a hearing of the House Committee on Un-American Activities. Granger stoked concern when he cited the idea (with which he disagreed) that Harlem was a "vast, seething hotbed of Communism," while Robinson assailed Paul Robeson for his alleged dearth of allegiance to his homeland.[33] In turn, Granger lavished effusive praise upon Robinson for his temerity.[34] "That was a lovely letter you sent, Jackie," chortled Branch Rickey, the baseball player's boss.[35] But it was the NAACP board member Alfred Baker Lewis who captured the anxiety of the age when he informed Granger, "Frankly, I believe they [CP] are more effective in infiltrating than many people realize."[36] It emerged subsequently that Granger actually wrote Robinson's explosive statement—at the behest of a U.S. diplomat, Chester Bowles, who thought it was necessary in order to "counteract anti-American Communist propaganda in India"—thus, ironically ratifying the potency of global pressure as it was being rejected.[37]

An unrepentant Patterson then turned up with his spouse and 1,500 others at the Soviet embassy—joined by Foreign Minister Andrei Vishinsky and W. E. B. Du Bois—at a celebration of the Bolshevik Revolution.[38] With Du Bois and Robeson, he sent warm birthday greetings to Josef Stalin as he turned seventy, highlighting his "leadership in uprooting racial discrimination"—an implicit slap at their homeland.[39] Patterson's foreign policy received a decided rebuff when, upon arrival in Toronto, he was held incommunicado for twelve hours. Drama ensued when he appeared on the platform of a local rally wearing a handkerchief gag, as his speech was read to the crowd.[40]

The homeland struck back. Walter White took to the pages of the monthly glossy journal founded by John H. Johnson, now well on his way to immense wealth, to discuss the "strange case of Paul Robeson." "There are many who attribute Robeson's conversion to William L. Patterson," he declared. "Certain frustrations, racial and personal, were believed responsible for Patterson's abandonment of a growing law practice in New York to become a party recruit. Patterson's assignment since appears to have been what someone has half seriously and half jocularly called 'the Monsignor. . . . of Negro Communism' and Robeson is often cited as one of his greatest triumphs. Persuasive, devout and indefatigable Patterson has devoted himself to efforts to indoctrinate and win over leaders or potential leaders of Negro opinion"—though, apparently, Robeson was his greatest triumph. White dismissed Patterson's relationship with Charles Hamilton Houston, now safely interred and unable to contradict his assertion, but the wider point was that if the CRC's leader could be quarantined, his putative contagion would not spread, as it apparently had to Robeson.[41]

Putting distance between the NAACP and Patterson's presumed contagion was not that difficult—except it left a lingering matter about what to do when his CRC was able to use its still formidable domestic and global apparatus to create a cause célèbre of a case involving evidence of racist bias. The NAACP could continue to ignore Patterson on such matters, but this ran the risk of eroding their own credibility, leaving the embarrassing query as to whether they cared more about anticommunism than antiracism. From the CRC's onset—and particularly after Patterson's accession to the leadership—this matter arose repeatedly, but most dramatically in the cases of Willie McGee, the Martinsville Seven, Rosa Lee Ingram, and the Trenton Six.[42] (Naturally, the many anticommunist prosecutions in the United States were greeted by an avalanche of protest from overseas,[43] largely generated by the CRC. But the NAACP was not under as much pressure here to intervene, though the civil-liberties issues involved were of moment to their very existence.)

McGee's case arose simultaneous with the founding of the CRC in 1946. The black Mississippi truck driver was slated for execution because of allegations of a forced sexual encounter with a Euro-American woman. Symptomatic of the contradictions involved with the NAACP's renewed relationship with U.S. elites was the credible assertion that Thurgood Marshall and his legal team had chosen not to become involved in this case, since they felt that the Magnolia State was much too dangerous for African American attorneys.[44]

There was good reason for this apprehension, as the future congresswoman Bella Abzug—the CRC's attorney in this case—could have told them. Her life was threatened in Mississippi—"It was so backward, it was unbelievable," she confided later. She spent two years on this case before McGee fell to executioners in 1951. "It was like being in a whole other world from the one I had been raised in," said this lifelong New Yorker. She was stunned when a local newspaper asserted that "they should have Willie McGee's white woman lawyer along with him in the electric chair." The stress no doubt contributed to a miscarriage she suffered. Unbowed, she and her CRC colleagues were able to keep the case embroiled in various courts, winning five stays of execution until his death. In the Grand Guignol, for which Mississippi was notorious, McGee was executed publicly as grimly satisfied Euro-Americans looked on. "I couldn't be there," said Abzug, "but an assistant held a phone. I could hear the bloodcurdling screams of delight from the crowd when he was executed."[45]

The NAACP stood down as Patterson toiled tirelessly to save McGee's life. He prodded Du Bois, now facing his own legal difficulties,[46] with little success, to travel to Mississippi. "I am placing tremendous stress upon the crusade into Mississippi," said Patterson, "and regard it as one of the most historic acts of the last 80 years," particularly the jump start it had given to a budding feminist movement, which had adopted McGee's case as its own. "This women's movement has limitless potentialities," he averred with enthusiasm.[47] He deployed his usual tactic of reaching out to the international community. "Willie McGee suddenly became a pawn in a world propaganda war," said *Life* magazine, the wildly popular organ of Henry Luce's journalistic empire. He became a "symbol with which Communism sought to convince Chinese and Indians and Indonesians that capitalism hates and tortures anyone who is not white. The 'McGee case,'" it was said, "became more famous in distant countries than in most of the U.S.," as "'Save Willie McGee' rallies blossomed in scores of cities from Los Angeles to Paris."[48]

Luce's organ was not exaggerating. Bella Abzug, the CRC lawyer on the ground in Mississippi, recalled later that "the local paper made a big thing about getting letters from Communist China in support of Willie McGee."⁴⁹ The State Department dispatched staff to Jackson, Mississippi, to monitor the case, since foreign embassies—prompted by inquiries from citizens back home—were demanding to know why an innocent man was being slated for execution. This concern was noticeably high in Paris. As McGee was being killed, Patterson was picketing at a familiar haunt: the White House. Across town at the Lincoln Memorial, a sizable group of trade unionists and war veterans chained themselves in a circle around the huge support column of the memorial's steps. "Lincoln freed the slaves," they chanted. "Truman free McGee."⁵⁰

Predictably, Patterson was outraged by the spectacle that was McGee's execution. "The moral conscience of white America has not been sufficiently awakened to the menace of Jim Crow, segregation, the ghetto, and lynch murders," he groaned, and that, along with "federal bi-partisan agreement with the Dixiecrats," contributed mightily to this state-sanctioned murder.⁵¹ Yet Patterson's detractors charged that he was the one responsible for McGee's cruel fate. As one white Mississippian exclaimed, "I don't think McGee is guilty of rape, but since he [was] hooked up with the Communists, I don't think he ought to be given another trial." McGee, it was reported, "was convicted because he was black and supported by Communists, not on any conclusive evidence."⁵²

The Martinsville case involved similar issues—and a similar result. As one scholar put it, "The NAACP's strident rejection of William Patterson's overtures also indicated that the CRC had emerged as a viable challenger to the NAACP for leadership of the civil rights movement," for the ILD under his leadership "earned a reputation among African-Americans as a reliable ally in the struggle for racial justice." The two cases—from Mississippi and Virginia—converged shortly after the war in Korea erupted, when Patterson escorted close relatives and associates of McGee and one of the Martinsville defendants to the front gates of the White House, where a guard refused to admit them because they did not have a scheduled appointment. While the delegation addressed reporters and passersby, Patterson busily telephoned White House aides, Justice Department officials, and representatives of the Democratic party—with little tangible result. This may have pleased officialdom and even the NAACP leaders, just as the charge was renewed that dastardly Communists had manipulated poor defendants for political ends—though this allegation rarely emerged from the defendants themselves or their relatives charged with burying them.⁵³

During the Martinsville case, the World Federation of Trade Unions—representing seventy-eight million globally—joined heartily in the protest.⁵⁴ Governor William Tuck of Virginia was bombarded with protests from abroad, particularly Scandinavia.⁵⁵ "Please remember," the chief executive was told, "that the eyes of Africa, Asia, Europe, and Latin America are upon you and the Commonwealth of Virginia. Group murders of innocent persons would not happen anywhere else in the world with the possible exception of Nationalist China, Greece, Spain, and

South Africa."56 At the same time, a Patterson ally was probably correct in declaring that, "had it not been for the intervention of the Civil Rights Congress" and their "brilliant and persistent" legal team, "all [these] men without question would have been executed by the state instantaneously."57

The case of the Trenton defendants was in the same category as the McGee and Martinsville cases, which was bared when Thurgood Marshall and his confederates in the American Civil Liberties Union took out a full-page advertisement in the *New York Times* on this controversial case involving an alleged racially charged robbery. They pointed with asperity to the "Communists"—actually meaning the CRC—who "have sought to make capital of this case by whipping up a worldwide hysteria against American treatment of Negro citizens." And, contrary to Martinsville, it was said, "our purpose was and is to secure to these humble men equal justice under law and not to leave the defense in the hands of Communists who attempted to exploit the case for their own ends."58 Per usual, Marshall and company had a point—insofar as Patterson (per usual) did see fit to deploy (or "exploit") this case as an exemplar of U.S. injustice and as a prod to erode Jim Crow. That was the import of the CRC requesting that the United Nations investigate this matter and why, to that end, he helped to foment demonstrations in Europe particularly. According to a British Labour parliamentarian, the case was known to "every Englishman," as consular officials were deluged with petitions of protest.59 CRC press releases alerted one and all when their "mass delegation" sought a meeting with Governor Alfred Driscoll. In what was becoming a macabre ritual, Patterson entered the death block of the state prison to meet with the defendants.60

Thus, in 1951, Marshall and others crowed about the Trenton case, "We have taken over the defense from a Communist-controlled organization. We believe it is time for patriotic Americans to undertake the defense of innocent man instead of leaving these cases to those who too often exploit for propaganda purposes."61 Marshall was assisted by the fact that Patterson and his fellow lawyers of the left were nudged out of the case by the authorities, charged with ethical violations after they blasted the trial as unfair, and were accused in turn of "studied discourtesy and contempt."62 The defendants in the cases that Patterson spearheaded were in a difficult dilemma: shun Patterson and waste away ignominiously like countless Negroes accused before and since, or embrace him and run the risk of becoming an unwanted cold-war symbol, with predictable untoward consequences. One writer adjudged that the "failure of justice in this case stemmed directly from the notion that the United States would somehow suffer a defeat in the Cold War with the Soviet Union if New Jersey were to fail to convict any person defended by the Civil Rights Congress."63

Patterson took a similar approach in the case of Rosa Lee Ingram, a Negro woman from Georgia convicted of killing a white man in the late 1940s. The facts of her case were presented to the U.N. General Assembly in the form of a petition written by Du Bois, who was now enjoying warmer relations with Patterson. Eighteen nations were targeted during this campaign.[64] "The patterns of racial-national terror change little," said Patterson, "whether it is Malan's South Africa, Britain's Kenya, or France's Indo-China. A white man had met his death in an attempt to exercise his will and 'divine right' over a Negro woman's body."[65]

Patterson's and the CRC's efforts were not solely concentrated abroad. Detroit, a center of union activism, was also a center of CRC activism—with an overlap between the two, to a degree. "Hooray!" exclaimed a CRC staffer there in late 1950, "we did it again. You never saw anything to equal the movement under way here around the Martinsville case," as they "took the town by storm" with massive union and religious outreach. There were two crucial aspects: "We've been hitting plant gates," and as a partial result, "the NAACP has had a hard time" in its usual role of blocking the CRC's path.[66] In Detroit, still buoyed by the presence of a progressive faction within the United Auto Workers union, the CRC was also strong. Fund-raisers were reasonably well attended, given the political climate.[67]

Patterson was promised a "magnificent place for the reception in your honor." Thus, he was informed, "we strongly urge you to fly out here and back for this event since we confidently expect that we can get close to 300 people to the reception and buffet dinner," since "the place is perfect."[68] Patterson had little reason to disbelieve the Detroit staff, since only recently they had organized a well-attended event where he was joined by the singer-activist Pete Seeger and Senator William Langer of North Dakota.[69]

A similar pattern could be espied in Richmond when Patterson led a delegation there that included the prominent writers Howard Fast and Dashiell Hammett.[70] "I arrived in Richmond," said Patterson much later, "on a sunny, summer like day," though it was actually "the winter season." This was his first journey there since the heyday of Scottsboro. That earlier trip was auspicious in that a mass meeting of Negroes was "held in a park the city was building over a garbage dump in the black ghetto," and "several hundred black men and women" were there, a considerable crowd for the time. Security for Patterson was tight, since police officers were "as thick as swarming bees and they [too] could sting." This trip for the Martinsville Seven presented similar circumstances, despite the passage of time. When Patterson showed up at the death house, the warden greeted him with "cordiality," though Patterson thought he detected an opposite though tacit message: "Someday I'll get you." He "was a burly man," said Patterson, resembling "a Negro whipper" of old. Patterson was escorted to the prison yard, and in this one-hundred-yard long venue, it was as if he had been transported back in time, for "it looked at first as if all of the inmates were black"—as if the year were 1864. It was almost with relief that he finally cast eyes upon a "small coterie of white prisoners." But upon descending the stairs to the death chamber, he was greeted with the startling presence of eleven men—nine of them Negroes, seven of whom were his clients. He spoke to each individually, and at that point an epiphany descended upon him. "I have pondered this case deeply," he said; prisons in Dixie were no more than "reservations for black political prisoners," for "every black American has an awareness when he leaves home in the morning that he may not return at night." There was a veritable national plot to make Negroes seem like a "criminal breed"—so as to justify genocide. Thus, when he reached the train station for his anguished departure, "it was hard to smile."

Such dismaying episodes drove Patterson's single-minded attempt to indict the U.S. authorities for genocide before an international body. "There was not a single state in the union," he concluded, "in which the black prison population was not in excess of the black man's percentage of the general population," capped by "one prison in Georgia [which] did not have a white inmate."[71]

This was one of many forays Patterson made into the former headquarters of the Confederacy. On his way to a meeting with the U.S. attorney general on this case, with a delegation he stopped in Richmond to see the governor. "I participated in several of the mass demonstrations" in Washington, he added. Reprising Scottsboro, he also "went to visit the men in the death house." Yet despite his ministrations, he confessed sadly, "about four months before Willie McGee" was executed, all the Martinsville defendants were "electrocuted, all of them."[72]

On the McGee case, Patterson led the charge. "From the start of the Civil War no white man has been sent to the electric chair for the crime of rape in any of the southern states," he proclaimed. And it was Patterson who coordinated the legal campaign and the mass defense: "I went over the pleadings," "prepared a draft for the defense with the lawyers," and organized a "mass picket-line in Washington and organized for the first time since the Civil War a mass demonstration in Jackson, Mississippi." Patterson recounts, "[I] spoke all over the country" and "spoke abroad on two occasions." At Madison Square Garden, as the Red Scare was brewing, there was a remarkable outpouring of "some 20,000 people"—"I chaired that meeting," Patterson said proudly. There were delegations to the state's governor and to the U.S. Attorney General and the Civil Rights Division, which he supervised. There was a "vigil" in Washington—"I was present there and played a leading part," he said. Though the vigil was silent, placards screamed in favor of "equal justice," "an end to discrimination and Jim Crowism," and "passage of an anti-lynch law [and] anti–poll tax law." In New York City alone, he orchestrated the distribution of fifty thousand leaflets to the religious community.[73]

Patterson was no stranger to the newfangled contraption that was television, discussing the various CRC cases and on one occasion, on WPIX in New York, asserting cagily, "I do not want change anything in our country in relation to the procedure and Constitution at this time."[74] Across the continent in Los Angeles, when he was honored at a testimonial dinner, it was deemed sufficiently newsworthy for the *Los Angeles Times* to take note, referring to him wondrously as the "stormy petrel in race issues."[75] In his remarks, Patterson—a practiced orator—did not disappoint, lambasting Truman and wondering why black soldiers had to die abroad for freedoms they did not enjoy at home.[76]

In Trenton, a few score miles away from his Harlem home, Patterson was even more active. The family of the defendants, he recalled, "requested that we defend these lads," and he recruited the exceedingly competent attorneys John Rogge and Emmanuel Bloch. Patterson "actively participated in all the legal phases" of the case "as counsel of record for the Six," and "on appeal" as well. They too "were in the death house," where Patterson visited them—"I pointed to the door leading to the electric chair." Yet, despite their extreme straits, the judge ruled that he and the counsel they desired should be removed, as this would be no replay of Scottsboro.[77]

Then there was the case of Robert Wesley Wells, an African American inmate in California facing the ultimate penalty. "I myself," Patterson informed inquiring investigators, "visited the heads of the National Council of Churches of Christ of America. I met with top leaders of the Methodist and Baptist churches on the Pacific coast. I went myself to the editors of the *Chronicle* in San Francisco, I called press conferences there," and "when abroad I spoke on the case." Patterson "met with the warden and his staff." "I, together with a delegation, presented this to the Governor of California," then "spoke in Vallejo, Oakland, Santa Rosa, Petaluma," and throughout the length and breadth of the Golden State.[78]

This constant—even incessant—travel was a reflection of the need, as his comrades were being jailed, forced into exile, or scurrying underground, while (as in 1919) Negroes assessing the postwar scene pushed even more aggressively toward justice, engendering a fierce counterreaction. "It was my contention," stressed Patterson, "that not only every jailed Communist but every jailed Negro was a *political prisoner*"—a contention that only magnified his workload. The traveling he had to endure as a result was a form of punishment in itself, since—he observed—"insults of all kinds were directed toward [Negro travelers] by white travelers. A clear sign of white supremacy was the unwillingness of a white person to sit beside a Negro in train, bus, railway, coach, or plane."[79]

The debilitating travel, the stress of descending into a death house, and the overweening surveillance was a prescription for worsening the health of a man who had now passed sixty years of age. Patterson used to be a good amateur boxer at college and continued to listen to the major matches on the radio. He was also a baseball fan and often spent the rare Sunday at home preparing a complex legal brief while listening to a game on the radio. Most of all, he exercised for half an hour every morning, even though his workday often extended to sixteen hours.[80] Yet this discipline was insufficient to rescue him from the desperate straits delivered by the Red Scare.

This regimen was necessary not only because of the grueling travel and draining visits to death chambers, but in part because of the often punishing rallies and meetings the CRC organized, with lengthy agendas and, at times, even lengthier lists of speakers. A troubling signal was sent when a member of the chapter in Los Angeles—one of their main bases of support—resigned in disgust after sitting through "nine (9—count 'em . . .) speakers plus entertainment, plus William Patterson." Aghast, he complained, "my brain can no longer take it. After 3 hours my backside can no longer take it." This, he said, "partially explains why people aren't turning out the way they used to."[81]

But no amount of personal discipline could prepare Patterson adequately for the increasingly unfavorable objective circumstances he faced. The centrists were fleeing in all directions from his embrace, while the U.S. ruling elite was having a hard time explaining why they should expend blood and treasure in fighting Communists abroad while tolerating them at home. Patterson's CRC may have had ten thousand members at its zenith and sparsely staffed offices in Manhattan, Detroit, Seattle, San Francisco, Los Angeles, and a few other key sites, but, like Archimedes, it had unparalleled ability to move the world not least because of its extraordinarily developed global contacts—thanks largely to the Communist movement—which only served to infuriate their domestic adversaries even more.

This was the backdrop of the startling confrontation between Patterson and a leading Dixiecrat at a congressional hearing called to interrogate him and the organization he led, which was a prelude to a concerted effort to put him behind bars. It was August 1950, shortly after war had erupted on the Korean peninsula, and the nation was more jittery than usual about Communists. This was the moment the subpoena arrived, summoning Patterson to Washington. Feisty as ever, he thought that the congressional bloodhounds "had bagged the wrong quarry." So he boarded the train southward, resting easily, dozing most of the time. He had departed before breakfast, so he ambled into the dining car, where he was recognized by a waiter—not an uncommon occurrence for a man who some deemed to be Public Enemy Number One—and like the postal inspector earlier, he was friendly, beckoning Patterson to sit at his table. He wanted to show his appreciation for the struggle the CRC was waging.

So bolstered, Patterson left the train refreshed and scurried to the capitol to confer with a remaining ally in these hallowed halls, Congressman Vito Marcantonio of East Harlem. Though he walked only a few blocks, he was dripping with perspiration, as Washington was enmeshed in a typical summer heat wave. The chilling remarks of his friend and counsel, the congressman, did little to alleviate his discomfort. "Pat, you're in a vise," he said. The inquisitors were fishing for names of CRC and Communist party members and said the man known colloquially as Marc, "If you don't give them the names [then] you are going to be in contempt of Congress. If you [do], you're going to be in contempt of all progressive mankind. Remember, you're a Red and a Negro and what they hate more than [a] Negro is one who knows both who and how to fight." Patterson realized that he had arrived to "come to grips with the eagle in her nest" as he walked into "one of the larger committee rooms, seating a gallery of a hundred or more." The legislators sat on a raised platform, below which was the witness chair. The crowd was small. "I wasn't in a vise," thought Patterson. "I was in a den of thieves and legal lynchers." Virtually every member of the committee was present, expecting a "Roman Holiday," said the presumed target of their ire, featuring "the twin sports of Red-baiting and Negro baiting." But as "the day wore on . . . the Committee got nowhere." Marc, his counsel, was tied up intermittently and was in and out of the room. The legislators demanded that Patterson go back to Manhattan and return with requested documents the next day, but he knew he would not get back in time, which would place him in contempt.

Marc was blunt: "You have got to make them make a mistake. Throw them off balance." Pondering his problem, Patterson returned to his hotel. He was not only anxious; he was also aware that he had not succeeded in compelling the committee to expose itself. The next morning he rose early, walked briskly to the corner drugstore for toast and coffee, then took another stroll to gather his thoughts. Arriving at the hearing, he found that the room was filling with Negroes, including Alice Dunnigan of the Associated Negro Press and a reporter from one of his favorite organs, the *Afro-American*. Chairing that day was H. L. Lanham of the Fifth Congressional District of Georgia, a congruous mix of thick and syrupy southern drawl and Harvard Phi Beta Kappa. He pounced immediately, demanding documents. Patterson, the experienced pugilist, bobbed and weaved until lunchtime, whereupon Marc escorted him to the House cafeteria, "much to the dismay of some of the gentlemen from the South," as Patterson recalled.

Between munches, Marc coolly informed him, "You have got to get Lanham riled up," forcing him away from the matter at hand: the offering up of membership lists and the like. Returning to the hearing armed with this wise counsel, Patterson began to aggressively interrogate the interrogators: "Why have you brought me down here?" he asked angrily. "You know that I am trying to prevent the legal murder of Willie McGee of Mississippi, and trying to put a stop to lynchings in Georgia." Rising to the bait, an outraged Lanham responded just as angrily, claiming there were no lynchings in his state. Patterson exclaimed, voice rising, "Georgia is a lynchers' state!" Lanham replied, "You're a liar." Patterson replied in kind, "How many Negroes have *you* lynched?" Touched to the quick, Lanham yelled blisteringly, "You god-damned black son-of-a-bitch!" He rose abruptly and started for the stairs leading down to the stunned witness. Some sought to restrain him as he shouted, "Let me go! Let me go!" He broke away with a burst of energy and hurled himself toward Patterson. He was rushing toward this experienced boxer when two police officers caught him about ten feet away from Patterson's furious visage. An officer stood beside Patterson, gun reputedly drawn—for what reason was unclear. Screams pierced the room as a journalist declaimed, "Don't kill him!"—meaning "me," Patterson added drily. Lanham, by now completely out of control, repeated his racially tinged epithet three times.

Patterson rose and eloquently demanded the floor. Lanham shouted, "Sit down!" The hearing was adjourned hastily. Lanham stormed out, shouting, "We've got to keep those black apes down!"

Patterson rushed to Marc's office, perhaps unaware that he had exchanged one snare for another, in that this episode did not deliver him safely away from the hoosegow. Temporarily, he was elated as this dramatic vignette hit the press like a thunderclap. *Time* magazine gave it a "double spread," Patterson said with a burst of pride. He was equally pleased that the "European and Latin American press highlighted it." He then hurried to the offices of the two Negro congressmen, both of whom he knew (they were "well acquainted," was his phrase), William Dawson of Chicago and Adam Clayton Powell of Harlem, suggesting that they press charges of misconduct against their congressional comrades. But Patterson had crossed swords with Dawson in Chicago, and he was none too embracing, while Powell was in the process of distancing himself from the organized left he once welcomed. Congressman Lanham, still fuming, preferred contempt charges against Patterson. The good news was that at a moment of national hysteria, Patterson received 106 votes in the body of 435 in his favor[82]—and that five thousand in Harlem rallied to his defense (though police officers on surrounding rooftops sent a contrasting message).[83] The bad news was that he now had to face a trial as he busily prepared to press an even more explosive charge of his own: dragging the country of his birth into the dock on the charge that it had perpetrated genocide against African Americans.

9

"We Charge Genocide"

William Patterson was tempting fate as the second half of the twentieth century dawned. He was fighting ferociously with Dixiecrats in Washington and their agents throughout the Deep South, including the cockpit of bigotry that was Mississippi, preparing the battlefield for an upsurge that soon was to blossom. Yet these Dixiecrats were bolstered by a concomitant surge in anticommunism—a philosophy of which they served in the vanguard, which allowed them to suggest that they were hell-bent on bashing Patterson not because of his "blackness" but because of his "Redness." He and the CRC—more than any others, to their everlasting credit—had taken the plight of the Negro to the global stage, helping to bring inordinate pressure upon Jim Crow, pressure that ultimately caused this system of bias to erode. However, this circumvention of Washington's jurisdiction only infuriated broader swathes of the U.S. population, wary about the erosion of sovereignty in the face of a Communist challenge abroad. Moreover, this rewarding activism had not gone unnoticed, as Congressman Lanham's outburst demonstrated, and carried the seeds of its demise. Thus, toward the end of this tumultuous year, the FBI was contemplating seizing Patterson's passport—which was to be done quite shortly, curtailing the oxygen supply for his activism.[1]

The genocide petition he filed abroad—mirrored by Robeson filing at U.N. headquarters in Manhattan—was a devastating indictment of the U.S. authorities' complicity and dereliction in lynching, murder, deprivation of voting rights, and all manner of crimes. Ominously for Washington, the petition virtually invited the international community to intervene forcefully in what had been seen traditionally as an internal U.S. affair. By early 1952, Patterson claimed that as a result of this petition, "the international offensive against racist terror" in his homeland had "reached unprecedented heights." Bedazzled, he found that "as fast as new editions" of this work were "printed, they are being sold out"—with twenty thousand copies sold by February 1952.[2] Cleverly, Patterson sought to win over Washington's foes by arguing that "the lyncher and the atom bomber are related."[3] When Eleanor Roosevelt felt compelled to disparage the petition, it suggested that this campaign could not be ignored easily.[4] Even in Seattle, which had been thought to be a liberal citadel, the public library banned the genocide book,[5] while the public-school system sought to bar the CRC from renting an auditorium.[6] Unsurprisingly, Patterson's antagonists had good reason to retaliate forcefully against him.

In April 1951, a racially integrated jury—seven blacks and five whites—in Washington, D.C., refused to convict Patterson on a charge of contempt of Congress, stemming from his confrontation with Congressman Lanham; it was a mistrial. A second trial was ordered by the Justice Department and set for June, but the intervention of seventeen bishops of the A.M.E. Zion church—of which Robeson's brother was a pastor—helped to compel the government to grant an extension until early 1952, by which time Patterson (quite conveniently) would have returned from his European journey, designed to place Washington on trial for perpetrating genocide against the Negro.[7] The trial was set for March 1952, and he was acquitted. But the authorities had not finished with him—Patterson was beginning to resemble a firefighter tied up in fighting blazes in the firehouse—and in 1954 he was sentenced to ninety days in prison, since the Internal Revenue Service desired the list of CRC donors, which he refused to relinquish. In early 1955, the circuit court of appeals reversed his conviction, but by then, both he and the CRC were virtually spent, with the latter to expire a scant year later.[8]

Certainly the U.S. authorities kept close tabs on Patterson's pulverizing travel schedule, and they were well aware that he arrived in London on September 8, 1950, where his schedule was filled with meetings with Robeson's friends and comrades from the time the performer resided in this capital, then it was on to Paris (only weeks after trading insults with Lanham), then to Hungary nine days later—"behind the Iron Curtain," to use the increasingly popular catch-phrase—then on to Prague about two weeks after that, then back to France, where he was to materialize a few months later with his genocide petition, which was to generate maximum worldwide publicity against Jim Crow. At various border checkpoints—particularly in Paris and New York—the anxious authorities searched rigorously his papers and documents.[9] J. Edgar Hoover was apprised as Patterson was seen "leaving the Russian Embassy,"[10] and it was duly noted when the French Communist newspaper carried a notice about his appearances in Paris.[11]

Thus, the U.S. authorities knew that in Budapest Patterson met with the minister of justice and was interviewed on the radio. He was pleased with a "very large and very interesting" press conference and undeterred by the presence of U.S. journalists who "tried to heckle." He met with numerous high-ranking diplomats about pressing the plight of the Negro in the global arena—particularly those from the Soviet Union and China, where the Communist party had only recently come to power. He was surprised pleasantly when the Chinese ambassador in Budapest "arose at 5 A.M. to see me off."[12] Perhaps he should have been not been surprised, for while in Paris, the Chinese ambassador appeared at a banquet in Patterson's honor, treated him wonderfully, took all the copies of the genocide petition that could be mustered, then saw that they were reprinted in Peking—and that U.S. prisoners of war received copies.[13]

The FBI, which was able to get ahold of Patterson's report about his journey, also filed away a newspaper column he penned, urging that drastic action be taken against the United States because of Jim Crow,[14] and his remarks in Prague, where he called the U.S. government a "criminal" enterprise and was said to have predicted that "armed resistance on the part of American Negroes against Ku Klux Klanism might increase."[15] These volatile words somehow were transmitted to a Clevelander, who then scribbled a note to J. Edgar Hoover—who needed no prompting. After terming Patterson correctly as a "radical," with similar insight this correspondent added that this Communist was "pulling no punches in his grudge against our government." Bringing coal to Newcastle, he instructed Hoover to "watch him, trail him to his hotel after he gets off ship, then trail him to his home. Please take action."[16]

When summoned to testify before the Subversive Activities Control Board, Patterson testified that he "presented" his prized petition directly to the U.N. leader Trygvie Lie and to "Mrs. Roosevelt" of the U.S. delegation—who refused, unsurprisingly, to sponsor it. So Patterson "immediately went to the Indian delegation," and that of Egypt as well. "While these two nations were considering the question," he recalled, "I was called up by the American Embassy in Paris." He "inquired why they wanted to see me, and they said the State Department had ordered them to . . . demand the surrender of my passport and to send me back to the United States." He spoke with the "secretary of the American Embassy in Paris" with no meeting of the minds, as "one of the leading *New York Times* reporters" hovered nearby. Those listening to his testimony may not have been pleased when Patterson recounted the "numerous meetings" he had while traipsing through Europe. "I spoke over the air twice in Paris," he said, and Hungary too. "I addressed the Hungarian Supreme Court. I spoke over the air twice in Czechoslovakia. I spoke over the air in Germany and addressed a number of meetings. I addressed meetings in Switzerland—in Austria and England. I spoke at the London University for Economics [sic]." He argued that since a petition was presented successfully on behalf of Namibia, then occupied questionably by apartheid South Africa, "I believed that the establishment of this precedent would be advantageous to me and that the same policy would be followed by the United States government when I presented our petition." It was striking for Patterson that Africa was blazing the trail for African Americans—but disconcerting for Washington. The same held true for his conferring with delegates from Liberia and "from the Gold Coast and other countries in Africa," where he found "tremendous sympathy."[17]

It is understandable why a wave of angst would wash over Patterson's opponents, for the CRC leader felt that the genocide petition would "offer tremendous possibilities for getting an income as well as the strongest political base we have yet [to] secure," since it would be printed in paperback and hawked globally. "There should be house affairs in which it is discussed and where money is raised," he advised.[18] That Patterson had zeroed in on an important issue was vindicated when in its first week, this powerful book sold out completely to the tune of five thousand copies.[19] "It is a scarce item on the book market," said one Negro journalist, "and copies in New York are at a premium."[20]

But if citizens were concerned about his European journey in the early fall of 1950, they may have been apoplectic about what occurred later, when Patterson turned up in Paris with his genocide petition. Departing on December 3, 1951, on Air France, he arrived the next day and stayed for three weeks, before heading to Vienna, then Budapest. After about a week there, it was off to Prague, then backtracking to Vienna and Paris, before decamping in London, where he spent six days. Arriving in New York City on January 23, 1952, his passport was snatched forthwith, along with a chest x-ray from a Hungarian clinic that revealed some spots. The FBI, which monitored his travel itinerary relentlessly, also found it curious that while in Paris he spent time at a certain spot in St. Germain, "which has been described as a hangout for American Communists in Paris."[21]

The FBI had reason to fret, for if Patterson's dream came true, they and not he would stand trial. Speaking as a seasoned attorney, Patterson counseled that the U.N. Charter "supersedes conflicting United States law," which meant that he was lengthening the battlefield, neutering the advantage enjoyed by the Dixiecrats and their advocates under domestic law. "Virtually all those who opposed ratification of the Genocide Convention before the United States Senate Committee on Foreign Relations," he recounted later, "did so precisely because the Genocide Convention specifically applies to the crimes being committed against the Negro people in the United States." The convention, he warned detractors, "having been ratified by twenty nations, is now in force and binding on all its signatories, including the United States"—a point angrily disputed by his opponents. Thus, said Patterson, "petitioners call upon the General Assembly to establish such a tribunal to the end that justice may be done and future acts of genocide prevented." Their specific targets, he asserted, should include the U.S. president, the Congress, and the high court. In a bold move, Patterson circumvented the levers of power that had executed misery against the Negro by placing them all in the dock.[22]

He had thought about this effort long and hard, befitting its importance and sensitivity. The FBI well knew that in 1946, while still in Chicago, Patterson "discussed the merit of addressing petitions to the United Nations" to "the effect that officials of that body lend their efforts toward ending discrimination against Negroes in the United States."[23] Like others, Patterson was deeply influenced by postwar flux. "I studied the reports of the War Crimes Court at Nuremberg," he said later.[24] In pressing this matter, Patterson thought that he had grasped the nettle: "If you study American History, you will know that in our country we have not solved one major crisis in all history and every one of them broke on the Negro Question; whether it is housing, jobs, education, TVA and water power, the Negro element has been the decisive feature."[25] Breaking the back of Jim Crow through the expert deployment of global pressure would open the floodgates to a new era of progressive reform, if not revolutionary upsurge. Patterson recalled the attempt in the World War I era by William Monroe Trotter to pressure Woodrow Wilson to terminate Jim Crow by raising the matter at Versailles. He recounted Du Bois's late-1940s petitions to the nascent United Nations and noted ruefully that "the leadership of that organization"—the NAACP—"had not been fully behind his efforts." His own National Negro Congress had ventured into this realm also—"I had written the draft introduction," he said, but "this, likewise, had not been followed up." This campaign, he pledged, would be different. He scrutinized intently the words of Secretary of State Dean Acheson, who maintained that Jim Crow had an "adverse impact upon our relations with other countries," a statement that signified the enormous leverage the international environment provided.

In between his many travels and cases to be handled (including his own), Patterson conferred at length, "several times," with the CP leader William Z. Foster, as well as discussing details with Finley Wilson of the Elks fraternal order and Hobson Reynolds, his chief lieutenant. "Both of them behind the scenes supported the project," apparently excited as Patterson was that "we were to be the first in history" to charge the government of the United States with the crime of genocide. In his spadework, he arrived quickly at a distressing conclusion. "A majority of the Negroes believed that the Genocide Convention should be invoked. The majority of the white liberals and personalities were of the contrary view. Some stated categorically that only a Communist could think of such a thing. I took this last expression as a compliment," he added. "Faculty members at law schools were without exception adamantly opposed to the project," all of which he found "amazing" but perhaps also an indication of the potency of such an effort.

Finally, he huddled with Robeson. The two had been through the fire of late, Peekskill being only the most riveting example. He was on board, and it was his accusing finger that appeared on the cover of the book that sold thousands of copies, a stunning figure given the rightward environment. It was Robeson who presented their petition to the United Nations in New York, as Patterson flew to Paris to do the same—after procuring a ticket in a name not his own and carrying twenty copies of the petition, while forwarding sixty each to London and Paris (most of which mysteriously disappeared). Comrades from the French Communist party coordinated his stay and an extensive public-relations campaign, underlining once more the value of a global network.

In Paris, Patterson bumped into Edith Sampson, a Negro woman of note whom he and his spouse had known "well" during their stay in Chicago. "She beckoned to me," said Patterson, and offered her hand—unlike Channing Tobias of the NAACP, who berated him and Ralph Bunche, now with the United Nations, who avoided him. She had read the petition, with its gruesome details about lynchings and state-sanctioned executions—and worse. According to Patterson, she "agree[d] with most of it." Naturally, seeking to preserve her fruitful options, she demurred from stating this publicly—though she provided the useful intelligence that the petition "had very much upset the delegation" of the United States to the United Nations.

Sampson was not the only Chicagoan he encountered in Paris. Ollie Harrington—the former NAACP staffer, now a permanent exile in Paris—brought him together with Richard Wright, also in exile. An entente ensued that was in the process of flowering before the novelist's sudden death less than a decade later.[26] Patterson had to be careful about such associations; per usual, he was being monitored by various authorities every step of the way. "I should like to write many things," he informed his spouse while overseas, "but if walls have ears in the USA, paper has eyes and an eternal memory. So I close."[27]

Patterson was sufficiently indiscreet to commit to paper his encounter with Ralph Bunche, now almost literally running away from his previous ties to the left and the reality that Patterson and the former professor had known each other for years.[28] "Friend Bunche has passed me several times," said Patterson, "and always avoids me. He ran out of the Polish Embassy when he saw me there at a reception." Others were more friendly, including the noted writers Ella Stewart and Donald Ogden Stewart.[29] Moderate Negroes, like Bunche and Tobias, were embraced by Washington, which moved to push more of them into the global arena in an attempt to subvert the charge that Negroes were maltreated atrociously.[30] This was a major import of Patterson's global initiative.

"Things are breaking splendidly," he said of his Parisian venture. Referring to an NAACP leader, he noted, "[Channing] Tobias and I had an extremely interesting talk in which he revealed great fear, asking me repeatedly if I was trying to discredit my government and even why I did not leave the country if I hated it so." Later, addressing the General Assembly, he was unsparing in his characterization of Tobias and his ilk: "I must confess with pain and emotion," he told the international delegates, "that there are men of my own color and nationality representing the government of the United States" and their policies of atrocity. "Negro America," he roared, "seeks through this world body, a redress of its grievances."[31] Responding like many in the international community, a Paris weekly said of Patterson's pained remarks, "reading it one can only be upset and angered by the violence of the criminal racism which oppresses 15 million Negroes in the United States."[32]

Patterson, by his own admission, made a splash in Paris, coordinating with Moscow's delegation, all of which served to "disturb Mrs. [Eleanor] Roosevelt's equilibrium" (Roosevelt was a critical leader of the U.S. delegation). He also conferred with "Krishna Menon of the Indian delegation," who "suggests talking with Prime Minister Nehru," but "facing a fight" in the region against U.S. allies

(Pakistan not least), he was reluctant. He conferred with the Egyptians too, but "the Suez trouble"—which was to explode in war a scant five years later—was a "handicap" there. Menon brought Patterson together with the few delegates representing independent Africa, who expressed "deep sympathy and desire" but, unlike Moscow, did not have the diplomatic leverage to move political mountains.

It was on December 17, 1951—an unrecognized turning point in the centuries-long struggle of Africans in North America—that Patterson presented his genocide petition to various delegations at the Palais de Chaillot. Patterson and the CRC "appreciated, in all respects," that the United Nations "was a higher forum than any we had ever reached before." If this body could debate and legislate concerning apartheid and Namibia, then why not Jim Crow? Thus, in his trailblazing turn on the global stage, Patterson was heartened, realizing that "the objective situation offers convincing proof that the struggles of black Americans are part of a world struggle." Likewise, this served to "testify to the need for Negroes to become interested in world affairs." Others were not as enthusiastic, such as the French authorities, who sought to hustle him out of Paris speedily. The U.S. Embassy also was not pleased with his initiative. They telephoned him and requested that he meet at their spacious site; they wanted him to surrender his passport.

Patterson evaded both by hopping a plane to Switzerland, stopping in Zurich before arriving in Budapest. There he was reacquainted with his old friend from Moscow, Endre Sik, now a high-level official in the Foreign Ministry. Unlike in France, he was greeted as if he were an important dignitary in Hungary, whisked through customs into a waiting car, then to a hotel, where he slept for hours, exhausted by the intensity of his duties. This was followed by a whirlwind of meetings, all with the aim of garnering global support to bring Washington into the dock of humanity, standing accused as a result of its lengthy abuse of the Negro. In Prague, Patterson was told by nervous African students that they had been approached with a proposal for them to leave the country and denounce the authorities for alleged racist practices, a deft counterattack by Washington designed to neutralize the sting of Patterson's biting accusation, a ploy that would escalate in coming years.

Then it was on to London, but by now the forces opposed to his initiative had been galvanized, and he was detained at the airport for seventeen hours before the eminent attorney D. N. Pritt—and a host of demonstrators—compelled his release. At Pritt's home he met with supporters about the circulation of the petition, then it was on to a meeting with the dean of Canterbury and a visit to Highgate cemetery, where he solemnly placed a wreath at the grave of Karl Marx.

By then, Patterson declared, it was "mission accomplished.... I meant that the struggle of American Negroes for their rightful place in their own nation was merging with the liberation struggles of the peoples of Asia, Africa, and Latin America." He was pleased that his petition would be translated into numerous languages, ratcheting up the pressure on Washington. "From the left wing" in Europe generally and "from every section of the socialist world," he stressed brightly, "I had learned much about the essence of the term *international working-class solidarity*." The "potential of the U.N. in the fight for peace and against racism was almost limitless," for at once it dodged the flatulent center-right discourse that was hegemonic among Euro-Americans, while thrusting the Negro Question boldly into a more favorable international arena, where antagonists of Washington were rising in strength.

Patterson may not have realized that he had scored a triumph for Negroes—but, paradoxically, this led to pain inflicted upon himself and the CRC, as the U.S. authorities seized the opportunity to place extraordinary pressure on both for their gumption, which led to Patterson's jailing and, ultimately, his organization's liquidation. As Negroes marched into the shining spotlight of a form of freedom, due not least to the global pressure Patterson helped to generate, he in turn was marched into a gloomy prison cell. "Most black leaders at the time," said Patterson disconsolately, "did not critically examine the world scene and how black masses related to it," which led them to think that the new dispensation emerged wholly from their alliance with domestic elites, ignoring the mighty force of global public opinion.

When he landed at Idlewild Airport in Queens in early 1952, Patterson received a foretaste of the bitterness that was to come. He was just about to place his bags on the conveyor belt for examination when the blow fell. Gently, politely, and without fanfare, an immigration inspector tapped him on the shoulder, and he was frog-marched away, walking the length of the vast hall to the far end. He was whisked into a small room where he saw three nondescript white men chatting amiably—not a harbinger of what he was to experience, for he was to be interrogated exhaustively and exhaustingly, while his baggage was searched thoroughly. Then they demanded that he be subjected to a strip search. He objected. What ensued was an even more minute search of a clothed Patterson.

Finally, he was ejected through a side door after an intentionally humiliating encounter—then had his spirits lifted when he set eyes on friends and comrades awaiting him, led by Robeson. From there it was off to a welcome rally at Harlem's Rockland Palace, with 2,500 eagerly awaiting his report. It was sponsored by Sojourners for Truth and Justice, a black feminist group in which his spouse played a leading role, and chaired by Hope Stevens, a rising Harlem attorney with roots—like Patterson—in the Caribbean. But then a moment ensued that crystallized the challenges to come for Patterson and his comrades. "I had referred several times to the Negro," he recalled "and the tasks ahead, when a woman stood up in the audience and cried, 'I'm not a Negro and don't call me one!'" A befuddled Patterson "could not see the principle involved"—he ascribed it all to the influence of his former comrade, Richard B. Moore, and his increased emphasis on the lineaments of African identity, an inevitable outcome, perhaps, of the anticolonial drive that Patterson embraced wholeheartedly. Still, demonstrating flexibility, he replied diplomatically, "In deference to your wishes, I won't use the term 'Negro' today." Satisfied, the woman took her seat.[33] But not reclining was the headlong rush that in the 1960s would involve an extensive plumbing of black identity, which had various aspects, including the rise of the Nation of Islam, which rose in strength—perhaps not coincidentally—as Patterson's influence began to decline.

A decline in his influence was not the note struck by the *Black Dispatch* of Oklahoma City: "Like Paul Robeson he represents the unqualified independent thinking of black men, without reservations." Patterson, it was reported, "was cast in the same mold as Robeson." Seemingly startled by his chutzpah, this periodical asserted, "He has actually made an issue of persecution of minorities in the United States in the court of world opinion. . . . May his tribe increase."[34] Even John H. Johnson's rapidly growing *Jet* magazine could not afford to ignore the CRC campaign.[35] Of course, the *Baltimore Afro-American* acted likewise.[36] "The press of the entire world has covered his trip," said this periodical; "He has made headlines in London, Paris, Geneva, Berlin, Prague, Warsaw, and Budapest." The U.S. delegation to the United Nations admitted, it was reported, that "the petition"—with its lengthy array of lynchings, murders, and the like—was "well documented." Even Eleanor Roosevelt asserted that the "petition would do some good in focusing world attention on the bad situation in America."[37] Naturally, Robeson, an essential part of the CRC team, elatedly proclaimed that the paperback version of the petition "has now become a world famous book, studied throughout the globe and particularly by oppressed colonial people," a testament to the fortitude of his friend, Patterson, a "heroic Negro fighter."[38]

The mainstream U.S. press was unimpressed. One study found it curious that the paper of record, the *New York Times,* gave the genocide petition skimpy coverage, and even that was festooned with extensive rebuttals, in dramatic contrast to the reception abroad. Other mainstream journals were not as reticent, with one alleging that the CRC was "one of the worst frauds and most mischievous fronts the Reds ever palmed off on the American public."[39] Patterson's former comrade Louis Budenz—now firmly in the grip of conservatism—charged that it was a "sample of the blunders of the State Department while Dean Acheson was Secretary of State that Patterson was permitted to go to Paris to make this attack upon the American nation, so helpful to Soviet aggression."[40]

It was left to the preeminent generator of tabloid scandal, Walter Winchell, to sound the alarm nationwide. While Patterson was still gallivanting around Europe, Winchell took to his microphone and informed his vast radio audience breathlessly—and incorrectly—that "a few months ago I revealed the name of the person now leading the Communist Party in Harlem, New York, the focal point for American Reds to win over the Harlems from coast to coast. This man's name is William Patterson, of the West Indies, one of the pets of the Civil Rights

Congress." It was telling that Patterson's Caribbean heritage, in a repetitive display, was wielded in an attempt to discredit him. Winchell's other point was intended to reassure: "Anyway, ladies and gentlemen, this is to make you feel good. Communist leader Patterson, now in France, has been given a swift kick in the seat by the Department of State."[41]

That Winchell reflected the sentiments of a broader audience was revealed when Eleanor Roosevelt, the totem of mainstream liberalism, condemned Patterson in the pages of the conservative *New York World Telegram and Sun*: "At a time when no visas are being given for Americans to visit Hungary, it seems a rather odd proceeding on his part and one wonders if he has decided to transfer his citizenship to the Soviets."[42] Patterson was of a different view, seeing Eastern Europe as—literally and figuratively—a source of warmth: "Today I was measured for a new overcoat," he said while in Budapest. "These people can't seem to do enough for one who fights American reaction in his own country."[43]

Patterson's Harlem address was the first of many, as he immediately set off on a whirlwind tour that featured addresses at Harvard, Princeton, and Cornell—which only served to guarantee more press coverage and more heartburn for his opponents.[44] Catapulted by the enormous press coverage globally, the CRC sponsored a full-page advertisement in the *Afro-American*, featuring pictures of Patterson and Walter White of the NAACP. It was "an open letter" from the former to the latter, making a "plea for real unity"—which was hardly forthcoming.[45] "It made quite an impact here," Patterson said from New York, "and I know Chicago felt it too. In my opinion it has considerable vitality."[46] Patterson swore that this advertisement did not augur a return to the conflicts that characterized the early days of the Scottsboro defense. "I do not, of course, want to engage in any fight of any kind with the NAACP," he said, underscoring that "one is not compelled to love everyone with whom one works," since "we have to subordinate our personal feelings to the struggle for political objectives."[47]

Rather deftly, White sought to leverage Patterson's initiative to his benefit, warning darkly about the influence the CRC was now wielding internationally. He conceded that "75 percent or more of the charges" against the United States presented by the CRC "are carefully documented ones taken from non-Communist sources and anticommunist sources."[48] Washington, he announced, "has been hit in its most vulnerable spot" by this "most damning indictment," which "will undoubtedly be used not only at Paris by the Soviets but in Asia and Africa as well as the United States" to "destroy faith in American democracy." Channeling civil-rights concessions through his hands to flummox the CRC was the preferred option,[49] though, to his credit, White reportedly refused to condemn the petition as a misrepresentation.[50] His refusal to disavow the petition may shed light on why Patterson discovered, while imprisoned, that a fellow inmate "said that he had read that book the NAACP put out, *We Charge Genocide*. He picked it up accidentally." "I told him," said Patterson, "that the NAACP did not put the book out nor did it welcome its issuance."⁵¹ Even Saunders Redding, a centrist Negro writer on the fast track to enhanced fortune because of the global pressure placed on Jim Crow, provided measured praise. "Compiled by skilled propagandists," its "anger is controlled and dignified," as "questions give way to the conviction that this book is true."⁵²

White's advice was followed—along with the concomitant idea that Patterson and Robeson should be effectively battered into submission, with the latter being referred to repeatedly—and, interestingly, abroad too—as "Black Stalin."⁵³ There was mordant concern throughout London's colonies in the Caribbean and Africa about his influence. Patterson moved quickly to take advantage of the impact of his own British journey by arranging for a concert by Robeson—whose concert arrangements were now being handled by his spouse, Louise—to perform (and raise funds) in London. "It is absolutely imperative," said Patterson "that my big friend"—whose name he dare not mention for fear of sabotaging the effort because of interference with his mail, which occurred nonetheless—"have an invitation to sing at a concert in the British Isles, England particularly and preferably London."⁵⁴ But soon, with the passports of Patterson and Robeson snatched, they were—in effect—under house arrest.

The left-wing journalist I. F. Stone backed Patterson's campaign, defying the gathering national consensus. "To browse through pages 57 to 191 of the genocide petition is an experience for any white man," he said, adding that it "may not be genocide. It is certainly Negro-cide."⁵⁵ At first he was "annoyed" by the petition, thinking it just "another case of Paul Robeson going off half-cocked again," but after reading more carefully, he concluded that "its claim of genocide is not to be lightly dismissed." In fact, he proclaimed, "the strongest legal argument in the document is that so many of those in this country who opposed the Genocide Convention did so on the ground that it might permit lynchings and race riots to be brought before international tribunals"—which was precisely the point and concisely explicated why and how the Dixiecrats were obliged to complete their slow and agonized retreat. Thus, before the U.S. Senate Committee on Foreign Relations, a witness from the National Economic Council asserted fearfully that the "real purpose" of this potent convention was to "set up an international FEPC," or the Fair Employment Practices Committee, whose specter and invocation had so outraged those who cherished Jim Crow. Hence, said Stone, "under the circumstances I see no reason why a Negro group should not utilize the Genocide Convention as a means of calling world attention more forcibly to the condition of the Negro in this country. If Communists were the first to do it, so much the worse for non-Communists."⁵⁶

Motoring on, Patterson entered into a maelstrom of activity seeking to capitalize upon his European venture. He made a proposal that the Communist labor leader Ben Gold "head a group organizing a Committee of One Thousand White Trade Unionists to Fight Genocide."⁵⁷ Patterson was told that "people in Detroit are very anxious to hear about your experiences in Paris," as a "huge mass meeting centered around you" was being organized.[58] They received an earful. "I spoke to representatives of many sections, including those of Egypt, India, Haiti, the British West Indies, Togoland, and Kenya." Racism, "and particularly American racism, is everywhere on the defensive," he enthused. "The international offensive against racist terror within the United States, which is a direct outgrowth of [the] U.S. government's war drive, has reached unprecedented heights."[59]

His subsequent tour, where he spread the word about this global triumph, was greeted gleefully by an embattled left reeling from one defeat after another. "All over the Northwest," he said rapturously, "the meetings were larger than I had ever experienced before." Even better, the more populous "Los Angeles presented a similar picture. Its meetings were a little larger."[60] This northwest advance of 1952 had been presaged the previous year when Patterson had visited that region, leaving an impression that reminded one veteran fighter of the "old days of the [19]17 strike," which had caused national ripples.[61]

This reception was foreshadowed when a debate on the petition was heard by an overflow crowd in Ann Arbor, with extensive coverage in the campus daily.[62] Further south in Chicago, the launch of the genocide-petition paperback was welcomed, since an outbreak of racism had scarred neighboring Cicero. "For the masses of Negro workers and farmers of the South," he declared, "this homeland is becoming a vast torture chamber."[63] In Cleveland, a journalist was struck by the juxtaposition of the "two most divergent positions on the Negro Question in existence today," as Patterson was "speaking at a luncheon group at the Phillis Wheatley Association," while a stone's throw away, Governor Eugene Talmadge of Georgia—Jim Crow personified—was singing a contrasting tune.[64] In his many speaking engagements, Patterson often drew directly from the petition, emphasizing that "54 percent of the state's prisons of New Jersey are Negro; in the fight for the lives of the Martinsville Seven, I discovered that approximately 70 percent of the state's inmates are Negro; in Louisiana the figure we found . . . was 80 percent."[65] Patterson was outraged when he ascertained that there existed a "whole series of houses of prostitution filled with Negro women who cater only to white men," a "conspiracy" that had "been forced upon the Negro ghetto."[66]

This recognition in the Negro press was indicative of the chord struck by the genocide petition. Perhaps a bit extravagantly, Patterson argued that the book-length version of this petition "can move white America as well as Black America to the extent that *Uncle Tom's Cabin* did." Still, he was sufficiently realistic to acknowledge that "the enemy" would move to "make concessions that will put Negroes on higher courts . . . perhaps ambassadorships and even cabinet officers and the like," but—akin to the "beans and rifles" strategy that Washington was soon to deploy in Guatemala—"the terror will increase and the 'honorees' will be expected to condone the terror and 'explain' the fact that it is not the terror of the government" but of a few misguided individuals.[67]

In New York, the writer Howard Fast hosted a reception for Patterson at his residence on the Upper West Side of Manhattan, 43 West Ninety-fourth Street. An agent of the FBI who was present reported in "confidential" words that there were "sixty present including fifteen to twenty Negroes," with a respectable $1,700 collected. In his remarks, Patterson said candidly that his then comrade—and Communist correspondent in Europe, Joseph Starobin—provided the "guidance," without which "he would have been severely handicapped in contacting people and getting around" the numerous nations he visited. Thus, in Budapest he spoke to the Chinese and North Korean ambassadors, "both of whom promised all war prisoners would get [a] copy" of his genocide petition. The agent seemed irritated that various European and Latin American nations "were secretly sympathetic to [Patterson] and would raise [the] Genocide Question in the General Assembly." India and Egypt were also thought to be part of this gathering alliance.[68]

Thus, at his moment of greatest triumph, Patterson was compelled to recognize that a new set of problems were unavoidably generated: one of which was the relatively weak state of CRC finances, strained to the breaking point by his extensive time spent abroad. Even before he departed, he was moaning about being "in a very tight place" and how he was "in desperate need of financial help."[69] "We are not growing, at a moment when a change in the political atmosphere would be discernible to anyone who is watching carefully," he said of the CRC, "but we are not planning a program of growth."[70] Just before departing for Paris, a strapped Patterson reported glumly, "There are no funds available for the cases now pending or for the fight for freedom of Mrs. Ingram and the Trenton [defendants], or for [his own] coming trial or [to] launch a mass campaign for the '11' [CP leaders] convicted under the Smith Act."[71] Despite the plaudits he received abroad, after his return home Patterson was still complaining about the "desperate financial condition": the "situation is far from being under control."[72]

Stalwart allies were also besieged. "It is a strange coincidence," said the International Workers Order (IWO), which had employed Patterson's spouse for years, "that the proposal to 'liquidate' the Order comes at a time when we in the Order were conducting a 'Human Appeal Campaign' to save the life of Willie McGee," which "presents a grave challenge to Negro Americans." When the IWO declared that they "would not be under attack if it adopted the practice of discrimination,"[73] it sent a distressing message that those against racial bias would be besieged if they somehow allied with the organized left.

As if that were not enough, the Bail Fund of the CRC, which was essential for an organization whose clients often ran afoul of the law, also came under assault.[74] Initially, the fund held firm, which George Charney—who eventually departed the Communist left—termed "one of the most remarkable experiences of this period."[75]

This episode was particularly disastrous for one of the key overseers of the fund, the celebrated mystery writer Dashiell Hammett.[76] Hammett wound up spending five months in detention as a result of his role in the fund.[77] Another overseer, who happened to be more affluent than the well-positioned Hammett, was Frederick Vanderbilt Field, the scion of a major fortune who did not elude censure.[78]

The tall, thin, and taciturn Hammett and the fabulously affluent Field were joined as overseers of the fund by W. Alphaeus Hunton, a stately and assured Negro academic, who formerly taught at Howard University and worked alongside Patterson's spouse at the Council on African Affairs,[79] which specialized in providing materials and influencing U.S. policy toward a mostly colonized continent. By July 1951, there was a sizeable $770,000 in the fund, contributed by about four thousand individuals and entities—who now faced the prospect of tireless inquisition. The overseers would not budge in relinquishing the list and, mimicking Patterson, they too wound up in prison.[80]

The noose was tightening on Patterson, as his comrades—first the CP leadership, then his CRC allies—were marched to prison or exile. The bell soon tolled for Arthur McPhaul of the Detroit chapter of the CRC. The auto giant for which he toiled—Ford—was upheld in firing him, severing a relationship that had endured for over two decades and that saw him rise to leadership of his union local. He had been charged with "boastful defiance" of a company ban against "political harangues during lunch hour."[81] Soon McPhaul was seeking more gainful employment, since he was a "plasterer by trade." This did not mean, he said mournfully, "that I am leaving CRC," as he planned to continue working there "on a voluntary basis rather than full time." There was a "tremendous strain placed on our organization," he added balefully,[82] which ultimately destroyed the CRC locally and nationally. At its peak, the chapter reported two thousand members.[83] Then, stunningly, the hard-working head of the CRC's San Francisco office, Ida Rothstein, was killed, struck by an automobile, as those around Patterson slowly began to disappear.[84]

Then Patterson's turn arrived to be punished for defiance. His first trial for contempt of Congress unfolded in Washington in April 1951. The most compelling witness against him was Congressman Lanham. Born in Georgia in 1888, he was a graduate of the University of Georgia and Harvard. A few years later he perished when his car struck a railroad crossing in his hometown of Rome, Georgia—but on this day, he struck out furiously at the man on trial.[85] "My anger was mounting," he told the jury, about the "false statements about the state of Georgia" said to be uttered by Patterson. "And when he called me a liar, as I think probably any Southern man would do, I jumped up immediately, and ran around the table to try to get him and I suppose I had to go 25 or 30 feet and go down a short stairway, and by that time two or three of the police officers, who had been stationed at the door, ran and got in front of me, and grabbed me." Stating the obvious about this disruption of decorum, the Georgian explained, "I was pretty much excited at the time." Vito Marcantonio, one of Patterson's attorneys, then asked, "Then why did you use the [word] 'black' in connection with the [incident]?" In that split-second moment, Lanham captured the transition of the era, as rank racism retreated to be supplanted in part by fierce anticommunism: "I should have used the word 'Communist,'" he conceded, "instead of the word 'black,' but it just rolled out." Marc suggested that he used the odious term "nigra" instead of "Negro," but Lanham dissented. He also denied calling Patterson a "black ape." Patterson escaped with a mistrial, though his other attorney, the distinguished jurist from Detroit, George Crockett, barely escaped with a contempt charge of his own because of his vigorous advocacy.[86] Marc was no less energetic, with the presiding judge frequently calling him to order[87]—though the judge could not save Lanham from the embarrassment of a correct pronunciation of the word "Negro."[88]

This vigor in the face of attack, followed by success, was seen as a positive signal by the CRC. "It is rare these days," said their organ, "almost unheard of—for a Washington, D.C., jury composed primarily of federal employees to refuse to convict a victim of government witch-hunting."[89] Eleven jurors were for conviction, but the twelfth would not budge. This Negro woman stiffened her spine and informed the judge, "Your Honor can keep me here the rest of my life. I won't vote him guilty." Later, when Patterson and his spouse met with this juror, she told them that one of her fellow jurors told her that the jury had to convict him because he was a Communist.[90]

The case was argued by jurors for an exhausting twenty-five hours. Asked by the judge if agreement could be reached after the apparent stalemate, the white foreman of the jury replied "yes"—but the Negro woman in question, Frances E. Armwood, disagreed sharply.[91] "I won't convict this man if you keep me here all summer," said this woman, described by Patterson as a "Negro heroine."[92] Her stubbornness contributed to Judge Alexander Holtzoff reportedly saying that the government "would never get a guilty verdict against Mr. Patterson here in Washington."[93]

In some ways, this trial was a reflection not only of Patterson's worldwide success but his success in Washington too, where he had become a constant lobbying presence. Just before his trial, he was to be found on Capitol Hill in a seventy-minute meeting with leading legislators, after "many brushes" with Senators Warren Magnusson of Washington and the notorious anticommunist Pat McCarran of Nevada. They "refrained from showing any open hostility," said Patterson, "and I was given the opportunity to expand extensively on a number of vital points." Senator William Langer, a friend, "went out of his way to demonstratively welcome me," he said. Reflecting the dilemma of popular-front politics, Patterson added, "I don't know whose party will condemn whom most—whether his party will condemn him for that, or my party will condemn me."[94]

Unimpressed with his coziness with various lawmakers, the authorities would not relent, forcing him to stand trial once more, with the consequent time tied up in trial preparation and fund raising, rather than shouting from the rooftops about "genocide." Du Bois, now a friend and soon to be a comrade, led Patterson's defense committee, along with the scholar E. Franklin Frazier, who observed archly that the new trial seemed to be a punishment for his successful advocacy.[95]

But Patterson still seemed to be more involved in fighting for others than for himself, causing a fellow New Yorker to worry on the verge of the second trial that "Pat's defense has also been neglected and is in dire need of funds. As a matter of fact," it was reported, "when I dropped into the office one day before the first trial, only one hundred fifty dollars were on hand to get defendants and lawyers to Washington, to maintain them there during [the] trial, to buy the transcript, to pay for research and other out of pocket expenses, let alone lawyer's fees."[96] The CRC scrambled to fill the breach, buttressed by the unique role played by Robeson, Fast, and the screenwriter John Howard Lawson, in his defense.[97] Then two bishops representing more than three million Negro churchgoers and their families led a delegation to the Justice Department to urge dropping of the charges.[98] A testimonial dinner that brought 750 cheering individuals into a crowded restaurant completed the comeback, with a much-needed five thousand dollars collected at the behest of speakers such as Claudia Jones, Eslanda Robeson, and Louise Patterson.[99]

Responding to the clarion call, Patterson's supporters jammed the courtroom in downtown Washington, featuring a core of pastors.[100] It was noteworthy, during this darkest day of the Red Scare, how many African Americans refused to flee from Patterson's side. This included Earl Dickerson, still reigning as the leading Negro attorney and businessman in Chicago; only preexisting commitments forbade him from joining the defense team.[101] Tellingly, the NAACP continued to turn a blind eye to Patterson, with White refusing to speak to a *Daily Worker* reporter about the case.[102] Patterson prescribed his traditional medicine for himself, mobilizing inside and outside the courtroom and managing to escape conviction once more. But the authorities were not finished with him, realizing that their trump card was his refusal to release membership and donor lists of the CRC. It was this adamant refusal that led him directly to a stint behind bars.

10

"I Am a Political Prisoner"

So spoke William Patterson in December 1954, as he wasted away behinds bars in the federal prison set amidst the undulating hills of Danbury, Connecticut.[1]

He was now well into his sixties, an age when many of his peers were contemplating a well-earned retirement. But Patterson remained in the trenches taking blows—and administering a few—though, in retrospect, his punishing imprisonment had a certain inevitability.

After all, he had reputedly besmirched the reputation of Washington while in Paris, raising difficult matters of Jim Crow as embedded in cases too numerous to mention from all parts of the land: McGee, Martinsville, Ingram, Trenton, Wells—the list was lengthy. While domestic elites were busily reassuring themselves that retreating on Jim Crow would not mean an advance for Communists—"no more than 1,400 Negroes ever belonged to the Communist Party at one time," claimed *Time* magazine in 1953—the ebony-hued Patterson stood tall globally as a symbol of the fact that a self-proclaimed Black Revolutionary could still win support in the midst of a Red Scare.[2] The *Afro-American,* in a powerful editorial, claimed that it was Jim Crow that was "creating Communists." The "Reds want tomorrow TODAY," it was emphasized, "and are willing to smash the clock to make time move faster."[3]

Washington was in a bind, forced by global pressure to retreat on Jim Crow so that human-rights violations in Moscow could be better argued, but fretting that this would present further opportunity for Moscow's domestic ally, the Communists. Just after the CRC was compelled to liquidate in early 1956, noted at a cabinet meeting at the White House was the idea that the CP was about to "concentrate" on the citadel of Jim Crow—including Alabama, South Carolina, and Mississippi. Fortunately, it was said, the "leader of NAACP" was not a Red, though this "cannot" be said "of all its locals." A supposed tie between the NAACP and CP only served to "aggravate" things.[4] In a "Memorandum for the President" presented near that same time, FBI director J. Edgar Hoover told the cabinet about "racial tensions in civil rights," that "extremist groups and individuals, including the Communists, are becoming bolder and more active," and that "threats of violence and bloodshed have been made publicly." As such, "The situation is serious enough to warrant Cabinet consideration."[5]

When the CP argued in mid-1955 that U.S. imperialism was facing an interlinked crisis implicating the Negro Question—a "crisis of [a] national minority" and a "crisis in the realm of political integrity"—they touched on an exceedingly sensitive point.[6] Imprisoning Patterson was a signal that tomorrow would arrive tomorrow, and those who argued otherwise were due for a rude awakening.

It was ironic that Patterson, who had strived tirelessly to explode the innards of Jim Crow, was locked away in the same year that the high court mandated that this odious system was illegal. Ironic, yes, but also logical in that with a Red Scare ascendant, it was virtually inexorable that those political outcasts who had fought an often lonely battle would now be sidelined, as domestic elites—pressed by international public opinion generated by Patterson in the first place—would rush to claim credit for a victory that was forced upon them.

Saunders Redding, a Negro writer who was to benefit enormously from the changed circumstance brought by desegregation, received a glimpse of how international public opinion viewed this new circumstance when he jetted into India on a mission for Washington. Initially, he was struck by the abhorrence of Senator Joseph McCarthy, then a rising star in his homeland. The Wisconsinite was an object of "scorn," he said, sounding amazed, propelled by the fact that "among Indian intellectuals with whom I had official association, there were those who admitted—even boasted, I thought—that organized Communist cells" were almost ubiquitous. Thus, he was asked, "Why has your government denied a passport to Paul Robeson?" He was hounded not only by class warriors but combatants on the racial front as well, since "many Indians were color conscious to a degree completely unimaginable even to American Negroes. . . . I was asked more than once whether the Negro community of America would join with the colored peoples of the world in a war against the white man." The Indians he encountered were outraged with "America's race prejudice. It was a shadow in which I moved." Most of all, he carped, "They were acquainted with and fully convinced of the frightful truth of the indictments brought against the American society by such an extremist Red publication as *We Charge Genocide*." Thus, like biblical verses, "lynching and riot statistics they knew by heart." Patterson's leading cases—McGee, Trenton, Martinsville—were grist for this mill, as well as the Peekskill incident. Redding's attempt to rescue the tarnished image of Uncle Sam was thwarted almost singlehandedly by Patterson.[7]

Patterson's advocacy on behalf of Julius and Ethel Rosenberg also proved upsetting to some. It was on June 19, 1953, when the future fervent anticommunist Ronald Radosh found himself at Union Square in Manhattan with "some ten or twelve thousand others," a remarkable turnout given that the issue at hand was the fate of two accused Soviet spies. "We stood with tears in our eyes" as the clock ticked down marking their executions. "Finally," said Radosh, "Howard Fast appeared to tell us that the unspeakable was occurring." The "photo of the event shows Fast at the sound truck's platform with William Patterson" as "singers started chanting the old hymn of slavery in Egypt land 'Let My People Go.'" With Patterson in the lead, "We marched with the crowd toward the Lower East Side, the last home of the Rosenbergs before they were sent to prison. Soon the police came on horseback, forcing us to back [off] and making us disperse."[8]

Subsequently, Patterson acknowledged that he and the CRC "came in immediately with the arrest" of the besieged duo and "played an active part in the later stages" of the case as well. At his initiative, the CRC "organized a large demonstration in Ossining," at Sing Sing where they were jailed, with about one thousand persons amassing. "I took two trips to Ossining," he said, and conferred "on both occasions with the Warden. . . . I went to the local press and pictures were taken of myself and published by the local press." Upon arriving at this hamlet due north of New York City, he was "met by a cordon of city and state police at the [train] station and . . . instructed by the chief of police that a march up the hill to a spot about a mile or a mile and a half from the gates . . . would be permitted." They were allowed to be "vocal" at the train station, "not in front of [the] prison, but they could be escorted with flowers to [the] gates of [the] prison." This delegation was "restricted to five individuals," which included Patterson, Howard Fast, and the actor Karen Morley. Like others, Patterson found the entire prosecution to be questionable, since "the atomic bomb could not be made a secret."[9]

Over eight hundred accompanied Patterson and Fast to Sing Sing, a site dangerously close to Peekskill, with fears erupting of an outcome akin to what had befallen the left in 1949. Patterson conferred repeatedly with the police, as the hearty band stood on a little hillock, huddled together in a pouring rain. Then Patterson, already renowned for his way with words, began to sing, his voice low and deep, the abolitionist anthem "Battle Hymn of the Republic," followed by an inspired follower reciting the Lord's Prayer—none of which spared the Rosenbergs from a state-administered execution.[10]

His presence in Manhattan on that deadly day reflected how the Rosenbergs' case had been added to his bulging portfolio. Saving their lives, he announced in Los Angeles in late 1952, was "the number one task before progressive America."[11] The Los Angeles leader of the CRC, David Brown, recalled—while testifying against his organization—the spring of 1953, when Patterson "got very excited" and told him forcefully, "They are not going to die. We are not going to let them die because I will not let them die as leader of my organization. I won't let this happen." Why the urgency? Patterson, it was recounted, remarked, "If they get away with this kind of business we may see another Warsaw here." Relating this story to his FBI handler, Brown noted chillingly that in Warsaw, "these people were executed," referring to those who were Jewish and/or Communists who were murdered during the war. "That man spoke with conviction," Brown said of Patterson. "I am a Jew, and I began to shiver all over . . . it shook me up badly." But, almost in a replay of Warsaw, the FBI man coldly told Brown, "'Well, you know what he is, you know what happens to his kind.' I said, 'What do you mean *his kind*?'" The response was, "'When his kind get up on top they get uppity. If you keep them down like they keep them down in the South, you will have no trouble, but once they get up to this point where they get on top of something, there is no keeping them down. We will take care of the kind like him.'"[12]

This agent was reflecting the unease that erupted as the Red Scare met a nascent and rising movement to uplift the downtrodden Negro. These two trends converged neatly in the person of Patterson, causing ever more fury to be directed toward him. Thus, like a slow-motion film dissolve, it was dawning on Patterson that as the Black moved to a form of freedom, the Red was assuming an enhanced polecat status. It was in May 1955 that Patterson dolefully informed the Subversive Activities Control Board (SACB) that "the leadership of the NAACP had been quite influenced by the wild Communist hysteria in this country," a sentiment that summed up neatly his own dilemma. Sounding surprised, Patterson found the "Negro press of America" to be "strangely silent" about this iconic case that was the Rosenbergs, as if speaking out might jeopardize concessions already in the pipeline. "Substitute the word 'spy' for the word 'rapist'" and "the Rosenbergs MIGHT AS WELL BE BLACK," he stressed, but few were paying attention as the material reality of the Negro was changing as he spoke.[13]

Patterson, who had been present in Germany when the seeds of the Holocaust were planted, was haunted by the possibility of this horrid phenomenon migrating across the Atlantic—even in micro—and frequently evoked it during his CRC tenure. Thus, said Patterson, we "wished to show the similarity of Willie McGee and the treatment of Jewish nationals in Germany under the Hitler regime," so he supervised the distribution of leaflets by the thousands, asserting, "Nazi murderers of American GIs are being freed but the Federal Government allows Virginia to execute the innocent Martinsville Seven."[14]

But Patterson's words, which once had been greeted with effervescent enthusiasm, were now being ignored by many. Undaunted, seeking to capitalize on what may have been the CRC's signal moment, Patterson was preparing a sequel of the "Genocide" petition, but as he acknowledged in mid-1953, "keeping all these projects moving is a very difficult thing and having such cases as Pittsburgh and the McCarran [cases] at the same time . . . presents a truly formidable job"—which was particularly the case when staff were being recruited as FBI informants or fleeing hither and yon.[15]

After returning from Europe and having his passport revoked,[16] Patterson was spending more and more time campaigning for various prisoners, as if he were gathering information for his own incarceration. Among these was the Communist leader Steve Nelson, jailed in Pittsburgh. Again, he found that his and the

CRC's time was better spent seeking to mobilize opinion abroad, particularly as concessions to the Negro leadership were disintegrating their remaining prop of support at home. "There is no meeting taking place in Europe today," he assured Nelson, "where your name and that of the Rosenbergs does not appear prominently."[17] He did not think that "the American scene in relation to the Pittsburgh fight can be characterized by indifference," though it was "true that the foreign scene reflects much greater maturity and activity and educational program than our own."[18]

The artful phrasing could not obscure the disconcerting reality that the United States was to the right of the international community and would become more so. As African Americans slowly came to enjoy basic rights, the scenario would alter to a degree, but the gap was to remain and continue to fester, for their ascension could not compensate for the decline of the organized left of which their empowerment was an unfortunate complement. Thus it was "French friends" who were "preparing a document" on "American violations of the Universal Declaration of Human Rights" that implicated Nelson's case,[19] just as the CRC sent a letter to a Pan-American gathering in 1954 "detailing the violation of civil liberties in the United States."[20]

A similar approach was taken with regard to his own case, though it did not prevent Patterson from winding up in Danbury on a rolling series of ninety-day sentences for contempt of court because of his refusal to turn over various donor and membership lists to the U.S. authorities. "I might be jailed for life," he told the historian J. A. Rogers, "for my refusal to betray my people."[21] "For the second time within six months," said the CP leader William Z. Foster in early December 1954, "Patterson has been sent to prison for 90 days on precisely the same charge." Moreover, "at the time of his two imprisonments Patterson was working to bring 'Genocide' up to date. Early in the current year Patterson also presented to the delegates to the recent Inter-American conference at Caracas, Venezuela, a document exposing the deterioration of civil and human rights in the United States entitled 'Six Years Retrogression toward a Police State.'"[22]

These actions did not endear Patterson to U.S. authorities, which sheds light on why in the spring of 1954 he had been asked to produce CRC records containing names and addresses of donors—a request that he chose not to observe, which led to the original ninety-day sentence for civil contempt of court, then again and again until finally in early 1955 he was released after the case had been fought up the federal ladder to the Second Circuit Court of Appeals, which ruled two to one in his favor.[23]

James Ford, still active in the CP, was there in 1954 as the grand jury convened to handle Patterson's fate. Patterson arrived and strode over to the gallery where Ford was sitting with other friends and comrades and murmured that it was a "hangman's jury" in this small room. Patterson's attorney, Milton Friedman, confronted his young counterpart from the government, who spoke haltingly, betraying his inexperience—but given the times, he did not have to be that persuasive to convince these jurors, for as the saying went years later, grand jurors would indict a ham sandwich if prompted by prosecutors. Patterson also spoke on his own behalf, providing what Ford termed a "magnificent defense" of himself, though the judge's swaying head and palpitating Adam's apple seemed to suggest otherwise. CRC records were at issue, and the judge was unconvinced by Patterson's remarks, asserting, "I don't believe the witness has physical possession of the records sought but he controls them wherever they are."[24] Ford denounced the "vengeful persecution" of his comrade, calling it "the most astounding abuse of civil liberties in the history of the republic."[25]

What Ford witnessed was only one aspect of Patterson's mounting difficulties. For simultaneously, while imprisoned for failure to produce CRC records, he was summoned before the Subversive Activities Control Board—a federal body meant to extirpate radical influence—on the ground that the CRC was ultimately an alien agent of Moscow. Adroitly, Patterson—then detained—sought to be transferred from detention to the hearing so he could perform as counsel and thus extend his ability to escape from a cramped prison cell. His attorney complained that her client was "subjected to an endless series of investigations" and "was being dragged into this court, before that proceeding or this proceeding," in a seemingly endless round-robin of procedures.[26] Part of the hearing that Ford witnessed—and, to a degree, the SACB hearing as well—was to ensnare Patterson in a perjury trap, grilling him until a contradiction in his words was unearthed, thus leading to yet another indictment in case the underlying alleged "crime" of not producing records did not lead to his jailing.

David Brown, thought to be a CRC leader in good standing but actually an informant for the FBI, recalled speaking to Patterson at a CRC conference in St. Louis in June 1954. "I went up to Mr. Patterson and shook hands with him," he testified. "I said, 'Here's luck to you. I know you are on your way to jail.' He looked at me and he held my hand and held it very strongly, and he said, 'I don't mind going to jail. First of all, it would be the first vacation I will have had for a long time. Secondly, more important than going to jail, it is the principle for which we are all fighting by refusing to turn informer.'" Brown, the informant, apparently did not blanch at the invocation of this despised status, and Patterson little knew that the man he was addressing was actually conspiring actively against him.[27]

In effect, as Patterson recounted later, "I was convicted of perjury even though not charged with it. When the court doubted my word it automatically charged me with perjury since it acted upon the doubt and against me. Pure speculation with no hearing, no attempt at confirmation."

Thus, as the paradigmatic case of *Brown v. Board of Education,* sounding the death knell for Jim Crow, was still being digested, Patterson found himself in Connecticut on a forced vacation. "This is beautiful country," thought Patterson. "We are in the midst of rolling hills." But the "repetitious" monotony seemed to be designed to make him daft, which led him to devise foiling means.²⁸ "There is so much reading I want to do," he said, seeking to put a positive spin on an unfortunate setback. "This is a school if one is willing to learn," he said, "only then can one teach."²⁹ "I watch the [*New York*] *Times* very carefully," he said, which left much to ponder.³⁰ At one juncture he was rereading Victor Hugo and emerging as impressed as he had been years ago; it "ought to be compulsory reading for some of the people who run this kind of institution."³¹ Since he estimated that "30 percent of the prison population is Negro" in Danbury, he had much work to do.³² "The majority here are under 30," and "especially the Negroes [are] mere kids just out of the army with no fundamental grasp of anything."³³ As for the "white lads" he met, they too were "openly expressing their hopelessness—'I am no good' . . . complete defeatism."³⁴

Patterson was not the only one unimpressed by this prison. His friend J. A. Rogers, the noted historian and columnist, said that it "sounds like one of those Communist slave camps we read about." Citing the former congressman, the conservative Parnell Thomas, who found himself incarcerated there, it was observed that this prison was "squalid and filthy," while the food was "awful," meaning that "four out of five prisoners . . . suffered from malnutrition." Medical facilities were "deplorable." About "30 percent of the prisoners were Negroes around 25 years of age," and they, along with those who were Jewish, were segregated. It was all, said Rogers, "a choice morsel for *Pravda*," the Soviet periodical.³⁵

The plight of his fellow inmates presented Patterson with an immediate dilemma. The high-court ruling had yet to trickle down to this federal facility, so Jim Crow reigned. If he spoke out, "especially against segregation," then that "would surely be un-American-subversive. I am not afraid to speak out," he assured, "but I don't seek further victimization." Then there was the atmospheric pallor of anticommunism. One inmate started a "tirade" against Communists. "I asked what they were," and "he said he didn't know but they all ought to leave the country," though Patterson apparently was restrained from administering a rebuff. "[I] hope you can learn [tolerance] to add to the intolerance one needs and patience to balance your impatience," he informed his spouse by way of reminding himself. "The experience is good if you come in strong but God help the mentally weak." Later he bumped into the militant anticommunist, who reiterated his "hatred" for Reds and added, "If he were on the street and a man said he was one, he would shoot him on the spot. I suppose he would."³⁶

"I walk around the cell block for exercise," said the elderly Patterson, conscious that "one can easily eat more than can be worked off here."³⁷ "I take a brisk walk around the cell block ten times each morning,"³⁸ he said shortly thereafter, increasing his pace. "I'm rounding into some kind of shape," he said days later. "Every day I do my ups and downs. Some of the belly is disappearing. Green stuff is plentiful on the table," thus, "physically, I feel splendid."³⁹ "This place is conducive to contemplation [and] meditative examination and analysis that action in the ordinary world does not provide ordinarily," he said of imprisonment. "One can seek and find the road to objectivity here."[40] Thus, he spoke frequently of the news of the day, adding, "I write of these things because they ease my mind."[41]

Stretching his muscles could not ease the pain of what he was enduring. His mail was censored,[42] then he was barred from writing anyone other than his spouse and his daughter.[43] For a while he was subjected to "quarantine," shielded from others, though not in solitary confinement, which would have been maddening. This meant no visitors and seven letters per week. He feared that "if I continue to agitate," he would be beaten physically by fellow prisoners, egged on by the authorities, which is what befell his fellow Communist, Bob Thompson. What particularly agitated him was the overrepresentation of Negroes behind bars. "With 40 percent of us in a place like this and every similar institution recording like percentages, it [is] time the Negro press began systematically to raise the question of a conscious policy to brand our youth as petty criminals." The possession of illegal drugs was a central reason for this mass incarceration, which, said Patterson, "indicates that the sale of dope in the ghettoes is smiled [on] rather than frowned upon." But it was hard to organize behind bars, which was restraining; he had "not heard one sustained conversation dealing with a serious national or international problem. Talking seriously is severely frowned upon."[44] Just in case, Patterson was placed "where I would have the least contact with other people and was not to be allowed to indoctrinate others," so he was compelled to toil in "an outside job—gardening. That's not too bad."[45]

There should have been a lot to discuss. Ironically, the year of his incarceration—1954—was the pivotal year that Jim Crow was declared to be verboten by the high court. "How they understand the weakness of their own position. How it sticks out on the school issue." While others were celebrating, Patterson opined that "'free' is not to include blacks for some years to come." He wondered why Washington tolerated Jim Crow in federal prisons, where it enjoyed "jurisdiction," while railing against Jim Crow in local school systems, where its remit did not reach as easily: "The hypocrisy stands out like an A bomb cloud and is as poisonous."[46] He realized instinctively that the high-court decision "will bring concessions to some Negroes, they must try to neutralize the Negro people, they cannot afford to let Negro thought become too greatly concerned with the freedom struggles of other colored people. That is one of the basic reasons for the segregation decision"—"prevent any discussion in broad Negro circles of the merger of our struggle with those of others." Yes, he offered, these were "concessions in the face of the revolts of the colonial peoples."[47] According to Patterson, "lots of people realize that it was foreign comment which played a great part in the segregation cases."[48] By underlining words like these produced by Patterson's comrades, J. Edgar Hoover underscored their significance.[49]

Writing behind bars, Patterson had few illusions about the increased tolerance among U.S. rulers.[50] It was as if great events were occurring, and an imprisoned

Patterson was left simply to comment on their significance rather than intervene forcefully as before.[51] Thus, he engaged the profound meeting of recently liberated mostly African and Asian nations at Bandung, Indonesia, in 1955. He hailed their shunning of South Africa and Australia as a "blow to racism" and urged the seating of "black American observers" as a "matter of vital concern," since "Negro Cadillac leadership will have to take cognizance of some of the happenings in the East, even though they continue their behind-kissing apologies for the genocidal policies of this government."[52]

Yet the new era inaugurated by the onset of desegregation paradoxically was to bring frustration to Patterson in the form of his awareness of the larger issues at play—"that the Negro press cannot see this period clearly while not amazing is at least very disheartening."[53] The "Negro press has apparently not reacted to the [anti-]subversive legislation," he said at one point, "yet no segment of America is more adversely affected by this campaign."[54]

It was not only the Negro press that he saw as failing to live up to its historic obligations. "What then is the difference between a man like Thurgood [Marshall] and Paul [Robeson]?" he asked. "Thurgood works *with* the enemies of the people," he stressed. "Paul works against them. The interests of the two cannot be reconciled. Thurgood compromises where his people are concerned with those who, when their interests are at stake, fight. His form of compromise jeopardizes the interests of his people," thus "Thurgood consciously or unconsciously works for the destruction of our constitutional form of government."[55]

It was just as well that Patterson had excoriated NAACP leaders, as they had no interest in aligning with him in any case and were equally dismissive of him besides. Still, such acerbic remarks may have hampered the ability of those who rallied to Patterson's side to broaden the coalition in his defense. Such considerations did not seem to hinder those who turned up in the thousands at a jam-packed Chicago's Tabernacle Baptist church where his praises were sung, despite a last-minute cancellation at the Civic Opera House downtown, which necessitated scrambling to the former venue.[56] Nor did this concern seem to bother the hundreds who crowded into the Renaissance Casino in Harlem in support of his cause. There Robeson spoke warmly of his longtime friend who "guided" him in his early days, while the increasingly popular actor Beah Richards provided poetry.[57]

These two events were part of a larger campaign by the CRC to free its leader. By mid-February 1955, a freed Patterson reported on his own case to conferees, elaborating on the "mass campaign" that led to his presence in Manhattan on this wintry day. He received "1,500 greeting cards in jail," while the U.S. attorney general, Herbert Brownell, "must have received a like number." "There were 9 mass meetings," while "some chapters got out their own leaflets and petitions." Articles about his plight appeared "in the left and Negro press," all of which necessitated that CRC staff be "expanded"—and yet the steep price was worth it, since otherwise it was conceivable that "prison for life" would have been his destiny.[58]

Patterson swallowed his own medicine, in other words, and campaigned inside and outside the courtroom for his own freedom—and this bore fruit. Yet his departure from Danbury brought no end to his misery. As the gates of prison were closing behind him, opening up before him was a maelstrom of misery, for the CRC was being plunged into a compelled liquidation, while the CP was undergoing a bout of internal wrangling that dwarfed that which had led to Browder's ouster about a decade earlier. Indeed, Patterson's life was entering the denouement, the final act of a three-act play: from birth to 1927 was the first; from 1927 to 1954 was the high watermark; and then from that fateful year to his passing in 1980 was a time of trial. During the second act, he emerged as an important Negro leader fighting globally and domestically against Jim Crow, but during the final act, Jim Crow retreated. In return—almost like a down payment for this concession—he was compelled to fight ostracism and increased anticommunist repression. This was not good news for Patterson, but in the long term, it was not necessarily in the best interests of U.S. Negroes either, for as they had a form of normalized citizenship thrust upon them, they were deprived simultaneously of their most battle-tested and internationally connected leaders—Patterson and Robeson—which ill prepared them to confront the complex challenges provided by an increasingly globalized world.

Some Communists sought to make the best of a bad situation by arguing that the new departure brought by the Montgomery bus boycott of 1955 meant that organizations like the CRC—which had been fighting an often lonely battle—were not as necessary. This struck James Ford as little more than piffle. "I simply have not had the courage to write you in recent years," he told his comrade, Ferdinand Smith, a Communist leader of the National Maritime Union [NMU] who had been forced by the U.S. authorities to return to his birthplace of Jamaica, "because of the state of affairs in this country (my organization)"—meaning the CP—"on which my influence was absolutely nil," was floundering. Ford complained that he had little clout to reverse changes he viewed as troubling. "We are liquidating and liquidating: African Council gone, CRC on way out, in the name of breadth," was his view in late 1955. As he saw it, "A lot of groundwork was laid in the thirties in trade unions among Negroes," but this was now being frittered away, as left "strength" was "sadly underestimated." Thus, "In a NMU convention recently a Negro delegate was beaten by [right-wing] thugs as he spoke at the mike"—"and not a word from our friends. Negro left leaders persecuted and imprisoned and very little done," all "in the name of breadth," or the idea that building broad coalitions precluded sharp focus on the difficulties of besieged Reds. The jailing and then deportation of the Communist leader Claudia Jones was "one grand scandal," he said. "Robeson's passport case, simply a scandal! Influence of bureaucracy and white chauvinism simply astounding." The murder of the Negro youth Emmett Till in Mississippi had created a firestorm of protest worldwide—made to order for Patterson and CRC—but, said Ford, "you would be ashamed to know that we are way behind developments" in this charged case. This lag was occurring "despite Geneva," which seemed to augur détente between Washington and Moscow and "most of all *Bandung*," trends that ordinarily Patterson would have been able to play upon adeptly like an expertly tuned piano. Sadly, he concluded, "the Negro Question is being neglected."59

Patterson sought to turn a sow's ear into silk by claiming that Jones's deportation meant that she could now act as an external agent and attack Jim Crow from abroad—which turned out to be accurate but did little to dissuade Ford's pessimism.60

There was some truth to what Ford said, but overall he seemed blind to the increased repression then being visited upon his comrades—Patterson and his CRC not least—which dramatically circumscribed the options available to the radical left: for 1956 was also the year in which an elevated crusade against the CP was launched by the FBI.61

Just before this momentous turn, the FBI reviewed Patterson's file "for the purpose of determining whether he is of such professed Chinese Communist sympathy that he would or could present a threat to the United States Government in the event of hostilities with Communist China." Particular note was taken of Patterson providing copies of the genocide book to a high-level Chinese official for distribution to U.S. prisoners of war in Korea.62 In a 228-page FBI report, again it was his foray abroad that seemed to enrage.63 This focus on territory beyond U.S. jurisdiction led to extensive—and "secret"—monitoring of Patterson's energetic campaign to restore Robeson's passport, which, the FBI believed, involved "the idea of smuggling Paul Robeson out of the U.S. for propaganda purposes. The plan was for Robeson to suddenly give a concert or make a speech in some foreign capital or large city in order to cause a sensation."64 The FBI snared a letter from Patterson to the East Berlin office of the Women's International Democratic Federation [WIDF] requesting they issue an invitation for Robeson to visit. Here Patterson was aghast in noting that the State Department mandated that Robeson "not leave the continental confines of the United States, even to go to any territories such as Alaska or Hawaii, or to go to those countries which do not require passport or visa for entry," on the premise that the actor's "defense of the independence fight of the South[ern] African nations interfered with government policy."65

So briefed, J. Edgar Hoover in a "personal and confidential" memo informed one of President Eisenhower's top aides about "propaganda concerning the case of [Rosa Lee] Ingram and her sons" generated by the WIDF; the attorney general, the State Department, and the Central Intelligence Agency were advised of the danger of allowing travel by radicals.66

Of course, when the NAACP leader Clarence Mitchell objected to the nomination of the former congressman—and Klan applicant—John Wood by Eisenhower to serve in the highest echelon of the Subversive Activities Control Board (whose mandate was to monitor relentlessly those like Patterson), there was hardly a murmur of concern.[67]

There was more involved politically, in short, than just the snatching of Patterson's correspondence. This was part of a larger scheme of isolating and debilitating the radicals, providing a wide berth to the Dixiecrats and obliging the Negro centrists not to complain too loudly, lest their vaunted concessions be halted. Patterson was incensed when the increasingly popular glossy magazine of John H. Johnson, an acquaintance from Chicago, glorified an FBI agent who infiltrated the CRC successfully.[68] This was symptomatic of the demonizing of the Reds to the point where disrupting the CRC and Patterson's political activity was viewed widely as being tantamount to patriotism.

Thus, a number of U.S. nationals made a good living infiltrating the CRC on behalf of the FBI.[69] Barbara Hartle was not alone in recruiting members to the CRC and then turning over their names to the authorities, which was a disincentive for any to be so bold as to join the ranks of the organized left.[70] Bereniece Baldwin of Detroit—who joined the CP in 1943, then ostensibly departed in 1952 (and was part of the CRC from 1948 to 1952)—acted similarly.[71]

By April 1955, Patterson had been freed from incarceration. Undaunted, he returned to the SACB hearing as a counsel, objecting vigorously at one point as a woman identified as Willie McGee's widow testified. After Patterson's words increased in velocity and intensity, opposing counsel referred to him contemptuously as a "creature," and an insulted Patterson replied, "I am going to warn you. . . . you should respect my dignity. I am sitting here as a human being," a fact that he felt needed emphasis in a nation scarred by apartheid.[72]

This tumultuous encounter was capped by Patterson's own testimony, where he said cautiously, "I am a graduate of a college in Eastern Europe . . . my mother told me that I was born in San Francisco" on "August 27, 1891." Yes, he said, he was elected to lead the CRC in April 1948 at a board meeting in Philadelphia, and under his leadership, chapters increased from nineteen to forty-two "or more" by 1952. And, yes, a measure of his effectiveness was revealed when he told how he was "run out of the city of Birmingham and by the officials of the City of Atlanta." Noting a frightening episode that left him seemingly unaffected, he remarked casually, "I had been threatened with lynching." Observing how his CRC organizing required stealth and nerves of steel, he noted that while toiling in Miami, New Orleans, and North Carolina, "I was very careful to come into those cities without any fanfare or notice and tried to meet with people secretly," since "the danger of Negroes being lynched was very great." After all, "terror against [the CRC] in Miami came almost instantaneously with the establishment of the chapter," and "in the Carolinas it was more difficult." The pressure meant that by 1951 the CRC board was not functioning, for it had taken note of what befell the board of the Joint Antifascist Refugee Committee—who were imprisoned. Strikingly, local boards in Los Angeles, San Francisco, and Oakland did not dissolve—but New Jersey's did.

Patterson's testimony incidentally revealed his effectiveness and why some sought the CRC's liquidation. When working to free jailed CP leaders, it was not unusual for Patterson to meet with high-level officials at the Justice Department in Washington. The counsel he secured for the CP leader John Gates earlier had represented the newspaper of Joseph Pulitzer, the *St. Louis Post-Dispatch*; it was also "Senator [Thomas] Hennings' firm in St. Louis." When campaigning for Steve Nelson, he recollected, "I spoke with the editorial board of the *Pittsburgh Post-Gazette*." For Smith Act defendants in this grimy steel town, "I went to the attorneys of the Mellon firm" to seek assistance. Though his appeals to high-powered law firms were not always successful, that he could meet with them was no less arresting. The same could be said of his meeting with the governor of New Jersey at the height of the struggle to free the Trenton Six.

Yet the overriding atmosphere of fear was hard to overcome. Patterson was stunned when an "extremely vital event had taken place in Madison, Wisconsin, where the Bill of Rights and the Declaration of Independence were handed out to people for them to sign and . . . they refused to sign saying that it was Communistic and that they were afraid to sign it."

Patterson's testimony, presented just before the compelled liquidation of the CRC, was similarly informative about why this eventuality occurred. The CRC vigorously defended the Communist leader Claude Lightfoot, since his case meant that "for the first time in the history of our country, membership in a political party with the right of the American people to select a party of their own choice"—guaranteed under the First Amendment ambit of the right to free association—was being challenged. Likewise, the CRC defended the Communist leader Junius Scales, whose prosecution raised similar issues; but unlike the Chicago-based Lightfoot, this case arose in North Carolina and thus "was bound to have a great effect upon the fight for Negro rights."[73]

Similarly illuminating was the fact that when Patterson wrapped up his testimony before the SACB in July 1955, the government's response was dismissive. "After seeing and hearing him on the witness stand," said counsel Posey Kime, "and reading some of the pleadings made in his behalf, and some of his writings, I do not believe anyone, except possibly a confirmed Communist, could put any credence in anything he said." He was, it was asserted, a "deliberate prevaricator, if not a perjurer"—as yet another series of criminal charges stared Patterson in the face.[74]

An indicator of the CRC's effectiveness at a time when it was in retreat was manifested in Los Angeles. There were three strong chapters there, and the overall leader was actually paid a considerable sixty-two dollars a week by the organization. However, the FBI paid him more than four times as much.[75] Indeed, perhaps the climax of these hearings occurred when David Brown, a CRC leader in the City of Angels virtually to the date of his testimony in May 1955, revealed himself as a stool pigeon. He too recruited members to the ranks and then turned over their names to the authorities. All told, he provided the FBI with two thousand names and addresses. Born in Kiev, he arrived in the United States in 1914 and before long was a leader of the left, joining the CP in 1931 and staying until 1948, helping to forge CRC chapters in Echo Park, Hollywood, and East Hollywood. He testified that his frequent conversations with Patterson caused him to regret his betrayal and admit that "all of my reports to [the FBI] contained both false and true statements and there was a great deal of falsity in most of the reports that I submitted." He confessed that "throughout my entire association with the FBI, I had periodic fits of remorse and depression. After a while I succeeded in burying these emotions and driving them away"—but that did not prevent an unsuccessful suicide attempt on his part.[76] Even his appalled spouse railed against his "shocking betrayal" targeting Patterson, the CRC, "my children, myself, and countless others."[77]

Brown's "betrayal" was a virtual deathblow for the CRC. Los Angeles may have had the strongest unit within the CRC, with access to an astonishing sixty attorneys to handle various cases.[78] He also recruited avidly on behalf of the Rosenberg Defense Committee—then too turned over their names to the FBI.[79]

Patterson was outraged when it was revealed that in his dealings with the FBI, the "rendezvous was for a period in the Mormon Church" where Brown's handler was "an active member." Apparently, Brown "had a key to the front and rear door," as this venerable institution was implicated in political destabilization.[80]

Once it became evident that the authorities would investigate the CRC relentlessly, a decision had to be made: Was it worth it to stay in business with the prime objective not being to defend victims of racist and political repression but, more so, to defend oneself? When the firehouse itself is constantly ablaze, an agonizing reappraisal is in order. A year before liquidation, in late February 1955, it was reported breathlessly that the CRC was tied to fraud. It had "collected" a small fortune and "diverted much of it," it was said at a public hearing in Manhattan that was marked by "anger and comedy"—and "long speeches." The august chambers of the Senate of the State of New York was the scene when Patterson angrily handed to Senator Edward Larkin a mimeographed statement that bristled with denunciations. The hearing was delayed when Patterson and then Robeson refused to take the witness stand unless their attorney, Milton H. Friedman, was permitted to sit alongside them. The senator insisted that the attorney remain at the counsel table, about twenty feet away, but said that his clients could consult with him. Irksomely, Patterson informed the lawmakers— to their dismay—that CRC had nineteen chapters in 1948 and "thirty-four or more" at that moment when repression had hit a new high. When asked about his fund-raising for CRC, an annoyed Robeson retorted, "I sing for Hadassah and the Sons of Israel and any number of worthwhile causes and no one asks me how much money they raise."[81]

But Robeson and Patterson were swimming against a mighty tide. The *Pittsburgh Courier*, apparently still upset with Patterson, had to be warned by his attorney to retract a "defamatory attack" on his client that suggested that the CRC leader "had been guilty of dishonesty and had appropriated to his personal use monies collected for [CRC]"[82]

The legislators were not the only ones dissatisfied with this testiness—as far afield as his old hometown of San Francisco, Patterson's activities had garnered negative attention[83]—and Patterson himself could sense how matters were changing severely as the Red Scare deepened. "The American political scene in some vital respects," he informed the eminent British jurist D. N Pritt, "gives cause for increasing alarm," since "for the first time in the history of the United States, men and women who advocate a political philosophy which does not conform to the dominant ideology in vogue at this time, and who advocate democratic political action which is considered unorthodox have been labeled criminals." Yet—and this is why he was reaching out to London—"never before were the rulers of this country more sensitive to reaction from abroad." Thus, he sent similar appeals to the World Federation of Trade Unions, influential foreign periodicals, and human-rights campaigners.[84] In return, Patterson encouraged the Vienna-based World Council of Peace to reach out to the Negro press in the United States with its concerns about Washington's orientation.[85] Patterson also encouraged the historian Herbert Aptheker to provide an analysis of anticommunist legislation for comrades in France.[86]

It was seemingly inexorable when in early 1956 the CRC was forced out of business. As a matter of virtual self-defense, nineteen chapters of progressive activists dissolved, just as the Montgomery bus boycott was marking a new stage in the struggle against Jim Crow.[87] An indicator of why this dissolution occurred came in early 1956, when Dr. Martin Luther King Jr. was told curtly by a leader of the National Baptist Convention that "millions are standing at your back"—yet "your stand has been so perfect that I trust there will be nothing done to mar it," a reference to the fact that King's comrade, the Rev. Ralph David Abernathy, was slated "to speak for the Civil Rights Congress," who were "on the subversive list." Abernathy was counseled "to withdraw because it might bring bad repercussion[s]."[88] Thus, those who had marked a new stage in the anti–Jim Crow struggle with Scottsboro were forced to retreat when the struggle reached a new stage in Montgomery—to the detriment of all—though both of these bends in the onrushing course of history were part of the same mighty river of freedom.

Nineteen fifty-six was also a year of profundity, not unlike 1941 or 1989, as France, Britain, and Israel waged war in Israel, while Soviet tanks rumbled into Budapest and—perhaps most important for the CP—revelations were unveiled about Stalin's crimes. The latter two developments in particular alienated numerous comrades, driving many from the ranks—though, strikingly, this was less true for Negro comrades who had fewer options in the United States and often were more determined to transform the nation radically. The split in CP ranks took the ostensible form of a standoff between a faction led by Ben Davis and William Z. Foster pitted against another symbolized by John Gates—who subsequently departed, with the issue of one's stance toward Moscow being a pivotal divide.[89] Since the Negro comrades had fewer illusions about the beneficence of the United States and a keener recognition of the need for global pressure to alleviate the plight of African Americans, they were more disposed to aligning with Moscow. For the most part, Negro comrades—including Patterson—stood alongside Davis and Foster, though not without friction.[90]

Surely, this internal wrangling was not helpful when Montgomery signaled a breath of fresh air. "This is not the time for panic," was the view of Ferdinand Smith. But when political earthquakes rumble, this is easy advice to discard. Echoing the views of many Negro comrades, Smith also denounced "the current hysterical anti-Soviet utterances which are now so prevalent in the New York *Daily Worker*"—Gates's bastion—sparked by "Stalin's excesses."[91]

As for Patterson, this internecine conflict was an added blow, compounded by the brusqueness of his recent imprisonment. The period from 1956 to 1960, said Patterson's comrade Claude Lightfoot, was "one of the worst periods in my adult life," as a result of the "factional disputes" that plagued the CP, and Patterson could have agreed easily.[92] He may not have realized it at the time, but Patterson, who had risen in prominence as Jim Crow waxed, was to decline likewise—and ironically—as domestic apartheid waned.

11

The CP's "FBI Faction" Rises

Forced away from the burgeoning civil-rights movement, seeking to avoid another incarceration, raising a young daughter, and trying to stay abreast of a rapidly changing global scene, the compelled death of the CRC did not necessarily lighten William Patterson's burden as he entered a brave new world in 1956. By April 1956, the FBI found that he and his family were residing in Brooklyn at 1268 President Street and that he was "self-employed as [a] Civil Rights Consultant."[1] Fortunately, his spouse, whose public life was not as well-defined as his, was able to find work, allowing the clan to persevere.[2] Still, the left was not wholly bereft; as the FBI reported, the Pattersons' 1956 income was a considerable $7966.30, with a portion of this sum coming from the recently organized hospital workers union in New York, organized with significant aid from the CP—a union in which Louise Patterson toiled, in her words, as a "technical worker."[3] Patterson received a monthly subsidy of $350 from the CP and was about to receive a pension from Social Security.[4]

Patterson was fortunate, since by mid-1958, some CP cadre—according to the FBI—had "worked for 4, 5, 6 weeks without any pay."[5] "Almost daily the burdens" of the party's organ "grow larger," *The Worker* reported agonizingly in mid-1958.[6] "Every week," said this paper, then under Patterson's leadership, "must see from $2,500 to $3,000 come in or *The Worker* is in jeopardy. We must either borrow or fail to pay wages." The "press run" then was eighteen thousand, a useful indicator of membership, and in "January the run was 6,000 less than that."[7] In April 1958, admitted FBI "surveillance" of CP headquarters at 23 West Twenty-sixth Street in Manhattan, captured Patterson lamenting the "poor health" of this periodical. Things were "extremely critical," he remarked. "I have a lot of leg work," he complained, "and don't even have a secretary."[8] Predictably, the paper's crack sportswriter, Lester Rodney, who played a significant role in the push to desegregate major-league baseball, was among those forced to flee: "I am sorry it had to come to this," he told Patterson with sadness, but "I am forced to take steps to protect my family."[9]

That was not all. The FBI captured Patterson's telephone conversation with Ben Davis, his fellow party leader, where the former CRC official complained that a "racketeer union" tied up distribution of the party newspaper. "I'm going down to the lawyers," he responded. "I'm trying to get it out now. It may come off the press at 2:45 this morning, but the racketeers wouldn't handle it and they are trying to force me to sign a contract"—besides which, the IRS was again breathing down his neck.[10] "Most dealers have been so terrorized by the FBI hooligans," Patterson complained in September 1959, "they fear to carry our weekly."[11]

Government harassment and surveillance further hampered his effectiveness. When Ferdinand Smith in Jamaica sought to contact Patterson, he cautioned, "maybe you can find a reliable 'cover,' non-political, where I can write you,"[12] which was neither simple nor easy.

In sum, Patterson had his hands full as a party official at this juncture. There was mulling over the consequences of the Stalin devaluation in Moscow, the import of the Bandung gathering of mostly Asian and African nations, the fierce confrontation over desegregation in Little Rock, battles to halt the isolation of iconic figures like Robeson and Du Bois, and lingering CRC matters, along with marches on Washington and congressional inquisitions in the same city. All of these matters—each weighty in themselves—were complicated tremendously by the then-unknown presence of a powerful FBI faction within the highest ranks of the party, led by the wily Morris Childs, who was quite effective in gumming up potentially far-reaching proposals and stoking internal conflict.

Looming above all else was the internecine conflict wracking the CP, fueled by Childs and providing a plethora of headlines for the U.S. press, which in turn alienated actual and potential members. At the sixteenth convention of the CP in February 1957, there were seventy correspondents from newspapers, television, and radio, including journalists from Italy, Poland, and the Soviet Union, not to mention—as the CP proudly (and ironically) noted—"all the great metropolitan dailies of New York" and "the great tv and radio networks," who did a credible job of presenting a portrait of disarray disrupting presumed agents of Moscow. Of the 298 delegates, fifty-four were Negroes—but only two were of Mexican origin, and only one Puerto Rican, though observers were present from fraternal parties in Cuba, El Salvador, and Guatemala.[13]

Despite party support collapsing all around—which became evident after this convention—as a Communist, Patterson found it necessary to find the time to survey the domestic (and particularly the global) scene when contemplating strategy and tactics. And even with the mass movement erupting in Montgomery, it was the world scene that seemed to hold much promise for advance. He greeted heartily the meeting at Bandung, Indonesia, in 1955 of mostly Asian and African nations, which prefigured the rise of an anti-imperialist "nonaligned" movement. Through "ties of ancestry," African Americans were being "drawn . . . more closely toward" Bandung, providing added strength to both and obliging

Washington to "use colored stooges to 'explain' the [Jim Crow] outlook of this country."[14]

It was in October 1955 that Patterson contacted Prime Minister U Nu of Burma; writing "as a Negro American," he made "an appeal" on Robeson's behalf that the basso profundo be allowed to address "the great peoples of Asian and African countries," since "colored peoples everywhere have an interest in this matter."[15]

More than this, he argued, "the rise of the Soviet Union," along with the 1949 revolution in China and "the rise of the [anti-]colonial liberation movements," were among the "historic changes in world relations that give impetus to the Negro liberation struggle" and "marked a decisive change in world history," as it forced "the world's strongest imperialists to take a second look at some phases of its policy of white supremacy." Thus, "when racism became an impediment to the imperialist fight for the oil of the Near East, control of the tungsten and iron ores of Korea, the markets of Indonesia, Malaya, and Ceylon, it was time to call a halt. Confronted by these facts, some American imperialists began to recognize that concessions to the Negro had become imperative." The confrontation in Little Rock in 1957 concerning desegregation of public education made this evident when the White House was compelled to intervene with federal troops.[16] The FBI was observant when—to that end—Patterson met with Hungary's deputy representative at the United Nations, Imre Hollai, then called CP headquarters to report.[17]

Patterson envisioned a revival of the genocide campaign.[18] "There is need," he said, "for Negroes on the Left to fight like hell for the realization of a Western Hemisphere conference" on the linked matters of the U.S. Negro and African liberation. Still, Patterson, who more than most sought to stay attuned to the balance of forces when promulgating initiatives, may have betrayed an undue optimism when he suggested that "[Dr.] King ought to be one of the promoters of this Western Hemisphere conference," styled as a regional "Bandung Conference."[19] Already being questioned about alleged radical ties, King was hardly in a position to ally himself with the man who was instrumental in converting Scottsboro into a worldwide campaign. Even his good friend George Murphy, scion of the clan that founded the popular Negro newspaper the *Baltimore Afro-American,* was not overly enthusiastic about this demarche.[20] Undeterred, while in Puerto Rico in 1956 Patterson broached the notion of a hemispheric gathering, taking advantage of the momentum brought by Bandung. But the proposal did not gain momentum there either,[21] though the recently deported Communist John Williamson, then in Britain, thought "the idea of a Western Hemisphere 'Bandung' would be terrific."[22]

Though rebuffed, this incident indicated that Patterson still wielded influence among Negroes, as he was being isolated from the U.S. mainstream (the editor of the *Pittsburgh Courier,* P. L. Prattis, presiding over a paper that had not been very friendly to him, thanked Patterson for "helping to keep on top of what is important.")[23] "I wish your cogent thinking had the benefit of a better moral and political climate," he informed Patterson in early 1958.[24] In praising the Scottsboro campaign for helping to bring the noxiousness of Jim Crow to a wider global audience, Ralph Matthews of the *Washington Afro-American* also echoed Patterson's outlook as he singled him out for lavish praise. The "protests" he led "were reflected in the May Day parades in Paris and Moscow and the cause of the Scottsboro Boys was shouted from soap boxes in Hyde Park in London and was echoed in anti-American speeches in Tokyo, Hong Kong and Bombay." The "National Negro Congress took on the mantle of the defender of the poor and almost sent the NAACP into eclipse," but now, "having driven the international agitators out of the assemblies and from the public platform and reduced the race problem to a homegrown variety of protest"—a lengthy trend, still in place in the twenty-first century—"what will be done about it?"[25] The answer was that the way desegregation arrived on these shores was not penalty-free.

Nonetheless, Patterson was compelled to rely upon his circle of radicals—Robeson, Du Bois, Ben Davis, and others—in organizing a "symposium" on the "Meaning of Little Rock" that soared far beyond what was being debated contemporaneously among most Negroes in that the focus included "the colonial liberation movement," "Bandung," and the "United Nations," with the emphasis that "America's relations with Negroes violates the Charter of the U.N."[26]

Even with the burst of progressivism brought by Dr. King's movement, anticommunism had sunk deep roots in the U.S. landscape, to the point where Patterson—who not only had global contacts but a demonstrated record of fearlessness in Dixie—was having difficulty finding an audience. Moreover, as he witnessed the racist mobs in Little Rock, Patterson justifiably expressed skepticism about the nature of the "white allies" aligned with the anti–Jim Crow movement; he thought that "such an alliance" between an effective "white social grouping and the Negro people" ended with Reconstruction; "the Negro people desperately need such an alliance," he stated, but as of the 1950s, "the Negro-white alliance exists only in the embryo."[27] Patterson may have had in mind the critique he shared with the *New York Times*, when recounting "the statement of William Faulkner that if the chips were down and 'if it came to fighting, I'd fight for Mississippi against the United States, even if it meant going out into the street and shooting Negroes.'"[28] This underscored further the need for global allies, but the reigning anticommunism—which too was a factor in blocking an effective "Negro-white alliance"—also hampered the ability of the anti–Jim Crow movement to forge international connections, effectively pushing this movement into an undesirable corner.[29]

Little Rock was not the only landmark effort in 1957; that year also featured a major march on Washington—a precursor of 1963—with, again, Dr. King in the limelight. The White House seemed concerned that Patterson "stated he is now responsible for the entire New York State CP activity in connection with the March on Washington. He said it is his feeling that the Party should be in the vanguard and that they should have 15,000 people from New York to attend."[30] Similarly, the FBI monitored the "youth march for integrated schools" in Washington in 1958; between ten and twelve thousand arrived at a time when somnolence was thought to be the order of the day, with "four busloads of students from Brooklyn College" alone. Speakers included Dr. King and Harry Belafonte—but the FBI seemed most concerned with the presence of Mary Lou Patterson, the daughter of the former CRC leader.[31]

When a follow-up march was being planned, the FBI seemed concern by Patterson's proposal of a petition campaign for school desegregation, seeking to gather signatures to the tune of "20,000 a day," with the aim of "getting a million" altogether, envisioning the cooperation of "labor delegations . . . youth, women, the PTAs," and "the NAACP branches." Patterson also envisioned "international solidarity" in this campaign and "some discussion of 'our brother parties to the south of us,'" a possible reference to his ties to Cuba, Puerto Rico, and Jamaica.[32]

Though the U.S. authorities had clipped Patterson's—and the CP's—wings at home, they were not as successful abroad, which meant that the party's dwindling membership was not met with dwindling attention on the part of Washington. By early 1958, Patterson was playing a major role as leader of the CP's largest district—that of New York State—while serving as the chief executive of the *Daily Worker*. Hoover seemed displeased when he got hold of a "draft of material" that Patterson sought to "circulate in the United States and abroad," which sharply rebuked Washington's shaky position on Jim Crow; this was deemed worthy of sharing with the CIA, military intelligence, and the State Department.[33]

Complicating matters further was the bitter wrangling that had descended upon the CP, which drained Patterson's time and energy, along with the debilitating governmental investigations that required rapt attention and substantial expenditures. As for the latter, his consul at the Subversive Activities Control Board pointed out in early 1956 that despite the liquidation of the CRC, there remained "grand jury investigations," "tax investigations, state and federal," and "legislative committee hearings." This was occurring despite the CRC 's expired lease and disconnected telephones and Patterson "looking for something else to do"—"he does not have a another job yet," his consul asserted.[34] By March 1957 Patterson was scheduled to be parked in a courtroom squaring off against the Internal Revenue Service, which had made assessments of seventy-five thousand dollars against the defunct CRC.[35] Patterson was not far wrong when he told readers of the *Afro-American* in mid-1957 that because he had brought Jim Crow before a global audience, particularly at the "General Assembly in Paris in 1951," "[this] has caused the government to seek to harass me interminably."[36] A year to the day after the high-court decision on desegregation, Patterson announced that there had been ninety-eight convictions of CP leaders in federal courts from New York to Honolulu, a remarkable decapitation—and not a coincidence, as

Jim Crow was being abandoned without the possibility of the radical left taking any credit or taking advantage of the altered political scene.[37]

Then there were the wrenching changes induced by the discrediting of Stalin and the subsequent revelations about misdeeds in Moscow, which were an essential component of internal party wrangling. Because Negroes had fewer career options in an apartheid society, they were less prone to flee party ranks, and besides, they were more attuned to the historic need of mobilizing global support against Jim Crow, a role filled by Moscow. Thus, the FBI thought in 1958 that—with the proliferating ailments of the CP leader William Z. Foster—it was actually the Negroes (Patterson and Ben Davis, in the first place) who were actually running the party.[38] Apparently, after Patterson lunched with his old friend Decca Truehaft (Jessica Mitford) of the defunct CRC, she was informed that it was actually the moral and political strength of Robeson that was the "main power" behind the Davis-Patterson duopoly.[39]

Patterson was thought to be part of the so-called pro-Moscow or anti-anti-Moscow faction, and this posed difficulties, since he too had a critique to make of the Soviet Union. (The FBI thought that Patterson "is not known to have become involved in any factional struggles.")[40] Patterson condemned "murderous attacks upon Jewish intellectuals, in particular upon Jewish professionals." "As a Negro in the United States," he declared, "the fate of any minority in a Socialist state is a matter of grave concern. This holds especially true for the Jews living in the Soviet Union." "A Negro must have an answer that satisfies the Negro people, otherwise they cannot be brought to believe that a socialist society holds the complete reward for them." Thus, he proclaimed, "treatment of the Jews in the Soviet Union is not only an internal matter."[41]

As for the other flashpoint of 1956—Soviet tanks in the streets of Budapest—Patterson was not as sympathetic as the U.S. mainstream, wondering where was the outrage about the "Cotton Curtain, the bombings of Negroes' homes." Washington, he harrumphed, "has lured the left away from a decisive and profound study of our own country and the Western Hemisphere at this historic moment," toward a focus on Hungary.[42]

Like others allied with the "anti-anti-Moscow" faction, Patterson was often harsh toward the titular leader of the other side, John Gates.[43] This fierce internal struggle stretched on for months through 1956 and 1957, which was only the epicenter of a conflict that lasted years and involved various twists.[44] The result was predictable: thousands left the CP. As the spouse of the CP leader Eugene Dennis, Peggy Dennis, put it, "Sharp internal differences over strategy, tactics, analyses, escalated throughout the 1960s decade" in a process aided by FBI infiltrators.[45]

Yet Patterson too came into conflict with those who had been seeking to reformulate the CP's theoretical position on the Negro Question. Ultimately, it was decided to drop the notion of a "Negro nation" seeking self-determination up to and including secession, a shift that did not please Patterson's old comrade,

Harry Haywood.⁴⁶ Patterson agreed with the shift but not the "reasons" for it. He thought that a "future socialist government in the U.S." would push for "self-determination" not only for "Puerto Rico and Hawaii," but "if at that time the Negro people constitute a nation it will apply to them" too. He acknowledged that "the Negro people have never considered that demanding the right was a good strategy in their fight for freedom. But to draw from this the conclusion that they have already exercised their right and have elected to merge with the rest of the U.S."—as the CP decided in the 1950s—"is unrealistic. All that they have decided is that the best strategy in their struggle for freedom is to demand equal rights with the white people." As he saw it, "The choice of integration which the Negro people have now apparently made was made under duress and is not binding." In any case, "no choice made under the right of self-determination is ever irrevocable."⁴⁷

Though deprived of the base provided by the CRC, Patterson still was enmeshed in various struggles, including the travails of his old friend, Paul Robeson. The FBI was noticeably concerned about the potential influence of Robeson and Patterson's impact upon him. The artist, it was thought, "first came into contact" with "Communist ideology as a result of his friendship with [Patterson] with whom he first toured the Soviet Union and with whom he has maintained close personal relations for many years."⁴⁸ The rattled FBI thought Patterson had "conceived the idea of smuggling Paul Robeson out of the United States for propaganda purposes. The plan was for Robeson to suddenly give a concert or make a speech in some foreign capital or large city in order to cause a sensation." As so often happened during this era, this novel idea was rejected by the CP—perhaps at the instigation of Morris Childs, the FBI's representative in leadership councils.⁴⁹ Unflappably, Patterson—as if the CRC had not been driven into death—aggressively took up the leadership of the fight to return Robeson's passport, resuming his identity as an attorney and once again linking the Negro struggle at home with the anticolonial struggle abroad, this time in the august chambers of the Circuit Court of Appeals in Washington, D.C.⁵⁰

It was Patterson, as well, who took the lead in the global campaign to free Henry Winston, a Negro leader of the CP whose health—in particular, his eyesight (he was to go blind in prison)—was in dire jeopardy. The FBI thought that his case "was used to arouse" the CP "emotionally"; Winston's difficulties were "the subject of stories, broadcasts, and newscasts in the socialist countries. Through efforts of William L. Patterson, it was front-page news in the *London Daily Worker* and *L'Humanite* in Paris."⁵¹

The FBI was alarmed when Patterson simultaneously took up the cudgels on behalf of W. E. B. Du Bois. Things had changed since they had crossed swords in the early 1930s, when the venerable intellectual had served on the staff of the NAACP. Now they were both under siege. Du Bois was actually tried—and acquitted—in the early 1950s in a premonition of what was soon to befall Patterson. Du Bois had moved closer to Patterson's views, actually endorsing the post-1956 actions of the Soviets in Budapest.⁵² His spouse, the former Shirley Graham, was often given credit for this apparent ideological shift, though Patterson's influence cannot be denied.⁵³ As part of his effort to merge the anticolonial struggle in Africa with the movement of U.S. Negroes, Patterson viewed Du Bois as the perfect person to spearhead such a campaign.

The campaign to highlight Du Bois's ongoing difficulties in his homeland was "designed to embarrass the United States internationally," complained J. Edgar Hoover. Patterson's plan was "to have as many as possible of the Soviet satellite [sic] nations, as well as Russia itself, elect Dr. Du Bois as an honorary member of the highest scientific academies of those nations." The "purpose" was to "show that Negroes, even those who are among the most prominent in the scientific field in the United States and particularly Dr. Du Bois, are not recognized in this country and are in fact humiliated. When this campaign gains momentum, Patterson indicated the possibility of having some of the satellite nations call international conferences of scientists for the purpose of honoring Dr. Du Bois." Hoover made sure that copies of his report were distributed widely, including to various intelligence agencies.⁵⁴

In fact, Patterson was campaigning avidly on Du Bois's behalf. "I have just returned from a trip that carried me to St. Louis, Chicago, and Pittsburgh," he told the elderly scholar in late 1957. "In each of these cities I raised the question of your birthday in February and its truly far-reaching significance, particularly to Negro Americans and their youth." He was keen to note his meetings with prominent Negro publishers and editors, such as Nathaniel Sweets (St. Louis), John Sengstacke (Chicago), and P. L. Prattis (Pittsburgh).⁵⁵ The White House carefully took note of this Patterson campaign,⁵⁶ along with his continuing effort to raise an international ruckus so that Rosa Lee Ingram—a hangover case from the CRC era—might be freed.⁵⁷

Though Adam Clayton Powell, the charismatic Harlem congressman and former close associate of Ben Davis, had flipped and even traveled to faraway Bandung to defend Washington, Patterson campaigned for his 1958 reelection—since the alternative would have been a right-wing victory.⁵⁸ This issue too got caught in a raging factionalism within the CP; as was becoming typical, Davis and Patterson were on the same side, with the latter asserting forcefully that the attack on Powell was "coming from labor reactionaries" and that "Powell will be [in] the most vital position any Negro has occupied since the Civil War," if reelected.⁵⁹ To that end, Patterson chaired a massive Harlem rally—the FBI thought that 2,500 had gathered at the crossroads of Harlem, at 125th Street and Seventh Avenue. "It became necessary for the police, who were not anxious to do so, and acted only under the pressure of the size of the crowd, to close off the block to downtown traffic, because the crowd could not be contained on the sidewalk." It was hard to say if the FBI were pleased or displeased to find that "party people and their contacts were a definite small minority of those who listened." Evidently, "several hundred" signed a petition calling for the arrest of Arkansas Governor Orval Faubus.[60]

Although Patterson campaigned for Powell, the prevailing atmosphere made it difficult for Powell to campaign for Patterson. A telling sign emerged after Powell's reelection when Patterson traipsed to New Haven and was drawn into a colloquy about the fabulous contralto Marian Anderson, who had catapulted into prominence in recent years. Patterson admitted that he was "personally acquainted" with her, having met her years earlier in Europe. Yet, according to an unnamed reporter, Patterson concluded mournfully—in an elegy for the era—that "since she has been placed in a position to help" the movement, "she has 'turned.' He said that he has written a letter which he has captioned, 'Marian—how could you?'"[61] Well, "Marian could," because like many who had formerly accepted the prospect of friendly relations with Reds during the high tide of Jim Crow, she blanched at the same idea as the contrasting trends of civil-rights expansion with civil-liberties retreat began to bite. It was at that moment that the powerful right-wing began to raise searching questions, such as the 1957 allegation that "ten top leaders" of the NAACP possessed "extensive Communist front records," including Patterson's old friend Earl Dickerson.[62]

Lorraine Hansberry diverged from the path trod by Marian Anderson in that she was known to be close to the organized left and Patterson notably.[63] Her signature play was an homage to Langston Hughes, and she traveled to Mississippi to save Willie McGee's life, for whom she wrote an affecting poem. She consulted Patterson in her writing, often in elevated philosophical terms.[64]

Hughes—a boon companion of Patterson's spouse and the former CRC leader as well—was comparable to Hansberry in this respect. He had been harassed by congressional authorities, though he did not retreat altogether from his radical commitments. Patterson had kept in touch during the CRC years,[65] and after his tenure there ended, they both had more time to pursue their relationship. After the collapse of the CRC, Patterson—in seeking to bring the Dean of Canterbury to Manhattan for a fund-raiser—consulted with the Harlem bard, who (according to the FBI) "told him that well known entertainers and spiritual singers could be obtained" for this "celebration" of *The Worker*.[66] Occurring at a time when the CP was under assault, this was no small thing.[67]

In mid-1957 Patterson, accompanied by his spouse and daughter, viewed Hughes's play, *Simply Heavenly*—"thanks" to gratis tickets provided by Hughes. After thanking him for a copy of his affecting memoir, *I Wonder as I Wander* (Patterson found it to be "excellent," the "best of the many fine things you have done"), he expressed grave reservations about what he had just viewed. "I cannot say that I liked it," he said chillily, while noting modestly that "I am not a theatrical critic." He remarked on Hughes's recycling of his fount of folk wisdom, a character based on Simple. Patterson admitted that "your use of the jazz medium to carry the dialogue along helped it to flow and gave it rhythm." But that was insufficient, he thought: "To me, Lang, the play was political. But the politics suited my enemy's," and "this is not the time to aid Simple's enemies, when his friends in Montgomery, Ghana, and elsewhere are fighting too desperately to effect fundamental changes."[68]

Hughes, in the difficult position of seeking to maintain ties with a reviled Communist leader while not alienating conservative U.S. rulers, was tactful in response, telling Patterson that his remarks were "greatly appreciated and [his] views valid in a number of ways." He reminded "Dear Pat" of artistic realities: "It's the old story—and the old problem I've been wrestling with for years—how to get everything to suit everybody into one piece. When it comes to plays, it is a struggle to end up with anything [one] wishes left in the play—after 20 or 30 other people have had a hand in the creation." After all, "in books one has 380 pages to work with, in a play only 80. In publishing, only one editor to contend with . . . but in the theater everybody pulls and hauls at a script. So, all I can say," he concluded resignedly, "is, I did the best I could under the circumstances."[69]

For all his grit, Hughes chose not to pursue the same path that had led to Robeson's and Du Bois's difficulties—and Patterson's too. For like Robeson and Du Bois, Patterson had difficulty garnering a passport to travel overseas—but he was able to reach the Caribbean. Wearing a brown suit, no hat, and carrying a large bag—or so reported the FBI[70]—he jetted southward. They thought his journey included an "attempt to influence" islanders "to send ship pilots to Suez."[71] The FBI thought that while in Jamaica, Patterson "described himself as the West Indies organizer for the Communist movement,"[72] which was a reflection of his close relationship with Ferdinand Smith, formerly of the United States, and the continuing effort to question the former CRC leader's authenticity by highlighting his roots in St. Vincent. Patterson was said to have made "an apparent attempt to stimulate Communist activities" there, while acting as a "liaison or courier between CPUSA and certain other Communist parties in this hemisphere."[73] Part of Patterson's stimulus was a donation of $150 to the movement in that poverty-stricken colony while mulling consideration of a further donation of an automobile. "The New York office must intensify its investigation of this aspect of Communist Party activities," said an FBI agent.[74] Part of the FBI's blocking of the Patterson tie to Jamaica was an apparently successful effort to thwart his attempt to have a Ferdinand Smith manuscript on the island published in the United States. Patterson had sent it to Arkansas and sought to have it translated in Norway, but somehow the U.S. authorities got wind of this initiative, as the potent Central Intelligence Agency was brought into the fray.[75]

Puerto Rico was also part of his itinerary, the Capitol Hotel in Santurce more precisely, where the FBI found that he conferred with "prominent Communist Party members in San Juan."[76] Naturally, the authorities reported that "through cooperation," Patterson's "luggage and briefcase were searched upon his arrival," where the most noteworthy items uncovered were "news bulletins on Suez Canal situation."[77]

Patterson provided the FBI with plenty of material for their frequent reports. He spoke at a public rally, denounced the trial of Communist leaders, and castigated the Smith Act—the anticommunist legislation used promiscuously to bludgeon Red leaders on the mainland. He again bruited the notion of a hemispheric conference along the lines of Bandung.[78] Such measures, designed to bring Washington's odious Jim Crow policies into the global spotlight, were not designed to lessen pressure on Patterson. The same could be said about another Caribbean initiative of his, seeking to enlist the founder of the American Civil Liberties Union—"Dear Roger" Baldwin—in joining a 1957 campaign to oust the U.S. ally Fulgencio Batista of Cuba in the face of a growing insurgency spearheaded by Fidel Castro.[79]

Seeking to mobilize a global front against Jim Crow (and Washington more particularly)—while bereft of a passport—Patterson took advantage of his presence in Gotham (and the proximity of the United Nations) to press this agenda: the FBI spotted him and his spouse entering the residence of the Bulgarian ambassador[80] and conferring repeatedly with a number of Hungarians and Poles whom he had met while conducting the genocide crusade.[81]

But as so often happened during this era,[82] Patterson's ambitious agenda encountered a buzz-saw of objections from Morris Childs. Patterson met with him in mid-1957 about his Caribbean journey and proposal for a hemispheric Bandung that would target Jim Crow, and how he would like to visit other nations to that end. Childs reminded him of his lack of a passport and the danger involved in such travel before asking him how it would be funded. As the FBI put it, "Patterson wrote the following on a piece of paper: the Poles and the Hungarians.... They remembered that he had made [an] exposé on genocide and would finance such a venture." Apparently Childs reported this news promptly to the FBI, then tied up the venture in bureaucratic maneuvers.[83]

Childs was also present at a high-level CP gathering in the summer of 1958. Shortly after noon on August 19, party leaders gathered at their Lower Manhattan office. Once more, said the FBI, "Patterson spoke and proposed that the party prepare a petition for presentation to the General Assembly to the United Nations ... concerning the plight of the Negro people in the South and requesting the [U.N.] to take note of this situation" and "recommended a picket line at U.N. headquarters" to that end. "Patterson further stated that this action would have a tremendous impact on the African and Asiatic press as well as the American press." Patterson "stated that this weekend he would take a trip to contact individuals concerning this U.N. petition. Informant"—Childs most likely—stated that "due to the added security of the use of the blackboard during this phase of the discussion the informant was unable to determine the location and identity of persons to be contacted by Patterson."[84]

In what was becoming routine—to the dismay of the FBI—Patterson also employed the "added security of the blackboard" when he "commented that Brazilian, Caribbean, and Latin American Negroes will come together" on a common agenda in which he wanted U.S. Negroes to join; this would be done in part through the vehicle of a "3rd [political] party" wherein "the Negro becomes a force second to none."[85]

The FBI was frustrated by its inability to glean details about such ambitious proposals. This information deficit seemed to spur on the agency concerning this "action on an international scale in regard to the mistreatment of the Negroes in the United States." Yet, at the same meeting, Childs was appointed to play a key role in "the fight against factionalism" internally—akin to making the town arsonist the fire chief, and he proceeded to act accordingly.[86]

Childs was ubiquitous. When the CP held its seventeenth national convention in 1959, it was he who announced the decision of the body that rejected the appeal of Harry Haywood to be readmitted to the CP, and it was he who provided the report on the CP treasury. When the former CRC stalwart Lottie Gordon objected to his ruling on Haywood, the FBI reported enthusiastically that she was "booed down by the convention."[87] Similarly, Patterson's attempt to have the U.N. Declaration of Human Rights and Declaration of the Rights of Children made part of the formal CP resolution on the Negro Question was also defeated,[88] with the FBI faction leading the charge.[89]

Blocked on this venture, Patterson pivoted toward another. Having forged a relationship with Earl Dickerson of Chicago, Patterson sought to develop ties between the Negro business community and his comrades in Eastern Europe. This could be mutually beneficial and allow both sides to press for eased relations in Washington. Patterson informed Moscow that they too could counter Washington, then seeking to employ more Negroes in responsible posts, by providing lucrative contracts to black business. One idea was for Patterson to be a partner in a venture that would deliver parcels, which could provide him and the CP with income. He was told that the U.S. Department of Commerce would be unlikely to provide him with the appropriate permissions—but that he could probably find a "front" to act on his behalf. This venture could be a "terrific public relations thing," he was told. Likewise, Patterson suggested that Moscow invite a group of Negro educators to visit the Soviet Union, then a relatively bold idea. Again, these ideas ran afoul of adroit bureaucratic maneuvering, aided by FBI meddling.[90] Still, it was in the summer of 1958 that Earl Dickerson of Chicago led a major delegation of Negro business persons to the Soviet Union with mutually satisfactory arrangements emerging.[91]

This seemed all a bit much for Washington. After all, the nation was expending buckets of blood and treasure fighting Communists worldwide and yet here in their backyard was a Communist—Patterson—who was continuing to wield a modicum of influence, seeking to embarrass the nation abroad by reminding one and all of the stain of Jim Crow, continuing to sway prominent Negro publishers and editors, attempting to influence artists from Lorraine Hansberry to Paul Robeson to Langston Hughes, rallying comrades in the sensitive neighborhoods of Jamaica and Puerto Rico, trying to forge ties between Moscow and Negro businessmen—all while playing a leading role in the highest ranks of the CP and serving as the chief executive of their primary organ of communication.

In late 1958, outraged Dixiecrats summoned Patterson to Washington, where they—in turn—were upbraided by the rhetorically nimble Communist leader.[92] The FBI did not seem elated when he raised sharply the issue of Jim Crow when confronting Senators Olin Johnston of South Carolina and James Eastland of Mississippi. Senator Johnston accused Patterson of slander and sought to connect him to "Soviet intelligence."[93]

This was a mere prelude to a bruising confrontation with the notorious House Un-American Activities Committee in April 1959. It was 10:00 A.M. in the Old House Office Building in Washington, D.C., when Patterson arrived, pursuant to a subpoena. The authorities were well prepared for the dodges Patterson intended to pursue to avoid a perjury trap and other legal snares.[94] Accompanied by his attorney, Abraham Unger, Patterson was feisty as ever: he adamantly refused to address certain questions based on his understanding of the First Amendment to the U.S. Constitution—though he agilely danced around inquiries concerning his activities in Moscow and Warsaw decades earlier. He flatly denied visiting South Africa, however, while parrying other queries by denouncing "gratuitous insults." "No act of all my life," he said pointedly, "has ever been directed by any foreign government." Sure, he confessed, while in Hungary during the genocide campaign, "I not only issued public statements but I spoke over the air on a number of occasions, broadcasting to the Far East and the Near East and setting forth the terror against my people," and yes, he admitted, "I spoke before the Supreme Court of Hungary." The lawmakers were decidedly unimpressed, with one accusing Patterson of shedding copious "crocodile tears" about racism: "How did you think you could help the Negroes in Alabama and Mississippi by attacking the United States in Prague?" he was asked. And what about his reported remarks from 1953, when he was cited as speaking in Harlem and asking those assembled to "bow our heads together with hundreds of millions of others who across the world mourn the death of Josef Stalin, the greatest peoples' champion that our world has known"? Agilely, Patterson responded, "Probably, I did" make these cited remarks—while declining to answer if he had changed his opinion since the revelations of 1956. When pressed further he responded by stating adamantly, "I must take my stand with the Soviet Union in its support of the freedom struggle of the Asian peoples, of Africa, and all progressive mankind."[95] "Let me assure you," he instructed the impaneled skeptics, "that your hatred for what I represent can never equal my contempt for that for which your committee stands."[96]

CHAPTER ELEVEN

The ostensible subject of this inquisition was "passport security," as by then, the U.S. authorities had been compelled to grant passports to Robeson, Du Bois, and others, worrying some about what these Patterson allies might reveal abroad about the iniquities of their homeland. Previously, the CRC had been so tied up with defending itself that it felt obliged to liquidate. Now Patterson was being summoned so frequently to Washington that perhaps he should have considered leasing an apartment there.[97] That same year, 1959, he was subpoenaed once more—though conveniently, Congress had convened in Lower Manhattan at Foley Square. "I am honored" to be beckoned to this hearing, he said, sarcasm dripping.[98] No less combative, Patterson challenged this hearing on "Communist Activities among Puerto Ricans in New York City and Puerto Rico": "I will not take the oath," he asserted in a brusque technicality, "but I will affirm." The truculent attorney started making his own requests: "I would like to look at the rules by which this committee was created before I enter into any of the proceedings," he declared. "I don't have to sit down, do I? I can stand?" he said with mock inquisitiveness, as he sought another advantage by hovering over the legislators. He was reprimanded, asked to "keep [his] voice down," and Patterson responded with irritation. But when asked about the supposed gravamen of the hearing, Patterson did not respond directly when queried on his travels to Puerto Rico. Finally, he was ordered to leave the room—which was an outcome to which he did not object,[99] a departure that, predictably, garnered headlines.[100]

But eluding the grasp of HUAC brought no relief, for it only meant a return to the vexing problems faced by the CP, under seemingly permanent siege with a constant outflow of members. "Well, I've got to have some money, Ben," Patterson was reported by the FBI as telling Davis in 1958. "We couldn't get $75.00?" It was for "Negro work," said Patterson, but Davis still replied, "I don't know." Then administering the major party organ, an exasperated Patterson confided, "I'm confronted with a real situation tomorrow" involving "typesetters" awaiting payment. The comrades in Detroit called, awaiting this newspaper eagerly, but said Patterson disconsolately, "[They] hadn't gotten it," though "they should have." Yes, said Davis, it was all "a peculiar situation," though no less confounding. Worst, thought Patterson, the FBI faction of the CP—which, unbeknownst to him, was headed by Childs—was probably responsible, "sabotaging" efforts.[101]

How large was this faction? This was unclear. What was evident was that they had played a crucial role in aiding the departure from the ranks of numerous comrades. By 1959, it was reported, there were about two thousand Communists in the state of New York and about 1,600 subscribers there to the party organ—a dramatic drop from the halcyon days of the late 1930s.[102]

What was also evident was that Childs despised Patterson's close comrade, Ben Davis. He was "extremely critical" of him at one CP meeting, the FBI reported, which was typical of the times.[103] Patterson was present at a meeting of CP leaders when Davis averred what to the former CRC leader was boilerplate: the Negro

Question "is not a central question but is *the* central question." Promptly, Childs—according to an informant present (probably Childs himself)—"launched into a verbal attack against Ben Davis" that soured moods. When Davis suggested that the CP accept a declaration by seventeen Communist parties worldwide, Childs objected, demanding "independent thinking" and not just cosigning documents. Childs, it was reported, "criticized Davis for shouting and pounding the table." Gus Hall, soon to be the top party leader, "agreed" with Childs, which was not unusual, since he too had problems with Davis. The record showed that "at this point the meeting was recessed for a couple of minutes to allow tempers to cool." The present informant "commented" that Childs "had probably made an enemy of Davis."[104]

The informant was probably correct. Just before this heated exchange, Patterson and Davis had conferred, with the latter berating—with expletives deleted—"the right wing in the Party," which was "responsible more than any other force inside the party for the downgrading of Paul [Robeson] and the Negro position," through both inattention and sabotage. Patterson responded simply, "You're absolutely correct on that angle."[105]

It was Childs who demanded that the CP and allies intervene in the ongoing dispute between the labor leaders George Meany and A. Philip Randolph, which, given the antipathy of both leaders to the Reds, would probably have not been well received—particularly since Childs wanted their debate to be highlighted and widely disseminated.[106]

As the tumultuous 1960s were dawning, Patterson had been dealt heavy blows but was still standing and dishing out a few of his own. He did not seem to realize that one of his fellow CP leaders—Morris Childs—was undermining what Patterson was seeking to build and complicating things mightily for him when he could least afford it.

12

Fighting Back

It should have been an unremittingly delightful moment for William Patterson. He departed the United States on March 13, 1960, headed to Czechoslovakia, Hungary, the Soviet Union, and China. In these difficult times, it was a monumental victory to gain a passport. When he applied for this document, the FBI stated the obvious: "In view of the subject's position and prominence in the Communist Party, this matter should be given preferred attention."[1] The CP leader Elizabeth Gurley Flynn evidently thought that Patterson would not receive a passport because of lingering resentment of the genocide campaign, a prognostication that proved surprisingly faulty.[2]

However, thanks to Morris Childs and those presumably not part of his FBI faction who were persuaded by him (which were at times indistinguishable), the FBI reported gleefully that "Party leaders have advised [Patterson] that he is not authorized to represent the CPUSA in discussions abroad." This was not only a stiff rebuke to one of the CP's leaders with probably the most extensive background in global affairs stretching over decades, it was also a rebuff to an African American leader, who was basically instructed to steer clear of that which had been a most potent ally for his people for centuries—the weight of the international community.[3]

This was even more unfortunate because Patterson was still negotiating with Eastern European leaders, seeking to forge business ties with Negro entrepreneurs. Moreover, he had gone further—as the FBI knew—and "asked members of the Czechoslovakian diplomatic corps in the United States for funds for Negro work in the United States."[4] As African nations were surging to independence, the possibility for material aid from these forces was also emerging. In late 1958 Patterson was in the process of conferring with a leader of what was soon to be the government of Cameroon, a man who apparently had close ties in China, where Patterson was now scheduled for a visit.[5] Thus, blocking Patterson's influence abroad was a real victory for the FBI faction, made all the more ironic when months before Patterson's departure, Childs returned from Moscow and, said the FBI, "stated that he had the opportunity to speak with many comrades from other countries."⁶ Perhaps Patterson should not have taken it personally; even William Weinstone, a comrade with a lengthy record of service to the CP, was blocked by Childs from reaching out to Moscow.⁷ Interestingly, Childs prevented Weinstone from raising in Moscow concerns about treatment of Soviet Jewry.⁸

Childs played unsuspecting Communists like a finely wrought bass fiddle. Claude Lightfoot, a leading Negro comrade from Chicago, told him "in strict confidence"—according to the FBI—that Patterson had "given some people the impression that he was going to [Prague] merely for a rest and a vacation, actually he was going with plans and proposals to submit to the Communist Party of Czechoslovakia," including "how to get money from [Prague] in order to carry on propaganda work among the Negroes in the United States" and "to induce [comrades there] to call a Latin American Congress" on the plight of U.S. Negroes and Africans.⁹ It seemed that Patterson also had in mind—or so thought the FBI—"plans for an international campaign charging mistreatment of children in the U.S.," with a focus on school-desegregation confrontations along the lines of Little Rock. The Latin American gathering was a revival of his long held idea of a "Bandung" for the Americas, targeting "racist practices and policy of American imperialism" along with pressing the Eastern Europeans to establish African institutes for study of the continent and placing U.S. Negroes in high-level posts in such organizations as the Women's International Democratic Federation so that a "program that will attract Negro women of the USA" could be more readily developed. Of course, these revelations buoyed Childs's preexisting idea to ensure that the brief Patterson carried abroad was exceedingly limited and constricting—though Dennis and Hall agreed to instruct Childs to provide Patterson with six hundred dollars for expenses "from the sums received by the CP ... from abroad."¹⁰

Patterson had continued to pursue these proposals with various U.N. agencies, though at one CP meeting, it was decided that the man then known as Hunter Pitts O'Dell—who under the name Jack O'Dell would go on to become a top aide to Dr. King—would replace Patterson as the chief liaison with these Eastern European forces.¹¹ This occurred, according to the FBI, when Patterson was "called in by the top brass" of the CP and "told 'to lay off the business enterprises.'" As a "result of Patterson's 'pushing at the embassies,'" his attorney, Milton Friedman, had "obtained a $15,000 retainer from Hungary," part of which apparently went to Patterson and part to *The Worker*. It was agreed that Childs should try to "confer regarding this situation."¹² The FBI reported further that Eugene Dennis "was also heard to tell Patterson that if he had to discuss these matters, he should only discuss them with Morris Childs." The various deals also involved "importing of motorized scooters from Hungary to the United States," which—apparently—Patterson thought had an "excellent chance of becoming a big business concern." However, he was "primarily interested in donations to *The Worker* or the Communist Party."[13]

But Patterson was checkmated. Gus Hall nominated Childs as Secretary of the Foreign Affairs Committee of the CP, and he was "elected unanimously" to what was deemed to be—quite conveniently—a "committee of one."[14]

Pressing on, Patterson counseled extensive foreign exchanges with Negro colleges, artists, entrepreneurs, and the like, along with "travel opportunities" for all, not least since it could allay the nagging suspicion in this community—cultivated in the United States—that "white racism" was not unique to Washington but was a veritable global norm among the melanin deficient, irrespective of nationality. The "Eastern People's Republics and progressive Asian countries" should employ a "Negro [law] firm," he urged, and should provide generous "retainers." He suggested that a firm headed by himself be "established at once."[15] Patterson, said the FBI, was reviving his idea to "determine if a Negro could get an agency for sending parcels to Russia or engage in foreign trade with the Russians"—but inertia and the FBI faction insured that this did not occur.[16]

This idea of one CP seeking support from another, in any case, was quite common and viewed as yet another example of "proletarian solidarity." At this same time, Cheddi Jagan of what became the nation of Guyana was soliciting Patterson—via Ferdinand Smith of Jamaica—for funds. "I am not against" this, Patterson replied.[17]

Despite Childs's energetic efforts, the fact was that in his many sojourns abroad, Patterson had made many friends, and simply because he was barred from conducting business on behalf of the CP did not mean that he was barred from renewing old acquaintances. Thus, while in China he conferred with leading members of the Communist party there, some of whom he had encountered during the height of the genocide campaign in the early 1950s. He arrived at a propitious moment, for PRC-USSR relations had plummeted, in part because of the Stalin devaluation—to which China objected. This tailspin contributed to an encirclement of the Soviets, which ultimately played a crucial role in the crisis in Moscow that decades later was to lead to the dissolution of the Soviet Union. Part of the dispute also concerned—ostensibly—Moscow's promulgation of "peaceful coexistence" with the imperialist camp, to which a number of Chinese leaders took strong exception on the grounds that it glossed over the fundamental concept of class struggle.[18] Patterson also thought that China's absence from the United Nations and its isolation generally contributed to the imbalance in relations between the two socialist giants—the rebel province, Taiwan, was to hold this seat for decades until China's entente with the United States years later. However, he did detect in his consultations an indication that China was not as convinced as the Soviet Union as to how the core concept of preventing World War III would occur.[19]

But even here Patterson—and the CP—were handicapped. When William Z. Foster, the top party leader, sought to pass on a message to Mao Zedong (Foster said that he knew the Chinese leader was "busy" but "would like him to read it carefully"), it was Childs who was given this important assignment—which was like asking Benedict Arnold to be the intermediary with George Washington.[20]

Initially, Patterson sought to straddle the emerging differences between Moscow and Peking, perhaps sensing that heightened tensions between the two could spell doom for the entire socialist project. Moreover, Patterson was of the view that "the giant leap of the Chinese people into history under the leadership of Communists and Communism has filled the racists of the world with paroxysms of fear," an opinion that shaped his overall view of the two nations' conflict.[21]

Patterson did not manage to escape controversy during his lengthy sojourn, for his stay in Moscow happened to coincide with a major diplomatic incident when the U.S. pilot Francis Gary Powers was placed on trial after his spy plane was brought down. Patterson spoke on television in Moscow, where the FBI recorded him as saying that Powers was lucky, for he might have been the victim of a lynch mob if he were a different color and had landed in certain areas of the United States instead.[22] "Patterson stressed that the prosecution had every reason to demand a death penalty," it was reported, which did not improve this radical's image in Washington.[23] "I have just left the last session in the historic trial of Francis Gary Powers," Patterson informed readers of the *Afro-American* in September 1960, as he praised "how magnanimously . . . the Soviet people dealt with this man"—in stark contrast to the "terrible [in]justice of the Scottsboro case."[24]

Earlier, Patterson had smoothed the path for Du Bois's visit to Moscow, a step toward his joining the CP himself in 1961.[25] When Du Bois did make this momentous announcement, Patterson provided the opinion that this "would not invite prosecution by the U.S. government," for "there is not an African in the United Nations . . . who would stand for that; and . . . prosecuting a man of his age would bring down the wrath of the Negro press."[26]

This reported Patterson opinion pointed to something else: though it is true that Communists like Patterson were under siege within and without during this period, harassed, subjected to pervasive surveillance, investigated, subpoenaed, and indicted, the reality was that they were not bereft of weapons, since the odious Jim Crow kept Washington on the defensive, not least among African nations coming to independence. As one comrade of Dwight Eisenhower confided, "The single most important development in Soviet Cold War planning for the encirclement of the North American continent is the emergence of the American Negro as an agent of the Kremlin for the conquest of Africa." It was thought that "Negro Communist agents have been infiltrating existing Negro organizations in this country and setting up other front organizations." Supposedly, these agents were "achieving a certain amount of success" because of the "current American

Negro schizophrenia, one part loyal American despite the pushing around he has received but also another part feeling his Negro oats" and a "third part pride in the emergence of black Africa." It was felt that "stirrings" in Angola were "being financed by U.S. Negro money"—ditto for Mozambique—with South Africa next. "I think that Adam Clayton Powell," it was reported, "will emerge as an important you-know-what in the woodpile"—all of which was "explosive and Orwellian."[27]

During his extensive tour abroad, Patterson did little to dissuade Eisenhower's comrade of his own "explosive" viewpoint. While in London, he conferred with Claudia Jones, the Trinidad-born former U.S. Communist leader, recently deported and rapidly becoming a leader of that metropolis's rapidly growing population of African descent. She informed him that her valiant efforts had been subsidized by Robeson, though his pecuniary strength was still ebbing. They met with Egyptian exiles, who were quite concerned that pressure on their homeland had not abated—and perhaps had increased—since London's (and France's and Israel's) spectacular inability to oust its leadership. He conferred with British CP leaders and attorneys about the possibility of bringing the question of U.S. Negroes to the International Court of Justice. While in France he lunched with the Communist leader Jacques Duclos, whose reproach of U.S. comrades in 1944 had led directly to the ouster of Earl Browder. Generously, Duclos assigned a number of French comrades to work with Patterson on his various campaigns, including internationalizing the plight of U.S. Negroes and freedom for the jailed Communist leader Henry Winston. A similar agenda unfolded in Prague and Moscow. In addition, Patterson conferred with a substantial number of Chinese comrades residing in Russia. There—and elsewhere—he also broached the matter of more teaching of Negro history; predictably, this was received favorably, along with the corollary notion of reprinting more material from the Negro press. Naturally, he met with the numerous African students then flocking to Eastern Europe, thirty-two from Guinea in Prague alone.[28]

Patterson also renewed old acquaintances during this journey—one personal, the other political, with the latter piquing the interest of the U.S. authorities. He met with his two daughters while in the Soviet Union, who he thought had perished during World War II; and while in France he spoke at length and amiably with the former Chicago-based novelist Richard Wright—who died shortly thereafter under mysterious circumstances.[29] On a happier note, Patterson was elated to find that his daughters were both happily married with children.[30]

A major purpose of Patterson's journey was to mobilize support for the freeing of Winston, and the publicity he generated about this heart-rending case ultimately led to Winston's release. The U.S. legation in Paris forwarded to the FBI an article from the widely circulated French Communist newspaper that welcomed Patterson as "Defender of the Scottsboro Negroes," who "arrived in Paris to tell us: Winston is in danger!" Winston, it was said, "is a Communist and he is colored. These are two unpardonable crimes in the United States," a nation that even non-Communists viewed with acute skepticism.[31] The press in Prague had a similar reaction to Winston's plight.[32] Assuredly, such activism was hardly embraced—or ignored—by the U.S. authorities. According to the FBI, while in France Patterson was told by a member of the cabinet that Paris had been asked to facilitate the seizing of his passport. In turn, Patterson told U.S. representatives there to "go to hell" when they contacted him.[33]

Then in Moscow, the FBI believed that Patterson met with the Chinese ambassador, who invited him to Peking. Patterson accepted the invitation, staying almost two months. Patterson then, said the agency, "spoke in glowing terms of the situation in Red China," all of which was in violation of "passport instructions"[34] and, perhaps, worthy of indictment and providing further evidence—if any were needed—that the now elderly Communist remained unready to make his peace with Washington. Retaliation was not long in arriving. Upon his return home, he faced yet another hearing with the Subversive Activities Control Board, demanding that he register as a Communist—and suffer the consequences of same.[35]

Washington had its hands full, in any case, wrestling with an emerging massive anti–Jim Crow movement while Patterson was traipsing across Europe and Asia preaching to all who would listen that it was precisely Jim Crow that discredited the former slaveholders' republic. Upon his return, Patterson was in touch with various African leaders, seeking to direct their students to the Soviet Union instead of the United States.[36] This proposal also included gaining the right of U.S. Negro students to attend university in Moscow and more opportunities for "Negro Marxists" to travel in Europe and Asia.[37]

Upon his return, Patterson remained in the midst of tumultuous events. When Robert Williams of the NAACP in North Carolina came under fire in 1961 at the behest of the local authorities, causing him to flee to socialist Cuba, the FBI overheard him informing Ben Davis about the "white mobs" who were "shooting into" his house. Patterson "had received the story" from a source on the scene, and Patterson and Davis quickly moved to mobilize forces to "call or send telegrams to the [Department of Justice] demanding he get protection."[38]

This charged episode was reflective of the reality that Patterson's extended time abroad was designed in the first place to generate support for the cause that had animated his existence since the 1920s—the anti–Jim Crow crusade. Often accompanied by Davis, Patterson was continuing to confer on the trajectory of this movement. For example, they met in the spring of 1961 to "discuss"—as the FBI put it—"the coming conventions of three mass organizations,"[39] the NAACP, the Negro American Labor Council, and the Negro Baptists, Dr. King's base of support. Patterson was to be continually disappointed with the NAACP, whose leadership was under enormous pressure, most notably in Dixie, and whose national leadership—particularly Roy Wilkins—had yet to forget the 1930s disputes over Scottsboro. Wilkins once told a national audience about how he had engaged in "many a joust" with the man he referred to familiarly as "Ben" (i.e. Davis), "an able and amiable fellow, as he sat in NAACP conventions."[40] He could have said the same about Patterson—except that their relations had become progressively testy. After the NAACP's 1959 convention, Patterson told CP leaders that this mass organization "did not meet its responsibility and ideologically took a step backward."[41]

Repeatedly, Davis and Patterson contemplated what the former referred to as "the stymie by the NAACP ... should the Party quarrel with them or try to get around them in another way."[42] Ultimately, the rise of Dr. King's movement—which was decidedly less anticommunist than the NAACP—effectively answered this question.

The FBI thought that the CP was "extremely influential in the Executive Board" of organized Negro trade unionists in New York, which included the anticommunist labor leader A. Philip Randolph—who refused to respond to Patterson's entreaties.[43] As time passed, Patterson's opinion of Randolph dropped precipitously; he eventually concluded that the "tragic turning point" for this leader was the 1920s, when he turned decisively against both the CP and Moscow, as the authorities objected strenuously to his own increasingly diluted professed socialist beliefs.[44]

A clandestinely gathered report of a Communist meeting revealed that Patterson—perhaps thinking of Wilkins and Randolph—felt that the "greatest weakness in the Negro struggle is the weakness of leadership." He proposed that the CP should confer with "white workers and leaders and give them an idea of how to fight and form a united front," a reflection of his perception that it was easier for the NAACP to look to the U.S. elite for support than those in the working class of a different ancestry—which weakened the working class as a whole and the Negro struggle.[45] The oft-touted "Negro-labor alliance," which the CP often hailed as the locomotive of progress, was not realizing its full potential, since labor—with a few conspicuous exceptions, such as the stevedores' union on the West Coast—"had not played a [meaningful] role in the Negro liberation movement."[46] As for the NAACP leadership, Patterson was quoted as objecting to their slogan of "integration" and opting instead for "complete equality."[47]

As time passed, Patterson had come to feel ever more strongly that the NAACP had mishandled a rare opportunity to push back against Jim Crow, since the U.S. ruling elite was under tremendous pressure to retreat from this compromising front in the 1950s. By opting for anticommunism, the association had not strengthened the struggle against domestic apartheid. Even during the waning days of the CRC, the NAACP chose—as one leader put it—"to throw down the gauntlet" and attack this weakened organization.[48] The attorney Herbert Simmons of Los Angeles, who was friendly with Patterson, was considered by the association as one of a number of "Communist suspects"[49] as a result of an organized protest emerging against this skilled lawyer's candidacy for NAACP leadership.[50]

Even after the CRC disappeared, the NAACP continued its aggressively anticommunist policy, actually physically removing alleged Communists from meetings, including Doxey Wilkerson, one of the most sophisticated intellectuals in the anti–Jim Crow circle.[51] A donation from Ben Davis was returned promptly and curtly—and then trumpeted widely.[52] "Please get some sense," one unnamed supporter asserted. "You have outlawed like Uncle Sam the best brains we have like our founder W. E. B. Du Bois, et al."[53] But the NAACP leadership felt that it had little choice.

NAACP leaders were under tremendous pressure from the right wing, who were threatening to impose a CRC-style liquidation upon them unless they complied. The glaring spotlight was on the affluent and prominent attorney-businessman Earl Dickerson,[54] who had personal ties to Patterson[55] and political ties with the NAACP, making him an attractive target. The FBI thought that Dickerson was actually a member of the party,[56] while subsequently it was charged that he was all too close to the similarly affluent Dr. Carleton Goodlett,[57] who was also a leading publisher and also close to Patterson. The NAACP could hardly afford to shun the few affluent Negroes who had managed to survive, simply because they were scorned as friends of Patterson, but that is precisely the direction in which they were moving.

Despite the strenuous efforts of detractors, there remained an informal CP caucus within the NAACP, and they met in March 1963—and were monitored by the FBI. They thought that they had evaded the authorities by convening at the Henry Hudson Hotel in Manhattan—not CP headquarters—but this proved to be wishful thinking. Patterson was present, along with Ben Davis, Claude Lightfoot, Ted Bassett, and others. Patterson set the tone when he argued that just as Moscow in the United Nations had pushed an anticolonial resolution—"unanimously adopted"—domestic Communists should follow in these footsteps. At the United Nations there was a "time limit after which there would be no colonialism," and Jim Crow should be subjected to a similar time constraint—and a "possible suit against these [Jim Crow] states under Article 4, Section 4, and under the 14th Amendment . . . drafted in such a way as to have international significance." Patterson also stated that he would "like to bring the genocide issue up to date, reintroduce it, and use this issue as a possible solution to the plight of the Negro in America."[58] But like so many initiatives during this era, this one failed to gain the support of the NAACP leadership.

With his mass base in the CRC forced out of existence, Patterson operated mostly as an "out-of-the-closet" Communist, which increased pressure on figures like Dickerson and Goodlett—and in response, the NAACP—to have no dealings with him. This was not easy, since those subjected to Jim Crow were not necessarily in a mood to accommodate those who were the guardians of this system of hatred. Still, the anti–Jim Crow movement, propelled—though often unacknowledged by participants—by global currents, often deluded itself into thinking that its herculean efforts alone accounted for its recent good fortune. When the Soviet leadership arrived in the United States in the fall of 1959, Patterson reprimanded Negro leaders "when they failed to insist that the State Department arrange a special meeting for them." The "Negro people have lost much as a result," he proclaimed. Patterson realized that support from U.S. elites—as reflected in the 1954 high-court decision that inaugurated this new era of struggle—was neither a sturdy nor reliable base of support. Strikingly, at the same time as the Negro newspaper in Arkansas operated by the heroic Daisy Bates was undergoing far-reaching financial difficulties,[59] so was the CP's own organ—a reflection of a U.S. movement that was enduring searching difficulties at a time when headlines seemed to suggest otherwise.[60]

What to do? Linking the U.S. movement to anticolonialism seemed to offer a way out.[61] After returning from his journey to Europe and China. Patterson began spending more time at the United Nations—1960 was the "year of Africa," as previously colonized nations surged to independence, and he sought to have this struggle take advantage of the Negro movement's successes, and vice versa.[62]

He joined the issue on the promising ground of linked opposition to Jim Crow and colonialism's troubled legacy. Returning from his journey abroad and energized and at a time when the United Nations was convening at a propitiously fortuitous moment, Patterson informed Davis, Lightfoot, and other Negro Communist leaders that these were "the most important weeks in the history of our time." The CP and its allies should "protest the treatment of the Negro delegates to the United Nations, in their hotels and other eating places." The route from Washington to New York was infamously pockmarked with Jim Crow, and as merchants often had difficulty distinguishing between African potentates and African Americans, it provided a confluence of circumstance for a victory against Jim Crow, as U.S. rulers were reluctant to alienate Africans further by barring them as they would domestic Negroes. If this bias did not cease, Patterson insisted, then the United Nations—and its millions in spending poured into Gotham—should be moved to another country.[63] By early 1961, Patterson and Davis were exulting after Davis joined many others at an unruly demonstration at the United Nations after the murder of Congo's Patrice Lumumba; it led to Harlemites congratulating his gumption, said Davis, while Patterson rushed to discuss following up on this development.[64] This portentous development emerged in the wake of another— the heralded journey of the newly installed Cuban leader Fidel Castro to Harlem, leading to further exultation by Ben Davis about this notorious event.[65]

Thus, at a secretly recorded CP gathering, Patterson was heard to say that they should seek to link the struggles of the United States and Africa in an "all-class struggle": "I . . . believe there is nobody more fit in [the] Party for this work than myself. I can make my greatest contribution to the Party, not as Party leader, but moving around to such cities as Baltimore, Chicago, and Pittsburgh,"[66] akin to the role he played during his—and the CP's—greatest successes, the Scottsboro,

Willie McGee, and similar campaigns. The record does not reveal if the FBI faction blocked this proposal too, though it did not seem to meet with enthusiasm.

With the momentum brought by anticolonialism and a growing spate of anti–Jim Crow demonstrations, Patterson had good reason to believe that the racism that undergirded the right wing was eroding—providing momentum for the CP. In late 1963, Ben Davis brought back heartening news from Detroit—news that the FBI, which was monitoring him relentlessly, did not find encouraging. Dr. King was in Detroit too, and there the Rev. C. L. Franklin, a prominent pastor and father of the increasingly popular chanteuse Aretha Franklin, told one and all, "We must consult with all groups politically, including the Muslims and Communists." Franklin punctuated his controversial remarks by adding that "he had the greatest respect for Ben Davis." Davis said that King's top aide, the Rev. Wyatt Tee Walker, "said the same thing," and when they spoke at this heavily monitored gathering, "he threw his arm around me and said Reverend King often mentioned me." With understatement, Patterson said in response that "Ben's report . . . poses a number of complex problems"—not the least of which was how to aid the anti–Jim Crow cause without compromising its most progressive figures.[67]

J. Edgar Hoover was not as impressed, charging that the "Negro situation is being exploited fully and continuously by Communists on a national scale," with the finger pointed not only at Dr. King and his ties to Jack O' Dell but to Du Bois as well.[68] It is unclear if Hoover was aware of Patterson's facilitation of O'Dell's contemporaneous journey to Moscow, but surely the FBI would have been keenly interested in receiving the former CRC leader's letter to the Soviet Union introducing his friend as "a figure of great importance as an ideologist of the Negro liberation movement" and requesting that he be extended every courtesy during his sojourn.[69]

Nevertheless, by early 1962, Patterson, the aging Communist, perhaps because of the strain induced by travel and stress-filled hearings, acknowledged that he was too ill to continue his full responsibilities as Communist cadre but took only a minor step back by relinquishing some of his duties but continuing as leader of the CP's largest and most influential district, that of New York State.[70] Certainly, the continuing travails he had to endure were not conducive to good health. That same year, 1962, Attorney General Robert F. Kennedy and the Subversive Activities Control Board continued to pursue him vigorously.[71] At this late date, he was still being pursued about the CRC, too.[72] In 1963, Patterson and Davis were among fourteen CP leaders being hounded by the federal authorities.[73]

Firing back, Patterson took to the pages of the *Afro-American* to denounce those same authorities for their failure to protect civil rights protesters in the Deep South from attacks by racists,[74] while energetically pursuing senior citizens like himself. Yet, the fact remained that at a time of intense activism, as Jim Crow's steady decline was accelerating, the membership of the CP was dwindling. This was a "profoundly alarming weakness," said Patterson, speaking of the "weakness of our position among the Negro masses"—but why would Negroes rush to join an organization under siege, riddled by a FBI faction? Thus, in the early 1960s he recalled a time when "we could count more than a thousand Negroes in our party, today the number is less than a hundred" in the state of New York. "In Harlem we have been reduced to half that number," while "movements such as the Muslims have sprung up out of the frustrations of black men and women at the failure of white men and women." He knew that the ruling elite could not "save American capitalism from itself except by making concessions to the Negro people seeking thereby to make them a force upon which American imperialism can depend for support in the decisive battles which it confronts." In other words, the ruling class could now make more attractive offers to Negroes than Communists could, and the forces that had driven the promising attorney William Patterson into the embrace of the CP in the 1920s had been eroded.[75]

Unsurprisingly, Patterson was still sparring with Morris Childs: at a meeting in early 1963, the leader of the FBI faction returned from Communist congresses in Sofia, Rome, and Prague with the news that the recently concluded showdown over Cuba in the fall of 1962—when the planet came close to nuclear destruction—featured the United States coordinating with China, as the latter seized the opportunity to wage war on Moscow's closest non-Communist ally, India.[76] Stirring the pot of controversy, Childs reported with seeming enthusiasm on conflicts between Moscow and Peking, exacerbated by the Soviet Union reportedly blinking during the showdown over Cuba. At this meeting, where Patterson was present, the informant noted that the leadership "formally and unanimously approved the thesis which had been presented by [Gus] Hall and Childs. Yet, the discussions that followed thereafter were full of contradictions."[77]

The CP felt compelled to opine—if not intervene—on such fraught international matters because, as Ben Davis put it, "other parties look upon the opinion of the CPUSA second only to those of the CPSU because the CPUSA is from the land of imperialism and is therefore closer to most of the facts."[78] Yet, once again, with Childs in the driver's seat of their international operations, the CP allowed a domestic infestation to spread worldwide, as Childs had succeeded in muddying the waters of a complex issue.

In the meantime, Patterson had passed the landmark age of seventy, headed toward his twilight. His birthday was marked by Communists worldwide,[79] while at home "Langston" saluted him.[80] Internal foes carped that he was "getting old and could not get around to organize things as in the past."[81]

Still, the hosanna from Hughes was emblematic of Patterson's dilemma at a time when the Jim Crow and colonialism that had defined most of his life were under severe strain. For shortly thereafter, Langston Hughes was being discussed at the White House, with concern expressed about some of his radical ties. A congressman had questioned why he was present at a luncheon hosted by President John F. Kennedy for the visiting Senegalese leader Leopold Senghor. "He was invited at President Senghor's request," it was said, since he "was responsible for translating the works" of this founding father of the philosophy of Negritude "into English."[82] This also reflected Washington's dilemma, now forced to curry favor with African leaders in the throes of decolonization, where once they might have been ignored, which often brought U.S. rulers into uncomfortable contact with those on the domestic scene they too would have preferred to ignore—if not indict.

Though it was reported in 1965 that the CP had "only 10,000 members," a downfall "from perhaps 100,000 in the 1930s,"[83] the authorities had not initiated a ceasefire. Indeed, in a report circulated in the White House, the FBI concluded that the "racial unrest" then buffeting the nation was the outcome of a "determined concentration of communist efforts." Singled out was Dr. King, who—it was reported—"has used the Communists and in turn has been used by them in an alliance that could have serious consequences both for the Negro movement and this nation." "In King's rise to national prominence [he] has been closely allied with Communists," particularly Jack O' Dell. There was "reluctance" on Dr. King's part, it was said, "to discontinue his association with O'Dell."[84]

One New York daily journal argued that "rarely in its checkered history has the party been so bold" as it was in the period leading up to this report's drafting.[85] The *Los Angeles Times* editorialized that there was "no doubt that in the last quarter-century the Communist approach to the Negro has grown in sophistication."[86] It was in this context that the *New York Times* speculated that Patterson was on the verge of becoming party chairman.[87]

It was also in this context that the leading Negro journal in New York City asked, "Does the Negro owe the Communist Party a debt of loyalty simply because the Communist Party . . . decided that it would be advantageous to support the Negro's fight against segregation and discrimination?" Patterson replied simply that the Negro did not necessarily owe the CP in the way the query was framed—but the Negro owed it to herself and himself and the nation to ally with the party.[88]

Now past seventy and with his best days behind him, Patterson still had to confront virtually perpetual surveillance of his every move and a meddling state apparatus that would not hesitate to place him behind bars—or worse—until he expired. Because his spouse was able to find work, his personal financial situation was not desperate, though it was constrained. Then there was the matter of their daughter, Mary Lou. Writing from prison in late 1954, Patterson fretted about his offspring: "I hope she doesn't begin to draw away from you and me," he informed her mother. "It is not easy for a child. She seems very solid but you can't tell what goes on in a young one's mind when the problems are so abstract. For her the ideals for which we struggle have not yet crystallized in concrete form. . . . [N]o one is there to answer the questions which loom large at an early age and truly are large."[89] For her part, his daughter admitted that during this turbulent era, she felt conflicted—at once proud of her parents, yet dreading being "found out" by schoolmates who would wish to inflict "public denunciation" and "rejection" upon her because of her parents' beliefs. Her high-school teacher did not help matters by calling her "Little Stalin." Along with her parents, she always marched in May Day and Labor Day manifestations, and she would "avoid looking at the faces of angry bystanders," while "trying to dodge the rotten eggs and tomatoes and epithets." Like her father, she too faced surveillance—the cook at her summer camp in Vermont was an informer for the FBI. Her situation was not improved when her father's family, which was "god fearing . . . excommunicated him." (She "irregularly" attended a Baptist church.) Her father, she said, "knew of my fears and respected my dilemma"; in any case, her plight was not as awful as others, since Patterson was "widely known outside the [CP] because of his involvement in mass protest." Thus, "perhaps because of this broad base, he wasn't as viciously or publicly hounded" as other CP leaders. She recalled "fun" at CP headquarters on Twenty-sixth Street, a "solid and impressive red brick townhouse" with a "rickety old self-service elevator, big enough for two, with a folding wrought-iron gate. The winding marble stairway had a highly polished dark wooden banister."[90]

At the end of the day, she may have gained an advantage in being the daughter of a controversial father when Patterson arranged for Mary Lou—she "made wonderful grades,"[91] said the proud father—to matriculate in Moscow, a step on her way to becoming a pediatrician. She was the "first Black medical graduate from a Soviet Union university," said the beaming papa, a breakthrough made all the more resonant since the school was "named for a great African leader," Patrice Lumumba of Congo.[92] Soon thereafter, the elated father announced that she was wedding a Cuban national, Roberto Camacho, in Moscow.[93]

The maturation and marriage of his daughter was enthralling, but Patterson had little time to savor this heartwarming episode, given the press of events. Jim Crow was under assault, along with colonialism, while Moscow-Washington relations had become ever more complicated. Though CP membership had declined, it was still viewed by the FBI as a combative antagonist; thus, in 1964, the FBI sought to destabilize Patterson via a "counterintelligence action exposing Patterson's one-sided approach to discrimination"—reference was made to his condemnation of "racist and discriminatory practices in the United States" and his alleged reticence concerning bias in the Soviet Union. "Consider circulation of anonymous documents within the Communist Party" to indict him was the recommendation, a maneuver that the FBI faction led by Childs would no doubt have enjoyed.[94] Evidently not cowed, Patterson continued his rhetorical barrage against the right wing, dismissing acidulously the GOP standard bearer for president, Senator Barry Goldwater of Arizona, in 1964 with the words, "in essence, Goldwaterism is a brand of Nazism or fascism."[95]

As if this enhanced campaign of discrediting were insufficient to shake Patterson's usually rock-solid demeanor, another blow was struck when his closest comrade at the highest level of the CP—Ben Davis—died prematurely in his early sixties. What Harlem's leading Negro newspaper said of Davis could have been said of Patterson: "[He] carved a place for himself in the hearts of Harlem's ordinary folk." Throngs stood quietly and respectfully outside of Unity Funeral Home in Harlem. Some sat atop parked cars, resting their chins on their hands, listening in silence, while others cascaded into the streets, overflowing the sidewalks, arms folded stolidly across their chests. Masses surged at the door to enter the chapel to view Davis's remains but were blocked by a detail of police. Then, when the crowds espied Paul Robeson—along with Patterson, the remaining giant of these men trained in the nation's best law schools (Columbia for Robeson, Harvard for Davis) who tossed away the possibility of accumulating fortune in pursuit of socialist revolution—they surged toward him, as if he were now the living embodiment of their hopes and dreams. They expended their unspent emotions on the now graying Robeson—and Patterson, as ever, was nearby. It was left to Patterson to handle the arrangements for the funeral, which was not simple, since political considerations led to the service being switched at the last minute from a Harlem church.[96]

Not long after joining Robeson in the burial of their comrade, Patterson planned to jet to West Africa. Decades earlier he had vowed to expatriate there, driven by disgust with Jim Crow, but a timely conversation in London obviated this. Now he was arriving in Ghana in more providential circumstances. Nkrumah, whose ties to the U.S. left congealed during his college days a few decades ago, was now ruling independent Ghana and had helped to bring W. E. B. Du Bois, now a Communist, and his spouse, Shirley Graham Du Bois, who had been and probably was still a member, to the country. It now seemed that another front had been opened in the battle against Jim Crow, this time in the ancestral homeland of U.S. Negroes. The trend did not escape the irked attention of the pugnacious J. Edgar Hoover: his view was that the CP "is of the opinion that Patterson, who has many contacts with African leaders, including Kwame Nkrumah . . . might be able to have these African leaders exert influence on the Americans in Africa and prevent them from forming a pro-Chinese core."[97]

This was a reflection of the deepening Sino-Soviet split that was to eventuate in a world-shaking U.S.-China entente a few years later, but Hoover no doubt knew that in journeying to the motherland, Patterson was more intent on rallying forces against Jim Crow and colonialism than anything else.

Health and related considerations forced Patterson to change his plans. The airline on which he departed advised the FBI that at 8:00 P.M. on November 4, 1964, he left New York for London with plans to go from there to Moscow,[98] where he spent a month hospitalized. He was given examinations and treatment, and, like his analogous medical journey there in the 1930s, the impecunious Patterson (he was then on the CP payroll to the tune of a meager $22.50 per week) was fortunate to be able to take advantage of this proletarian largesse.[99] ("Being in a poor man's business," he once said, "where you are paid only if the revolution is successful, I must await the final victory before settling my bills.")[100] The medics also recommended that he postpone his visit to Ghana.[101] Though spending a considerable amount of time with the faculty at the University of Leningrad and students and faculty at Moscow University, Patterson reported upon his return that he felt "physically stronger."[102] However, Patterson's weight was felt nonetheless in Accra as he began writing for newspapers there; this "famed U.S. jurist," as he was termed, praised "socialism in Romania."[103]

By the mid-1960s, Patterson had far surpassed the life expectancy of the typical African American man, though he had lived a life that was hardly stress-free. When the Australian Bert Klesing encountered him at a hotel in Moscow in May 1965, he was fooled: "I had summed you up. About 55, I thought, or maybe even 60."[104] The saying was that the "movement keeps you young," and Patterson, with his sprightly stride and still fiery oratory, was a walking advertisement for this slogan.

Nonetheless, bedeviled by external foes and internal ones, too (though, like most, he could not confirm that Morris Childs and his followers were actually in the pay of the FBI, only that they acted like it), and beset by a small income, he was still able to wield influence, not least because he was buoyed by the reality that the balance of forces had shifted decisively in favor of his twin causes: anti–Jim Crow and anticolonialism. Both had enjoyed major victories with the passage of civil-rights legislation and the independence of African states too numerous to mention. Still, in a sense, the years to follow, which marked the rise of the Black Panther party and the campaign to free Angela Davis, could well be considered the highlight of his political career.

13

Patterson and Black Power

Black America was buffeted by contradictory trends in the 1960s. On the one hand, the edifice of Jim Crow had begun to crumble, a reality that received legislative sanction in 1964 and, notably, 1965, with the passage of the Voting Rights Act. On the other hand, this victory was attained while the most sophisticated, cosmopolitan, and battle-ready fighters—W. E. B. Du Bois, Shirley Graham, Claudia Jones, Paul Robeson, Ben Davis, and William Patterson—were under attack, with courage required to associate with them. Like a cold front and a warm front colliding over the plains of Nebraska, this served to create a political tornado that created new realities.

Among these were the spectacular rise of the group that came to be called the Nation of Islam, which had been founded decades earlier but only gained traction in the 1960s when the "other" radical alternative—that represented by Patterson—was battered and bludgeoned. Their contention that Euro-Americans were "devils" complicated interracial relations, which—as Patterson's career well showed—were not in the best of shape, in any case. Indeed, their rise was probably a direct result of this parlous condition.

As early as 1961, Patterson and Claude Lightfoot drafted an "Open Letter to the Negro People," focused on "Unity, the Muslims, and their Traducers," where responsibility for this group's meteoric rise was laid firmly at the doorstep of white supremacy. After a lengthy contextual introduction sketching the contours of racism, the role of the ruling class, foreign policy, and their interactions producing Jim Crow, they limned the increasingly hysterical atmosphere. "In magazines, on the radio, over the TV, Negro leaders, with the exception of Communists, are being asked for articles, given time singly or in symposiums to comment on the nature, scope, aims, and purposes of the Muslim Movement." Despite the best efforts of these leaders, "attacks" against them were "mounted" nonetheless—not coincidentally, since many of these media organs were not necessarily convinced of the correctness of the anti–Jim Crow cause. As for the "Muslims," said these Communists, "theirs is a belief that the white masses cannot be freed from the spell of racist mythology. Credence is given to it because of the apathy of the white masses in the face of racist terror. This . . . tends to breed a hatred of whites because they are white. It obscures the misery of the white jobless and hungry." While acknowledging that the "Muslims are not the main danger," and "certainly white progressives should not select them as a major target," which was to occur, they wondered plaintively, "Why don't the Muslims and their traducers expose the mutual foe?" After all, "in this battle the Negro needs allies. So too do the white masses."[1] In early 1962, Patterson mused that "naturally among [the] frustrated and especially Negroes new currents arise. The Muslims return in considerable numbers, and there are the nationalists."[2]

Subsequently, Patterson denounced the "brain damage caused by racism" and the "passivity of tens of thousands of white worker and slum dwellers," which "built up a wall of distrust and even hatred among hundreds of thousands of Negroes for and towards whites regardless of their station in life."[3] He rejected the still-resonant idea that there was a kind of equivalence—as the *New York Times* put it—between "black racism and white." Patterson found this outrageous. "What a vicious distortion of historical fact!" he roared. "There is no such thing as black racism," he countered, in the sense of Negroes systematically depriving and oppressing Euro-Americans. The reality was that "millions of black Americans have concluded that there are few whites ready and willing to fight for a democracy freed from the criminal taint of racism," and they have reacted accordingly. "White racism must go—black racism, there ain't no such thing."[4]

There were those who took sharp exception to this formulation, including Sid Resnick of New Haven. He singled out Patterson's declaration that "instead of white progressives being greatly disturbed by the hate-white, ultra-nationalist, and even obscurantist attitudes of the Muslims, they should be greatly and really disturbed by the hate-black, ultra-nationalist, chauvinist and mythological and obscurantist attitudes of those white Americans, whose class collaborationist practices . . . [have] made our country a warren for racism." Resnick disagreed and longed for "criticism of the ideology of the Muslims," along with a "more profound critique and polemic" by Patterson and the Negro comrades most notably. "Can one really equate the nationalism of a Malcolm X," he asked with exasperation, "with the nationalism" of "Latin America, Asia, and Africa"?[5] While Resnick assailed him from one angle, another critic took the opposite tack, declaring that the Communist leader "spends a great deal of time justifying the actions of 'do good' whites. . . . [I]f I didn't know he was Black," said Winston Hall, "it is quite possible that I might have confused him with being a white liberal."[6]

Mainstream opinion was more sympathetic to Resnick than Hall. Benjamin Gitlow, a former Communist converted into a fierce adversary, declared that the Reds "intend to arouse to a fever heat the nationalist and chauvinist sentiments now finding expression in segments of the Negro population into a drive for the separation of the Negroes from the whites through the establishment of an independent Negro republic in the United States [to] such an extent that it can be turned into a civil war, [thus] the Communists hope to so undermine to American government and our social structure that they can take over power. In the racial civil war they envisage, they are sure Negroes will be in the front ranks, the shock troops of the Communist revolution." Earlier, he argued, "Stalin hoped by utilizing Negro nationalism in the United States to develop revolutionary Negro Nationalist movements on a world scale"—and now it appeared that with Patterson as the vector, this aspiration was being realized.[7]

The NAACP was also told that the earlier CP policy on self-determination provided the template for the 1960s black nationalism—which was ironic, it was thought, since "this policy was imposed upon the American party leadership," and since "Communists and Russians are, after all, mostly white people."[8] An alarmed Roy Wilkins blasted these "American Negro cultists . . . so-called Muslims who teach black supremacy."[9] Undoubtedly, the NAACP felt that this emerging tendency compromised their carefully crafted alliances with Euro-American elites; the association reacted accordingly, boosted by a tidal wave of hate mail blaming them—ironically—for the resurgence of black nationalism into a form that was to be denoted subsequently as "Black Power."[10]

It was not as if Patterson agreed with what he termed a "narrow nationalist position," a divergence that arose sharply when his friend Paul Robeson was described as adhering to such a view.[11] While some may have been nonchalant about such trends, Patterson in the 1960s noted ruefully that "anti-Semitism grows in the Negro ghettoes of this country."[12] When Robert F. Williams, whom Patterson had defended when he was harassed in Dixie, wrote the provocative book *Negroes with Guns*, Patterson took issue with the left-wing writer Phillip Abbott Luce—who was soon to attack Patterson from the right, and who endorsed this militant book in hyperbolic terms.[13] Unlike the 1960s' militants, Patterson was no fan of Marcus Garvey, who—he asserted forcefully—"carried . . . his errors . . . with him to the grave but left a disturbing heritage to confuse those sincerely seeking a solution to one of the greatest problems of the day." X-raying the term "sincerely" exposes why Patterson found it difficult to renounce these militants, while he remained critical of their provenance: he knew that a raging anticommunism had warped the political atmosphere and that this was a transnational phenomenon with transnational repercussions, including the strengthening of "narrow nationalism" globally,[14] as a counterweight to the struggle for socialism.[15]

And it is not as if he capitulated to every aspect of the program of these new militants. When addressing the recently formed National Conference of Black Lawyers in New Orleans—which the present writer once led—he observed, perhaps unnecessarily, "I do not believe that we confront Black Revolution as you have asserted."[16] While praising the 1965 urban revolt in the Watts neighborhood of Los Angeles—"this youth, magnificent in its courage"—Patterson lamented that they "lacked clarity of vision regarding the social forces it faced," which contributed to their shedding barrels of blood in the streets.[17] More than once during this conflicted era, Patterson reproved "a narrow nationalist view" that presented black liberation as "something independent, separate, and apart from other fights." This was "emotionalism" that, sadly, "now characterize[d] the position" of all too many.[18]

Still, the allegation that Patterson was insufficiently harsh toward this rising ideological trend did not emerge solely from concerned Euro-Americans like Resnick. Joseph Hayden, who was viewed widely as a political prisoner, reported that "I nearly lost my life as a result of the contradictions that exist between the Black Muslims and the progressive elements in the struggle behind these walls," speaking of the ironically named Green Haven prison in New York State. He had a "narrow escape from the clutches of death," as a rising nationalist trend confronted elements of the left that were in a forced retreat.[19]

As the "Muslim movement" continued to grow, Patterson hammered what he saw as the condition precedent—white racism, whose compelled retreat at the behest of global forces only seemed to increase its nagging toxicity. "White America," said Patterson, "by and large has been dehumanized as we were degraded," but now they were confronted with a "new morality" that viewed "former colonials as equals," which was quite jarring. In this world-historic process, he saw the Communists as "modern Abolitionists," and like their ideological ancestors, they too were viewed as a "fanatical minority"—though on a "world scale we are no longer a minority."[20] This was true globally, but at home Paul Robeson Jr. was probably correct in asserting that "the younger generation of black radicals were unaware" of Robeson and by extension Patterson (though this was probably untrue of the leaders).[21] That those who were giants not so long ago were reduced drastically in size was a major victory for anticommunism and those who held Jim Crow dear—but it complicated mightily the political clarity of what was coming to be called the "civil-rights movement."

Perhaps because Patterson did not join the mainstream in a full-throated denunciation of the renewed black militancy that was arising, and also because the CP was a convenient scapegoat, when the epoch of urban unrest began to erupt—Harlem 1964, then Watts 1965—the Communists were often blamed. Patterson's critics may have noticed that, for example, when the Black Arts Repertory opened its doors in Harlem during this era with such luminaries as Ishmael Reed, LeRoi Jones, and Larry Neal present—the latter two particularly identified with the rising black militancy—Patterson happened to be present.[22]

Thus, the inflammatory author Phillip Abbott Luce, who was also a consultant to HUAC, did not mince words in blaming the Reds for the "Harlem Riot" of 1964, though like most of these episodes, police brutality was a more likely cause. "CPUSA leaders participated in violence-inciting rallies in Harlem prior to the riots," he said accusingly. "William L. Patterson, then Chairman of the New York state District Committee of the CP," just "happened to attend a rally where Communist Jesse Gray"—a future member of the state legislature and former leader of the left-led National Maritime Union—"called openly for 'guerilla warfare' to stop 'police brutality.'" He went on to lay at the feet of Patterson and the CP all manner of ills.[23] (Even the U.S. Congress found it curious that Patterson was present when Gray reportedly made his call for "guerilla warfare.")[24]

The *New York Daily News* found it suspicious when, in July 1964, Patterson was present at a meeting at Mount Morris Presbyterian church at 122nd Street in Harlem when a speaker supposedly called for "one hundred black revolutionaries" who were "ready to die" to fight police brutality.[25] Patterson was then asked if he had "ever offered a person one thousand dollars to form a Black Nationalist Organization in New York City. Patterson," said the FBI, "denied this." Patterson was then "asked to comment on charges that Communist agitators are trying to create disorder in New York City."[26]

Patterson, for his part, reprimanded the Soviet press for their coverage of "the long hot summer," as this burst of revolts was termed, since the admiring journalist condescendingly asserted that Negroes were no longer willing to "grovel."[27] Patterson, contrarily, spoke of the "heroic rebellion" in Watts in 1965.[28]

Nevertheless, the idea of Patterson's complicity in these conflagrations was not Luce's alone and was gaining currency in ultra-right-wing circles, with one analyst berating Patterson particularly for stressing the global dimensions of the anti–Jim Crow movement.[29] "Martial law" was approaching as a result of these urban rebellions, screamed one analyst, with umbrage taken to a picketer in Harlem carrying a sign proclaiming, "U.N. must intervene to stop U.S. genocide now." Though this viewpoint was attributed to Malcolm X—who in turn was connected to the reviled Muslims—the author made clear that he was aware of the supposed role of Patterson in this unfolding drama that featured "Communist Terror in the Streets."[30]

The hysteria was sufficiently intense that Patterson, Gus Hall, and the recently freed Henry Winston felt compelled to hold a press conference where they stoutly denied instigating unrest in Harlem. "Even so," said one observer, it was "reported that a 'five month investigation by dozens of top detectives, working in close cooperation with the FBI has disclosed widespread Communist infiltration, so much that they command 1,000 young fanatics dedicated to violence.' Americans wonder why nothing official is done about it." Why, it was bewailed, was nothing done about the reported tie between the emerging Nation of Islam and the CP, whose now-shelved Black Belt thesis seemed to mirror the Muslims' platform.[31] Bewildered as black militancy rose while civil-rights concessions were wrenched away, propagandists were reduced to musty Red Scare tropes to explain what they refused to comprehend.

Rather than dwell on the differences that separated him ideologically from what came to be referred to as Black Power, Patterson engaged with this phenomenon, assuming correctly that it is easier to win others to your view if you are working alongside them—as opposed to tossing rhetorical spitballs at them. After all, *Muhammad Speaks,* the widely circulated journal of the Nation of Islam, often featured articles by writers of the left—including the present writer—and, naturally, provided Patterson more favorable coverage than the mainstream press, which urged him to renounce this periodical.[32] (His ecumenical approach did not prevent Patterson from reproving their unfavorable coverage of Du Bois.)[33]

Though anticommunism and anti-Sovietism were undeniable factors in U.S. political life, African Americans were accustomed to paying attention to causes that many elites found distasteful—human rights for Negroes, for example—and, as a result, there were those who held a certain reverence for Patterson, despite the political baggage he carried. He was consulted by young militants even when it was guaranteed that he would take exception.[34] In addition to the Black Panther party, he had particularly bounteous relations with the Student Non-Violent Coordinating Committee (SNCC)—the shock troops of the movement, whose valor on the frontlines of racism in the Deep South was well documented. Following in his footsteps, in 1967 SNCC chose to apply—as Patterson was told—for "Non-Governmental Organization status at the United Nations, as you suggest[ed] in your letter." Elizabeth Sutherland of the leadership of SNCC also desired to "reprint an updated 'We Charge Genocide.'" She informed Patterson that SNCC had sent an urgent report to "all African and Asian nations in the United Nations" with the message that "unwarranted and brutal suppression of black people in the United States is a matter of international concern." Their leader, then known as Stokely Carmichael, had addressed a major protest against the war in Vietnam, where he invoked the theme "we charge genocide," an acknowledgment of Patterson's earlier crusade.[35] James Forman, yet another militant leader of SNCC, termed the genocide campaign "extraordinary."[36] Julian Bond, perhaps SNCC's most distinguished alumnus, joined with the future Detroit mayor Coleman Young and the future congressman George Crockett in a 1960s tribute to Patterson.[37]

SNCC knew more than most of the calcified biases that girdled the United States and how external force was desperately needed if progress were to be made. No doubt these young militants agreed with Patterson when he hailed the passage of the International Convention on the Elimination of all Forms of Racial Discrimination, which, he said, had direct implications for the Deep South.[38]

Yet, of all the groups that came to define the upsurge of 1960s militancy, it was the Black Panther party that had the closest relationship to Patterson and the CP. This was no secret to the ultra-right foes of both, as conservatives repeatedly pointed to Patterson's contention that his party "should stand in the forefront in the defense of the Black Panthers," referring to the group founded by Huey P. Newton and Bobby Seale in Oakland in 1966. This writer cited Patterson's contention that the BPP "now have organized contingents in approximately 33 states," which—according to the writer—suggested that the "situation in America today is comparable to that in Russia before the Red conquest of that nation in 1917."³⁹ Linking black Communists to the Black Panthers was de rigeur for the ultra-right, and not without reason.⁴⁰

The BPP, said one conservative, was "obviously an important phase of Communist operations in the United States."⁴¹ This tendency affected Norman Hill, a close comrade of A. Philip Randolph, who in editing a book that referred to the BPP as a "menace" and "Neo-Nazis" also managed to include the "role of international communism" in their development.⁴² A congressional investigation asserted that Newton's attorney—Charles Garry—was a Communist comrade of Patterson; even the minority report pointed to "extensive Communist involvement" with the BPP, a tendency that rose as their "activists became increasingly involved in legal problems." It was then that "Communist Party support became more apparent," for here the CP had developed a corps of experienced attorneys and, thanks to Patterson, a skill in "mass defense."⁴³

Congressional investigators had a point. The leading contemporaneous analyst of 1960s black radicalism—Robert L. Allen—termed Patterson "remarkable" and gave him principal credit for the trailblazing Scottsboro defense, noting what has since been ignored—that the CP was for "twenty years . . . the most influential radical force in the black community." Allen underscored that Patterson's genocide book was "presently on the reading list of the Black Panther Party." And confirming congressional supposition, he added, "It was on his [Patterson's] advice that the Panthers engaged a white attorney prepared to conduct a militant defense, Charles Garry, as lawyer for Huey P. Newton, paramount leader of the BPP. It was also on his advice that the Panthers conducted the mass-demonstration 'Free Huey' campaign in defense of Newton."⁴⁴ Garry in turn served as an intermediary between Patterson and Newton, once telling the elderly Communist that the BPP leader was "indeed touched" by the "warm and flattering" words accorded him.⁴⁵ Actually, Garry's relationship with Patterson stretched back to the tensest moments of the CRC era.⁴⁶

The U.S. Congress was taken with the lengthy articles in the BPP organ lavishing praise on Patterson, Patterson's reciprocal praise of Newton, his various contributions to the newspaper, and the multiple analyses of the genocide crusade.⁴⁷ When one hysterical analyst, seized with fear, claimed in the early 1970s that "the attack has begun! Communists plan 1973 as a year of mass terror,"⁴⁸ this party's tie to the BPP added ballast to the otherwise fanciful claim.

In other words, the U.S. Congress was not wholly wrong. The BPP repeatedly praised Patterson as one of their key influences, and he was deployed as a means of providing legitimacy to themselves, suggesting that militant struggle had deep roots, as reflected in the life of this now elderly Communist. Patterson was complimented as a "crack warrior, strategist, and organizer of the Black liberation and working class movements." Such admiration apparently forced the BPP cofounder, Bobby Seale, to deny that his group was dominated by the

CP—though he added quickly, "We're not against Communism—we dig Communism." After all, while others were hiding when the BPP came under attack by the authorities, the CP "actually came out and did some degree of work" on their behalf, said Seale.[49] The BPP organ sought to walk in Patterson's footsteps, urging that comrades "take black genocide before U.N.," with a photograph of Patterson nearby, accompanied by his words.[50]

A key member of the Oakland hierarchy of the BPP, David Hilliard, referred to Patterson as "an historic figure," giving him credit for developing the schema of the "Free Huey" campaign that rocked the nation after the paramount leader had been placed on trial. Patterson happened to be in Oakland when Newton was shot in a brutal confrontation with a police officer, leading to his incarceration. "Drawing on his experience," said the impressed Hilliard, "Patterson [explained] . . . the need to create a defense committee that can operate separately from the party, raise legal defense funds and propagandize about the trial." Instinctively, Patterson recommended internationalizing this struggle, "to carry Huey's story to . . . Eastern and Western Europe." An appreciative Hilliard concluded that though Patterson's "dedication to political radicalism may be a little outside my immediate experience," he acknowledged that he "merits respect: no one can have put themselves on the line and lived as long as he has without knowing something."[51]

Patterson averred that it was a "distinct pleasure" to attend a birthday party for Newton, and rehashing a tactic that worked so well for the Scottsboro defendants, he tried to "organize a world tour for Huey's mother."[52] "This young freedom fighter," he said appreciatively of Newton, "commands one of the most politically significant fronts of the Black Liberation conflict." Newton was "one of our own," he said, adding, "I am proud to say that Huey Newton is black." Adopting the jargon of the BPP, he concluded with passion, "All power to the people! . . . RIGHT ON!"[53] Patterson did more than adopt their lingo; he provided a legal and moral justification for their confrontational tactics. While pointing to the "more than 5,000 lynchings of Negro citizens [that] have gone unpunished," he pointedly observed that the U.N. Charter demonstrated that "self-defense is an inalienable right." It was the "duty of each and every citizen," he added.[54] The mutuality was reinforced when the countercultural *Berkeley Barb*, in stating the obvious—"Oakland's Panthers Know Pat"—pointed to the balding, bespectacled Communist as the "Genuine Original Black Panther."[55]

During this epoch of militancy, Patterson affirmed that the 1971 uprising at a dank prison in upstate New York was a "great battle in the national liberation struggle," while the dozens of murders that occurred at Attica were "a form of fascism [that] haunts our country."[56]

This bonhomie was not limited to Newton and Hilliard. The incarcerated BPP cofounder Bobby Seale told Patterson, "When Ericka [Huggins, a BPP leader] and I are freed from here . . . I must talk with you. I have much more to say."[57] Among other things, Seale may have wanted to thank Patterson for his avid support, as he termed the BPP leader then on trial in Chicago—where he was bound and gagged in court—as an "inspiring" leader; elevating Seale in the pantheon, he compared him to the virtually mythic Georgi Dimitrov, who famously stared down the Nazis in a 1930s courtroom.[58] Even after the BPP split,[59] a faction leader, Donald Cox, then of the Afro-American Liberation Army and the Revolutionary People's Communication Network, greeted "Pat" warmly, adding wistfully, "Its been a long time."[60] The BPP leader Kathleen Cleaver, while remonstrating against the presumed inadequacies of Negro lawyers, listed Patterson—"of Scottsboro Boy fame"—as one of the few attorneys "in the entire span of Afro-America" who were "prominent in the struggle."[61] Her spouse at the time, the faction leader Eldridge Cleaver, was known to call Patterson from exile in Algeria and—asserted the aging Communist—"said that he wanted to collaborate on genocide [campaign]." "'Rap' Brown is there" too, he said, speaking of the former SNCC leader's presumed residence in Algiers.[62]

Cleaver may have been calling to thank Patterson for his enthusiastic defense of Brown, who was then in desperate flight from the U.S. authorities. The FBI found it curious that Patterson sent a telegram from Moscow—of all places—to the BPP congratulating them for the conference on the "United Front against Fascism," held in Oakland.[63] Patterson joined the future congressman Bobby Rush of Chicago, the attorney William Kunstler, the activist Tom Hayden, and others in this effort.[64]

Thus, the FBI's concern was understandable to a degree. In that vein, certain ultra-rightists were struck by the presence of CP leaders, such as Herbert Aptheker, at critical BPP gatherings—which led one analyst to term the Oakland-based group as no more than "Communist Guerillas in the Streets."[65]

Rather rapidly, when Newton ran afoul of the California authorities, Patterson signed on as a lawyer.[66] Newton's defense committee was quick to request that Patterson "set up speaking engagements" on their behalf.[67] BPP supporters turned to Patterson when they needed to reach notables for a full-page advertisement in the *New York Times* backing the increasingly besieged activists.[68] When the BPP was in dire straits, it was Patterson who suggested "Hollywood talent" to come to their assistance—"Sidney Poitier, Harry [Belafonte], Jane Fonda, Shelley Winters, and such like."[69] Though often ailing and approaching the age of eighty during the BPP's heyday, Patterson repeatedly rallied diverse forces against the "savage attack" on the party.[70] When twenty-one Panthers in New York were swept up in a dragnet and then tried, Patterson stood by their side, along with Ossie Davis—the actor and playwright with whom he shared a close relationship—and Afeni Shakur, who was to claim a share of fame decades later as the mother of the prominent rapper and actor Tupac Shakur.[71]

This support from Patterson came clear at the March 1970 Emergency Conference to Defend the Right of the Black Panther Party to Exist at Chicago's Malcolm

X College. This conference came in the bitter aftermath of the slaying of the BPP leaders Fred Hampton and Mark Clark in the wee hours of the morning as they were in bed. Over five hundred from twenty-three states (and Canada and Germany) registered for this militant gathering, with 128 organizations represented. Strikingly, revival of the genocide petition was high on the agenda, as well as dragging the U.S. authorities to the dock of the World Court and the United Nations.[72] Unsurprisingly, it was Patterson himself—joined by Ossie Davis, Dick Gregory, and the former chief aide to Dr. King, Ralph David Abernathy—who led the session that "endorsed unanimously" a resuscitation of the genocide initiative; it was also from the Patterson session that a proposal emerged for a massive demonstration in New Haven to free Bobby Seale.[73]

In the follow-up U.N. petition, Patterson was joined by Shirley Chisholm, soon to be renowned as a stellar congresswoman from Brooklyn and candidate for U.S. president.[74] Patterson's relationship became so intimate with the BPP that he contributed his immense legal skills to a book prepared by Charles Garry that tutored attorneys on how to pick juries in politically charged cases—the problem that ensnared Newton. According to the book's introduction, "[I]t took the enthusiastic prodding of a militant black Communist lawyer who organized the defense of the 'Scottsboro' defendants, 77 year old William L. Patterson, to get the project moving."[75]

After suffering through years of imprisonment, investigation, surveillance, and harassment, Patterson's mutually beneficial relationship with the BPP was a refreshing tonic. He was pleased with the "flattering words [that] were said about me" in their newspaper. At this point—mid-1968—he was "in more or less regular correspondence" with BPP leaders and charitably admitted that "if they are making mistakes, it's on the side of militancy as I view the scene from afar."[76] While visiting BPP leaders in Oakland, he found their meetings of "vital significance" and was warmed by "the class character of those fighters," the ultimate compliment from Patterson. "It is so clear and pronounced and so healthy. No pretense. They are what they are. Bobby [Seale]'s confessions of his mistaken attitude toward some whites was [for] me an outstanding event. . . . I think we started them thinking of the principles," an apparent reference to Marxist analysis—though he reminded, "We had better learn how not to try to pose our advice and assistance in terms of our own yesterdays precisely because by the manner in which we made our yesterdays, we changed their todays." Animated with a renewed drive after conferring with these young fighters, Patterson wanted to "tell them they added 20 years to my life."[77]

When CP comrades visited Patterson in Harlem from Oakland, he was informed that "Bobby Seale and Cleaver both sent regards," for while visiting there in 1967, "we talked long about them and their organization. As for Bobby, I was deeply impressed by him," and "as for Cleaver"—notice the use of the surname in this instance—"I would like to see what the success of authorship and its cash rewards do to him. Success is, on many occasions, a thing that makes for one's undoing." Cleaver's future embrace of conservatism, after the acclaim brought by his writings, may have been anticipated by Patterson's reservations. "I have *Soul on Ice*," he said of Cleaver's premier text, "but have not finished reading it. When I spoke of his success I had in mind the book." "As for the [BPP as a whole], I think that there are some splendid young men in it," said Patterson, who apparently did not encounter any of the women leaders of this group. Communist comrades were "talking of joining up with them," though he warned of one comrade, "if he does, I am afraid that they will capture him."[78]

As the Communist lawyer John Abt observed, "There were even a few cases of comrades holding membership in both" the CP and BPP: "My old friend Bill Patterson constantly impressed upon me the importance of the Panthers as a national development."[79] Abt knew this well, since Patterson importuned him energetically for funds for Newton—"his Defense Committee is in dire need of help."[80] Patterson played a major role when his comrade George Murphy, of the publishing clan based in Baltimore, issued a mock complaint: "I've been raising funds for the Black Panther Party Defense and have also depleted my small checking account."[81]

While visiting his birthplace, now the headquarters of a resurgent form of militancy, Patterson was confronted with one of those rare and delicious moments when the past embraces the present. Meeting him at the airport was the publisher Dr. Carlton Goodlett, an affluent former leader of the NAACP in San Francisco, who drove Patterson to meet Charles Garry and the local CP leader Roscoe Procter.

This was in 1969, when the BPP was under tremendous pressure, a condition exacerbated by Newton's imprisonment—meeting with him was a prime purpose of Patterson's visit. Procter thought that the visit was important, given an incipient split in BPP ranks. According to Patterson, Garry, perhaps prematurely, "expressed complete confidence in Bobby and David as to loyalty to Huey and devotion to Marxism-Leninism. [He] felt however that [the] CIA and FBI had infiltrated [the] ranks," which proved to be prescient. Patterson listened attentively as Garry explained that he "saw Huey as [a] brilliant tactician and strategist and revolutionary." He did compliment Garry on his "splendid"—one of Patterson's favorite words—"fight" on Newton's behalf. Garry further informed him that the leading East Coast attorneys Arthur Kinoy and William Kunstler were collaborating on BPP cases. Patterson and Garry spoke for two hours before calling on Seale at BBP headquarters in Oakland and speaking for a few more hours with him on various political matters. Then Patterson and Procter conferred hours more with other BPP leaders, including David Hilliard and Raymond "Masai" Hewitt. They wanted to tape the meeting, which made Patterson a tad uneasy, but he agreed once it was explained that the words spoken were "to be used by them as instructions" for the "entire" BPP. While in this latter meeting, it became "obvious that although Bobby S." was "officially top nabob," David Hilliard "ran affairs." Still a bit skeptical, Patterson revealed that "numerous pictures [were] taken of me, allegedly for use in [the] paper." The meeting revealed that the "degree of dependence upon us"—meaning the CP—was "very great," in terms of their seeking to develop their own version of Marxism, learning how to fend off state harassment, how to organize a "mass defense," and, not least, basic strategy. "Their adaptation of Dimitrov 7th Congress report on UF [United Front] purely mechanical" and "not suitable in my opinion to [the] objective situation that obtained" in 1969. "Neither in form or content did they see what they had initiated,"[82] which on the positive side was a proliferating party of young militants, many of whom were deeply imbued with the notion of socialism, along the lines of FRELIMO in Mozambique and the MPLA in Angola and Sekou Touré in Guinea, all of whom paid some form of obeisance to the now-deposed Kwame Nkrumah; on the negative side, their very presence had infuriated Washington—the FBI not least, which thought that it had undermined Patterson in the 1950s and now years later found him influencing and directing a new generation of activists bent on bringing socialism to North America.

Patterson was impressed with the energy, enthusiasm, militancy, and fundamental intelligence of the BPP, but he worried that they would not be able to handle effectively the outraged onslaught from Washington. This concern was not alleviated when Patterson crossed the bridge spanning the bay and arrived back in San Francisco, where he chatted with the legendary leaders of the stevedores' union, Harry Bridges and Louis Goldblatt, both of whom were known to be close to the CP, which played a critical role in 1934 when the union came into being.[83] Two hours were spent with them. "Both very skeptical on future of BPP" was his conclusion, and they were reluctant to throw in their lot with the Panthers.[84] These two grizzled warhorses of labor did provide a financial contribution to facilitate Patterson completing his autobiography, however, a token of their overall goodwill.[85]

Patterson well understood their apprehensions, but, correctly, he felt that he had no choice at that juncture: he had to mobilize all the resources at his disposal to aid the BPP, a reality that was propelled by the ongoing unrest in the Bay Area and nationwide.[86] Speaking at Nashville's Fisk University in October 1969 at an anti-Vietnam War rally, the Communist Claude Lightfoot signaled the onset of a new era, while noting that his visit there "marks the first time I have been asked to speak on a black campus"; by way of comparison, "in the last five years I have spoken in at least twenty . . . universities in foreign lands."[87]

Despite the promising portent, the budding relationship between Patterson and the BPP endured a spectacular flameout. Just as the rise of the Nation of Islam was a local manifestation of a transnational phenomenon—the decline of the organized left and the rise of "narrow nationalism"—the once-promising relations between Patterson and the BPP reflected yet another global trend: the ever sharpening Sino-Soviet conflict and its domestic repercussions.

As one Panther put it, "I couldn't understand why Mao Tse-Tung was so important to Huey."[88] Neither could Patterson; or more precisely, he found it hard to accept the BPP's increasingly passionate tie to China—along with preexisting flaws, such as the glorification of the "lumpen," a beatification that was all too congruent with a nation where organized crime was prominent. All this made it difficult for him to continue his passionate support for this beset organization. For while Newton and the BPP heaped adoring praise on Mao, Patterson observed that "on the issue of war and peace, there is a chilling similarity between the 'thought of Mao' and Hitler's thought."[89]

This was more than just an ideological dispute—though it was certainly that. It was also a sharp disagreement about the feasibility of armed struggle in the United States—indeed, an unavoidable difference concerning the deifying of armed struggle as an all-purpose remedy for every ill worldwide, with those unwilling to adhere to this deeply held belief denounced. These militants also renounced a belief in "peaceful coexistence" between socialism and capitalism, which Patterson supported, as an indicator of their advocacy of armed struggle. Patterson was no pacifist; however, unlike the BPP, he tended to see armed struggle as a means, not an end, a tactic, not a strategy, which was not necessarily the view of the new rising militancy.[90]

Global factors propelled this rift between Patterson and his erstwhile Panther comrades. In 1971 an entente between China and the United States was forged, fundamentally on an anti-Soviet basis, and this created the condition for the rise of a domestic left-wing, particularly among youth, that could engage in the national sport of hostility to Moscow—while still, theoretically, retaining militant and Marxist credentials. This entente emerged after years of frosty relations between China and the Soviet Union, with the former power berating the latter for the doctrine of "peaceful coexistence," which was perceived as antithetical to anti-imperialism and armed struggle. Elaine Brown, a top BPP leader, argues that their delegation to China, led by a newly freed Newton, was one of the "central factors" in the paramount leader's evolution.[91]

This polemic metastasized when the activist then known as Stokely Carmichael joined the leadership of the BPP, bringing with him some SNCC cadre. Patterson was distraught. He worried that a "Black Panther partisan movement as projected by Carmichael demands the creation of a 'defense' wing from which provocateurs can readily operate"—already a real problem in the BPP—and the CP too, for that matter, as the still lingering (and undetected) presence of Morris Childs attested.[92]

Patterson was troubled—to put it mildly—with the "impossibility" of converting the lumpen into a vanguard political force, an idea that was a reflection of

Newton's own descent into strong-arm tactics and drugs, fueled by extensive destabilization by the state. His reservations about Cleaver then blossomed.[93] "Blacks in the USA are not a colony," argued Patterson, countering a central BPP thesis—though the once-heralded Black Belt thesis may have suggested otherwise. "The black bourgeoisie is not a colonial bourgeoisie," he said, perhaps thinking of his close friends Earl Dickerson and Dr. Carlton Goodlett, "although it has some of the characteristics" of this class. "We are not Africans," he argued—weakly in my opinion—"any more than are the blacks of Cuba or Brazil," which begged the question. He assailed the notion of "picking up the gun," which did invite further destabilization and, in any case, was driven by an inexpert reading of the Cuban Revolution and the then-current idea that a small group—like the BPP, a "subjective" factor—could by its heroism alter decisively and accelerate the "objective" factor, the ongoing crisis of capitalism. "The Black Panther Party became the far left wing of the liberation movement. That is not a vanguard role," he argued.[94]

Yes, Patterson stressed, "*the Black liberation movement is the Achilles' heel of American imperialism*," and, yes, the BPP was skilled in playing upon this frailty. But he was worried—as early as 1970—about their "weaknesses," which, if not arrested, would mean "deterioration," a tendency propelled internally by "left sectarians." Still, it was his and the CP's duty to "fight increasingly for the constitutional rights" of this self-proclaimed vanguard.[95] Despite this salve, there was little doubt that a full-scale polemic had erupted between the CP and BPP—or more precisely, between Patterson and Newton—with neither frail force standing to benefit from such a confrontation.[96]

It was unfortunate that this bitter break could not have been hashed out behind closed doors, but this was not to be. A crescendo was reached with the publication of Newton's curiously titled *Revolutionary Suicide*, which encapsulated the dilemma of BPP leaders then being mowed down systematically. It was "bankrupt," said Patterson, a "political fiasco," a "hare-brained scheme," "divisive," "fanning putschist tendencies," "anarchistic" (an intended epithet), reflecting "political immaturity." Going in the other direction, he thought, was the once-praised Seale, who now "seeks to organize and stabilize a fraction of the Democratic Party among his ghetto neighbors"—though "both courses lead to new disasters," "both are forms of narrow Black Nationalism adverse to unity." This "debacle" was not due to "the anarchism of Eldridge Cleaver alone" but had to do "with an ideology that could not bear the weight of revolutionary struggle" and thus became "counterrevolutionary in a new form."[97]

Thus, it was in 1972 that Newton publicly spoke of what "Chairman Mao teaches us," as he denounced Patterson in no uncertain terms. This was after Patterson gently analyzed the BPP, seeking to sketch the objective conditions that led to their emergence: failures of the labor leadership manacled by a fierce anticommunism, a central weakness of the NAACP as well. "White philanthropists and their Black sycophants" seemed to have attained hegemony, Patterson said. But then came the BPP with a radically different approach: "The Panthers did not lift the Black Liberation movement to an international level. The Communist Party of the US had already done that," said Patterson, but there was little doubt that the BPP had walked with agility and creativity in their footsteps. "For the first time in the history of the Black Liberation struggle," enthused Patterson, "an exclusively Black-led political party had sought the aid of science in its leaders' efforts to find a solution."[98]

Newton was outraged. Patterson's questioning of the notion that Negroes were a colony was "crap," while his neglect of Malcolm X was unconscionable. "This is not what Chairman Mao teaches us," he repeated. He scorned Patterson's "bourgeois ideology," dismissed the CP peremptorily as not constituting a "threat" to the status quo (unlike the BPP), and added derisively, "I see very little difference between their line and the Democratic Party line,"[99] which in some ways was the ultimate insult. Patterson, he asserted, using a term then popular in China to describe their erstwhile comrades in Moscow, was "revisionist and opposed to armed struggle," and a factotum of "bourgeois ideology" besides. "I think the Black Panther Party has done more in three years to mobilize the masses than the American Communist Party has in twenty years," he announced. "I think that in the whole history of the Communist Party in the USA, only about five or six people have been incarcerated for a lengthy period," he charged.[100]

One positive outcome of this flare-up was that Patterson was developing a relationship with Newton's editor, the future Nobel laureate Toni Morrison. "Huey's name calling serves no constructive purpose," Patterson told her, while adding, "I would indeed like to meet with you."[101] Morrison "read with a great . . . interest your book, *We Charge Genocide*, and wonder if you have other writings you might care to discuss with me with a view toward publication." She also admitted, "I share your sentiments regarding the title and thrust of the book," speaking of Newton's, as she pushed for a "meeting" at "lunch."[102]

But a pleasant lunch was not on the Patterson-Newton agenda. As the polemics rose in intensity, and as Newton descended into a farrago of drug binges and an exile propelled by escalating government harassment, the BPP entered an irreversible spiral of decline—which certainly was no boon for Patterson nor the CP. Still, by being obliged to retreat from the more egregious aspects of Jim Crow while embroiled in a quagmire in Southeast Asia, Washington had uncorked forces in the streets that it could hardly control. Unsurprisingly, it was during this era that the CP's organ resumed its daily publication—after a lengthy hiatus as a weekly—as it was propelled by the dual forces of anti–Jim Crow and antiwar protests.

In this context—simultaneous with the rise of the BPP—came a similarly crucial development: the global campaign to free Angela Davis, the intellectual and Communist who had been charged with assisting an attack on a courtroom in Marin County, California, in a failed attempt to free men deemed to be political prisoners, then on trial. That fatalities occurred, including a judge, in an attack on a reigning symbol of state power heightened the attention on this case. As he did with Huey P. Newton, Patterson played a central role in organizing a mass defense—except that here his role was even more enhanced, since she was a Communist and, thus, it was easier to tap Communist networks worldwide in her defense. This case, along with the BPP's ascendancy, helped to introduce a younger generation to Marxism, a tendency already driven by events in Indo-China and Southern Africa—a remarkable trend, contrary to the still-reigning anticommunism.

Though almost eighty at the time of her arrest, Patterson became a focal point of this global effort,[103] as did his spouse, who traveled to Europe on Davis's behalf[104]—a journey that caught the eye of the U.S. legation in London, which promptly informed the FBI.[105]

When Davis's defense fund held a board meeting in August 1972, the first three points of discussion on the agenda were led by Patterson.[106] It was a "political case of the first magnitude," he argued, adding that "blacks have been attracted to it largely because of its moral essence."[107] Besides, it was a "crime of government,"[108] his specialty since he had joined the CP almost a half century earlier. Though often slowed down by various ailments not uncommon in one of his advanced years, he toiled ceaselessly on her behalf. Consequently, at his birthday party in Chicago in late 1971, at the Midland Hotel on West Adams, with three hundred in attendance, the mother of Angela Davis said pointedly to Patterson, "We will never forget how tenaciously you have worked in Angela's behalf."[109] This tireless labor also involved generating positive press coverage, particularly in the black press.[110]

Marvel Cooke—a Harlem Communist whose sister married the brother of Roy Wilkins (she was once engaged to the NAACP leader and helped place him in that post in the first place)—was drawn into the Davis case, like so many others, by Patterson. She got a call from this man whom she viewed with "awe": "He called me and said he wanted to see me and could he come up. I said, 'Certainly.'" He arrived with "another party functionary," and "they talked about Angela and Angela's case and they asked me if I would work for Angela," which she did. Working alongside Patterson, she became aware of the immense reach of this case. "One day," she recalled, "I got a letter from some little woman in Austria, enclosing $4,000" for the defendant. "These little workers in Austria had sent it"—and they were joined by other "little workers" globally and within the United States itself.[111]

The British legation in Budapest reported that "much publicity has been given in the Hungarian press" to the case; "members of the American embassy told us that they are receiving an enormous amount of mail on the subject," which—it was said—were rife with "misinterpretations" that "so nettled the Americans that they have begun to reply." It reminded this diplomat of "the Rosenberg case in the early 1950s"—another example of Patterson's activism—which "culminated in the naming of a Budapest street after them," and he saw history repeating itself.[112] Speaking in East Berlin in May 1971, Patterson congratulated those in the German Democratic Republic who had protested Davis's detention. Speaking alongside the well-known writer Alex La Guma, then in exile from apartheid South Africa, Patterson praised the "widespread knowledge in the GDR about the current status of the struggles of Black Americans and the relation of these struggles to the national liberation struggles throughout the world. Meetings, demonstrations and mass letter writing involving hundreds of thousands people are taking place" there in solidarity with Professor Davis specifically and black America generally.[113]

At this symposium celebrating Robeson, Patterson was keen to "relate the current battle to free black political prisoners in the U.S. to the value of Paul's ideas," pointing to a number of Panthers, including Seale and Ericka Huggins.[114]

Patterson was not exaggerating the importance of the Davis case, and this placed his old fencing partners in the NAACP on the horns of a dilemma. It was like Scottsboro all over again, but this time with a conscious intellectual in the bullseye, guaranteed to appeal to African Americans who had placed a high value on education, since there had been a concerted effort to shield them from this precious commodity. "The Legal Department has received numerous inquiries from some branches," Roy Wilkins was told in October 1970, concerning "the Angela Davis case." The NAACP counsel, Nathaniel Jones—a future federal judge—was inclined to let her fend for herself, since "she will have at her disposal considerable financial resources."[115]

But times had changed. Just a few years earlier, NAACP leaders and HUAC had engaged in a love-fest of anticommunism, outdoing each other in their denunciation of Patterson and the CP.[116] But now Margaret Bush Wilson, the feisty St. Louis–based attorney who once worked alongside the Progressive party and now served as a leader of the NAACP board, was "affronted" when a "black woman of dignity and superior academic training [was treated] as a dangerous criminal."[117] An irate Wilkins informed her that Professor Davis "is not indigent," and besides, he said, playing the "race card" despite his repeated denunciations of black nationalism, "there is no record of Miss Davis' having requested at that time a black attorney"—which elided the roles of Howard Moore and Margaret Burnham. Anyway, he concluded triumphantly, "Miss Davis herself has reiterated her affiliation with the Communist Party," and "in the minds of a vast number of American people, the people involved remain, to use your words, 'dangerous criminals.'"[118]

Gloster Current, a self-described "ardent anticommunist," told Wilkins of his "reservations" about his posture. "First, I don't know any issue in the last twenty years which has so captivated our people, especially the young"—"this case transcends the usual NAACP concern," he emphasized. The NAACP ran the risk of being inflicted with a "propaganda black eye, if we show disinterest," and this "will not enhance our image in the Negro community," particularly since there were "rising Negro emotions on this issue," as suggested by "branches" that were now "absorbed in fund-raising" for this case.[119]

Thus, the *Chicago Defender* was among those who hailed the NAACP statement on the case—"a courageous departure from an outworn restrictive policy" on radicalism.[120] This important organ may have sought to emulate the *Baltimore Afro-American*, in which Patterson's comrade George Murphy played a leading role. It was Murphy who made what he called an "important act" in lobbying the National Association of Black Students on Davis's behalf, "with whom I operate as a sort of big brother and advise them . . . as a trustee of the Angela Davis fund." Thus, he continued, "I would expect of them [to] bring out a good, strong resolution that supports Angela"—which occurred according to plan.[121] It was Murphy who facilitated the placement of Patterson's frequent correspondence in the newspaper—at times in the face of opposition.[122]

This multifaceted grassroots support that altered the NAACP's normalized anticommunist calculus was—in a real sense—a retreat by the association, marking what may have been the most significant of Patterson's final triumphs. His jaunts to San Francisco airport were now routine, bringing him full circle to the region where he had first seen the light of day. On one of these many occasions, he drove to the Marin County Jail, where he met with his client, Professor Davis, for a tense four hours. He and his comrade, Henry Winston, passed through a metal detector before proceeding. Their comrade Kendra Alexander and the attorney Margaret Burnham were there and were thoroughly searched. They were forced to take off their shoes and blouses or shirtwaists before being admitted. Patterson was struck by the contrast between the striking edifice designed by Frank Lloyd Wright and the awful conditions under which his client was held. It was a "vicious form of solitary confinement," he said, though "she was obviously happy to see us." The "day spent with Angela was one of foremost political organizational importance," he declared, with much discussion of the plight of her codefendant, Ruchell Magee. The next day they met with local CP leaders, he reported, "on questions affecting the Bay Area and its preparation to absorb the influx of new party forces, white and black, that the Angela case and objective conditions generally make possible."[123]

Patterson was correct. The present writer resided in Berkeley during those hotly charged days and actually attended the celebration party for the defendant after she was acquitted. This case did bring more individuals, "white and black" and otherwise, to the left, including the CP. Patterson was now in his early eighties; he had less than a decade to live.

14

Death of a Revolutionary

"May I still be called your protégé?"[1]

Such was the rather droll query put to Patterson by Dr. Carlton Goodlett, the affluent Negro publisher, medic, and political activist whose influence reached into the White House, and who maintained extensive ties to diverse strata within black America. Born in Florida in 1914, he grew up in Omaha and served as leader of the NAACP chapter in Patterson's own San Francisco in the late 1940s. There he cooperated with the organized left[2]—often energetically[3]—even as Roy Wilkins was pointing toward a different course.[4] Dr. Goodlett's newspaper, the leading purveyor of news in black San Francisco, was praised by Patterson in 1962, particularly for its coverage of Moscow's peace initatives—"none equals yours in any respect," said the Communist leader.[5] Dr. Goodlett, like Earl Dickerson—"my great friend covering many years" was the Chicagoan's description of Patterson[6]—was among the black affluent with whom Patterson maintained a close relationship. "[I] hear regularly from Carlton," was Patterson's 1968 remark that could easily be extended backward and forward in time.[7] Dr. Goodlett—Patterson's "protégé"—also had access to the U.S. ruling elite: "We spent an entire day on the 16th visiting at the State Department discussing fair employment practices with the top personnel, including Dean Rusk. . . . [W]e started the day with breakfast with Hubert Humphrey and spent two hours with LBJ . . . [and] briefly presented him the proposition that the U.S. should stop bombing North Vietnam." Dr. Goodlett, planning to visit the Soviet Union and then Bulgaria, signed off—quite typically—with the arresting words: "Cordially, your protégé."[8]

As Patterson's lifespan wound down, it became evident that despite his association with a reviled organization—the CP—it was difficult to isolate him altogether, not only because of his track record, which inspired admiration, but also because many African Americans were not necessarily prone to bow to those who only recently had declared their unwavering support for Jim Crow. Thus, a man who made no secret of his desire for a revolutionary transformation of the United

States, a nation where conservatism was ingrained, continued to win adherents even as his debilities mounted and his life was expiring.

Even Patterson, at times, had to be reminded of the reality that African Americans were not as affected by the ascendant Red Scare as others. The Communist historian Herbert Aptheker felt compelled to inform him—after Patterson had questioned the receptivity to the scholar's ideas within the profession—that the "*Journal of Negro History* and *Journal of Negro Education* generally welcomed and encouraged my work—and this was true above all of Dr. Carter G. Woodson," the doyen of the field.[9]

Dr. Goodlett was also active in the international peace movement, where Communists from various regions played pivotal roles and also maintained ties to Dr. King and his top deputy, Ralph David Abernathy.[10] Weeks after King's murder, Goodlett, who knew this deputy "both as a patient and a friend," invited Patterson and Abernathy to a meeting, then agreed that "your ideas will be communicated directly to Ralph," while requesting that Patterson discuss his ideas with leading African American Reds such as "[James] Jackson, [Henry] Winston, and probably [Claude] Lightfoot and John Pittman."[11] It was Dr. Goodlett who attended to Patterson in April 1977 when he needed care in San Francisco. He was "Pat's doctor while we were there and attended him very solicitously," said Louise Patterson, which was needed, since Patterson "was quite ill" and "had to be hospitalized."[12]

Patterson had his own ties to King and his deputy. Ruth Reese—who called herself the "Black Rose"—resided in Oslo and, like others, referred to her comrade as "Pat." She knew Dr. King—"I gave a concert in his church in 1949 and renewed acquaintance with him and his wife when they came here to Oslo in 1964" to receive a Nobel Prize. Coretta Scott King "took sick while they were in Oslo," she told Patterson chattily, days after Dr. King's murder, and "Dr. and Mrs. King asked me to spend as much time with her as possible."[13] She was yet another conduit between Dr. King and Patterson; the latter leader was "deeply moved" when she chose to "dedicate" her book to him—though, he conceded, "I can't read Norwegian."[14]

In 1977, when Patterson was approaching the age of ninety, Dr. Goodlett acknowledged freely that "I have attempted to make the shadow cast by this great man a guiding signpost in marshalling my peers."[15] Thus, Dr. Goodlett strived to exert his influence on his friend's behalf, mentioning in 1980, "While in Moscow on my return home from Ethiopia I discussed critically the failure of our Soviet friends to grant Pat the [lucrative] Lenin Peace Prize during the 1970s. They were apologetic and asked for resubmission of the nomination."[16] (Patterson did receive from Moscow the Lenin Centennial Memorial Medal, delivered to him by the Soviet ambassador Anatoly Dobrynin at the U.N. Mission of the Soviet Union.)[17]

Dr. Goodlett was also the publisher of the leading black paper in San Francisco and, along with Patterson's comrade George Murphy—of the *Afro-American* chain, whose circulation was in the hundreds of thousands[18]—worked with Patterson in seeking to place a correspondent in Moscow. In that regard, Goodlett traveled to the Soviet Union in the early fall of 1973,[19] a journey duplicated by Murphy shortly thereafter, which brought warm endorsement from Patterson.[20] The issue was joined further when in 1974, Patterson praised Murphy's newspaper for detailing Moscow's aid to anticolonial projects in Africa.[21] All of these men were disappointed by the past performance of Homer Smith, who had served the Negro press for years as Soviet correspondent, at a time when Smith boasted, "it happened that I was the only Negro journalist ever stationed in Russia" and "the only Negro war correspondent on the Russian-German front."[22] Patterson revealed the importance he placed on his tie to the black press when confronting the U.S. escalation in Southeast Asia: in a move that caught the eye of the FBI, Patterson argued that the CP should stress "the racist issues," which would attract attention "from the Negro papers."[23]

Still, Dr. Goodlett's ties to Communists were so extensive that it was rumored that he had more than perfunctory ties to the CPUSA, which would have been a coup, since his newspaper, the *San Francisco Sun-Reporter*, was said to have a circulation of over one hundred thousand.[24] One of Patterson's major bases of support over the decades was the black press, not only Goodlett's organ but Murphy's too. The Murphy-Patterson tie stretched back to 1932, when they encountered each other—in a trio that included Louise Thompson—at a Scottsboro demonstration.[25]

The close relationship between Patterson and Goodlett belies the popular notion of ideological rigidity among Communists, since the publisher did not hesitate to disagree with his mentor[26]—including on the presumed bedrock issue of approach to Moscow[27]—while pursuing associations with those in Communist circles, including Paul Robeson.[28] The popular notion also is inconsistent with the tendency of figures like King and Abernathy to reject the widespread animus toward Communists, for example in 1972, when Goodlett and Abernathy joined Patterson at the United Nations—along with the civil-rights icon Ella Baker—at an "emergency conference on racism [as] as a threat to world peace."[29]

The problem for Washington was that the retreat from the egregious aspects of Jim Crow was not rapid enough for many blacks—and too fast for many whites, as reflected in the popularity of the presidential races of Alabama's segregationist governor George Wallace in 1968, then in 1972. Many blacks had failed to forget Patterson's herculean struggle against Jim Crow, which began decades ago, and saw little reason to shun him simply because Washington had seemingly changed its tune about apartheid. Thus, he remained close to the Sutton family of San Antonio, which produced the prominent Manhattan politician Percy Sutton and John Sutton, who had his own sojourn in the Soviet Union, where he and Patterson had met in the 1930s.[30] What a close relative of Sutton said about his years in what was then the first land of socialism could have been said about Patterson: "John did love the Soviet Union," not least because of its support for African liberation at a time when U.S. allies were the central proponents of colonialism.[31]

Actually, it was Robeson and his still-stellar image across class lines in black America—even as he was expelled from the mainstream in the nation at large—who not only helped to bring added attention to Patterson but also helped to attract those who aspired to walk in the actor's activist footsteps. Among these were Ossie Davis, who acted in Hollywood productions and wrote plays for Broadway and, like Goodlett, was Patterson's intermediary, allowing the Communist access to a broad array of personalities. Davis honed his skills by directing a play on the Martinsville Seven in 1950 and subsequently declared that he was attracted to Robeson and Patterson because "traditional black leadership always treated foreign affairs as the province of white folks"—quite unlike these two leaders of the left.[32] Davis, in his own argot, seemed perpetually interested in "rapping" with Patterson.[33] Following in Patterson's footsteps, Davis had a favorable opinion of the BPP and went as far as nudging Roy Wilkins in a similar direction.[34] Davis referred to him familiarly as "Pat," as the CP chairman, Henry Winston, was termed "Winnie," and in 1976 he decided that he "would most certainly appreciate a chance to chew the fat with [Patterson]."[35] It was probably more effective for Davis, not Patterson, to contact the Soviet leader Alexei Kosygin in 1972, as the latter had the ear of the White House, about the widespread "genocidal racist terror and violence" then besetting black America. Whereas President Richard Nixon was pressing the case for Soviet Jewry in Moscow, Davis countered, "We can only humbly request that you present to the President the facts of genocidal murders of their own Black nationals."[36] A copy of this message was delivered promptly to Patterson.

Patterson was one of eight members of the Board of Trustees of the Angela Davis Legal Defense Fund; Davis was the chairman.[37] "The more I hear about the party in support of Angela Davis that took place at your home," Patterson told Davis in the spring of 1972, "the more I regret our absence."[38] So close was Davis to the CP that Anthony Montiero, then a CP leader serving alongside Patterson, recalled that at the 1975 party convention, chairman Henry Winston had to intervene forcefully to bar Davis from addressing those assembled, on the grounds that it could unnecessarily jeopardize his public persona.[39] Unsurprisingly, Patterson informed Dr. Goodlett that "for my money Ossie Davis stands heads and shoulders above" other celebrities and notables—"save and except Beah."[40]

This was a reference to the actor Beah Richards, who had attained a certain prominence when playing the mother of her actual contemporary, Sidney Poitier, in the iconic movie *Guess Who's Coming to Dinner*. The Pattersons had sheltered this struggling performer for years before she was able to establish herself. To her, he was simply "Mr. P"—also the title of a poem she wrote in his honor.[41] "The most fortunate event of my life," she told him in 1978, well after she had established herself as a formidable presence in the entertainment industry, "was meeting you, your family and associates. Each day confirms it."⁴² "Tell Beulah I think of her quite often," Patterson told his spouse from his cramped prison cell in 1954. "Her poetry helps me. What wonderful growth she has shown since her eyes began to open."⁴³ "Tell Beulah," he instructed his spouse in early 1955, while still jailed, "that while she was born in an era in which her splendid talents could be ignored, there is some great consolation in knowing that she lives in the twilight of that horrible period," then adding, "give Beulah one or two" kisses on his behalf.⁴⁴ "You are a superb artist," he told Richards, "you must be helped to continue,"⁴⁵ which she did, going on to climb the greasy pole of success in Hollywood.

Richards was joined in her praise by Josephine Baker, the renowned singer, actor, and dancer, who departed Jim Crow St. Louis for fame and fortune in Paris.⁴⁶ The sadly unsung black playwright Theodore Ward had been supported financially by Patterson at a time when the Communist leader could hardly support his family; Patterson was thanked accordingly for his "generous loan."⁴⁷ The poet and journalist Frank Marshall Davis, who knew Patterson from Chicago before decamping to Honolulu, where he became a close friend of the family that produced U.S. President Barack Obama, was sufficiently bold to write an incarcerated Patterson in 1954 (guaranteeing further scrutiny at a time when the powerful left in Hawaii was already being bombarded)⁴⁸ and joining a tribute to him in 1967.⁴⁹ Davis and Dickerson had worked alongside Patterson in the Chicago branch of the CRC.⁵⁰ Echoing Davis, the prolific Hollywood screenwriter and historian John Howard Lawson, the embodiment of the infamous "blacklist," summed up the sentiments of numerous creative artists when he said simply, "I salute William Patterson."⁵¹ In this context, Patterson dipped into critiques of popular television comedies.⁵²

The celebrated muckraking writer of British descent Jessica Mitford called Patterson "one of my best friends,"⁵³ a relationship that endured even after she sharply criticized his CP in her well-reviewed book: he referred to it dismissively as not a "positive contribution to the struggle."⁵⁴ Mitford nonetheless provided the Pattersons with a bouquet of praise in 1975; she reminded the politicized couple—quite appropriately—that though the Freedom Riders were the immediate "catalysts for change" in the Deep South, it was cases like that of Willie McGee that had "laid the foundation."⁵⁵ Anne Braden, who, like Mitford, received some of her earliest political tutelage in a rich history of activism in the ranks of the CRC, deemed Patterson her "mentor"; his "advice set a course for the rest of her life," particularly about the shockingly neglected topic of "organizing whites."⁵⁶

In other words, as Patterson reached the twilight of his lengthy career, marked by stunning victories and ignominious defeats, he was still wielding influence in diverse circles.

Ironically, his influence was reflected in the corridors of power in London, Washington's close ally. In a "confidential" report in 1966, Sir Patrick Dean conceded that the accelerating "revolution in the status of the American Negro owes an incalculable amount . . . to the new international role of the United States." The "placing of the headquarters of the United Nations with its insistence on human rights not much more than a mile or so from the greatest slum in America was bound to foster a feeling if not of identification, certainly a sympathy with the young African nations," which was reflected in the work of Patterson's other protégé, Lorraine Hansberry. Hansberry exemplified this "increasingly identifiable Negro viewpoint on matters of foreign policy," which could circumscribe the republic's unilateralism.[57] London's man in Liberia noticed that this trend had crossed the Atlantic, as those Africans tended to "follow events in the Negro struggle" in the United States "with close interest" and uncertain impact on North Atlantic interests.[58] Even President Lyndon Johnson conceded to his British counterpart that "you are certainly right when you say that this is only part of a world-wide problem," meaning Jim Crow and its torturous legacy.[59]

In some ways, Patterson's example was rising as he was expiring; he had come full circle in his dying days, returning to spirited sparring with his combatant from the 1930s, Roy Wilkins of the NAACP. The latter's reluctant support for Angela Davis did not becalm Patterson. In the 1970s he was still pursuing Wilkins aggressively, hammer and tong. He was a "reformist"—not a compliment—"and ideologist who supports the existing establishment"—and an apologist for "imperialism" besides.[60] "He has never with exactitude and clarity designated the enemy of the people," charged Patterson.[61] He was incensed by Wilkins's attack on the recently slain political prisoner George Jackson, killed by prison guards during an alleged escape,[62] just as he was irked by attacks on Dr. King's antiwar views.[63]

Though some of these comments were conveyed privately, as Patterson became increasingly infirm, he wrote more—particularly for the *Afro-American*—and became a stern critic of mainstream leaders who did not meet his exacting standards. At times this was at the instigation of George Murphy, such as when he advised Patterson to assail the longtime NAACP leader Alfred Baker Lewis.[64] Wilkins's close colleague Clarence Mitchell was also reproved sharply when he was deemed to be insufficiently critical of the high-court nomination of William Rehnquist.[65] As for Ralph Bunche, who had taken a long journey from the left to the citadel of power at the United Nations, Patterson acidulously commented that "[he] did not serve the people black or white. He did not serve labor."[66]

Given his past association with Abernathy, it was foreseeable that Patterson would support the Atlanta-based pastor when he came into conflict with his deputy, the Rev. Jesse Jackson of Chicago; Patterson worried that Jackson would "give priority to the problems of black business," while expressing "deep regret in the break among freedom fighters."[67] He bewailed the fact that the Congress on Racial Equality (CORE) was "splintering" and like Jackson, as he saw things, "going into the business field with the ghetto market its objective." Whitney Young of the National Urban League "gives them bombastic support," though "the ghetto market will not worry imperialism in the least, while CORE as a militant organization presents many dangers." The NAACP "youth is in rebellion," which "may mean that a split off will feed militancy everywhere," he said with optimism.[68]

As for Wilkins's fellow anticommunist and leading politician, Hubert Humphrey, Patterson dismissed him as a "racist law and order man," while in the pivotal 1968 presidential election he touted this presidential candidate's opponents: "Why should one forget [Dick] Gregory, [Eldridge] Cleaver, and [Charlene] Mitchell?"[69] Humphrey, he spat out, "offered no positive choice."[70] Humphrey's opponent, Richard M. Nixon, was no prize either, he thought, applauding when Nixon was driven out of office in 1974, since "had Watergate succeeded, the gateway to an American brand of fascism would have been opened wide."[71] Subsequently, Humphrey's counterpart, the Democratic presidential candidate Jimmy Carter, was derided as a "peanut vendor" allied with a "crew of demagogues, political mesmerizers, and jingoists." In 1976, as ever, he asked, "Do we not need [then] an independent party?"[72] Ample evidence for this provocative proposition was provided, he thought, by the rise to the U.S. Senate of Daniel Patrick Moynihan—on the Democratic party ticket, since he was "always" a "confusionist [sic] in matters of race."[73] Meanwhile, the Democrats' labor supporters "fail to fight for civil rights," he added, unlike Congressman Adam Clayton Powell, who was besieged at the time.[74]

Even after the BPP had weakened severely, Patterson continued to adopt a militant view of what he routinely called the "black liberation movement" of the United States, which was a "pivotal point in all the struggles against American reaction on the internal front. It is part and parcel of the revolutionary struggles waged on a world scale against the imperialists [and] neo-colonialists, The situation could not be otherwise," he declaimed.[75] As he saw it in 1970, "The American domestic situation is becoming a threat to international peace, so we will take it to the U.N."—"the racism suffered by 40 million Americans cannot be regarded as strictly an American affair." Making the transoceanic connection, he observed that "the U.N. has intervened in some affairs in African nations where the domestic-foreign line was curiously fuzzed," and since "American racism has also become an export commodity, spreading the germs of dehumanization overseas," there was all the more reason for external intervention.[76] Jim Crow and its troubled legacy, he said, "falls under U.N. jurisdiction as rightfully as does the racism of South Africa."[77]

This continued militancy was unaccompanied by implicit defense of the disappearing legacy of the BPP. In commenting on a screenplay concerning the zenith of their activism, he conceded, "Emotionally I was deeply moved"—yet, he also conceded, neither "'kill the pigs! [nor] 'Burn baby burn!' are . . . slogans of the day or hour."[78] Because—conceptually—he continued to place the freedom struggle of African Americans in a context not unlike what was unfolding, for example, in Southern Africa, he sought parallel remedies for both: internationalization and repeated appeals to the United Nations, not unlike the genocide petition, a call he reiterated in the BPP organ in 1970[79] and again in 1974.[80] He accompanied this with an impassioned appeal for the United Nations to oust apartheid South Africa from membership,[81] not least because apartheid itself "weakens the national liberation struggles of all colonials and the liberation battles of the 'colored' people of these United States," meaning blacks, indigenes, and those of Mexican origin—groups he increasingly addressed as his final days wound down.[82] Patterson also paid attention to the plight of the blacks in Brazil, which he envisioned as an essential part of this Pan-African circle of solidarity.[83] It was also at the United Nations that Patterson endorsed the controversial 1975 resolution that basically equated Zionism and racism,[84] a view of his that was driven in part by an attempt to provide cover for other black leaders.[85]

Inevitably, this political initiative was accompanied by globetrotting, now a Patterson specialty, well into his ninth decade. When in 1970 he and his spouse departed Kennedy Airport in Queens for Prague, the FBI—per usual—took note.[86] "My wife and I have just returned from one of the most spiritually exciting, inspiring, politically informative vacations of my life," he said in the spring of 1974, speaking of socialist Cuba, his first journey there since the 1930s.[87] That same year he was pleased to welcome a trans-Atlantic visitor, his Soviet daughter, Anna Patterson, whom years ago he had thought had perished. Resembling him (she had a sizable "Afro" hairdo), this thirty-five-year-old journalist resided in Leningrad and seemed to resemble her father in other ways: "The main thing that I do not understand," said the befuddled scribe during a visit to the office of the *Afro-American*, "is the idea of private ownership of many things." Appropriately enrolled in the International Working Class Movement Research Institute, she was in the United States for months while completing work for an advanced degree.[88]

During that same jam-packed year, Patterson and his spouse visited Mexico City, where they communed with the formidable sculptress Elizabeth Catlett and her husband, Pancho Mora. "They were wonderful to us," said Louise Patterson, "met us, housed us, fed us and took us everywhere." Havana "reminded" her of "Uzbekistan skies though there the blue is deeper," with this capital following a stop in Camaguey.[89] Perhaps the high point of their enthralling visit was meeting Pham Van Dong of Vietnam, at a time when the U.S. war was still raging.[90]

The FBI also was able to discover what occurred months later, while Patterson in Prague became "very ill. He has been confined to a hospital and he also has a hairline break in his hip," along with having suffered a "heart attack," all ominous turns for a man of his age.[91] During that same year, 1972, he reported that while visiting East Germany, "for the greater part I was either in the hospital or a rest home" near Potsdam.[92]

In late 1979, Louise Patterson told the novelist Alice Childress that the aging Communist leader was again quite ill, and though he was receiving the "best of care (private nurses and his personal physician's daily visits)," he "doesn't seem to respond too well." The harried Mrs. Patterson was "so concerned" that "I haven't done much other than [go] to the hospital every day."[93]

Some of Patterson's health problems were exacerbated during his stay in prison. He lost weight,[94] and once his hay fever had flared up with such intensity that, he confessed, it "has truly left me feeling so miserable."[95] This latter ailment, in his own words, "wrought havoc" on his well-being.[96] Yet even before his stay in a prison cell, he was diagnosed as having a "descending colon diverticulitis with a palpable mass."[97] By 1971, the CP leader Helen Winter was lamenting that Patterson, "for health reasons," was "unable to participate and make the contributions that you usually do."[98] Patterson revealed simultaneously that he had "been out now about a month" and was reeling from "pains in the back which are extremely persistent"—which may have been an indicator of the kidney problems that eventually took a severe toll upon his increasingly frail body.[99]

Still, apparently hale and hearty, at his seventy-fifth birthday party Patterson boasted, "I have the best doctor in the world," and thus he expected to live another twenty-five years, at which point he expected to say to Henry Winston, "Congratulations, Comrade President!"[100] At his eightieth birthday celebration in Chicago, an optimistic Patterson was "encouraged to suggest that we look ahead to another birthday dinner twenty years from now" that "could be in a Socialist United States."[101]

By February 1980, Mary Lou Patterson reported glumly that "twice over the past four months Pat . . . has been in the hospital in critical condition. Each time he rallied and improved. The last hospital admission one month ago was for kidney failure. He required and continues to receive 24 hour special nursing care," which was a "very expensive $90.00 per day," requiring her to request that those so solicited to "please send your contribution."[102] A few weeks after this plea—on March 5, 1980—Patterson died [103] at Union Hospital in the Bronx.[104] He was eighty-nine years old.[105]

The salutations in his honor already had been immense. An exhilarated supporter of Patterson, impressed with his versatile contributions, had chosen to designate him as "the Frederick Douglass of our times."[106] The historian and Communist Herbert Aptheker had upped the ante by terming Patterson "a giant in the mold of Douglass, Robeson, and Du Bois."[107] The affluent and progressive black publisher Dr. Carlton Goodlett, who resided in San Francisco, asserted at the time of Patterson's death that "his passing represents the going home of the last of the great triumvirate of the twentieth century—Du Bois, Paul [Robeson], and now Patterson. . . . As I look back upon the lives of these three great men whom I have had the privilege of knowing, it seems that Pat had the greatest effect."[108] Naturally, Robeson had termed his ally "one of the greatest of men, known throughout the world."[109]

His death led predictably to his being showered with such effusive praise. Condolences poured in from all over the world, including from the past and future leader of Guyana, Cheddi Jagan;[110] leaders from South Africa, including the Communist party[111] and Nelson Mandela's African National Congress (the representative of which praised the genocide petition, which "facilitated the beginning of the international campaign for the isolation of the apartheid regime [for] a similar crime");[112] Congressman Ronald V. Dellums of Oakland;[113] and Communist parties too numerous to mention, including Vietnam,[114] were among the praise singers.

The memorial for Patterson in Los Angeles took place in the church of Dr. King's old comrade, the Rev. James Lawson, with the actors William Marshall, Beah Richards, and Frances Williams providing remarks.[115] At the memorial in Oakland at the St. Augustine Episcopal church at Twenty-ninth and Telegraph Avenue, remarks were provided by Angela Davis and Maya Angelou.[116] At Harlem's Convent Avenue Baptist church on West 145th Street, Beah Richards appeared again, along with Ruby Dee, Judge Bruce Wright, and Ossie Davis, who spoke effusively and metaphorically.[117]

Patterson left behind memories of a life of struggle shaped by an all-pervading hatred of Jim Crow and imperialism; more than that, he saw the path to socialism as paved by the struggle for democratic rights—and to that ideal he was devoted to his last breath. What about his devotion to Moscow and the socialist camp? Does that discredit his accomplishments? After all, Patterson informed the intellectual Loften Mitchell in 1972, "See East Germany—see the Socialist World. It's the future and it works."[118] Even the continued existence of Cuba, Vietnam, China, and North Korea, as I write, does not erode the reality that—like many—Patterson did not envision the earth-shaking changes of 1989 (though little has been made of the fact that socialism suffered rollback in Europe but not elsewhere). Does this allegiance eviscerate his contribution to the anti–Jim Crow cause? I don't think so. Does the repeated attempt by Abraham Lincoln to deport Africans from the United States discredit his accomplishments? Does the crime of Jim Crow discredit the accomplishments of Franklin D. Roosevelt, who presided over this outrage? Or do we countenance a kind of "victors' history," where only those who are not overthrown are worthy of praise? A major reason for Patterson's solidarity with Moscow was Soviet aid to national liberation in Africa—a cause generally opposed by Washington; in other words, his view of Moscow was not unlike that of Washington itself during the 1941–45 era.

In analyzing the post-1945 scene, Patterson asserted correctly that "most black leaders at the time did not critically examine the world scene and how black masses related to it."[119] This is not just an accurate assessment, it is also a devastating and ongoing critique insofar as it remains true. The rise of China, Brazil, and India and the radically transformed global relations of forces today bids fair to turn the entire planet upside down, destabilizing what were thought to be eternal verities and demanding new thinking—thinking that is largely absent in black America, not least because of the discrediting and ignoring of those like Patterson who contributed so heavily to the erosion of Jim Crow and possessed the kind of global analysis that is needed now more than ever. This great ideological divide was solidified during the Red Scare when—ironically—black rights received a boost, but this was a ultimately a limited and limiting reform because the price of the ticket (the diminished influence of leaders like Patterson) hardly prepared a now-beset black America for the Copernican changes that have swept across the globe. Whatever criticism can be made of Patterson, it cannot be said that he committed the profound error of ignoring the world when making a domestic analysis.

And what about the victims of Jim Crow, to whom he devoted most of his life, to the point where this once relatively affluent attorney, when expiring, barely had enough in his bank account to cover his medical expenses? Did African Americans gain when the organized left—Patterson, Du Bois, Ferdinand Smith, Claudia Jones, Shirley Graham, and Ben Davis—were cast into an ideological purgatory? Or was the right wing strengthened when the left was weakened to the detriment, most notably, of African Americans, who tended to share a common terrain—the Deep South—where conservatism was strongest and meanest?

"Don't forget," said Patterson in 1967, "the revolution is ahead. It can't be stopped. We won't make it," he instructed his friend, Matt Crawford, "but the words we use may help those who will." These were his parting words as he looked forward to a time "when the normal way of life itself will be revolutionary."[120] "Au revoir but not goodbye."[121]

NOTES

Introduction

1. Draft Autobiography of William L. Patterson, box 14, folder 15, William L. Patterson Papers, Howard University, Washington, D.C (hereafter William Patterson Papers). Also present in Paris was the well-known U.S. diplomat Ralph Bunche—an African American—then on a path from left to center. See also William Patterson to Louise Thompson Patterson, December 1951, box 17, folder 22, William Patterson Papers: "Bunche was there until he saw me then he ran for cover. Several times he has come face to face with me at the Palais des Chaillot [sic] and on each occasion he has turned aside." Unless otherwise indicated, all references to the William Patterson Papers refer to those at Howard.

2. Gerald Horne, *Red Seas: Ferdinand Smith and Radical Black Sailors in the United States and Jamaica* (New York: New York University Press, 2005).

3. Paul Robeson on William Patterson, August 1951, in *Paul Robeson Speaks: Writings, Speeches, Interviews, 1918–1974*, ed. Philip S. Foner (New York: Brunner Mazel, 1978), 283–85.

4. *Baltimore Afro-American,* 2 February 1952.

5. *Black Dispatch* [Oklahoma City], 29 March 1952.

6. Barbara Foley, *Wrestling with the Left: The Making of Ralph Ellison's* Invisible Man (Durham, N.C.: Duke University Press, 2010), 31.

7. Michael Brown, *The Historiography of Communism* (Philadelphia: Temple University Press, 2009).

8. Roy Wilkins to Walter White, 1 May 1946, box II, A369, folder 2, NAACP Papers, Library of Congress, Washington, D.C. (hereafter NAACP Papers).

9. Marian Perry to Walter White, 7 May 1946, box II, A369, folder 2, NAACP Papers.

10. Roy Wilkins to Rowland Watts, 15 December 1949, box II, A369, folder 2, NAACP Papers.

11. Roy Wilkins to C. B. Baldwin, 10 January 1950, box II, A369, folder 2, NAACP Papers.

12. *Pittsburgh Courier,* 25 August 1951.

13. Genna Rae McNeil, *Groundwork: Charles Hamilton Houston and the Struggle for Civil Rights* (Philadelphia: University of Pennsylvania Press, 1983), 101, 108.

14. Houston repeatedly donated funds to the ILD. See Charles Hamilton Houston to William L. Patterson, 6 January 1933, receipts and acknowledgments for Houston donations to ILD, 2 August 1931, 12 September 1931, 30 December 1932, 11 April 1933, 23 December 1932, box 26, Charles Hamilton Houston Papers, Howard University, Washington, D.C. (hereafter Charles Hamilton Houston Papers).

15. Charles Hamilton in debate with Bernard Ades before the Liberal Club of Howard University, 28 March 1935, box 26; Charles Hamilton Houston to ILD, 4 May 1933, box 26, Charles Hamilton Houston Papers.

16. Gerald Horne, *Negro Comrades of the Crown: African Americans and the British Empire Fight the U.S. before Emancipation* (New York: New York University Press, 2012).

17. Remarks by William Patterson, ca. 1956, box 1, William Patterson Papers, New York University.

18. Press Release, 6 November 1950, Press Releases Concerning the Martinsville Seven, University of Virginia, Charlottesville.

19. Blas Roca, *The Cuban Revolution: Report to the Eighth National Congress of the Popular Socialist Party of Cuba* (New York: New Century, 1961), 71.

20. Maria Holm, "Love across the Color Line: The Limits of German and American Democracy, 1945–1968," in *Germans and African-Americans: Two Centuries of Exchange*, ed. Larry A. Greene and Anke Ortlepp (Jackson: University Press of Mississippi, 2011), 105–25, 110.

21. Abram Harris, "Lenin Casts His Shadow upon Africa," *The Crisis* 31.6 (April 1926): 272–75, 272.

22. *Pittsburgh Courier*, 24 May 1951.

23. This insight was recognized by the renowned Soviet writer Maxim Gorki, addressing a U.S. audience. *Negro Worker* 2.1–2 (January–February 1932): 13–16, 14.

24. Walter White to President Hoover, 13 November 1930, box 107, Presidential Papers: Subject Files, Herbert Hoover Presidential Library, West Branch, Iowa.

25. Walter White to President Hoover, 20 October 1930, box 107, Presidential Papers: Subject Files, Herbert Hoover Presidential Library, West Branch, Iowa.

26. Benjamin Davis Sr. to President Hoover, 4 August 1930, box 521, Presidential Papers: Secretary's File, Herbert Hoover Presidential Library, West Branch, Iowa.

27. Kampfgemenschaft fuer Rote Sportsinheit to U.S. Government, 3 March 1932, Record Group 59, Decimal File, 1930–39, 811.4016, National Archives and Records Administration, College Park, Md. (hereafter NARA-CP).

28. Felix Cole to Secretary of State, 18 February 1932, Record Group 59, Decimal File, 1930–39, 811.4016, NARA-CP.

29. Memorandum, 18 April 1932, RG 59, Decimal File, 1930–39, 811.4016, NARA-CP.

30. M. K. Moorhead, U.S. Consulate to Secretary of State, 27 August 1931, Record Group 59, Decimal File, 1930–39, 811.4016, NARA-CP.

31. James Ford, "Scottsboro before the World," *Labor Defender* (April 1932). According to this Negro Communist leader, "[W]e received protests" on the Scottsboro case "from workers in colonial countries. As far away as Australia, New Zealand, and Japan. . . . German workers held demonstrations before the American consulate at Hamburg . . . Berlin, Dresden, and Cologne. . . . [B]ottles were hurled thru windows of American consulates. . . . [I]n South Africa protest meetings were held. . . . [O]n the occasion of the holding of the World Congress of the Second 'Socialist' International in Vienna in July 1931, this writer spoke," though afterwards Ford was "arrested, held in jail three days, and deported." (This ILD journal can be found at New York University. It can also be found at the University of North Carolina at Chapel Hill.)

32. G. S. Messersmith to Secretary of State, 17 February 1932, RG 59, Decimal File, 1930–39, 811.4016, NARA-CP.

33. Roy Wilkins, "Stalin's Greatest Defeat," *American Magazine* 152.6 (December 1951): 21, 107–10, 108, box II, A68, folder 6, NAACP Papers.

34. Qtd. in Glenda Elizabeth Gilmore, *Defying Dixie: The Radical Roots of Civil Rights, 1919–1950* (New York: Norton, 2008), 124.

35. Testimony of William L. Patterson, 24 May 1955, Part II, Reel 27, Records of the Subversive Activities Control Board, 1950–72, NARA-CP. See Allison Blakely, *Russia and the Negro: Blacks in Russian History and Thought* (Washington, D.C.: Howard University Press, 1988), 87. Patterson married Vera Gorokhovskaia in 1929, with whom he fathered two daughters. See also FBI Report, 11 June 1943, 100-39-22, William Patterson/FBI/FOIA File, Gerald Horne Papers, Schomburg Center, New York Public Library (hereafter Patterson/FBI/FOIA File): Patterson reported that he married "Tamara Efremova" born in Siberia in 1907 on December 1, 1934.

36. Draft Autobiography of William L. Patterson, box 13, folder 35, William Patterson Papers.

37. Benjamin Gitlow, *I Confess* (New York: Dutton, 1940), 482. For more on this point, see Sheridan Johns to Otto Huiswood, 8 August 1961, Hermina Huiswood Papers, New York University.

38. Report from U.S. Embassy, Havana, to U.S. Secretary of State, 25 May 1934, Record Group 59, Decimal File, 1930–39, 837.00B/145, NARA-CP

39. Gitlow, *I Confess,* 480.

40. Michael Gold, "William Patterson: Militant Leader," *Masses and Mainstream* 4.2 (February 1951): 34–43, 35, 37, 38.

41. Draft Autobiography of William L. Patterson, box 13, folder 36, William Patterson Papers.

42. Report, 17 June 1952, 100-139-202, Patterson/FBI/FOIA File. In the same collection, see also Special Agent, New York, to FBI Director, 21 July 1961, 100-39-402: Patterson "admitted membership in the CP underground in Germany in 1934–1937."

43. Testimony of William Patterson, 26 July 1957, Part II, Reel 27, Records of the Subversive Activities Control Board, NARA-CP.

44. Mollie Moon to "Darling Boys," 11 May 1933, George Padmore Collection, Princeton University, Princeton, N.J.

45. Draft Autobiography of William L. Patterson, box 13, folder 13, William Patterson Papers.

46. Louise Thompson, "Southern Terror," *The Crisis* 41.11 (November 1934): 327–28.

47. Ossie Davis to Frances Williams, 14 February 1989, box 10, folder 18, Frances Williams Papers, Southern California Library for Social Studies and Research, Los Angeles. Davis—along with other luminaries of the black literati—referred to William Patterson as the "Communist Guru." See, for example, Ossie Davis and Ruby Dee, *With Ossie and Ruby: In This Life Together* (New York: Morrow, 1998), 178, 292.

48. *Los Angeles Times,* 16 September 2000. See also Testimony of Julia Brown, U.S. Congress, House of Representatives, Committee on Un-American Activities, 87th Cong., 2d Sess., "Communist Activities in the Cleveland Area, Part 1," 4–5 June 1962 (Washington, D.C.: Government Printing Office, 1962).

49. Interview with William Patterson, n.d., box 3, folder 7, William Patterson Papers.

50. Julian Mayfield to "Dear Louise," 27 April 1980, box 24, folder 1, Louise Thompson Patterson Papers, Emory University (hereafter Louise Thompson Patterson Papers).

51. Arnold Rampersad, *The Life of Langston Hughes,* vol. 2 (New York: Oxford University Press, 1988), 93.

52. *Midwest Daily Record* [Chicago], 7 October 1939. See also Davarian Baldwin, *Chicago's New Negroes: Modernity, the Great Migration, and Black Urban Life* (Chapel Hill: University of North Carolina Press, 2007).

53. See Claude Lightfoot, *Chicago Slums to World Politics: The Autobiography of Claude M. Lightfoot* (New York: International, 1986), 83. Dickerson described Patterson as "my great friend covering many years." Earl Dickerson to Louise T. Patterson, 13 March 1980, box 19, James Jackson Papers, New York University.

54. Ben Burns, *Nitty Gritty: A White Editor in Black Journalism* (Jackson: University Press of Mississippi, 1996), 4, 36. Burns served as executive editor of Johnson's *Negro Digest*. Contributing editors included Frank Marshall Davis, Eslanda Robeson, Earl Conrad, and Carey McWilliams. See *Negro Digest,* October 1947, box 16, Arthur Capper Papers, Kansas Historical Society, Topeka. See also John H. Johnson, *Succeeding against the Odds* (New York: Warner, 1989), 120.

55. *Midwest Daily Record,* 16 December 1939.

56. *Chicago Defender,* 3 June 1944.

57. *Baltimore Afro-American,* 26 December 1942. See also FBI Report, 6 October 1944, 100-5912, 100-39-59, Patterson/FBI/FOIA File.

58. Claude McKay, *Harlem: Negro Metropolis* (New York: Dutton, 1940), 252.

59. *Pittsburgh Courier,* 12 August 1950.

60. Junius Scales to "Dear Friend," 2 May 1955, box 4, folder 6, John Daschbach Papers, University of Washington, Seattle.

61. Testimony of David Brown, 3 May 1955, Reel 26, Part II, Records of Subversive Activities Control Board, NARA-CP.

62. Gerald Horne, *Communist Front? The Civil Rights Congress, 1946–1956* (London: Associated University Presses, 1988).

63. *Pittsburgh Courier,* 20 November 1954.

64. Lawrence P. Jackson, *The Indignant Generation: A Narrative History of African American Writers and Critics, 1934–1960* (Princeton, N.J.: Princeton University Press, 2011), 404. See also J. Saunders Redding, *An American in India: A Personal Report on the Indian Dilemma and the Nature of Her Conflicts* (Indianapolis: Bobbs-Merrill, 1954).

65. William Patterson to Louise Thompson Patterson, 27 July 1954, box 5, folder 2, William Patterson Papers.

66. Article by William Patterson, June 1954, box 11, folder 33, William Patterson Papers.

67. Press Release, 6 November 1950, Press Releases Concerning the Martinsville Seven, University of Virginia, Charlottesville.

68. Alex Heard, *The Eyes of Willie McGee: A Tragedy of Race, Sex, and Secrets in the Jim Crow South* (New York: HarperCollins, 2010), 328.

69. *East Bay Express* [Oakland], 20 March 1992, box 4, folder 10, Louise Thompson PattersonPapers. It was in 1956 that the FBI formulated COINTELPRO—an upgraded counterintelligence program—that initially targeted Patterson's party but quickly expanded. The program sought to influence organized crime to attack the CP. In 1975, five years before Patterson's death, the FBI reported that it had launched 1,388 COINTELPRO initiatives between 1956 and 1971: unsurprisingly, membership shrunk from eighty thousand in 1946 to less than two thousand by the time of Patterson's death. See, for example, Ward Churchill and Jim Vander Wall, eds., *The COINTELPRO Papers: Documents from the FBI's Secret War against Dissent in the United States* (Cambridge, Mass.: South End, 2002), 40, 42, 47.

70. Gerald Horne, *Black Liberation/Red Scare: Ben Davis and the Communist Party* (Newark: University of Delaware Press, 1994).

71. Meredith L. Roman, "Another Kind of Freedom: The Soviet Experiment with Antiracism and Its Image as a Raceless Society, 1928–1936" (Ph.D. diss., Michigan State University,

2005, 1). On December 1, 1958, amid a panoply of crises, U.S. Senator Hubert Humphrey had an eight-hour meeting with the Soviet leader Nikita Khruschev. At one point, according to the garrulous senator, his counterpart "tore off on a whole long lecture like I wish I could remember [because it would have been] the best speech I could ever make in my life on antiracism. Boy, he gave me a talk on that." In Moscow, "'speaking antiracism' became one form of "speaking Bolshevik." See also William Taubman, *Khrushchev: The Man and His Era* (New York: Norton, 2003), 406–7; Lyubov Ginsburg, "Confronting the Cold War Legacy: The Forgotten History of the American Colony in St. Petersburg, a Case Study of Reconciliation" (Ph.D. diss., University of Kansas, 2010), 115. As evidenced by the prominence of Alexander Pushkin, Russia's stance toward those of African descent diverged sharply from the pattern that existed in the United States. Thus, there were "quite a few Americans of African descent" in Russia in the nineteenth century, to the point that "many Russians believed that the Negroes they saw were typical Americans; they thought that all the English-speaking white men were British." See Mina Curtiss, "Some American Negroes in Russia in the Nineteenth Century," *Massachusetts Review* 9.2 (Spring 1968): 268–96.

72. *Washington Afro-American,* 29 June 1957.

73. Memorandum, 3 February 1959, 100-23825-6956, Ben Davis, FBI/FOIA Files, Gerald Horne Papers, Schomburg Center, New York Public Library (hereafter Ben Davis/FBI/FOIA File). At the Patterson memorial in Chicago in 1980, the writer Richard Durham "said he first met Patterson while a reporter assigned to interview him" and later "quoted Dr. Martin Luther King Jr. as having said during the Selma [Alabama] marches that his campaign to expose national oppression was encouraged by Patterson's own civil rights campaign earlier. King said that those campaigns led by Patterson gave him hope that a national movement against oppression could be built." *Daily World,* ca. March 1980, box 24, folder 5, Louise Thompson Patterson Papers.

74. Howard Fast, *The Naked God: The Writer and the Communist Party* (New York: Praeger, 1957), 7, 50.

75. Howard Fast, *Being Red: A Memoir* (Boston: Houghton Mifflin, 1990), 183, 316.

76. John Barron, *Operation Solo: The FBI's Man in the Kremlin* (Washington, D.C.: Regnery, 1996). For more on Childs, see Tim Weiner, *Enemies: A History of the FBI* (New York: Random House, 2012).

77. Director, FBI to SAC, Chicago, 25 July 1957, 100-3-81, 100-33729, Patterson/FBI/FOIA File. Also blocked was Patterson's attempt, in the FBI's words, "to determine if a Negro could get an agency for sending parcels to Russia to engage in foreign trade with the Russians." Patterson "revealed he had also spoken to [Juliusz] Katz-Suchy about this matter in connection with Poland." See also Special Agent, New York, to Director of FBI, 2 October 1957, 100-39-311; FBI Report, New York, 31 December 1959, 100-39-356, Patterson/FBI/FOIA File. Patterson "has had contact with an unnamed member of the Czechoslovakian Diplomatic Corps. According to this informant, Patterson talked about the need for money for work in the Negro field and he was informed that his request for funds would be given consideration."

78. Report by FBI, New York office, 29 April 1960, 100-39-376, Patterson/FBI/FOIA File. Patterson was "pushing plans for an international campaign charging mistreatment of children in the U.S. This campaign would charge that there is a denial of integration in education, particularly in Little Rock . . . and other places in the Southern part of the U.S. An effort will be made to take this charge of mistreatment of children before the U.N. . . . Patterson said he had discussed this campaign with the First Secretary of the Czechoslovakian Embassy."

79. William Patterson to Matt Crawford, 22 December 1967, box 17, folder 3, Matt Crawford Papers, Emory University. See also Special Agent, New York, to FBI Director, 13 February 1969, 100-161993, 105-165705, 105-165706–873, Patterson/FBI/FOIA File.

80. Fay Stender to H. V. Field, 19 June 1969, box 4, folder 18, Louise Thompson Patterson Papers. On Patterson's pervasive influence on the BPP, see the memoir by David Hilliard and Lewis Cole, *This Side of Paradise: The Autobiography of David Hilliard and the Story of the Black Panther Party* (Boston: Little Brown, 1993), 145, 171.

81. *Black Panther,* 4 May 1969. See the huge photograph and glowing story in *Black Panther,* 13 June 1970, which was reprinted in the *San Francisco Sun-Reporter,* 13 June 1970, which covered black San Francisco and was controlled by Patterson's friend, Carlton Goodlett.

82. Aaron L. Fridberg, *A Contest for Supremacy: China, America, and the Struggle for Mastery in Asia* (New York: Norton, 2011); Henry Kissinger, *On China* (New York: Penguin, 2011).

83. Martin Jacques, *When China Rules the World: The End of the Western World and the Birth of a New Global Order* (New York: Penguin, 2009).

Chapter 1. The Road to Revolution

1. Michael Gold, "William Patterson: Militant Leader," *Masses and Mainstream* 4.2 (February 1951): 34–43, 35.

2. "CRC Bulletin," September 1951, box 10, Civil Rights Congress of Michigan Papers, Wayne State University, Detroit (hereafter CRC-Michigan Papers).

3. Notes, undated, box 13, folder 6, William Patterson Papers.

4. Nancie L. Solien Gonzalez, *Sojourners of the Caribbean: Ethnogenesis and Ethnohistory of the Garifuna* (Urbana: University of Illinois Press, 1988); Christopher Taylor, *The Black Carib Wars: Freedom, Survival, and the Making of the Garifuna* (Jackson: University Press of Mississippi, 2012).

5. "Certified Copy of an Entry Birth" of James Patterson, 27 April 2011, St. Vincent and the Grenadines, Registration District: Second, Volume Year: 1872, p. 375, Entry No. 2248 (in possession of the author; thanks to Leroy Adams, who obtained this document for me).

6. Draft Autobiography of William L. Patterson, box 13, folder 21, William Patterson Papers.

7. Ibid. See also Lynn M. Hudson, *The Making of "Mammy Pleasant": A Black Entrepreneur in Nineteenth-Century San Francisco* (Urbana: University of Illinois Press, 2003).

8. William Patterson to Matt Crawford, 13 March 1968, box 8, folder 3, Matt Crawford Papers, Emory University.

9. Douglas Henry Daniels, *Pioneer Urbanites: A Social and Cultural History of Black San Francisco* (Berkeley: University of California Press, 1990), 17.

10. Draft Autobiography of William L. Patterson, box 13, folder 21, William Patterson Papers.

11. Oakley Johnson, "William Patterson at Seventy," *Mainstream* 14.10 (October 1961): 45–54, 45.

12. Annual Report, Tamalpais Union High School, 1958, box 30, folder 4, William Patterson Papers.

13. See FBI Report, 1 December 1954, 100-39-244, Patterson/FBI/FOIA File: "Records of U of C, Berkeley, set forth subject's birth date as 8/27/90. Attended U of C during 1912 and 1913. Dropped from the rolls on 3/13/? for 'failure to respond to military notice.'"

14. Draft Autobiography of William L. Patterson, box 13, folder 26, William Patterson Papers.

15. Draft Autobiography of William L. Patterson, box 13, folder 25, William Patterson Papers.

16. William L. Patterson, *The Man Who Cried Genocide: An Autobiography* (New York: International, 1971), 15, 19, 27, 37, 39.

17. Draft Autobiography of William L. Patterson, box 13, folder 26, William Patterson Papers.

18. Draft Autobiography of William L. Patterson, box 13, folder 13, William Patterson Papers.

19. Draft Autobiography of William L. Patterson, box 13, folders 27, 30–31, William Patterson Papers. See also Undated Notes, box 2, Hermina Huiswood Papers, New York University; and William Patterson to Ted Vincent, 10 April 1972, box 2, folder 23, William Patterson Papers.

20. Autobiography, n.d., box 10, Nemmy Sparks Papers, Wayne State University, Detroit.

21. Patterson, *Man Who Cried Genocide*, 65, 67.

22. *New York Amsterdam News*, 20 January 1926.

23. William Patterson to Langston Hughes, 7 June 1957, box 127, folder 2379, Langston Hughes Papers, Yale University, New Haven, Conn.

24. *Baltimore Afro-American*, 28 March 1925.

25. *Baltimore Afro-American*, 1 January 1927.

26. *New York Times*, 17 January 1926.

27. *New York Times*, ca. 1919, reel 14, L. S. Alexander Gumby Papers, Columbia University. See also R. M. Whitney, *Reds in America* (1924; reprint, Boston: Western Islands, 1970), 197–214. Whitney argues that the Communist party, from its beginnings in the postwar era, saw Negroes as the revolutionary vanguard.

28. "Labor Defense: Manifesto, Resolutions, Constitution," Adopted by the First National Conference held in Ashland Auditorium, Chicago, 28 June 1925. International Labor Defense, 1925, University of Kansas, Lawrence.

29. *New York Times*, 11 August 1927. See also *New York Herald Tribune*, 30 June 1927; William Patterson to D. H. Kaufman, 25 August 1927, box 6, folder 32, CPUSA Papers, New York University.

30. Abram Harris, "Lenin Casts his Shadow upon Africa," *The Crisis*, 31.6 (April 1926): 272–75, 272. See also Bryan A. Palmer, *James B. Cannon and the Origins of the American Revolutionary Left, 1890–1928* (Urbana: University of Illinois Press, 2007): "[B]y the end of the 1920s the ANLC boasted only five active chapters and 180 members" (214).

31. W. E. B. Du Bois, "Judging Russia," *The Crisis* 33.4 (February 1927): 189–90.

32. Newspaper Clipping, ca. 1920s, box 11, folder 41, William Patterson Papers.

33. William Patterson, Remarks at Jack Stachel Memorial Meeting, 9 June 1966, box 8, folder 18, William Patterson Papers.

34. See, for example, Paul Avrich, *Sacco and Vanzetti: The Anarchist Background* (Princeton, N.J.: Princeton University Press, 1991).

35. Gold, "William Patterson."

36. Johnson, "William Patterson at Seventy," 48–49.

37. *New York Times*, 11 August 1927.

38. *New York Times*, 24 August 1927.

39. Gold, "William Patterson."

40. *Baltimore Afro-American*, 17 September 1927.

41. Testimony of William Patterson, 26 July 1957, Records of the Subversive Activities Control Board, 1950–1972, part II, reel 27, NARA-CP. See also *Labor Defender,* September 1934.
42. See the article by Patterson in the ILD journal *Labor Defender,* September 1934.
43. Gold, "William Patterson."
44. Draft Autobiography of William L. Patterson, box 13, folder 31, William Patterson Papers.
45. Johnson, "William Patterson at Seventy," 54.
46. Draft Autobiography of William L. Patterson, box 13, folder 31, William Patterson Papers. On Lovestone's objection, see Joy Gleason Carew, *Blacks, Reds and Russians: Sojourners in Search of the Soviet Promise* (New Brunswick, N.J.: Rutgers University Press, 2008), 36. See also Jay Lovestone, *Pages from Party History* (New York: Workers Library, 1929); and Robert J. Alexander, *The Right Opposition: The Lovestoneites and the International Communist Opposition of the 1930s* (Westport, Conn.: Greenwood Press, 1981).
47. Draft Autobiography of William L. Patterson, box 13, folder 35, William Patterson Papers.

Chapter 2. Moscow Bound

1. Report, 11 June 1943, 100-39-22, Patterson/FBI/FOIA File.
2. Draft Autobiography of William L. Patterson, box 13, folder 13, William Patterson Papers. I thank Glenda Gilmore for generously sharing with me her research notes from the archives in Moscow, which have shaped this chapter.
3. Draft Autobiography of William L. Patterson, box 13, folder 35, William Patterson Papers.
4. Horne, *Negro Comrades of the Crown.*
5. Claude McKay, "Soviet Russia and the Negro," *The Crisis* 27.2 (December 1923): 61–65, 63, 64.
6. Claude McKay, "Soviet Russia and the Negro," *The Crisis* 27.3 (January 1924): 114–18, 115, 117. See also Claude McKay, *A Long Way from Home* (New York: Harcourt Brace, 1970), 167; and Mary M. Leder, *My Life in Stalinist Russia: An American Woman Looks Back* (Bloomington: Indiana University Press, 2001). The contemporary Russian personality Yelena Khanga—a descendant of enslaved African Americans—confirms McKay's insight. See Yelena Khanga, *Soul to Soul: A Black Russian Jewish Woman's Search for Her Roots* (New York: Norton, 1992), 63.
7. *New York Amsterdam News,* 12 September 1928.
8. John L. Garder, "African Americans in the Soviet Union in the 1920s and 1930s: The Development of Transcontinental Protest," *Western Journal of Black Studies* 23.3 (Fall 1999): 190–200, 197.
9. Sheila Tully Boyle and Andrew Buni, *Paul Robeson: The Years of Promise and Achievement* (Amherst: University of Massachusetts Press, 2001), 305.
10. Woodford McClellan, "Africans and Black Americans in the Comintern Schools, 1925–1934," *International Journal of African Historical Studies* 26.2 (1993): 371–90, 371, 376. See also Barbara Keys, "An African American Worker in Stalin's Soviet Union: Race and the Soviet Experiment in International Perspective," *The Historian* 71.1 (Spring 2009): 33–54, 40, 41; and Jonathan Derrick, *Africa's Agitators: Militant Anticolonialism in Africa and the West, 1918–1939* (New York: Columbia University Press, 2008), 214.

11. Robbie Aitken, "From Carmeroon to Germany and Back via Moscow and Paris: The Political Career of Joseph Bile (1892–1959), Performer, 'Negerabeiter,' and Comintern Activist," *Journal of Contemporary History* 43.4 (2008): 597–616, 611.

12. *Cincinnati Enquirer*, 29 June 1927, box IIL249, folder 12, NAACP Papers, Library of Congress, Washington, D.C. (hereafter NAACP Papers).

13. Statement on ANLC, ca. 1925, I: D, box 1, National Urban League Papers, Library of Congress, Washington, D.C.

14. Theodore Draper, *American Communism and Soviet Russia* (New York: Viking, 1960), 321.

15. Bryan D. Palmer, *James P. Cannon and the Origins of the American Revolutionary Left, 1890–1927* (Urbana: University of Illinois Press, 2007), 215.

16. Horne, *Negro Comrades of the Crown*.

17. Margaret McCarthy, *Generation in Revolt* (London: Heinemann, 1953), 127, 165, 216.

18. James Allen on visit to Soviet Union in 1927, box 5, James Allen Papers, New York University.

19. Memorandum from U.S. Embassy, London, 10 August 1928, on Minutes of 31 July 1928 meeting in Moscow on "Negro Proletariat," Record Group 59, Decimal File, 1910–29, 800.00B, NARA-CP.

20. Harry Haywood, *Black Bolshevik: Autobiography of an Afro-American Communist* (Chicago: Liberator, 1978), 312–13. Haywood, who joined the CP in 1921, was one of five Negroes sent to the University of the Peoples of the East in 1925. See Interview with Harry Haywood, 28 November 1958, box 31, Theodore Draper Papers, Stanford University. For more on the Negro experience in Moscow, see John Sutton to George Murphy, 2 November 1976, box 1, John Sutton Papers, Howard University, Washington, D.C. See also Material on Maude White Katz, 8 December 1981, box 2, Mark Solomon and Robert Kaufman Research Files, New York University (hereafter Solomon and Kaufman Research Files).

21. Harvey Klehr, *Communist Cadre: The Social Background of the American Communist Party Elite* (Stanford, Calif.: Hoover Institution Press, 1978), 60.

22. Patterson, *Man Who Cried Genocide*, 105.

23. Draft Autobiography of William L. Patterson, box 13, folder 36, William Patterson Papers. See also Tim Tzouliadis, *The Forsaken: An American Tragedy in Stalin's Russia* (New York: Penguin, 2008).

24. Patterson, *Man Who Cried Genocide*, 109.

25. Patterson, *Man Who Cried Genocide*, 108. See also "Chicago Journal," 10 June 1981, box 1, Hermina Huiswood Papers, New York University.

26. Mark Solomon, *The Cry Was Unity: Communists and African-Americans, 1917–1936* (Jackson: University Press of Mississippi, 1998), 76.

27. Minutes of Political Committee of Communist Party USA, 30 May 1928, box 2, Daniel Bell Papers, New York University: "[T]he greatest need of our present work among the Negroes is the development of sufficient Communist Party cadres and the full utilization of the Negro comrades.... [T]ake into consideration not only the race problems of the Negroes in the United States and its colonies."

28. "International Press Correspondence," 1928, box 2, Solomon and Kaufman Research Files. See also "Report to the PolComm. Negro Department—Communist Party USA," 4 December 1930, Records of the Communist Party, USA, Library of Congress, Washington, D.C. (hereafter Records of the CPUSA).

29. Translation of article from *Pravda,* 30 October 1928, Record Group 59, Decimal File, 1910–29, 800.0B, NARA-CP.

30. John Pepper, *American Negro Problems* (New York: Workers Library, [ca. 1928]), University of Kansas at Lawrence: "The meetings of the Communist Party have been broken up in Arizona, in Texas, in Delaware and in other southern states, because the Communist spokesman dared to tackle the Negro Question and was bold enough to call the Negro workers to their meetings."

31. Political Committee Minutes of CPUSA, 9 April 1928 and 30 May 1928, box 2, Daniel Bell Papers, New York University.

32. Steve Nelson, James R. Barrett, and Rob Ruck, *Steve Nelson, American Radical* (Pittsburgh: University of Pittsburgh Press, 1981), 125.

33. *Pravda,* 30 October 1928, Decimal File, 800.0B, 1910–29, Record Group 59, NARA-CP.

34. Manning Johnson, *Color, Communism, and Common Sense* (New York: Alliance, 1958), 10.

35. See "Final Text of Resolution on the Negro Question in the United States," 26 November 1930, Reel 140, Records of the CPUSA.

36. Claude McKay to "Com. Kolaroff," 23 December 1922, Reel 5, Records of the CPUSA

37. On the influences of preexisting black nationalism on U.S. Communists, see for example Interview with Harry Haywood, 15 December 1958; Cyril Briggs to Theodore Draper, 24 March 1858; Cyril Briggs to Theodore Draper, 7 March 1958; Cyril Briggs to Theodore Draper, 17 March 1958; and Theodore Draper to Cyril Briggs, 11 March 1958, Theodore Draper Papers, Stanford University.

38. See Clipping, 21 October 1933, and Bulletin No. 1, the National Council, the National Movement for the Establishment of a Forty-ninth State, 417 East Forty-seventh Sreet, Chicago, box 23, folder 1, Loren Miller Papers, Huntington Library, San Marino, Calif. At the same site, see also "Stalin's Speeches on the American Communist Party," published by Central Committee, CPUSA, n.d., esp. Speeches of 6 May 1929 and 14 May 1929. In 1935, the NAACP demonstrated the concordance between this movement and the Black Belt thesis by publishing accounts of both, side by side. See Oscar C. Brown, "What Chance Freedom!" and James Allen, "The Communist Way Out." The conservative George Schuyler attacked both propositions. See *The Crisis* 42.5 (May 1935): 134–37, 148. The socialist leader Norman Thomas argued that the Black Belt thesis was "fantastic"—in the negative sense. See Norman Thomas, "Socialism's Appeal to Negroes," *The Crisis* 43.10 (October 1936): 294–95, 315.

39. James Edward Smethurst, *The New Red Negro: The Literary Left and African American Poetry, 1930–1946* (New York: Oxford University Press, 1999), 61.

40. Christopher E. Linsin, "Not by Words but by Deed: Communists and African-Americans During the Depression Era" (M.A. thesis, Florida Atlantic University, 1993), 11, 148.

41. Jacob Andrew Zumoff, "The Communist Party of the United States and the Communist International, 1919–1939" (Ph.d. diss., University College–London, 2003).

42. Roman, "Another Kind of Freedom," 121.

43. See, for example, the words of the columnist William Jones in the *Baltimore Afro-American,* 15 August 1931: "When you boil Communism down to a low gravy, there are few policies about it that most of us . . . do not believe in." For other positive assessments in this vein, see, for example, *Chicago Defender,* 7 May 1932, 28 December 1929, 23 July 1932, and 13 April 1929.

44. William Patterson, "Awake Negro Poets!" *New Masses* 4 (October 1928): 10.
45. William Patterson, Letter to Editor, *New Masses* 4 (June 1928): 16.
46. Langston Hughes, Letter to Editor, *New Masses* 6 (December 1930): 23.
47. It has been suggested that Patterson had a hand in the slaying of his fellow Negro comrade, Lovett Fort-Whiteman, in the Soviet Union. See Carew, *Blacks, Reds, and Russians,* 182. See also Gilmore, *Defying Dixie,* 33, 59, 69, 154, 244; Statement by Fort-Whiteman, 15 October 1919, box 2, Solomon and Kaufman Research Files; Palmer, *James P. Cannon and the Origins of the American Revolutionary Left.* Apparently, Fort-Whiteman ran afoul of the Moscow authorities, which led to a premature death. See *Washington Post,* 13 January 2008.
48. "William Wilson" (probably Patterson using a pseudonym), "The Negro Movement," International Press Correspondence, box 2, Solomon and Kaufman Research Files.
49. K. Kratov, "Working among the Negro Toilers in the Southern Part of the United States," n.d., Reel 155, Records of the CPUSA. See also Meeting of National Committee, St. Louis, 16 November 1930, Reel 140, Records of the CPUSA.
50. *New York Times,* 22 July 1929; William Patterson, *Man Who Cried Genocide,* 110–14.
51. Testimony of William L. Patterson, 26 July 1957, Part II, Reel 27, Records of the Subversive Activities Control Board, 1950–72, NARA-CP.
52. "Report of Proceedings and Decisions of the First International Conference of Negro Workers," Hamburg, 7–8 July 1930, box 2, Solomon and Kaufman Research Files. The Provisional Executive Committee includes James Ford, Otto Hall, and Kenyatta. See also "Report from U.S. Embassy, London, 14 May 1930, Record Group 59, Decimal Files, 1930–39, 800.00B, NARA-CP.
53. Draft Autobiography of William L. Patterson, box 13, folder 13, William Patterson Papers.
54. S. Ani Mukherji, "'The New Negro Will Not Be an Aesthete': Anticolonialism and Black Radical Politics in the Comintern," unpublished paper in possession of the author.
55. James Ford to "Comrade Flynn," 10 December 1954, James Ford Papers, New York University.
56. George Washington Carver to John Sutton, 25 January 1931, John Sutton Papers, Howard University, Washington, D.C.
57. FBI File of John Sutton, 10 May 1967, John Sutton Papers, Howard University, Washington, D.C. See Associated Negro Press Release, ca. 1938, box 203, folder 4, Claude Barnett Papers, Chicago Historical Society. See also Press Release, ca. 1938, box 202, folder 4, Claude Barnett Papers, Chicago Historical Society.
58. William Patterson to John and Bessie Sutton, 19 November 1972, box 2, folder 23, William Patterson Papers.
59. Report, 11 June 1943, 100-39-22, Patterson/FBI/FOIA File.
60. Draft Autobiography of William L. Patterson, box 13, folders 9 and 13, William Patterson Papers.
61. Testimony of William Patterson, 23 May 1955, Reel 27, Part II, Records of Subversive Activities Control Board, NARA-CP.
62. Theodore Kornweibel, *"Seeing Red": Federal Campaigns against Black Militancy, 1919–1925* (Bloomington: Indiana University Press, 1998), 177. See also Chief, Division of Eastern European Affairs of State Department, to J. Edgar Hoover, 29 January 1929, Record Group 59, Decimal File, 1910–29, 800.00B, NARA-CP.
63. *Baltimore Afro-American,* 11 April 1931.

64. *Chicago Defender*, 4 April 1931.
65. Roman, "Another Kind of Freedom," 52.
66. *Time*, 13 April 1931, box IIL249, folder 12, NAACP Papers.
67. "Negro Editors on Communism," *The Crisis* 41.4 (April 1932): 117–18.
68. W.E.B. Du Bois to Herman Babich, 10 December 1930, Reel 33, No. 740, W. E. B. Du Bois Papers, Duke University, Durham, N.C.
69. T. Arnold Hill, "Communism," *Opportunity* 8.9 (September 1930): 278.
70. Asbury Smith, "What Can the Negro Expect from Communism," *Opportunity* 11.7 (July 1933): 211–13, 219.
71. Loren Miller, "One Way Out—Communism," *Opportunity* 12.7 (July 1934): 214–16. See also Kelly Miller, "Should Black Turn Red," *Opportunity* 11.11 (November 1933): 328–32.
72. Roger Baldwin, "Negro Rights and Class Struggle," *Opportunity* 12.9 (September 1934): 264–66, 265.
73. John Louis Hill, *National Asset or Liability* (New York: Literary Associates), 1930.
74. "Report to the PolComm. Negro Department—Communist Party, USA," 4 December 1930, Reel 140, Records of the CPUSA.

Chapter 3. The World Confronts Jim Crow

1. *Daily World*, 5 April 1969.
2. Draft Autobiography of William L. Patterson, box 13, folder 39, William Patterson Papers. See also "Meeting of the Negro Department" of the CPUSA, 26 March 1929, box 224, Jay Lovestone Papers, Stanford University.
3. Clarence Norris and Sybil D. Washington, *The Last of the Scottsboro Boys: An Autobiography* (New York: Putnam's, 1979), 60. See *Daily World*, 13 March 1980; J. R. Uhlmann, "'A Bunch of Jews Defending Them Damned Niggers!': Radical Jews in the ILD's Scottsboro Campaign" (M.A. thesis, Australian National University, 1997).
4. "Draft Resolution on Negro Work," ca. February 1932, Reel 213, Records of the CPUSA. See also "Excerpts from Report of CI . . . instructor, August 16, 1931. . . . statistics on Negro Workers. . . . Negroes in Party. . . . New York," Reel 167, Records of the CPUSA; ILD, "Legal Defense Work among Negroes," 29 December 1931, box 45, Printed Ephemera, New York University.
5. "National Buro Letter No. 1," 11 February 1932, box 45, Printed Ephemera, New York University.
6. Government Report, 23 April 1933, box 2, Solomon and Kaufman Research Files.
7. William Patterson, "Does Russia Love the Negro?," box 1, Solomon and Kaufman Research Files.
8. Editorial, *The Crisis* (December 1934), box 2, Solomon and Kaufman Research Files. In the same collection, see Martin Bank, "Workers of the World—'Scottsboro,'" September 1932, for more on global protests.
9. Report by U.S. Consul, Sydney, 4 January 1932, Record Group 59, Decimal File, 1930–39, 811.4016, NARA-CP.
10. Report by U.S. Embassy, Madrid, 31 December 1931, Record Group 59, Decimal File, 1930–39, 811.4016, NARA-CP.
11. Felix Cole, Riga, to Secretary of State, 5 June 1931, Record Group 59, Decimal File, 1930–39, 811.4016, NARA-CP. Attached is a copy of an article in the Moscow periodical *Trud*, protesting Scottsboro as an example of U.S. racism.

12. Robert Skinner, U.S. Legation, Riga, Latvia, to Secretary of State, 5 February 1932, Record Group 59, Decimal File, 1930–39, 811.4016, NARA-CP.

13. *Labor Defender,* November 1932.

14. *St. Louis American,* 19 May 1934.

15. Frank Walter, "Scottsboro Again Re-Echoes over the World," 29 February 1934, International Press Correspondence, box 2, Solomon and Kaufman Research Files.

16. Report, 21 March 1932, Record Group 59, Decimal File, 1930–39, 811.4016, NARA-CP.

17. Julius Wadsworth to Secretary of State, 9 May 1932, Record Group 59, Decimal File, 1930–39, 811.4016, NARA-CP.

18. *Daily Worker* [London], 1 July 1931.

19. J. Louis Engdahl, "Scottsboro Campaign in England," *Negro Worker* 2.8 (August 1932): 18–30.

20. "Panama and Canal Zone workers" to President Hoover, 12 April 1932, Presidential Papers, Secretary's File, box 842, Herbert Hoover Presidential Library, West Branch, Iowa.

21. Report from Oscar De Priest, ca. 4 April 1932, Presidential Papers, Secretary's File, box 842, Herbert Hoover Presidential Library, West Branch, Iowa.

22. *Southern Worker,* 20 June 1931, box 4, James Allen Papers, New York University.

23. Charles Hathaway, U.S. Consul, to Secretary of State, 11 March 1932, Record Group 59, Decimal File, 1930–39, 811.4016, NARA-CP.

24. *Baltimore Afro-American,* 22 August 1931.

25. Speech by James Ford, 6 July 1934, Madison Square Garden, box 1, Clarina Michelson Papers, New York University.

26. *Baltimore Afro-American,* 5 January 1935.

27. *Brooklyn Eagle,* 6 September 1931.

28. Committee for the Deliverance of the Victims of Scottsboro to President Hoover, 4 July 1931, Presidential Papers, Secretary's File, box 842, Herbert Hoover Presidential Library, West Branch, Iowa.

29. Susan D. Pennybacker, *From Scottsboro to Munich: Race and Political Culture in the 1930s* (Princeton, N.J.: Princeton University Press, 2009), 75.

30. Hunt Frazier, Selma, Alabama, Chamber of Commerce to Cordell Hull, 7 September 1935, Record Group 59, Decimal Files, 1930–39, 811.00B/1647, NARA-CP.

31. J. Edgar Hoover to Gordon Gray, 11 June 1959, FBI Series, box 2, White House Office, Office of the Special Assistant for National Security Affairs: Records, 1952–61, Dwight D. Eisenhower Presidential Library, Abilene, Kans.

32. J. Louis Engdahl to Henry Stimson, 22 September 1931, Record Group 59, Decimal Files, 1930–39, 800.00b-engdahl, NARA-CP.

33. *Labor Defender,* January 1933. See also a leaflet announcing a memorial for Engdahl, 18 December 1933, box 3, Clarina Michelson Papers, New York University.

34. "Confidential" Memorandum, 19 December 1932, Record Group 59, Decimal Files, 1930–39, 800.00b-engdahl, NARA-CP.

35. Remarks by William Patterson and Joseph North, n.d. (ca. 1931), File on J. Louis Engdahl, box 2, CPUSA Papers, New York University.

36. Testimony of Carl Hacker, 1955, Part II, Reel 24, Records of the Subversive Activities Control Board, NARA-CP.

37. "Minutes of Enlarged Meeting of Negro Buro," ca. 14 July 1932, Reel 213, Records of the CPUSA: "[W]e inform the Secretariat that the Negro Buro is unanimously opposed to

placing Comrade Patterson into a lower function in the ILD, such as Negro Department of the ILD."

38. Elsa Brock to "Secretariat, CPUSA," 7 June 1932, Reel 213, Records of the CPUSA.

39. *Labor Defender,* November 1932.

40. Haywood, *Black Bolshevik,* 664.

41. Harvey Klehr, John E. Haynes, and K. M. Anderson, *The Soviet World of American Communism* (New Haven, Conn.: Yale University Press, 1998), 360. See also Allen Weinstein and Alexander Vassiliev, *The Haunted Wood: Soviet Espionage in America—the Stalin Era* (New York: Random House, 1999).

42. Patterson, *Man Who Cried Genocide,* 117.

43. Joy Gleason Carew, *Blacks, Reds, and Russians,* 182.

44. J. Edgar Hoover to Robert F. Kelley, 4 December 1929, Record Group 59, Decimal File, 1910–29, 800.00B, NARA-CP.

45. Dan T. Carter, *Scottsboro: A Tragedy of the American South* (Baton Rouge: Louisiana State University Press, 2007), 148.

46. George Maurer, "The Tasks of the ILD," March 1930, box 2, Solomon and Kaufman Research Files.

47. Charles H. Martin, "The International Labor Defense and Black America," Paper presented at the American Historical Association, Dallas, 27 December 1977, box 45, Printed Ephemera, New York University.

48. J. Louis Engdahl, "The ILD after Four Years," n.d., box 2, Solomon and Kaufman Research Files.

49. *Labor Defender,* May 1931.

50. William Patterson, rev. of *Scottsboro: A Tragedy of the American South,* by Dan T. Carter *Freedomways* 9 (1969): 265–72, 269.

51. William L. Patterson to Nancy Cunard, ca. December 1933, Record Group 59, Decimal Files, 1930–39, 800.00B, NARA-CP.

52. "Secret" Report from U.S. Embassy, 4 April 1933, Record Group 59, Decimal Files, 1930–1939, 800.00B-cunard, NARA-CP. See also Confidential Report of James A. Norton, December 1931, Manuscript: "Report on Communism in the State of Kansas," Kansas Historical Society, Topeka.

53. William Patterson, "Manifesto [to] the Negro People," November 1932, box 2, Solomon and Kaufman Research Files.

54. *St. Paul Pioneer Press,* 24 June 1931, ID69, NAACP Papers.

55. Roman, "Another Kind of Freedom," 78, 118, 218, 226. See also Louise Thompson Patterson, Oral History, n.d., box 6, folder 32, CPUSA Papers, New York University; Louise Thompson Patterson Interview, 16 November 1981, Oral History of the American Left, Series I, New York University; Homer Smith, *Black Man in Red Russia: A Memoir* (Chicago: Johnson, 1964), x, 57, 105, 172, 206–7. The U.S. Negro, Robert Robinson—who spent part of his childhood in Cuba—found the Soviet Union to be terribly racist. See Robert Robinson, *Black on Red: My 44 Years inside the Soviet Union* (Washington, D.C.: Acropolis, 1988). The accomplished Negro actor Wayland Rudd agreed with Smith, as he told the readers of the NAACP journal. See Wayland Rudd, "Russian and American Theatre," *The Crisis* 41.9 (September 1934): 270–71, 278. A future NAACP leader also agreed with Smith. See Henry Lee Moon, "Woman under the Soviets," *The Crisis* 41.4 (April 1934): 108.

56. See, for example, George Padmore, *What Is the International Trade Union Committee of Negro Workers* (Hamburg: ITUCNW, n.d.), University of Kansas, Lawrence.

57. William Patterson, "Race Hatred on Trial," *Negro Worker* 1.6 (June 1931): 21–22.

58. *Labor Defender,* April 1932.

59. "World Congress of International Labour Defense," *Negro Worker* 2.9–10 (September–October 1932): 5–6. See also Hermina Huiswood to "Natinale Voolichtings Dienst, NVD ... Surinam," 20 November 1985, and Biography of Otto Huiswood, n.d., box 1, Hermina Huiswood Papers, New York University.

60. Langston Hughes, "The Same," *Negro Worker* 2.9–10 (September–October 1932): 31–32: See also Wilson Record, *The Negro and the Communist Party* (New York: Athenaeum, 1971), 52.

61. See the new masthead in the following issue: George Padmore, "Negro Toilers Speak to the World Congress of ILD," *Negro Worker* 3.2–3 (February–March 1933): 1–6, 2. See also T. Jackson, "The International Labour Defense and the Negro Peoples," *Negro Worker* 3.2–3 (February–March 1933): 9.

62. Leaflet for Rally, 16 December [year unclear], box 3, Clarina Michelson Papers, New York University.

63. Solomon, *Cry Was Unity,* 145; *Liberator,* 19 September 1931 and 4 November 1932.

64. *New York Times,* 2 August 1931.

65. Officers and National Council of the League of Struggle for Negro Rights, 29 October 1933, box 2, Solomon and Kaufman Research Files.

66. W. Burghardt Turner and Joyce Moore Turner, eds., *Richard B. Moore, Caribbean Militant in Harlem: Collected Writings, 1920–1972* (Bloomington: Indiana University Press, 1988), 58.

67. *Baltimore Afro-American,* 2 May 1931.

68. *Baltimore Afro-American,* 20 August 1932..

69. *Labor Defender,* May 1933.

70. William Patterson, "Maryland Gets a Jolt," September 1932, box 2, Solomon and Kaufman Research Files. See also Negro Press Service: William Patterson, Remarks to students at Howard Law School, 12 May 1933, box 5, folder 7, Matt Crawford Papers, Emory University.

71. Johnson, "William Patterson at Seventy," 54.

72. Charles Hamilton Houston to Editor, *New York Amsterdam News,* 25 December 1933, box 12, folder 8, Charles Hamilton Houston Papers.

73. Kenneth Robert Janken, *White: The Biography of Walter White, Mr. NAACP* (New York: New Press, 2003), 149, 150.

74. Oakley Todd to Editor, *Harper's,* 18 January 1932, ID71, NAACP Papers. See also *Southern Worker* [Chattanooga], 2 May 1931: "William Pickens calls for support of ILD."

75. Walter White, "The Negro and the Communists," *Harper's,* December 1931, ID71, NAACP Papers.

76. Walter White to Fred R. Moore, *New York Age,* 17 August 1931, ID70, NAACP Papers.

77. *Waterbury [Conn.] Republican,* 13 December 1931, ID71, NAACP Papers.

78. J. Finley Wilson to Walter White, 13 November 1931, ID71, NAACP Papers. See also Howard Kester to "Dear Friend," 15 August 1931, ID71, NAACP Papers.

79. Magdeleine Paz to Walter White, 25 June 1932, ID72, NAACP Papers.

80. Translation by Herb Seligman, October 1932, ID72, NAACP Papers.

81. Charles White to William Andrews of the NAACP, 12 August 1931, ID70, NAACP Papers.

82. David A. Canton, *Raymond Pace Alexander: A New Negro Lawyer Fights for Civil Rights in Philadelphia* (Jackson: University Press of Mississippi, 2010), 39.

83. Notes by William Patterson, 1931–35, Alexander comments on 17 September 1931, box 12, folder 36, William Patterson Papers.

84. Raymond Pace Alexander to Walter White, 25 September 1931, ID70, NAACP Papers.

85. Raymond Pace Alexander to William Andrews, 22 April 1931, ID68, NAACP Papers.

86. *Norfolk Journal and Guide,* 15 August 1931.

87. William Pickens to Walter White, 30 May 1931, ID69, NAACP Papers.

88. *Atlanta Daily World,* 12 October 1932. For a similar report, see *Baltimore Afro-American,* 17 September 1932.

89. Gold, "William Patterson," 37.

90. Testimony of William Patterson, 26 July 1957, Records of the Subversive Activities Control Board, 1950–1972, Part II, Reel 27, NARA-CP.

91. Gold, "William Patterson."

92. *Freedom,* August 1951, qtd. in Foner, *Paul Robeson Speaks,* 383–85.

Chapter 4. Scottsboro—and Collapse

1. William Patterson, "Scottsboro Protest Must Grow," February 1934, box 2, Solomon and Kaufman Research Files.

2. William Patterson, "Labor Defense—Renegade Style," April 1934, box 2, Solomon and Kaufman Research Files.

3. *Communists in the Struggle for Negro Rights* (New York: New Century, 1945), Emory University.

4. Walter White to Will Alexander, 16 April 1932, ID72, NAACP Papers.

5. Membership Figures, 28 May 1933, box 2, Clarina Michelson Papers, New York University.

6. *Labor Defender,* 2 August 1933.

7. James Ford and Louis Sass, "Development of Work in the Harlem Section," *Communist* 14.4 (April 1935): 312–21, 319.

8. "Report for ILD Branch Organizers Made Out Each Week for Section," 9 August 1933, box 2, Clarina Michelson Papers, New York University.

9. "Directive on the Immediate Tasks of the LSNR of Greater New York," n.d., box 2, Clarina Michelson Papers, New York University.

10. Roy Wilkins to John Haynes Holmes, 14 April 1933, ID73, NAACP Papers.

11. Press Release, ca. April 1933, ID73, NAACP Papers.

12. Roy Wilkins to Walter White, 7 May 1931, ID68, NAACP Papers. Toiling as a journalist in Kansas City at the time, Wilkins complained about NAACP lethargy on the Scottsboro case.

13. Walter White to "Dear Pat," 19 April 1933, ID73, NAACP Papers.

14. William Patterson to Walter White, 20 April 1933, ID73, NAACP Papers.

15. Walter White to Editor, *Afro-American,* 6 July 1933, ID73, NAACP Papers.

16. There were numerous problems with the NAACP and the non-Communists involved in the Scottsboro defense. See, for example, Alfred Baker Lewis to Walter White, 3 June 1931, ID70, NAACP Papers; William Pickens to Walter White, 15 May 1931, ID69, NAACP Papers. Meanwhile, the non-Communist attorney for the Scottsboro defendants had many problems of his own. See, for example, *Chicago Defender,* 29 August 1931.

17. *Chicago Defender,* 29 April 1933.

18. William Patterson to Charles Martin, 25 May 1970, box 3, folder 30, William Patterson Papers.

19. Walter White to William Patterson, 14 June 1933, Reel 260, Records of the CPUSA.

20. Walter White to William Patterson, 13 July 1933, Reel 260, Records of the CPUSA.

21. ILD Press Service Release, 2 June 1933, box 5, folder 8, Matt Crawford Papers, Emory University.

22. ILD Press Service Release, 3 July 1933, box 5, folder 8, Matt Crawford Papers, Emory University. Of the seven thousand dollars collected by the NAACP for Scottsboro, said Patterson, two thousand went to Clarence Darrow and sixteen hundred for NAACP-related travel.

23. ILD Press Release, 22 July 1933, box 5, folder 8, Matt Crawford Papers, Emory University.

24. Acting Secretary, NAACP, to Will Alexander, 27 May 1930, box IC310, NAACP Papers.

25. Earl Browder interviewed by Joseph Starobin, 1965, box 1, folder 10, Theodore Draper Papers, Emory University.

26. *Labor Defender*, October 1932.

27. *Labor Defender*, June 1933.

28. Minutes of National Committee of League of Struggle for Negro Rights, 29 October 1933, Reel 260, Records of the CPUSA.

29. *Chicago Defender*, 20 May 1933.

30. Theodore Dreiser, *Mr. President: Free the Scottsboro Boys!* (New York: ILD, 1934), University of Kansas, Lawrence.

31. William Patterson to Mary Church Terrell, 10 May 1934, box 10, Mary Church Terrell Papers, Library of Congress.

32. William Patterson to Mary Church Terrell, 18 May 1934, box 10, Mary Church Terrell Papers, Library of Congress.

33. Letter from Louise Thompson, ca. April 1933, box 3, Clarina Michelson Papers, New York University.

34. Louise Thompson Patterson, Interview, 16 November 1981, Oral History of the American Left, Series I, New York University.

35. *New York Times*, 30 December 1932.

36. Testimony of William Patterson, 26 July 1957, Records of the Subversive Activities Control Board, 1950–72, Part II, Reel 27, NARA-CP. Patterson also "led a delegation to Harvard University to intercede with Felix Frankfurter," the future U.S. Supreme Court Justice, on Mooney's behalf. "We talked at length," he said. In 1933, Patterson and his delegation met with Vice President John N. Garner. See *Black Communists Speak on Scottsboro: A Documentary History*, ed. Walter Howard (Philadelphia: Temple University Press, 2007), 121.

37. Negro Press Service, 12 May 1933, box 5, folder 7, Matt Crawford Papers, Emory University. See also Testimony of William Patterson, 26 July 1957, Records of the Subversive Activities Control Board, Part II, Reel 27, NARA-CP. The 1933 meeting at the White House concerned both Mooney and Scottsboro. "We were ushered in to see Mr. Early. . . . [H]e phoned from his office to see President Roosevelt and stated that the President would not see us. I took the phone from his hand and myself spoke to President Roosevelt. The President did not, however, see us."

38. Mark Naison, *Communists in Harlem during the Depression* (Urbana: University of Illinois Press, 1983), 79.

39. *Baltimore Afro-American*, 11 July 1933.

40. "Great United Front Scottsboro-Mooney Mass Meeting, Bronx Coliseum," n.d, "Welcome Scottsboro Delegates from Washington!" "Hear Ruby Bates," leaflet, 10 May 1933, 8 P.M., Rockland Palace, box 3, Clarina Michelson Papers, New York University. See also leaflet on Scottsboro rally, 20 April 1932, St. Lukes Hall, 125 West 131st St.: Patterson speaks; leaflet announcing rally, 26 April 1933, 8 P.M., Mt. Calvary church, 140th St. and Edgecombe Ave: Patterson and Thompson speak; leaflet announcing meeting, 3 May 1933, 8 P.M., Bethel A.M.E. church, box 3, Clarina Michelson Papers, New York University. In box 2, see leaflet announcing rally at 159 West 132nd St., n.d.: Patterson speaks; LSNR, "Greater New York Council," "Advisory Committee." *New York Age* reported: "3,000 pack Holy Trinity Church and overflow streets in Scottsboro protest meeting," as "Patterson stirs audience" (29 April 1933).

41. *Chicago Defender*, 11 November 1933.

42. *Philadelphia Tribune*, 9 February 1933.

43. *Baltimore Afro-American*, 11 February 1933.

44. *Baltimore Afro-American*, 23 December 1933.

45. *Baltimore Afro-American*, 15 April 1933. Scottsboro not only placed the odious Jim Crow system on trial and in the process achieved a breakthrough in bringing global attention to the Negro's plight; by focusing on an uncomfortable collision between "race" and gender, it was possible to engage in open discussion about sexuality in a manner hardly attempted to that point. See *Baltimore Afro-American*, 25 November 1933.

46. *Baltimore Afro-American*, 12 May 1934.

47. See ILD Press Service Release, 22 July 1933, box 5, folder 8, Matt Crawford Papers, Emory University. See also ILD Minutes, 6 October 1933, meeting in office at 799 Broadway, New York City, box 2, Clarina Michelson Papers, New York University.

48. See Report on "International Persecution," 26 March 1932, box 2, Clarina Michelson Papers, New York University.

49. Gerald Horne, *Black and Red: W. E. B. Du Bois and the Afro-American Response to the Cold War, 1944–1963* (Albany: State University of New York Press, 1986).

50. *Baltimore Afro-American*, 30 June 1934.

51. ILD Press Service Release, 9 June 1933, box 5, folder 8, Matt Crawford Papers, Emory University.

52. Leaflet Announcing Rally, 14 April [1933?], 5 P.M., Union Square, New York, box 3, Clarina Michelson Papers, New York University.

53. *Labor Defender*, November 1933

54. *Norfolk Journal and Guide*, 17 June 1933

55. Memorandum from Mr. Bagnall, 6 May 1931, ID68, NAACP Papers.

56. Minutes of meeting of LSNR, 14 May 1934, box 1, Clarina Michelson Papers, New York University.

57. Gilmore, *Defying Dixie*, 128.

58. *Freedom,* August 1951, qtd. in Foner, *Paul Robeson Speaks,* 283–84.

59. Testimony of William Patterson, 26 July 1957, Records of Subversive Activities Control Board, NARA-CP.

60. Carter, *Scottsboro,* 148.

61. See ILD leaflet announcing rally in Washington, D.C., ca. February 1934, ID77, NAACP Papers. See also *Washington Post,* 8 February 1934; *Washington News,* 7 February 1934.

62. Charles Hamilton Houston to "Dear Pat," 13 October 1933, and William Patterson to "Dear Charlie," 14 October 1933, box 12, folder 12, Charles Hamilton Houston Papers.
63. Charles Hamilton Houston to William Patterson, 28 April 1933, box 26, folder 1, Charles Hamilton Houston Papers.
64. Charles Hamilton Houston to William Patterson, 20 April 1933, box 26, folder 1, Charles Hamilton Houston Papers.
65. William Patterson to Charles Hamilton Houston, 21 April 1933, box 26, folder 1, Charles Hamilton Houston Papers.
66. William Patterson to Charles Hamilton Houston, 13 May 1933, box 26, folder 1, Charles Hamilton Houston Papers.
67. Charles Hamilton Houston to William Patterson, 16 October 1933, box 12, folder 12, Charles Hamilton Houston Papers.
68. Charles Hamilton Houston to William Patterson, n.d. [ca. 1933], box 12, folder 12, Charles Hamilton Houston Papers: "I have asked Walter to get in touch with you."
69. William Patterson to Charles Hamilton Houston, 10 November 1933, box 26, folder 10, Charles Hamilton Houston Papers.
70. William Patterson to Charles Hamilton Houston, 31 December 1931, box 26, folder 10, Charles Hamilton Houston Papers. See also Charles Hamilton Houston to William Patterson, 11 April 1933, and Charles Hamilton Houston to ILD, 23 December 1932, box 26, folder 10, Charles Hamilton Houston Papers.
71. Assessment of Scottsboro campaign, n.d., box 26, folder 13, Charles Hamilton Houston Papers.
72. Charles Hamilton Houston Debate with Bernard Ades, 28 March 1935, box 26, folder 14, Charles Hamilton Houston Papers.
73. Charles Hamilton Houston Interview, December 1949, box 3, folder 31, William Patterson Papers.
74. Leaflet on Patterson for Mayor campaign, 14 October 1932, box 3, Clarina Michelson Papers, New York University.
75. *Norfolk Journal and Guide,* 4 November 1933.
76. *New York Times,* 17 April 1933.
77. Scottsboro Press Service, 17 April 1933, ID73, NAACP Papers.
78. William Patterson to Morris Hillquit, 28 September 1932, box 4, folder 4, Morris Hillquit Papers, State Historical Society of Wisconsin, Madison. See *New Leader,* 21 June 1930. See also Patterson's rebuke of the SP: *Daily Worker,* 14 October 1933, and William Patterson, "We Indict the Alabama Lynchers," *Labor Defender,* March 1933.
79. Morris Hillquit to William Patterson, 3 October 1932, box 4, folder 4, Morris Hillquit Papers, State Historical Society of Wisconsin, Madison. In the same collection, see also Blanche Watson to "Comrade Hillquit," 10 November 1932, folder 5. Cf. Harry Haywood, *The Road to Negro Liberation: Report to the 8th Convention of the CPUSA* (New York: Workers Library, 1934), University of Kansas, Lawrence.
80. Carl Murphy et al., "The Afro: Seaboard's Largest Weekly," *The Crisis* 45.2 (February 1938): 44–46, 50.
81. *Baltimore Afro-American,* 29 October 1932.
82. *New York Times,* 26 August 1932: Patterson speaks at Carnegie Hall to two thousand delegates assembled, representing seventy thousand from various organizations.
83. *New York Times,* 1 November 1932.
84. See, for example, Terry Martin, *The Affirmative Action Empire: Nations and Nationalism in the Soviet Union, 1923–1939* (Ithaca, N.Y.: Cornell University Press, 2001); Gerald

Horne, *Reversing Discrimination: The Case for Affirmative Action* (New York: International, 1992).

85. Tom Brandon and Harriet Silverman to Negro Department, CPUSA, 6 June 1932, Reel 213, Records of the CPUSA.

86. William Jelani Cobb, "Antidote to Revolution: African American Anticommunism and the Struggle for Civil Rights, 1931–1954" (Ph.D. diss., Rutgers University, 2003), 314. See also Interview with Louise Thompson Patterson, 16 November 1981, Oral History of the American Left, Series I, New York University.

87. Statement, n.d., box 2, Hermina Huiswood Papers, New York University. When Thompson and her crew arrived, "the Moscow public would vie with each other to give up their seats in the streetcars or would allow them to go the head of the line if waiting to enter a theater or whenever they turned up."

88. Statement, ca, 1932, Reel 213, Records of the CPUSA.

89. Leaflet, 27 October 1932, box 2, Clarina Michelson Papers, New York University.

90. Ted Poston to Claude Barnett, 21 September 1932, box 202, folder 4, Claude Barnett Papers, Chicago Historical Society.

91. Johnson, William Patterson at Seventy," 50.

92. *New York Amsterdam News,* 25 October 1933.

93. *Labor Defender,* November 1933.

94. Gold, "William Patterson," 35.

95. Draft Autobiography of William L. Patterson, box 13, folder 13, William Patterson Papers.

96. Draft Autobiography of William L. Patterson, box 13, folder 12, William Patterson.

97. *Chicago Defender,* 20 September 1930.

98. Legation in Port au Prince to State Department, 3 January 1933, Record Group, Decimal Files, 1930–39, 838.00b/10, M1246, Roll, 6, NARA-CP.

99. *Chicago Defender,* 11 July 1931. See also the edition of 30 April 1932, where Cuban writers again protest.

100. *Chicago Defender,* 10 February 1934.

101. *Labor Defender,* January 1935 and February 1935.

102. Gustavo Urrutia, Havana, to Herbert Seligman, 15 April 1932, ID72, NAACP Papers.

Chapter 5. Back in the USSR

1. Gold, "William Patterson," 35. See also *Labor Defender,* June 1935. On Patterson's collapse, see *Baltimore Afro-American,* 28 July 1934. See also *Chicago Defender,* 21 October 1939.

2. Draft Autobiography of William L. Patterson, box 13, folder 21, William Patterson Papers.

3. The FBI also confirmed that from 1934 to 1937, Patterson studied at Lenin University, while noting that he was in and out of Germany during this same period. Report, 11 June 1943, 100-39-22, Patterson/FBI/FOIA File.

4. Statement by James Ford, ca. 1932, Reel 213, Records of the CPUSA.

5. Report, 22 January 1947, 100-39-91, Patterson/FBI/FOIA File.

6. Report, 29 June 1955, 100-23717, Civil Rights Congress/FBI/FOIA File, Gerald Horne Papers, Schomburg Center, New York Public Library.

7. *Negro Worker* 7.2 (February 1937): 10.

8. *Midwest Daily Record,* 12 November 1938.

9. William Patterson, "West African Youth and the People's Front," *Negro Worker* 7.3 (March 1937): 8–9, 13.

10. William Patterson, "The Scottsboro Case," *Negro Worker* 7.7–8 (September/October 1937): 5–6.

11. Mollie Moon to "Darling Boys," 11 May 1933, George Padmore Collection, Princeton University.

12. Draft Autobiography of William L. Patterson, box 13, folder 12, William Patterson Papers.

13. Anna Damon, *The Work of the International Labor Defense for Aid to Labor's Prisoners and to Maintain and Enlarge Democratic Rights* (New York: ILD, 1937), University of Kansas, Lawrence.

14. Geroge Charney, *A Long Journey* (Chicago: Quadrangle, 1968), 91. See also James Cannon, *The First Ten Years of American Communism: Report of a Participant* (New York: Pathfinder, 1973).

15. Jackson, *Indignant Generation,* 57. However, see also J. Edgar Hoover to Robert Cutler, ca. 1950s, "The Communist Party and the Negro," FBI Series, box 16, White House Office, OSANSA Records, Dwight D. Eisenhower Presidential Library, Abilene, Kans.

16. Interview with Earl Browder, 28 June 1955, box 1, folder 6, Theodore Draper Papers, Emory University. Draper stated: "I checked up on the membership of the Communist Party between 1930 and '38 and just by looking at the rate of growth, something emerges. . . . 1930 about 7500; 1931 about 9000; '32, 14,000; '33, 18,000 . . . '34, 26,000; '35, 30,000; '36, 40,000; '37, about 50,000; '38 about 75,000. . . . [I]n the years '34 to '38, when the deepest period of the Depression has passed, there is a real momentum. . . . [T]he real momentum of growth comes between the ninth and tenth convention, between 1936 and 1938. . . . [T]he party jumps from about 40,000 to about 75,000 in two years—almost double." Browder replied: "The New York organization from the middle '30s on usually had about 40 percent of the party membership." Then Draper asserted: "In the '20s about ¹/₅, maximum ¹/₄ of the party was actually Jewish," though, Browder countered, "at the high point there was [sic] about 7 or 8 percent Jews" (most of these in the Northeast and California). Thus, if you analyze nationally, "there wouldn't be 1 percent" of the membership denoted as Jewish. Similarly, Draper noted that "in [the] 1928 presidential election, the Communist vote is 48,000, the Socialist vote 289,000. . . . [I]n '32 the Communist vote is 102,000, the Socialist vote 918,000." See Draper interviewing Browder, 10 October 1955, box 1, folder 8, Theodore Draper Papers, Emory University. In 1939, the estimated membership of the CP (including the Young Communist League) was approximately one hundred thousand. See also "Proceedings, 10th Convention Communist Party, New York State, 20–23 May 1938," University of Kansas, Lawrence.

17. *Baltimore Afro-American,* 25 May 1935.

18. *Baltimore Afro-American,* 24 August 1935.

19. *Baltimore Afro-American,* 21 September 1935.

20. See Gregg Andrews, *Thyra Edwards: Black Activist in the Global Freedom Struggle* (Columbia: University of Missouri Press, 2011).

21. *Baltimore Afro-American,* 29 August 1936.

22. James R. Hooker, *Black Revolutionary: George Padmore's Path from Communism to Pan-Africanism* (London: Pall Mall, 1967), 37.

23. *Chicago Defender,* 1 June 1935.

24. Sheila Tully Boyle and Andrew Bunie, *Paul Robeson: The Years of Promise and Achievement* (Amherst: University of Massachusetts Press, 2001), 477.

25. Carew, *Blacks, Reds and Russians*, 147. See also Fred E. Beal, *Proletarian Journey: New England, Gastonia, Moscow* (New York: Hillman-Curl, 1937), 225, 248.

26. Paul Robeson Jr., *The Undiscovered Paul Robeson: An Artist's Journey, 1898–1939* (New York: Wiley, 2001).

27. *Midwest Daily Record*, 6 May 1939.

28. See also S. Ani Mukherji, "'Like Another Planet to the Darker Americans': Anticolonial Cultural Work in 1930s Moscow," unpublished paper in possession of the author.

29. Lois Gordon, *Nancy Cunard: Heiress, Muse, Political Idealist* (New York: Columbia University Press, 2007), 205, 206.

30. Pennybacker, *From Scottsboro to Munich*.

31. *Chicago Defender*, 16 June 1934. Cuba, France, and Argentina were listed as the other members of this charmed circle. See also article by Frank Marshall Davis, 14 April 1937, box 202, folder 4, Claude Barnett Papers, Chicago Historical Society.

32. William Patterson, "The Negro People and the Centenary of Pushkin," *Negro Worker* 7.4 (April 1937): 7, 14.

33. See Eugene Gordon on Pushkin, 24 February 1937, box 202, folder 4, Claude Barnett Papers, Chicago Historical Society. See Sergius Kara-Mourza, "Ira Aldridge in Russia," *The Crisis* 40.9 (September 1933): 201–2, 201. A Euro-American family in the Soviet Union was confounded by knowledge of the United States and struck by revulsion toward U.S. racism there. See Harry Timbres and Rebecca Timbres, *We Didn't Ask Utopia: A Quaker Family in Soviet Russia* (New York: Prentice Hall, 1939), 89.

34. Thelma Nurenberg, *This New Freedom* (New York: Wadsworth Press, 1932), 157.

35. William Jelani Cobb, "Antidote to Revolution: African American Anticommunism and the Struggle for Civil Rights, 1931–1954" (Ph.D. diss., Rutgers University, 2003), 36.

36. See, for example, Chatwood Hall, "A Black Woman in Red Russia," *The Crisis* 44.7 (July 1937): 204.

37. *Pittsburgh Courier*, 21 November 1931.

38. Consul General, Berlin, to Secretary of State, 28 April 1931, in *Foreign Relations of the United States: Diplomatic Papers, 1932*, vol. 2, *The British Commonwealth, Europe, Near East and Africa* (Washington, D.C.: Government Printing Office, 1947), 521–22.

39. *Philadelphia Tribune*, 2 August 1934.

40. Jonathan Derrick, *Africa's Agitators: Militant Anti-Colonialism in Africa and the West, 1918–1939* (New York: Columbia University Press, 2008), 288. See also George Padmore, "Why I Left the Communist International," ca. 1934, George Padmore Collection, Princeton University; *Daily Worker* [London], 18 April 1934; George Padmore to Secretariat of CPUSA, 2 March 1934, and George Padmore to Earl Browder, 9 August 1934, George Padmore Collection, Princeton University. Cyril Briggs joined Patterson in disputing Padmore's account. See *New York Amsterdam News*, 23 July 1934.

41. See Release by Crusader News Agency, 4 August 1934, and George Padmore to Henry Moon, 25 August 1934, George Padmore Collection, Princeton University.

42. William Patterson, "The Abyssinian Situation and the Negro World," *Negro Worker* 6.5 (June 1935): 16–19, 18. The CP leader Earl Browder told NAACP readers that Padmore was ousted by a committee that included Patterson because of his pro-Tokyo views, the idea that "the Mikado is the guardian of the 'darker races,'" and his possible role in the detention of progressive seafarers, of which Hamburg had plenty. See Earl Browder, "Replies," *The Crisis* 24.12 (December 1935): 372.

43. William Patterson, "Helping Britain to Rule Africa," *Negro Worker* 6.10 (December 1936): 7–11.

44. William Patterson, "World Politics and Ethiopia," *The Communist* 14.8 (August 1935): 723–34, 723, 724.

45. Hooker, *Black Revolutionary*, 37.

46. *Pittsburgh Courier*, 25 August 1934.

47. *Pittsburgh Courier*, 17 June 1933.

48. William Patterson to Professor Rukudzo Muropa, 17 July 1972, box 2, folder 23, William Patterson Papers.

49. *Labor Defender*, June 1934. This ILD journal can be found on microfilm at the University of North Carolina, Chapel Hill, within the ILD Papers.

50. *Labor Defender*, October 1932.

51. *Labor Defender*, May 1934.

52. See also *Labor Defender*, April 1935. An audited statement reveals that ILD total assets were just over three thousand dollars, with eighteen thousand having been spent on Scottsboro and sixteen thousand on the Angelo Herndon case.

53. "Meeting with Negro Comrade of Harlem, Aug. 23, 1932," box 9, folder 46, William Patterson Papers.

54. Reverend Adam Clayton Powell Jr. to "Dear Friends," 8 October 1937, box 6, folder 1, Richard B. Moore Papers, Schomburg Center, New York Public Library.

55. Louise Thompson, "What Happened in Harlem: An Eye-Witness Account," n.d., box 2, Solomon and Kaufman Research Files.

56. William Patterson, "Negro Harlem Awakes," *Negro Worker*, July/August 1935. See also William Patterson, "The ILD Faces the Future," *The Communist* 13.7 (July 1934): 718–27.

57. See, for example, Harry Haywood, "The Road to Negro Liberation" and "Report to the Eighth Convention of the Communist Party of the USA, Cleveland, April 2–8, 1934" (New York: Workers Library, 1934), University of Central Florida, Orlando.

58. Patterson, "World Politics and Ethiopia," 734.

59. Martha Gruening, "The Truth about the [George] Crawford Case: How the NAACP 'Defended' a Negro into a Life Sentence," *New Masses* 14.8 (January 1935): 9–15.

60. Charles Hamilton Houston to William Patterson, 22 June 1933, box 12, folder 10, Charles Hamilton Houston Papers.

61. William Patterson to Charles Hamilton Houston, 10 November 1933, box 12, folder 10, Charles Hamilton Houston Papers.

62. *Cleveland Call and Post*, 21 April 1934.

63. Charles Hamilton Houston to William Patterson, 17 May 1934, box 12, folder 10, Charles Hamilton Houston Papers. See also Roy Wilkins to Charles Hamilton Houston, 15 November 1933, ID73; William Pickens to William Patterson, 1 May 1934, ID73; Walter White to "My Dear Pat," 17 May 1934, ID73, box 12, folder 10, Charles Hamilton Houston Papers.

64. Charles Hamilton Houston–Bernard Ades debate, 28 March 1935, box 12, folder 10, Charles Hamilton Houston Papers.

65. Ben Davis to Charles Hamilton Houston, 12 June 1933, box 12, folder 9, Charles Hamilton Houston Papers.

66. Roy Wilkins to William Patterson, 24 May 1933, ID73, NAACP Papers.

67. Roy Wilkins to Adam Clayton Powell Jr., 6 May 1933, ID73, NAACP Papers.

68. John H. Holmes to Roy Wilkins, 13 April 1933, ID73, NAACP Papers.

69. ILD Press Service, 24 April 1933, box 17, folder 3, Matt Crawford Papers, Emory University.

70. Walter White to Louise Thompson, 18 April 1933, ID73; and Louise Thompson to Walter White, 21 April 1933, ID73, NAACP Papers.

71. L. F. Coles to Walter White, 13 May 1933, ID73, NAACP Papers.

72. Arthur Spingarn to Walter White, 24 April 1933, ID73, NAACP Papers. See also Walter White to "My Dear Patterson" [no longer "Dear Pat"], 27 April 1933, ID73, NAACP Papers.

73. L. F. Coles to Walter White, 13 May 1933, ID73, NAACP Papers. Thompson "lives in 409 [Edgecombe, Harlem] your building, with young Ben Davis."

74. *New York Herald Tribune,* 5 July 1933; *Daily Worker,* 11 July 1933.

75. William Patterson to NAACP, 12 June 1934, ID73, NAACP Papers.

76. Walter White to William Patterson, 13 June 1934, ID73, NAACP Papers.

77. Kelly Miller, "Should Black Turn Red, White Would Be to Blame," ca. 1935, box 17, folder 3, Kelly Miller Papers, Emory University. See also Miller's 21 May 1935 column, box 17, folder 4, and Miller's 31 August 1935 missive: "Communism among Negroes, an Open Letter to the President of Howard University," box 17, folder 5, Kelly Miller Papers, Emory University.

78. See, for example, Stephen B. Tallackson, "The Chicago *Defender* and its Reaction to the Communist Movement in the Depression Era" (M.A. thesis, University of Chicago, 1967); Charles Russel Branham, "The Transformation of Black Political Leadership in Chicago, 1864–1942" (Ph.d. diss., University of Chicago, 1981).

79. St. Clair Drake and Horace R. Cayton, *Black Metropolis: A Study of Negro Life in a Northern City* (New York: Harcourt Brace, 1945); Christopher Robert Reed, *The Chicago NAACP and the Rise of Black Professional Leadership, 1910–1966* (Bloomington: Indiana University Press, 1997); Paul Clinton Young, "Race, Class, and Radicalism in Chicago, 1914–1936" (Ph.d. diss., University of Iowa, 2001).

80. *Midwest Daily Record,* 16 May 1938.

81. *Baltimore Afro-American,* 30 October 1937.

82. *Labor Defender,* June 1937.

83. Lester Granger, "The National Negro Congress: An Interpretation, " *Opportunity* 14.5 (May 1936): 151–53, 152. See *Cleveland Call and Post,* 13 April 1935.

84. Remarks by Kelly Miller, ca. March 1936, box 18, folder 1, Kelly Miller Papers, Emory University.

85. William Patterson to Charles Hamilton Houston, 27 November 1939, box 12, folder 12, Charles Hamilton Houston Papers; *Midwest Daily Record,* 4 March 1939 (for more praise by Patterson of Dickerson, see the edition of 1 April 1939). See also *Midwest Daily Record,* 9 November 1939.

86. William Patterson to Charles Hamilton Houston, 27 November 1939, box 12, folder 12, Charles Hamilton Houston Papers.

87. Robert J. Blakely with Marcus Shepard, *Earl B. Dickerson: A Voice for Freedom and Equality* (Evanston, Ill.: Northwestern University Press, 2006).

88. *Chicago Defender,* 9 September 1939.

89. *Norfolk Journal and Guide,* 17 June 1939. See also *Midwest Daily Record,* 3 June 1939.

90. *Chicago Defender,* 11 March 1939.

91. *Baltimore Afro-American,* 5 August 1939 and 8 July 1939.

92. *Midwest Daily Record,* 10 September 1938.

93. *Midwest Daily Record,* 11 November 1938. For more praise of FDR, see Patterson's columns: *Midwest Daily Record,* 6 January 1939, 20 January 1939, and 9 December 1938.

94. *Baltimore Afro-American,* 29 August 1939. Patterson stated, "I remember when I last spoke with Marian Anderson. It was in Chicago the night before she gave her great 1938 recital. I asked her then to sing for the relief of the Spanish children. She said that would be taking sides in politics. I answered that all men must take sides, whether they desired or not. She demurred. I did not press the issue. Time has proclaimed the correctness of my position. . . . I had seen Paul Robeson go through the same inner struggle. . . . I saw Paul Robeson change. . . . Marian Anderson is moving in that direction. Life itself is the greatest propagandist."

95. Report from CPUSA, circa 10 May 1937, Reel 306, Records of the CPUSA.

96. "Proposals for the Solidarity Movement in the USA," 13 April 1937, Reel 306, Records of the CPUSA.

97. *Midwest Daily Record,* 18 June 1938.

98. *Midwest Daily Record,* 13 August 1938

99. *Midwest Daily Record,* 23 July 1938.

Chapter 6. Black Chicago

1. Michelle Yvonne Gordon, "Black Literature of Revolutionary Protest from Chicago's South Side: A Local Literary History, 1931–1959" (Ph.d. diss., University of Wisconsin, 2008). See also Gerald Horne, *Fighting in Paradise: Labor Unions, Racism and Communists in the Making of Modern Hawaii* (Honolulu: University of Hawaii Press, 2011).

2. *Midwest Daily Record,* 2 August 1939.

3. William Patterson, editorial, ca. 1938, box 11, folder 32, William Patterson Papers.

4. *Midwest Daily Record,* 14 September 1938.

5. *Midwest Daily Record,* 12 September 1938.

6. See, for example, *Midwest Daily Record,* 7 May 1938.

7. Ben Burns, *Nitty Gritty: A White Editor in Black Journalism* (Jackson: University Press of Mississippi, 1996), 56, 65. See also Louis Francis Budenz, *Men without Faces: The Communist Conspiracy in the USA* (New York: Harper and Bros., 1948); Louis Francis Budenz, *The Bolshevik Invasion of the West* (Linden, N.J.: Bookmailer, 1966). See also *Midwest Daily Record,* 16 September 1939: Budenz makes frantic appeal for funds for the journal. See also Report, 5 May 1953, 100-39-214, Patterson/FBI/FOIA File. Joseph Alsop, "The Strange Case of Louis Budenz," 1952, Series I, box 4, Ernest Goodman Papers, Wayne State University, Detroit. See also Testimony of Louis Budenz before House Subcommittee on Foreign Relations, Washington, D.C., 20, 25 April 1950, p. 548, Series I, box 4, Ernest Goodman Papers, Wayne State University, Detroit. In November 1937 Budenz became an editor at the *Record*—then charged that "it was financed by the secret conspiratorial bund under Robert William Weiner."

8. See, for example, *Midwest Daily Record,* 6 May 1938. See also *Midwest Daily Record,* 12 September 1938. See Report, 6 October 1944, 100-39-59, Patterson/FBI/FOIA File.

9. See, for example, U.S. Congress, House of Representatives, Committee on Un-American Activities, 79th Cong., 2d Sess., On House Resolution 5, "Investigation of Un-American Activities in the United States," Testimony of Louis Budenz, 22 November 1946 (Washington, D.C.: Government Printing Office, 1947), 19.

10. Report, 11 September 1941, 100-39-7, Patterson/FBI/FOIA File. See also Patterson passport, 2 December 1958, box 1, folder 17, William Patterson Papers. (Here his height is listed as five feet, seven inches, with gray hair and brown eyes.)

11. J. Edgar Hoover to L. M. C. Smith, 27 March 1941, 100-39-6, Patterson/FBI/FOIA File.

12. Gil Green, *Cold War Fugitive: A Personal Story of the McCarthy Years* (New York: International, 1984), 122.

13. Remarks by William Patterson, 11 March 1949, box 1, Civil Rights Congress of Illinois Records [in Chicago Committee to Defend the Bill of Rights Papers], Chicago Historical Society.

14. *Midwest Daily Record*, 3 March 1939. For more on the Workers School, see *Midwest Daily Record*, 9 October 1939,

15. Report, 6 October 1944, 100-39-59, Patterson/FBI/FOIA File.

16. *Midwest Daily Record*, 3 October 1939.

17. *Midwest Daily Record*, 24 February 1939.

18. *Midwest Daily Record*, 1 September 1939. See also *Midwest Daily Record*, 6 October 1939.

19. *Midwest Daily Record*, 7 October 1939.

20. *Midwest Daily Record*, 20 September 1939.

21. *Midwest Daily Record*, 29 October 1938. See also *Midwest Daily Record*, 8 November 1939.

22. NNC document, n.d., box 6, folder 7, Richard B. Moore Papers, Schomburg Center, New York Public Library. See also *Midwest Daily Record*, 8 November 1939.

23. Printed Ephemera, ILD, 28 April 1948, box 45, New York University.

24. Proceedings of the Third Biennial National Conference of the International Labor Defense, 4–6 April 1941, box 13, Counterattack Papers, New York University.

25. *Midwest Daily Record*, 2 December 1939.

26. Bill V. Mullen, *Popular Fronts: Chicago and African-American Cultural Politics, 1935–1946* (Urbana: University of Illinois Press, 1999), 52, 53. Patterson's column often appeared in this journal. See, for example, *Chicago Defender*, 21 October 1939. See also Report, 26 July 1940, 100-39-5, Patterson/FBI/FOIA File.

27. *Chicago Defender*, 4 November 1939.

28. Report, 13 January 1945, 100-39-45, Patterson/FBI/FOIA File.

29. Report, 28 August 1943, 100-39-32, Patterson/FBI/FOIA File.

30. Report, 21 April 1945, 100-39-69, Patterson/FBI/FOIA File. For Patterson's writings—sans pseudonym—in the *Daily Worker*, see the editions of 27 August 1944, 1 October 1944, 12 November 1944, and 14 January 1945.

31. Campaign Material, 1940, box 30, folder 13, William Patterson Papers.

32. *Midwest Daily Record*, 16 September 1939.

33. *Midwest Daily Record*, 26 September 1939 and 2 October 1939.

34. Jeffrey Hegelson, "Striving in Black Chicago: Migration, Work and the Politics of Neighborhood Change, 1935–1965" (Ph.d. diss., University of Illinois at Chicago, 2008), 283.

35. J. Edgar Hoover to Harry Hopkins, 28 December 1943, box 151, Harry Hopkins Papers, Franklin D. Roosevelt Presidential Library, Hyde Park, N.Y.

36. Report, 21 April 1945, 100-39-69, Patterson/FBI/FOIA File.

37. Report by J. Edgar Hoover, 26 June 1943, 100-39-23, Patterson/FBI/FOIA File.

38. Report, 31 December 1943, 100-30-41, Patterson/FBI/FOIA File.
39. Report, 6 October 1944, 100-39-59, Patterson/FBI/FOIA File.
40. *Midwest Daily Record,* 18 November 1938.
41. Report, 23 July 1946, 100-39-85, Patterson/FBI/FOIA File.
42. Report, 17 March 1944, 100-39-51, Patterson/FBI/FOIA File.
43. Report, 7 March 1944, 100-39-59, Patterson/FBI/FOIA File.
44. Report, 21 April 1945, 100-39-69, Patterson/FBI/FOIA File.
45. Ruth McKenney, "Meet the Communists," *New Masses* 27 (24 May 1938), 3–6: "Take any day last week. Take Monday. On Monday the Communist Party . . . organized half a dozen big relief demonstrations in six big American cities; went to press with a weekly Chinese American paper in Chinese; sat in on four peace meetings and talked collective security until all hands were hoarse; organized eighteen dances for benefit purposes, in New York City, chief feature of which [was] red hot swing music; published three newspapers in English. Collected money for Spain, China, Tom Mooney, the Scottsboro Boys and twenty-two other labor victims, most of them not famous; organized tenants' rent strikes in four slum districts of New York, Chicago, and Philadelphia; issued seven new nickel pamphlets . . . raised hell with four public officials in New York and other towns via telephone calls and letters; held 324 committee meetings in eighty-nine cities and villages on subjects ranging from industrial insurance to what we'll do about getting a free swimming pool for Northside slum districts; pushed the sale of eighteen different books in twenty-four workers' bookshops; and issued 114 mimeographed shop papers distributed at the gates of 114 factories in forty-three cities."
46. *Midwest Weekly Record,* 18 November 1939.
47. Arthur J. Sabin, *Red Scare in Court: New York versus the International Workers Order* (Philadelphia: University of Pennsylvania Press, 1993), 262. See also James Gavin, *Stormy Weather: The Life of Lena Horne* (New York: Atria, 2009), 220.
48. William Goldsmith to Professor Richard Kip, Wharton School, 10 July 1956, box 1, International Workers Order Records, New York University. Goldsmith emphasized the "importance of the [IWO] in the vast network of Communist dominated and Communist oriented organizations. . . . [The IWO] served as a principal source of contacts, fund, jobs, and recruits and was an important outlet for propaganda for the Communist Party in America for many years. One of the reasons it succeeded . . . brilliantly in these functions was that it fulfilled an important role, particularly in the various immigrant communities. The IWO offered cheap insurance to thousands of workers."
49. Maxim Matusevich, "'Harlem Globetrotters': Black Sojourners in Stalin's Soviet Union," in *The Harlem Renaissance Revisited: Politics, Arts, and Letters,* ed. Jeffrey O. G. Ogbar (Baltimore: Johns Hopkins University Press, 2010), 211–44, 230. See also James R. Barrett, "Was the Personal Political? Reading the Autobiography of American Communism," *International Review of Social History* 53 (2008): 395–423: "Important African-American leaders like William Patterson, Claudia Jones, Lovett-Fort Whiteman, Abner Berry and Harry Haywood all had white partners" (412). See also Louise Thompson Patterson Interview, 16 November 1981, Oral History of the American Left, Series I, New York University.
50. Pennybacker, *From Scottsboro to Munich,* 94.
51. NNC Program, 15–17 October 1937, Philadelphia, Metropolitan Opera House, 16 October, 4:30–6:30 P.M., box 6, folder 7, Richard B. Moore Papers, Schomburg Center, New York Public Library.

52. Louise Thompson Patterson Interview, 16 November 1981, Oral History of the American Left, Series I, New York University.

53. William Patterson to Langston Hughes, 5 January 1938, box 127, F2379, Langston Hughes Papers, Yale University: "Dear Lang. . . . my love to the boys in the trenches" of Madrid.

54. Erik S. Gellman, "Death Blow to Jim Crow: The National Negro Congress, 1936–1947" (Ph.d. diss., Northwestern University, 2006), 119.

55. Faith Berry, *Langston Hughes: Before and Beyond Harlem* (Westport, Conn.: Lawrence Hill, 1994), 190, 157.

56. Patterson, *Man Who Cried Genocide,* 140. Thompson too had been married previously, to the writer Wallace Thurman, who was born in 1902 in Utah. By 1934 he was dead of tuberculosis. At the time of their marriage, Thurman said that his wife was a "very intelligent woman who has her own career and who also does not believe in marriage and who is as anxious as I am to avoid the conventional pitfalls into which most marriages throw one." But within months, the marriage was collapsing. Dorothy West, a writer who was part of the film project headed by Thompson, assailed her for supposedly abandoning him on the night his Broadway play opened, a prelude to an acrimonious divorce and the unveiling of his having been arrested in 1925 for having sex with a man in a bathroom at the 135th Street subway station in Harlem. Thompson felt that his "sexual ambivalence" was a factor in the termination of their marriage: "He took nothing seriously . . . and he would never admit that he was a homosexual. *Never, never,* not to me at any rate." See Martin Summres, *Manliness and Its Discontents: The Black Middle Class and the Transformation of Masculinity, 1900–1930* (Chapel Hill: University of North Carolina Press, 2004), 149, 327.

57. Draft Autobiography of William L. Patterson, box 13, folder 12, William Patterson Papers.

58. Ibid.

59. Mary Louise Patterson to Gerald Horne, 14 July 2010, in possession of the author. See also Report, 21 September 1943, 100-39-34, Patterson/FBI/FOIA File.

60. Report, 8 July 1940, 100-39-3, Patterson/FBI/FOIA File.

61. *Midwest Daily Record,* 16 April 1938.

62. *Midwest Daily Record,* 19 September 1939. See also *Midwest Daily Record,* 13 May 1939.

63. *Midwest Daily Record,* 19 November 1938.

64. *Midwest Daily Record,* 24 September 1938.

65. *Midwest Daily Record,* 30 April 1938. See *Midwest Daily Record,* 8 July 1938. A mass movement erupted that was sparked when a Negro, John Robinson, was slain by police: "There has never been anything like it before here in Chicago," said Patterson. See also *Midwest Daily Record,* 17 September 1938.

66. *Midwest Daily Record,* 14 May 1938.

67. *Midwest Daily Record,* 21 May 1938. See also *Midwest Daily Record,* 24 June 1938.

68. *Pittsburgh Courier,* 9 July 1938.

69. *Midwest Daily Record,* 4 June 1938.

70. *Midwest Daily Record,* 1 July 1938. Louis's victory, said Patterson, was a "definite advance in the Negro struggle" that was "ushering in a new stage of struggle," since "defeat of the color line in boxing makes the struggle against it in politics, in economics, on the cultural field, [and] in other spheres of the sporting world more easy." Since "he who fights to save himself must master the theory and art of fighting," this victory was all the more important.

71. *Midwest Daily Record*, 19 November 1938.

72. *Midwest Daily Record*, 9 December 1938. Patterson said that "certain elements among the Czechs and Slovaks . . . when they held their mammoth anti-fascist meeting here in Chicago Stadium, did not desire the presence of a Negro speaker."

73. *Midwest Daily Record*, 9 July 1938.

74. *Midwest Daily Record*, 30 July 1938.

75. *Midwest Daily Record*, 2 September 1938. In 1918, said Patterson, the *Tribune* published "145 articles" that "placed Negroes in an unfavorable light," and "it printed 88 other articles in which it ridiculed the Negro soldiers . . . [and] succeeded in creating a lynch atmosphere out of which flowed the 1919 attacks upon the Negro people. . . . [T]he *Tribune* has not changed. . . . [W]hy then read it when you have the *Daily Record*. . . . [A]s I walked into the 'L' this morning the hands of almost every man and woman clutched at the *Tribune*."

76. *Midwest Daily Record*, 28 October 1938.

77. Gerald Horne, *Race War! White Supremacy and the Japanese Attack on the British Empire* (New York: New York University Press, 2004).

78. *Midwest Daily Record*, 13 September 1939.

79. *Midwest Daily Record*, 7 January 1939.

80. *Midwest Daily Record*, 9 September 1939.

81. *Midwest Daily Record*, 31 August 1939.

82. *Midwest Daily Record*, 9 September 1939. See also Remarks by Eugene Davidson, 9 February 1941, box 2, folder 44, Eugene Davidson Papers, Howard University. "The attitude some Negroes take on this question is not loyalty, not disloyalty, but, if I may coin a word, 'unloyalty,' and their position is understandable."

83. *Midwest Daily Record*, 25 October 1939.

84. *Midwest Daily Record*, 10 November 1939.

85. *Midwest Daily Record*, 6 January 1940.

86. *Midwest Daily Record*, 19 October 1939. See the 26 October 1939 issue for further material on Patterson's antiwar activism. See also Letter to Associated Negro Press, 30 July 1939, Series H, Reel 6, Claude Barnett Papers, Chicago Public Library.

87. Patterson, *Man Who Cried Genocide*, 149. See also Draft Autobiography of William L. Patterson, box 14, folder 2, William Patterson Papers; Special Agent, New York, to Director, FBI, 21 March 1951, 100-39-142, Patterson/FBI/FOIA File.

88. *Midwest Daily Record*, 20 September 1939.

89. *Midwest Daily Record*, 13 November 1939.

90. *Midwest Daily Record*, 20 January 1940.

91. *Chicago Defender*, 4 May 1940.

92. See George Padmore, "Race Relations, Soviet and British," *The Crisis* 50.11 (November 1942): 345–48, 362. The former Red leader acknowledged the obvious: that Moscow's record in this realm was infinitely superior to that of its rivals.

93. William Patterson on A. Philip Randolph, ca. 1940, box 10, folder 42, William Patterson Papers.

94. William Patterson to Langston Hughes, 2 August 1942, box 127, F2379, Langston Hughes Papers, Yale University.

95. Draft Autobiography of William L. Patterson, box 14, folder 2, William Patterson Papers.

96. William Patterson to Langston Hughes, 25 July 1944, box 127, F2379, Langston Hughes Papers, Yale University.

97. William Patterson to Langston Hughes, 4 March 1947, box 127, F2379, Langston Hughes Papers, Yale University.

98. *Chicago Times,* 7 February 1943.

99. *Chicago Daily News,* 9 February 1943.

100. Report, 17 March 1944, 100-39-51, Patterson/FBI/FOIA File. See William Patterson, "A Negro Looks at Russia," *Chicago Defender,* 26 September 1942.

101. Report, 17 March 1944, 100-39-51, Patterson/FBI/FOIA File.

102. William Patterson to Langston Hughes, 23 February 1943, box 127, F 2379, Langston Hughes Papers, Yale University.

103. William Patterson to Langston Hughes, 17 September 1943, box 127, F2379, Langston Hughes Papers, Yale University.

104. William Patterson to Langston Hughes, 25 July 1944, box 127, F2379, Langston Hughes Papers, Yale University.

105. Report, 28 May 1943, 199-39-20, Patterson/FBI/FOIA File. See also K. Keith Kane to Lucien Warner, 25 November 1942, box 29, Philleo Nash Papers, Harry S. Truman Presidential Library, Independence, Mo.

106. "Report from the Field on the Chicago Race Situation," 29 June 1943, box 29, Philleo Nash Papers, Harry S. Truman Presidential Library, Independence, Mo.

107. Report, 12 December 1945, 100-39-75, Patterson/FBI/FOIA File.

108. *New York Post,* 28 September 1945.

109. FBI Report, 23 November 1943, 100-3299, box 154, National Lawyer Guild Papers, New York University.

110. FBI Report, 3 June 1943, 100-45805, box 154, National Lawyer Guild Papers, New York University.

111. *Daily Worker,* 6 June 1943. See also FBI Report, 10 August 1950, 100-3299, box 154, National Lawyer Guild Papers, New York University.

112. FBI Reports, 23 November 1943 and 10 December 1953, 100-3299, box 154, National Lawyer Guild Papers, New York University.

113. *Chicago Star,* 24 August 1946. See also Irwin Silber, *Press Box Red: The Story of Lester Rodney, the Communist Who Helped Break the Color Line in American Sports* (Philadelphia: Temple University Press, 2003).

114. William Patterson, "Against Jim Crow in Baseball," in *A Documentary History of the Negro People in the United States, 1933–1945,* ed. Herbert Aptheker (New York: Citadel, 1968), 375–78, 375, 376. Patterson's newspaper carried numerous articles about this sports issue. See, for example, *Midwest Daily Record,* 8 August 1939.

115. Ishmael Flory to *Chicago Daily Defender,* 29 September 1971, box 3, folder 13, William Patterson Papers.

116. Article by Patterson, 16 January 1973, box 4, folder 29, William Patterson Papers.

Chapter 7. Turning Point

1. William Patterson to "Dear Revels and Matt," 2 July 1945, Reel 17, No. 428, National Negro Congress Papers, Chicago Public Library. See also *Washington Daily Times,* 22 June 1943; Remarks of James Ford, 7 May 1943, box 2, James Ford Papers, New York University.

2. William Patterson, *The Communist Position on the Negro Question* (New York: New Century, 1947), box 2, folder 4, Pettis Perry Papers, Schomburg Center, New York Public Library.

3. *Midwest Daily Record,* 20 January 1939.

4. Report, 7 March 1944, 100-39-58, Patterson/FBI/FOIA File.

5. *Midwest Daily Record,* 20 January 1940.

6. *Chicago Defender,* 12 August 1944.

7. *Chicago Defender,* 17 June 1939.

8. *Midwest Daily Record,* 31 December 1938. See Biography of James Ford, n.d., box 12, folder 32, William Patterson Papers. See also *Pittsburgh Courier,* 2 March 1940.

9. *Chicago Defender,* 26 February 1944.

10. For a more elaborate articulation of this point, see, for example, Gerald Horne, *Black Liberation/Red Scare: Ben Davis and the Communist Party* (Newark: University of Delaware Press, 1994). See also "Proceedings of the Constitutional Convention of the Communist Political Association," New York, 20–22 May 1944, University of Kansas, Lawrence; Cristobal Davis, "Cuba: A Fascist Weakens," *New Masses* 25 (14 December 1937): 5–6.

11. *Chicago Defender,* 3 June 1944.

12. "Stenogram of CPUSA National Board meeting, June 18–20, 1945," box 36, folder 4C, Phillip J. Jaffe Papers, Emory University. On Jacques Duclos, the French Communist leader who helped to spark this internal wrangling in the U.S. party and who was no stranger in North America, see Raoul Damiens, "Duclos: Worker-Statesman," *New Masses* 20 (8 September 1936): 15–17.

13. Louis Budenz, *This Is My Story* (New York: Whittlesey House, 1947), 294.

14. Frederick Vanderbilt Field, *From Right to Left: An Autobiography* (Westport, Conn.: Lawrence Hill, 1983), 178.

15. Howard Fast, *The Naked God: The Writer and the Communist Party* (New York: Praeger, 1957), 139.

16. Joseph Starobin, *American Communism in Crisis, 1943–1957* (Cambridge, Mass.: Harvard University Press, 1972), 94.

17. Bella V. Dodd, *School of Darkness* (New York: Kenedy, 1954), 186, 172.

18. Testimony of Bella V. Dodd, 5 April 1955, Part II, Reel 26, Records of the Subversive Activities Control Board, NARA-CP.

19. Browder rejected the widespread notion that his ouster was the result of a directive from Moscow. Earl Browder to the Editor, 29 September 1950, box 4, folder 8, Theodore Draper Papers, Emory University.

20. *Communists in the Struggle for Negro Rights* (New York: New Century, 1945), Emory University. See also *The Communist Party and the Negro People* (New York: CPNYS, 1945), University of Kansas, Lawrence.

21. Mark A. Huddle, ed., *Roi Ottley's World War II: The Lost Diary of an African-American Journalist* (Lawrence: University Press of Kansas, 2011), 183.

22. Ben Burns to John Pittman, 5 April 1946, box 2, John Pittman Papers, New York University.

23. John Pittman to Ben Burns, 9 April 1946, box 2, John Pittman Papers, New York University.

24. See, for example, "Charges Preferred against Angelo Herndon by Richard B. Moore, Submitted to the Harlem Section and to the New York State Discipline Committee," 8 January 1942, box 6, folder 1, Richard B. Moore Papers, Schomburg Center, New York Public Library.

25. Report, 27 March 1946, 100-39-80, Patterson/FBI/FOIA File.

26. Report, 31 October 1945, 100-39-73, Patterson/FBI/FOIA File.

27. See the 1946–47 news articles on Patterson's activity, 100-39-93, Patterson/FBI/FOIA File.

28. *Daily Worker,* 22 May 1947.

29. *Chicago Times,* 1 May 1947.

30. Bill to "Dear Ken," 19 November 1947, box 33, Counterattack Papers, New York University.

31. Bill to "Dear Ken," 28 October 1947, box 33, Counterattack Papers, New York University.

32. See, for example, John H. Johnson, *Succeeding against the Odds* (New York: Warner, 1989), 195. This most affluent Negro attributes desegregation to "impersonal forces like the Cold War."

33. "American Anticommunist Association" v. J. A. Krug, 1947, box 41, folder 758, NAACP Papers, Howard University.

34. *Washington Daily News,* 26 May 1947.

35. For a fuller exposition of the CRC and details of Patterson's role in it, see Gerald Horne, *Communist Front? The Civil Rights Congress, 1946–1956* (London: Associated University Presses, 1988).

36. Roy Wilkins to Walter White, 1 May 1946, box II, A369, folder 2, NAACP Papers.

37. Gloster Current, 2 May 1946, box II, A369, folder 2, NAACP Papers: "The branches represented were Louisville, Kentucky, Philadelphia, South Carolina, Boston and Houston, Texas." In the same folder, see Marian Wynn Perry to Walter White, 7 May 1946.

38. Lulu White to Walter White, 26 January 1949, box II, A369, folder 3. See also Merline Pitre, *In Struggle against Jim Crow: Lulu B. White and the NAACP, 1900–1957* (College Station: Texas A&M University Press), 2010.

39. Holland Roberts, Educational Director of the CP in San Francisco, to Dr. Goodlett, President of the NAACP chapter, 1947–49, Reel 2, Carlton B. Goodlett Papers, State Historical Society of Wisconsin, Madison.

40. See, for example, Norman Wilson to CRC, 14 December 1946, box 5, Civil Rights Congress–Michigan Papers, Wayne State University, Detroit (hereafter CRC-Michigan Papers). Shockingly, the writer attached his address to his vitriol, suggestive of the putrid climate: "You want the DAMNED BLACK NIGGER to get hold in this country. That's your chief aim and no GOOD WHITE SOUTHERNER is going to see it done.... [I]t is our duty to see that the nigger has been destroyed with the Jew.... [W]e Southerners think and will support ... T. G. Bilbo to the fullest extent.... [W]e will follow through only to destroy the NIGGER, JEW loving Civil Rights Congress."

41. Remarks by Charles Hamilton Houston, 1939, National Conference of ILD, Washington, D.C., Printed Ephemera, New York University.

42. CRC Newsletter, 26 August 1949, box 1, folder 17, John Daschbach Papers, University of Washington, Seattle.

43. William Patterson to Langston Hughes, 17 August 1948, box 127, F2379, Langston Hughes Papers, Yale University.

44. Testimony of Len Goldsmith, 8 December 1954, Part I, Reel 22, Records of the Subversive Activities Control Board, 1950–72, NARA-CP.

45. Testimony of Bella V. Dodd, 5 April 1955, Part II, reel 26, Records of the Subversive Activities Control Board, 1950–72, NARA-CP.

46. Louis Budenz, *The Techniques of Communism* (Chicago: Regnery, 1954), 32. See also Henry Foner and Lorraine Foner, eds., *"In This Corner": Columns by Bill Mardo in the* Daily Worker, 1948, New York University.

47. Bud Schulz and Ruth Schulz, *The Price of Dissent: Testimonies to Political Repression in America* (Berkeley: University of California Press, 2001), 127.

48. Testimony of Dewey Price, 10 January 1955, Part II, Reel 24, Records of the Subversive Activities Control Board, 1950–72, NARA-CP.

49. Testimony of Herman Thomas, 6 January 1955, Part II, Reel 24, Records of the Subversive Activities Control Board, 1950–72, NARA-CP.

50. Testimony of Mary Stalcup Markward, 12 January 1955, Part II, Reel 24, Records of the Subversive Activities Control Board, 1950–72, NARA-CP.

51. Testimony of Barbara Hartle, 12 January 1955, Part II, Reel 24, Records of the Subversive Activities Control Board, 1950–72, NARA-CP.

52. For an examination of the CRC's role in Seattle, where it had one of its strongest chapters, see Michael Bieshuevel, "What Cold War Consensus? Anti-McCarthyism in Washington State, 1947–1955" (M.A. thesis, Western Washington University, 2009).

53. Testimony of Clark M. Harper, 17 and 21 February 1955, Part II, Reel 25, Records of the Subversive Activities Control Board, 1950–72, NARA-CP.

54. Testimony of Rev. Obidiah Jones, 15 February 1955, Part II, Reel 25, Records of the Subversive Activities Control Board, 1950–72, NARA-CP.

55. Testimony of James Glatis, 3 January 1955, Part II, Reel 23, Records of the Subversive Activities Control Board, 1950–72, NARA-CP.

56. Testimony of Matt Cvetic, 13 December 1954, Part II, Reel 23, Records of the Subversive Activities Control Board, 1950–72, NARA-CP. See also Harvey Matusow, *False Witness* (New York: Cameron and Kahn, 1955).

57. Letter to Steve Nelson, 30 September 1988, box 9, Steve Nelson Papers, New York University. See also Daniel Leab, *I Was a Communist for the FBI: The Unhappy Life and Times of Matt Cvetic* (University Park: Pennsylvania State University Press, 2000).

58. Testimony of William Patterson, 26 July 1957, Reel 27, Part II, Records of the Subversive Activities Control Board, 1950–72, NARA-CP.

59. Testimony of Timothy Evans, 21 February 1955, Reel 25, Part II, Records of the Subversive Activities Control Board, 1950–72, NARA-CP.

60. Testimony of John Lautner, 15 November 1954, Reel 22, Part I, Records of the Subversive Activities Control Board, 1950–72, NARA-CP.

61. Pettis Perry, "Destroy the Virus of White Chauvinism," 16 May 1949, Speech Delivered at National Committee of CPUSA, Wilcox Collection, University of Kansas, Lawrence.

62. Dick Reuss to "David (and Barbara) Kopple, 16 January 1980, box 3, Barbara Kopple Peekskill Riots Collection, New York University. See also Howard Fast, *Peekskill USA: A Personal Experience* (New York: CRC, 1951).

63. Louise Thompson Patterson, Oral History, 1979–81, box 3, Barbara Kopple Peekskill Riots Collection, New York University.

64. "Sunday at Peekskill," *American Heritage*, n.d., box 2, Barbara Kopple Peekskill Riots Collection, New York University.

65. James Rorty and Winifred Raushenbush, "The Lessons of the Peekskill Riots: What Happened and Why?" *Commentary* 10.4 (October 1950), box 2, Barbara Kopple Peekskill Riots Collection, New York University.

66. Griffin Fariello, *Red Scare: Memories of the American Inquisition* (New York: Norton, 1995), 78, 79.

67. Arthur Miller, "The Year It Came Apart," *New York*, n.d., box 2, Barbara Kopple Peekskill Riots Collection, New York University.

68. Nicholas diGiovanni, "When Peekskill Saw Red," *Westchester Illustrated* 3.3 (August 1978): 34–39, 58–60, box 2, Barbara Kopple Peekskill Riots Collection, New York University.

69. Testimony of William Patterson, 26 July 1957, Part II, Reel 27, Records of the Subversive Activities Control Board, 1950–72, NARA-CP.

70. Joseph Walwik, "Good Americans: The Peekskill Riots of 1949" (Ph.d. diss., American University, 1994), 4, 117.

71. CRC Statement, 28 August 1949, box 39, Paul Robeson Papers, Howard University.

72. *Baltimore Afro-American,* 10 September 1949.

73. Suzzane Braun Levine and Mary Thom, *Bella Abzug* (New York: Farrar Strauss Giroux, 2007), 111; Heard, *Eyes of Willie McGee,* 108. Heard says that the "permanent scar" was on her chin.

74. Moses Miller, "Victory and Omen," *Jewish Life* 3.12 (October 1949): 3–4, box 2, Barbara Kopple Peekskill Riots Collection, New York University.

75. William Patterson to the *New York Times,* 17 October 1949, PE 036, box 22, Printed Ephemera, New York University.

76. Rorty and Raushenbush, *Lessons of the Peekskill Riots.*

77. Paul Robeson Jr., *The Undiscovered Paul Robeson: Quest for Freedom, 1939–1976* (New York: Wiley, 2010), 174, 158.

78. William Patterson, "Introduction of Paul Robeson," n.d., box 26, Paul Robeson Papers, Howard University. See also Kenneth Greenberg, "Anti-Communism in Harlem during the 1940s: Reactions to Benjamin Jefferson Davis Jr. in the City Council," box 4, Barbara Kopple Peekskill Riots Collection, New York University.

79. Rorty and Raushenbush, *Lessons of the Peekskill Riots.* See also *New Africa,* October 1949, box 64, CRC-Michigan Papers. Robeson received messages "from individuals and organizations all over the United States and from Africa, China, the Soviet Union, England, France and other countries."

Chapter 8. Prison Looms

1. *New York Times,* 22 February 1951.
2. *New York Times,* 3 December 1947.
3. See Horne, *Race War!*
4. Roy Wilkins to Branches, 18 October 1949, box II, A369, folder 2, NAACP Papers.
5. William R. Ming to Thurgood Marshall, 12 August 1947, box II B12, NAACP Papers.
6. *New York Times,* 10 December 1996.
7. David Caute, *The Great Fear: The Anti-Communist Purge under Truman and Eisenhower* (New York: Simon and Schuster, 1978), 178.
8. See Joint Biography of Ernest Goodman and George Crockett, 1992, box 87, Ernest Goodman Papers, Wayne State University, Detroit. Crockett visited Thurgood Marshall in his hotel room at the Cadillac Hotel in Detroit at an NAACP convention. He requested that the association file an amicus brief in the trial of the CP leaders on the grounds that potential jurors on a list had "C" for "colored" accompanying their names. Marshall agreed that this was objectionable but refused to act on anticommunist grounds. Crockett says that his esteem for Marshall fell sharply after this incident. See also Sarah Hart Brown, *Standing against Dragons: Three Southern Lawyers in an Era of Fear* (Baton Rouge: Louisiana State University Press, 1998).

9. Draft Autobiography of William L. Patterson, box 14, folder 10, William Patterson Papers.

10. Mark Naison to Milton Cantor, 26 February 1974, box 2, Barbara Kopple Peekskill Riots Collection, New York University.

11. See the "Hate Mail" from the 1950s forward, carton 69, NAACP Papers, University of California, Berkeley.

12. Franklin Williams to Gloster Current, 6 December 1949, box 1, James C. Clarke Papers, University of Central Florida, Orlando.

13. Thurgood Marshall to William Patterson, 9 June 1950, box II, A369, folder 2, NAACP Papers.

14. William Patterson to Thurgood Marshall, 15 June 1950, box II, A369, folder 2, NAACP Papers.

15. Press Release, 16 June 1950, box 62, CRC-Michigan Papers.

16. Daniel E. Byrd to William Patterson, 12 March 1951, box II, A369, folder 4, NAACP Papers.

17. William Patterson to Jack Raskin, 12 July 1950, box 63, CRC-Michigan Papers.

18. Gloster Current to Walter White, 29 June 1950, box II, A521, folder 3, NAACP Papers.

19. Haywood, *Black Bolshevik*, 572.

20. Statement by Walter White, 6 July 1950, box II, A521, folder 3, NAACP Papers.

21. Thurgood Marshall to Roy Wilkins, 16 November 1949, box II, A193, folder 1, NAACP Papers.

22. Roy Wilkins to William Patterson, 22 November 1949, box II, A193, folder 1, NAACP Papers.

23. William Patterson to Roy Wilkins, 29 November 1949, box II, A193, folder 1, NAACP Papers.

24. *Atlanta Daily World*, 20 May 1949.

25. Roy Wilkins statement on "Patterson-Wilkins Correspondence," 23 November 1949, box II, A193, folder 1, NAACP Papers.

26. Cecile Cooper, NAACP-Queens College, to Roy Wilkins, 8 January 1950, box II, A193, folder 1, NAACP Papers.

27. Roy Wilkins to Rowland Watts, National Secretary of Workers Defense League, 15 December 1949, box II, A193, folder 2, NAACP Papers. See also Alan Wald, *The New York Intellectuals: The Rise and Decline of the Anti-Stalinist Left from the 1930s to the 1980s* (Chapel Hill: University of North Carolina Press, 1987), 110.

28. Roy Wilkins to Fred Korth, Assistant Secretary of Army, 23 December 1952, box II, A200, folder 1, NAACP Papers.

29. Wilson Record, *Race and Radicalism: The NAACP and the Communist Party in Conflict* (Ithaca, N.Y.: Cornell University Press, 1964), 154, 155.

30. "Delegate's Report on the National Civil Rights Mobilization," 17 January 1950, Reel 3, Carlton B. Goodlett Papers, State Historical Society of Wisconsin, Madison. On the barring of students and professors and the like, see *Baltimore Afro-American*, 17 January 1950. On the antiracist record of the ILWU, see Horne, *Fighting in Paradise*.

31. *Baltimore Afro-American*, 20 August 1949; *Daily Worker*, 12 August 1949.

32. "CRC Liberator," February 1949, box 10, CRC-Michigan Papers.

33. Hearings Regarding Communist Infiltration of Minority Groups, Part I: Hearings before the Committee on Un-American Activities. House of Representatives, 81st Cong., 1st Sess., 13–14, 18 July 1949 (Washington, D.C.: Government Printing Office, 1949).

34. Lester Granger to Jackie Robinson, 19 July 1949, I: A, box 155, National Urban League Papers, Library of Congress, Washington, D.C.

35. Branch Rickey to Lester Granger, 20 July 1949, I: A, box 155, National Urban League Papers, Library of Congress, Washington, D.C.

36. Alfred Baker Lewis to Lester Granger, 6 September 1949, I: A, box 155, National Urban League Papers, Library of Congress, Washington, D.C.

37. Memorandum from Lester Granger, 15 October 1954, I: A, box 12, National Urban League Papers, Library of Congress, Washington, D.C.

38. *Baltimore Afro-American*, 19 November 1949.

39. *Baltimore Afro-American*, 31 December 1949.

40. Press Release, 15 December 1949, box 6, CRC-Michigan Papers. See also S. M. Goodman, Civil Rights Congress, New Jersey, to Secretary of State, 16 December 1948, Record Group 59, Decimal File, 842.111/12-1648, NARA-CP.

41. Walter White, "The Strange Case of Paul Robeson," *Ebony*, February 1951, Reel 14, Alexander Gumby Papers, Columbia University.

42. For a fuller exposition of these cases, including Patterson's role, see Horne, *Communist Front?*

43. See, for example, William Patterson to Governor John S. Fine, Pennsylvania, 10 December 1952, Record Group 59, Decimal Files, 741.001/12-1052, NARA-CP.

44. Leandra Zarnow, "Braving Jim Crow to Save Willie McGee: Bella Abzug, the Legal Left, and Civil Rights Innovation, 1948–1951," *Law and Social Inquiry* 33.4 (Fall 2008): 1003–41, 1010.

45. Levine and Thom, *Bella Abzug*, 33, 47, 48, 51, 52, 53.

46. Horne, *Black and Red*.

47. William Patterson to Anne Shore, 17 May 1951, box 3, CRC-Michigan Papers.

48. *Life*, 21 May 1951, box 63, CRC-Michigan Papers.

49. Bella Abzug, Oral History, 1995, Columbia University.

50. Heard, *Eyes of Willie McGee*, 4, 272, 328.

51. CRC "Chapter Bulletin," 14 May 1951, box 10, CRC-Michigan Papers.

52. *The Nation*, 5 May 1951, box 63, CRC-Michigan Papers.

53. Eric Rise, *The Martinsville Seven: Race, Rape, and Capital Punishment* (Charlottesville: University Press of Virginia, 1995), 69, 55, 112–13.

54. Press Release, n.d., box 62, CRC-Michigan Papers.

55. Kenneth Cameron, Department of English, Trinity College, to Governor Tuck, 19 June 1949, box 116, Executive Papers, Papers of Governor William Tuck, Library of Virginia, Richmond.

56. Ray O. Thomas, Salem, Oregon, to Governor Tuck, 29 June 1949, box 116, Executive Papers, Papers of Governor William Tuck, Library of Virginia, Richmond.

57. *Daily Compass*, 1 July 1949.

58. *New York Times*, 28 November 1951.

59. Press Release, n.d., box 63, CRC-Michigan Papers.

60. CRC Press Release, n.d., Series II, box 56a, National Lawyers Guild Papers, New York University.

61. Dr. Edward Corwin et al., "Joint Committee to Secure a Fair Trial of the Trenton Six," 4 April 1951, box 575, H. Alexander Smith Papers, Princeton University.

62. Judge Charles P. Hutchinson, Mercer County, N.J., to William Patterson et al., 16 December 1949, Wilcox Collection, University of Kansas, Lawrence. See also "U.S. District Court, District of New Jersey, Ralph Cooper et al. vs. Charles Hutchinson," University of Kansas, Lawrence. Patterson "being duly sworn, deposes" that he has been "admitted

'pro hac vice'" in Illinois and Pennsylvania and "in good standing" as a member of the bar in New York for twenty-five years.

63. *The Nation,* 21 July 1951, box 64, CRC-Michigan Papers.

64. "Ingram Newsletter," March 1950, box 62, CRC-Michigan Papers. Among these nations were India, Mexico, France, Panama, Egypt, Denmark, the USSR, Uruguay, Belarus, Ukraine, and Yugoslavia.

65. William Patterson on Rosa Lee Ingram, ca. 1954, Reel 2, R7472, "Communist Party Misc. Newspapers," *Negro Affairs Quarterly,* New York University.

66. Anne Shore to William Patterson and Aubrey Grossman, 11 November 1950, box 62, CRC-Michigan Papers.

67. Invitation to dinner for William Patterson, 16 June 1951, box 3, CRC-Michigan Papers.

68. Anne Shore to William Patterson, 21 May 1951, box 3, CRC-Michigan Papers.

69. "CRC News," 24 March 1949, box 2, CRC-Michigan Papers.

70. Press Release, n.d., box 62, CRC-Michigan Papers.

71. Draft Autobiography of William L. Patterson, box 14, folder 8, William Patterson Papers.

72. Testimony of William Patterson, 26 July 1957, Part II, Reel 27, Records of the Subversive Activities Control Board, 1950–72, NARA-CP.

73. Testimony of William Patterson, 26 July 1957, Part II, Reel 27, Records of the Subversive Activities Control Board, 1950–72, NARA-CP. See also *New York Amsterdam News,* 22 July 1950: Patterson addresses a pro-McGee rally in Manhattan at Second Avenue and 101st Street.

74. *Daily Worker,* 3 August 1951, box 2, Phil Bart Clipping Files, CPUSA Papers, New York University.

75. *Los Angeles Times,* 11 January 1951. See also *California Eagle,* 4 January 1951.

76. Remarks of William Patterson, 14 January 1951, box 9, folder 1, Civil Rights Congress, Los Angeles Papers, Southern California Library for Social Studies and Research.

77. Testimony of William Patterson, Part II, Reel 27, Records of the Subversive Activities Control Board, 1950–72, NARA-CP.

78. Testimony of William Patterson, Part II, Reel 27, Records of the Subversive Activities Control Board, 1950–72, NARA-CP. For more on Wells, see *Freedom,* February 1954, box 11, folder 51, William Patterson Papers.

79. Draft Autobiography of William L. Patterson, box 14, folder 5, William Patterson Papers.

80. Gold, "William Patterson: Militant Leader," 35.

81. Jim Maas to CRC-L.A., 15 September 1951, box 9, folder 2, Civil Rights Congress–Los Angeles Papers, Southern California Library for Social Studies and Research.

82. Draft Autobiography of William L. Patterson, box 14, folder 10, William Patterson Papers. See, for example, *New York Times,* 5 August 1950; and *Daily Worker,* 8 August 1950: "A guard stood over Patterson fingering his gun."

83. *Daily Worker,* 14 August 1950.

Chapter 9. "We Charge Genocide"

1. Guy Hottel, Special Agent, Washington, to Director, FBI, 12 October 1950, 100-39-123, Patterson/FBI/FOIA File.

2. "Chapter Bulletin," 2 February 1952, box 1, folder 18, John Daschbach Papers, University of Washington, Seattle.

3. *Daily Worker,* 21 November 1951.

4. Clipping, 29 November 1951, box 2, folder 3, John Daschbach Papers, University of Washington, Seattle.

5. "The Washington State Liberator," February 1952, box 5, folder 11, Naomi Benson Papers, University of Washington, Seattle.

6. Legal Complaint, early 1950s, box 4, folder 10, John Caughlan Papers, University of Washington, Seattle.

7. William Patterson, "We Demand Freedom! Two Addresses by William Patterson," November 1951, box 9, folder 17, Civil Rights Congress Papers, Southern California Library for Social Studies and Research, Los Angeles (hereafter CRC-LA Papers).

8. Johnson, "William Patterson at Seventy," 50.

9. Legal Attache, London, of U.S. Embassy to J. Edgar Hoover, 8 November 1950, 100-39-131, Patterson/FBI/FOIA File.

10. Guy Hottel to J. Edgar Hoover, 29 November 1950, 100-139-134, Patterson/FBI/FOIA File.

11. Legal Attache, Paris, to J. Edgar Hoover, 14 November 1950, 100-139-134, Patterson/FBI/FOIA File.

12. Truncated Report by William Patterson, ca. 1950, 100-39-31, Patterson/FBI/FOIA File.

13. Testimony of William Patterson, 23 May 1955, Reel 27, Part II, Records of Subversive Activities Control Board, NARA-CP.

14. *Daily Worker* [London], 26 September 1950, Patterson/FBI/FOIA File.

15. Clipping, ca. 1950, 100-39-124, Patterson/FBI/FOIA File.

16. Clevelander to J. Edgar Hoover, 12 October 1950, 100-39-123, Patterson/FBI/FOIA File.

17. Testimony of William Patterson, 26 July 1957, Reel 27, Part II, Records of Subversive Activities Control Board, NARA-CP.

18. William Patterson to Anne Shore, 24 October 1951, box 2, CRC-Michigan Papers.

19. *Daily Worker,* 2 December 1951.

20. *Baltimore Afro-American,* 2 February 1952.

21. Report, 11 August 1952, 100-39-203, Patterson/FBI/FOIA File.

22. William Patterson, ed., *We Charge Genocide: The Crime of Government Against the Negro People* (New York: Emergency Conference Committee, 1970), 35, 41, 43, 52, 157, 191, 196.

23. Report, 9 December 1946, 100-39-88, Patterson/FBI/FOIA File.

24. William Patterson to Doris Brin Walker, 15 June 1970, box 4, folder 22, William Patterson Papers.

25. William Patterson to Margie Robinson, 17 November 1949, box 9, folder 17, CRC-LA Papers.

26. Draft Autobiography of William L. Patterson, box 14, folder 15, William Patterson Papers.

27. William Patterson to Louise Thompson Patterson, ca. 1951, box 17, folder 22, William Patterson Papers.

28. *Baltimore Afro-American,* 2 February 1952.

29. William Patterson to Louise Thompson Patterson, December 1951, box 17, folder 22, William Patterson Papers.

30. Richard Lentz and Karla K. Gower, *The Opinions of Mankind: Racial Issues, Press, and Propaganda in the Cold War* (Columbia: University of Missouri Press, 2011), 72–73.

31. William Patterson to Louise Thompson Patterson, December 1951, box 17, folder 22, William Patterson Papers.

32. *Droit et Liberté,* 11 January 1952, box 17, folder 23, William Patterson Papers.

33. Draft Autobiography of William L. Patterson, box 13, folder 10, and box 14, folders 15 and 26, William Patterson Papers. See also in the same collection Remarks by William Patterson, 12 November 1951, box 7, folder 44. At various points, he crossed out "Negroes" and scribbled "Blacks."

34. *Black Dispatch* [Oklahoma City], 29 March 1952.

35. Emil Freed to John Johnson, 31 January 1952, box 9, folder 17, CRC-LA Papers.

36. *Baltimore Afro-American,* 2 February 1952.

37. *Baltimore Afro-American,* 26 January 1952.

38. Paul Robeson to "Dear Friend," n.d., box 16, folder 17, William Patterson Papers.

39. *Washington Daily News,* 4 August 1951.

40. Budenz, *Techniques of Communism,* 264.

41. Radio Report, 30 December 1951, box 16, folder 14, William Patterson Papers.

42. *New York World Telegram and Sun,* 8 January 1952.

43. William Patterson to Louise Thompson Patterson, December 1951, box 17, folder 22, William Patterson Papers.

44. Testimony of 26 July 1957, Reel 27, Part II, Records of Subversive Activities Control Board, NARA-CP.

45. *Baltimore Afro-American,* 23 February 1952, box 9, folder 16, CRC-LA Papers.

46. William Patterson to Arthur McPhaul, 23 April 1952, box 2, CRC-Michigan Papers.

47. William Patterson to Charles Howard, 28 February 1950, box 16, folder 21, William Patterson Papers.

48. Remarks by Walter White, ca. 1951, box 9, CRC-LA Papers.

49. *Detroit Free Press,* 2 December 1951, "Chapter Bulletin," 7 December 1951, box 10, CRC-Michigan Papers.

50. *Baltimore Afro-American,* 8 December 1951.

51. William Patterson to Louise Patterson, 5 July 1954, box 5, folder 3, William Patterson Papers.

52. *Baltimore Afro-American,* 22 December 1951.

53. Clipping, ca. 1950, KV2/1829, National Archives of the United Kingdom, London.

54. William Patterson to Desmond Buckle, 16 August 1950, KV2/1830, National Archives of the United Kingdom, London.

55. *Daily Compass,* 21 December 1951.

56. Clipping, 20 December 1951, box 72, CRC-Michigan Papers.

57. William Patterson to Arthur McPhaul, 27 May 1952, box 8, CRC-Michigan Papers.

58. Arthur McPhaul to William Patterson, 25 January 1952, box 4, CRC-Michigan Papers.

59. "Chapter Bulletin," 2 February 1952, box 10, CRC-Michigan Papers.

60. "Chapter Bulletin," 3 November 1952, box 10, CRC-Michigan Papers.

61. Memorandum, 29 January 1951, box 4, folder 26, John Daschbach Papers, University of Washington, Seattle.

62. "Michigan Daily," ca. early 1952, box 72, CRC-Michigan Papers.

63. Remarks by William Patterson, 21 November 1951, box 2, Civil Rights Congress of Illinois Records.

64. *Cleveland Call and Post,* 15 September 1951.

65. William Patterson to Reverend James Simmons, 13 February 1951, box 3, folder 9, William Patterson Papers.

66. William Patterson to Ralph Reynolds, 13 February 1951, box 16, folder 21, William Patterson Papers.

67. William Patterson to Anne Shore, 4 April 1952, box 2, CRC-Michigan Papers.

68. "Confidential" Teletype, 30 January 1952, 100-139-196, Patterson/FBI/FOIA File.

69. William Patterson to Anne Shore, 22 June 1950, box 7, CRC-Michigan Papers.

70. William Patterson to Anne Shore, 24 October 1951, box 2, CRC-Michigan Papers.

71. William Patterson to Arthur McPhaul, 25 October 1951, box 7, CRC-Michigan Papers.

72. William Patterson and Aubrey Grossman to "Dear Friends," 14 May 1952, box 7, CRC-Michigan Papers.

73. *IWO News Bulletin,* April 1951, New York University.

74. Minutes of CRC Bail Fund, 18 January 1952, box 6, Labor Research Association Papers, New York University.

75. Charney, *Long Journey,* 201.

76. Bernard Smith, *A World Remembered, 1925–1950* (Atlantic Highlands, N.J.: Humanities Press, 1994), 79.

77. Julian Symons, *Dashiell Hammett* (San Diego: Harcourt Brace, 1985), 146.

78. Field, *From Right to Left,* 214, 222.

79. Louise T. Patterson to Esther V. Cooper, 28 March 1950, box 2, CRC-Michigan Papers.

80. Victor Rabinowitz, *Unrepentant Leftist: A Lawyer's Memoir* (Urbana: University of Illinois Press, 1996), 140–41.

81. *Detroit Free Press,* 25 August 1950.

82. Arthur McPhaul to "Dear Friend," 18 May 1954, box 5, CRC-Michigan Papers.

83. *Detroit Free Press,* 8 June 1974.

84. William Patterson to Steve Nelson, 18 January 1954, box 7, Steve Nelson Papers, New York University.

85. *New York Times,* 11 November 1957.

86. "In the United States District Court for the District of Columbia," U.S. v. William Patterson, Criminal No. 1787-50, 5 April 1951, Transcript of Proceedings, box 3, CRC-LA Papers; Memorandum, Special Agent, Detroit, to Director of FBI, 17 February 1964, 100-31597, box 280, National Lawyers Guild Papers, New York University; *Daily Worker,* 16 April 1950.

87. Gerald Meyer, *Vito Marcantonio: Radical Politician, 1902–1954* (Albany: State University of New York Press, 1989), 84

88. Associated Negro Press story, 18 April 1951, Series H, Reel 6, Claude Barnett Papers, Chicago Public Library.

89. "Chapter Bulletin," 30 April 1951, box 10, CRC-Michigan Papers.

90. Draft Autobiography of William L. Patterson, box 14, folder 10, William Patterson Papers.

91. Associated Negro Press story, 18 April 1951, Series H, Reel 6, Claude Barnett Papers, Chicago Public Library.

92. Draft Autobiography of William L. Patterson, box 13, folder 13, William Patterson Papers.

93. *Baltimore Afro-American,* 21 April 1951.

94. William Patterson to George Marshall, 12 August 1949, box 16, folder 20, William Patterson Papers.

95. W. E. B. Du Bois and Ollie Harrington, n.d., box 8, CRC-Michigan Papers.

96. Letter to Anne Shore from unnamed New Yorker, 10 May 1951, box 8, CRC-Michigan Papers.
97. Report by William Patterson, 7 July 1952, box 5, CRC-Michigan Papers.
98. "Chapter Bulletin," 25 June 1951, box 10, CRC-Michigan Papers.
99. "Chapter Bulletin," 21 May 1951, box 10, CRC-Michigan Papers.
100. William Patterson and Aubrey Grossman to "All Chapters, Committees, Friends of CRC," ca. 1952, box 9, folder 17, CRC-L.A. Papers. In the same collection and box, see also Undated Press Release and pamphlet from "National Committee to Defend William L. Patterson."
101. Draft Autobiography of William L. Patterson, box 14, folder 10, William Patterson Papers. See also File on Earl Dickerson, 1950s, Series II, box 6, National Lawyers Guild Papers, New York University.
102. Walter White to Mr. Moon, 8 August 1950, box II, A369, folder 2, NAACP Papers.

Chapter 10. "I am a Political Prisoner"

1. William Patterson to Louise Thompson Patterson, 13 February 1954, box 5, folder 3, William Patterson Papers.
2. *Time*, 11 May 1953, box 29, Ben Burns Papers, Chicago Public Library. See House Un-American Activities Committee, "The American Negro and the Communist Party," 22 December 1954, Western Reserve Historical Society, Cleveland. Of the 5,395 "leading members" of the CP, "only 411 were Negroes." See also J. Edgar Hoover to Robert Cutler, ca. 1950s, box 16, FBI Series, White House Office, OSANSA Records, Dwight D. Eisenhower Presidential Library, Abilene, Kans.: At present, "only 1,994 active, disciplined, dues paying Negro members in the Communist Party." It is alleged here that in 1939 there were 5,005 Negro members in the CP, and in 1946, according to William Z. Foster, CP leader, Negroes were 14 percent of the party; 17 percent in 1947; 14 percent in 1949; and 15 percent in 1950. Thus, 3,701 "at present" is based on an estimated membership of 24,674 in August 1952.
3. *Baltimore Afro-American*, 7 July 1951.
4. Notes from Cabinet Meeting, 9 March 1956, box 16, Maxwell Rabb Papers, Dwight D. Eisenhower Presidential Library, Abilene, Kans.
5. "Memorandum for the President," 7 March 1956, box 16, Maxwell Rabb Papers, Dwight D. Eisenhower Presidential Library, Abilene, Kans.
6. Minutes of Discussion, 30 June 1955, box 2, folder 13, Junius Scales Papers, University of North Carolina at Chapel Hill.
7. Saunders Redding, *An American in India: A Personal Report on the Indian Dilemma and the Nature of Her Conflicts* (Indianapolis: Bobbs-Merrill, 1954), 75, 105, 114, 128, 169, 218, 253.
8. Ronald Radosh, *Commies: A Journey through the Old Left, the New Left, and Leftover Left* (San Francisco: Encounter, 2001), 47. See also Michael Meeropol, ed., *The Rosenberg Letters: A Complete Edition of the Prison Correspondence of Julius and Ethel Rosenberg* (New York: Garland, 1994).
9. Testimony of William Patterson, 26 July 1957, Reel 27, Part II, Records of Subversive Activities Control Board, NARA-CP.
10. Howard Fast, *Being Red* (Boston: Houghton Mifflin, 1990), 316.
11. William Patterson to Marguerite Robinson, 20 November 1952, box 9, folder 3, CRC-LA Papers.

12. Testimony of David Brown, 3 May 1955, Reel 26, Part II, Records of Subversive Activities Control Board, NARA-CP.

13. *Freedom* [New York], January 1953.

14. Testimony of William Patterson, 26 July 1957, Reel 27, Part II, Records of Subversive Activities Control Board, NARA-CP.

15. William Patterson to Ann Shaw, 3 July 1953, box 3, CRC-Michigan Papers.

16. *New York Times,* 24 January 1952.

17. William Patterson to Steve Nelson, 29 November 1952, box 7, Steve Nelson Papers, New York University.

18. William Patterson to Steve Nelson, 18 September 1953, box 7, Steve Nelson Papers, New York University. See also Steve Nelson, *The 13th Juror* (Leipzig: Panther, 1956), 121.

19. William Patterson to Steve Nelson, 4 December 1953, box 7, Steve Nelson Papers, New York University.

20. CRC Press Release, 9 March 1954, Printed Ephemera, New York University.

21. William Patterson to J. A. Rogers, 14 October 1954, box 16, folder 23, William Patterson Papers.

22. *Daily Worker,* 8 December 1954.

23. "U.S. vs. Patterson," 27 January 1955, *Civil Rights Law Letter* 1.1 (February 1955): 1, New York University.

24. Article by James Ford, ca. 1954, box 2, James Ford Papers, New York University.

25. James Ford to "Comrade Flynn," 10 December 1954, James Ford Papers, New York University.

26. Testimony of Patterson's Counsel, 8 February 1955, Reel 24, Part II, Records of Subversive Activities Control Board, NARA-CP.

27. Testimony of David Brown, 3 May 1955, Reel 26, Part II, Records of Subversive Activities Control Board, NARA-CP.

28. William Patterson to Louise T. Patterson, 12 July 1954, box 5, folder 3, William Patterson Papers.

29. William Patterson to Louise T. Patterson, 2 July 1954, box 5, folder 3, William Patterson Papers.

30. William Patterson to Louise Patterson, 8 July 1954, box 5, folder 3, William Patterson Papers.

31. William Patterson to Louise T. Patterson, 16 July 1954, box 5, folder 3, William Patterson Papers.

32. William Patterson to J. A. Rogers, box 16, folder 23, William Patterson Papers.

33. William Patterson to Louise T. Patterson, 2 July 1954, box 5, folder 3, William Patterson Papers.

34. William Patterson to Louise T. Patterson, 16 July 1954, box 5, folder 3, William Patterson Papers.

35. *Pittsburgh Courier,* 20 November 1954.

36. William Patterson to Louise Patterson, 16 July 1954, box 5, folder 3, William Patterson Papers.

37. William Patterson to Louise Patterson, 5 July 1954, box 5, folder 3, William Patterson Papers.

38. William Patterson to Louise Patterson, 8 July 1954, box 5, folder 3, William Patterson Papers.

39. William Patterson to Louise Patterson, 16 July 1954, box 5, folder 3, William Patterson Papers.

40. William Patterson to Louise Patterson, 23 February 1955, box 5, folder 3, William Patterson Papers.

41. William Patterson to Louise Patterson, n.d. [ca. early 1955].

42. William Patterson to Louise Patterson, 8 July 1954, box 5, folder 3, William Patterson Papers.

43. William Patterson to Louise Patterson, 17 July 1954, box 5, folder 3, William Patterson Papers.

44. William Patterson to Louise Patterson, 20 July 1954, box 5, folder 3, William Patterson Papers.

45. William Patterson to Louise Patterson, 17 July 1954.

46. Ibid.

47. William Patterson to Louise Patterson, 25 July 1954, box 5, folder 3, William Patterson Papers.

48. William Patterson to Louise Patterson, 8 September 1954, box 5, folder 3, William Patterson Papers.

49. J. Edgar Hoover to Robert Cutler, ca. 1950s, box 16, FBI Series, White House Office, OSANSA Records, Dwight D. Eisenhower Presidential Library, Abilene, Kans. The following words of the CP were highlighted: "The Negro Question in the United States is no longer just a domestic question . . . it is now an international question. The new stage of the Negro liberation movement merges with the struggle of the colonial and darker peoples of the Far East—as well as Africa—against the common enemy—Wall Street Imperialism."

50. William Patterson to Louise Patterson, 11 August 1954, box 5, folder 3, William Patterson Papers.

51. William Patterson to Louise Patterson, n.d., box 5, folder 3, William Patterson Papers.

52. William Patterson to Louise Patterson, 6 January 1955, box 5, folder 3, William Patterson Papers.

53. William Patterson to Louise Patterson, 17 January 1955, box 5, folder 3, William Patterson Papers.

54. William Patterson to Louise Patterson, 25 August 1954, box 5, folder 3, William Patterson Papers.

55. William Patterson to Louise Patterson, 23 February 1955, box 5, folder 3, William Patterson Papers.

56. *Daily Worker,* 30 March 1953.

57. *Daily Worker,* 10 November 1954.

58. William Patterson Keynote Address, 19–20 February 1955, box 5, folder 4, William Patterson Papers.

59. James Ford to "Dear Ferdi" Smith, 15 December 1955, James Ford Papers, New York University.

60. Carol Boyce Davies, *Left of Karl Marx: The Political Life of Black Communist Claudia Jones* (Durham, N.C.: Duke University Press, 2008), 157.

61. Ward Churchill and Jim Vander Wall, eds., *The COINTELPRO Papers: Documents from the FBI's Secret Wars against Dissent in the United States* (Cambridge, Mass.: South End Press, 2002).

62. J. H. Kleinkauf to A.H. Belmont, 4 February 1955, 100-39-246, Patterson/FBI/FOIA File.

63. FBI Report, 15 February 1955, 100-84-275, Patterson/FBI/FOIA File.

64. FBI Report, 5 August 1955, 100-3-75, Patterson/FBI/FOIA File.

65. William Patterson to WIDF, 5 October 1955, 100-39-273, Patterson/FBI/FOIA File.

66. J. Edgar Hoover to Dillon Anderson, 9 January 1956, box 2, White House Office, Office of the Special Assistant for National Security Affairs: Records, 1952–61, FBI Series, Dwight D. Eisenhower Presidential Library, Abilene, Kans.

67. "BR" to Maxwell Rabb [on White House stationery], 10 May 1955, box 51, Maxwell Rabb Papers, Dwight D. Eisenhower Presidential Library, Abilene, Kans.

68. William Patterson, "A Study in Infamy," *Mainstream* 14.6 (June 1961): 63–64.

69. Testimony of Arthur Paul Strunk, 11 January 1955, Reel 24, Part II, Records of Subversive Activities Control Board, NARA-CP. See also Testimony of Daniel Scarletto, 24 February 1955, Testimony of Anita Bell Schneider, 7 March 1955, and Testimony of Robert Dunn, 19 April 1955, Reel 26, Part II, Records of Subversive Activities Control Board, NARA-CP.

70. Testimony of Barbara Hartle, 9 February 1955, Reel 24, Part II, Records of Subversive Activities Control Board, NARA-CP.

71. Testimony of Bereniece Baldwin, 9 Febuary 1955, Reel 24, Part II, Records of Subversive Activities Control Board, NARA-CP.

72. Testimony of "Georgia Lee Magee," 2 May 1955, Reel 26, Records of Subversive Activities Control Board, NARA-CP.

73. Testimony of William Patterson, 12 May 1955, Reel 27, Part II, Records of Subversive Activities Control Board, NARA-CP.

74. Closing Argument of Posey Kime, 5 July 1955, Reel 27, Part II, Records of Subversive Activities Control Board, NARA-CP.

75. Testimony of William Patterson, 26 July 1957, Reel 27, Part II, Records of Subversive Activities Control Board, NARA-CP.

76. Testimony of David Brown, 9 May 1955, Reel 26, Part II, Records of Subversive Activities Control Board, NARA-CP.

77. Sylvia Brown to William Patterson, 1 February 1955, box 16, folder 16, William Patterson Papers.

78. Testimony of David Brown, 9 May 1955.

79. Testimony of David Brown, 2 May 1955, Reel 26, Part II, Records of Subversive Activities Control Board, NARA-CP.

80. William Patterson to David McKay, 2 February 1955, box 16, folder 24, William Patterson Papers.

81. *New York Times,* 25 February 1955.

82. Milton Friedman to William Nunn, 9 March 1955, box 16, folder 25, William Patterson Papers.

83. U.S. Congress, House of Representatives, Committee on Un-American Activities, 83d Cong., 1st Sess., "Investigation of Communist Activities in the San Francisco Area—Part I" (Washington, D.C.: Government Printing Office, 1954), 3161.

84. William Patterson to D. N. Pritt, 27 July 1955, box 1, William Patterson Papers.

85. Jean Lafitte to William Patterson, 20 September 1956, box 1, William Patterson Papers.

86. Herbert Aptheker to William Patterson, 30 September 1953, box 3, folder 17, Herbert Aptheker Papers, Stanford University.

87. *San Francisco Examiner,* 10 January 1956; *Daily Worker,* 9 January 1956.

88. Leonard G. Garr to Dr. Martin Luther King Jr., 5 March 1956, in *The Papers of Martin Luther King, Jr.,* vol. 3, *Birth of a New Age, December 1955-December 1956,* ed. Clayborne Carson (Berkeley: University of California Press, 1992), 156.

89. John Gates, *The Story of an American Communist* (New York: Nelson, 1958). See also Peggy Dennis, *The Autobiography of an American Communist: A Personal View of a Political Life, 1925–1975* (New York: Lawrence Hill, 1977).

90. James Ford to Editors, 8 November 1956, James Ford Papers, New York University: "During my thirty years in the Communist Party I have found that it has been the practice of some white comrades to play Negroes against each other or to 'line them up' in the most unprincipled manner."

91. Ferdinand Smith to Editors, 16 November 1956, James Ford Papers, New York University: "I was a member of the New York Seamens' Branch of the [CP] at the time the Browder proposals were under discussion and our branch was, if I remember correctly, the only one in New York to reject the proposals."

92. Claude Lightfoot, *Chicago Slums to World Politics: The Autobiography of Claude Lightfoot* (New York: New Outlook, 1988), 120.

Chapter 11. The CP's "FBI Faction" Rises

1. FBI Report, 13 April 1956, 100-39-281, Patterson/FBI/FOIA File.

2. Louise Thompson Patterson, Interview, 16 November 1981, Oral History of the American Left, Series I, 065-063, New York University.

3. FBI–New York Report, 9 January 1958, Patterson/FBI/FOIA File.

4. FBI Report, 9 January 1958, 100-39-319, Patterson/FBI/FOIA File.

5. FBI Report, 16 June 1958, 100-23825-5583, Patterson/FBI/FOIA File.

6. *The Worker*, 27 July 1958.

7. *The Worker*, 3 August 1958.

8. FBI Director to SAC–New York, 24 April 1958, 100-8064, Patterson/FBI/FOIA File.

9. Lester Rodney to William Patterson, 17 May 1958, Patterson/FBI/FOIA File.

10. William Patterson conversation with Ben Davis, 24 January 1958, 100-23825-3-448, ELSUR [Electronic Surveillance], Ben Davis/FBI/FOIA File, Gerald Horne Papers, Schomburg Center, New York Public Library (hereafter Ben Davis/FBI/FOIA File).

11. *The Worker*, 6 September 1959.

12. Ferdinand Smith to "Dear Pat," 12 February 1954, box 4, folder 13, William Patterson Papers.

13. *Proceedings of 16th National Convention of Communist Party, USA, 9–12 February 1957* (New York: New Century, 1957), University of Kansas, Lawrence.

14. William Patterson, "The Fight against Racism: The Monumental Contributions of Bandung and Geneva," ca. 1955, box 12, folder 1, William Patterson Papers.

15. William Patterson to Prime Minister U Nu, 21 October 1955, box 2, folder 18, William Patterson Papers.

16. William Patterson on Little Rock, 1957, box 53, George Murphy Papers, Howard University. See also William Patterson, Remarks, ca. 1956, box 1, William Patterson Papers. See also Patterson's remarks in the *Baltimore Afro-American*, 1 September 1956; William Patterson, "The Negro and the Suez Canal," ca. 1956, box 10, folder 33, William Patterson Papers.

17. J. A. Sizoo to A. H. Belmont, "Confidential," 10 September 1957, 100-39-308, Patterson/FBI/FOIA File.

18. J. Edgar Hoover to Dennis Flinn, 11 March 1954, 100-39-226, Patterson/FBI/FOIA File.

19. William Patterson to George Murphy, 7 March 1957, box 53, George Murphy Papers, Howard University.

20. George Murphy to William Patterson, 1 November 1957, box 53, George Murphy Papers, Howard University.

21. *El Imparcial* [San Juan, P.R.], 6 October 1956, imbedded in Report, San Juan, FBI, 31 October 1956, 100-39-299, Patterson/FBI/FOIA File. This was not Patterson's first journey to Puerto Rico. See also FBI Report, New York City, 24 August 1954, 100-39-232, Patterson/FBI/FOIA File: "Patterson also reported to have been expected in Puerto Rico in late April 1954 under pseudonym of William Livingston to investigate possible civil rights violations of Puerto Rican Police Department in March and April arrests of Nationalists and CP members."

22. John Williamson, Communist Party–Great Britain, to "Dear Pat," 30 July 1957, 100-84275, Patterson/FBI/FOIA File.

23. P. L. Prattis to William Patterson, 7 January 1958, box 11, folder 9, P. L. Prattis Papers, Howard University.

24. P. L. Prattis to William Patterson, 11 February 1958, box 11, folder 9, P. L. Prattis Papers, Howard University.

25. *Washington Afro-American,* 29 June 1957. Matthews recalled the "hectic days of the middle '30s when civil rights were brought into sharper focus than they are today, despite the fact that this is [now] one of the major issues before the present Congress. The reason for it then was the struggle between the races was projected on the world scene with greater impact through the propaganda machinery of International Communism than it is today." Scottsboro meant that "the plight of the colored race in America was as familiar to the people of Europe, Asia, and Africa as it was at home." Though the NAACP survived by purging the radical left, he wondered if it was worth it. Rhetorically, he asked, were U.S. authorities "most concerned with crushing Communist infiltration or did they use the excuse of Communism to eradicate all militant groups which could help advance the cause of the colored race through inter-racial cooperation?" Thus, he added balefully, "this brings us now to the crossroads."

26. William Patterson to W. E. B. Du Bois, Paul Robeson, Ben Davis, James Jackson, James Allen, Alexander Trachtenberg et al., 14 January 1958, Reel 73, No. 338, W. E. B. Du Bois Papers, Duke University.

27. William Patterson remarks, ca. 1956, box 1, William Patterson Papers. At the same site in the same collection in the same box, see William Patterson, "Behind the Scenes at Little Rock," ca. 1957.

28. William Patterson to Editor, *New York Times,* 18 April 1956, box 16, folder 27, William Patterson Papers. In the same collection, see also in box 4, folder 31, William Patterson to *New York Times,* 18 April 1956. The writer hails Du Bois's "splendid challenge to debate William Faulkner on the great issue of desegregation" and scorns the "refusal of William Faulkner to debate Dr. Du Bois."

29. *Baltimore Afro-American,* 21 July 1956. See also William Patterson, "The Negro and the Suez Canal," n.d. [ca. 1956], box 10, folder 33, William Patterson Papers.

30. Report, 26 April 1957, FBI Series, box 2, White House Office, Office of the Special Assistant for National Security Affairs: Records, 1952–61, Dwight D. Eisenhower Presidential Library, Abilene, Kans.

31. FBI Report, 27 October 1958, 100-136272, Ben Davis/FBI/FOIA File.

32. SAC–New York to FBI Director, 4 March 1959, 100-23825-7074, Ben Davis/FBI/FOIA File.

33. J. Edgar Hoover to Robert Cutler, 31 January 1958, FBI Series, box 2, White House Office, Office of the Special Assistant for National Security Affairs: Records, 1952–61, Dwight D. Eisenhower Presidential Library, Abilene, Kans.

34. Remarks of Rhoda Laks, 10 February 1956, Reel 27, Part II, Records of the Subversive Activities Control Board, NARA-CP.

35. Milton Friedman to William Patterson, 7 December 1956, box 16, folder 17, William Patterson Papers.

36. *Baltimore Afro-American,* 10 August 1957.

37. Remarks by William Patterson, 17 May 1955, Reel 27, Part II, Records of Subversive Activities Control Board, NARA-CP.

38. FBI Report, 30 May 1958, 100-47142, Patterson/FBI/FOIA File.

39. FBI Report, 29 May 1958, 100-25861, Patterson/FBI/FOIA File. See Davis conversation with Robeson, 17 February 1958, 100-23825-3-472, Ben Davis FBI/FOIA File.

40. SAC–New York to FBI Director, 18 February 1960, 100-23825-8761, Ben Davis/FBI/FOIA File.

41. *Daily Worker,* 12 July 1956.

42. William Patterson, "Aspects of the Negro Struggle in America," box 1, William Patterson Papers. See also Patterson remarks in Chicago, 10 May 1953, box 8, folder 26, William Patterson Papers: "I have read the Soviet Constitution. The substance is there. But a few short days ago some innocent doctors [were] framed up in the Soviet Union by men high in government. Today they have been freed and those who sought to incite to national chauvinism at their expense are in jail. They will be punished. I ask you to compare this case to that of the innocent Willie McGee, the Martinsville Seven, the Rosenbergs or that heroic Negro woman, Rosa Lee Ingram."

43. William Patterson to John Gates, 11 June 1956, box 1, William Patterson Papers.

44. FBI Report, 22 July 1955, 100-81-7037, Patterson/FBI/FOIA File.

45. Peggy Dennis to "Dear Friend," June 1982, box 9, Steve Nelson Papers, New York University.

46. Although Negroes were more prone to stick with the CP through good times and bad, not least because of a dearth of other opportunities, in mid-1958 the FBI cited the Red leader James E. Jackson as asserting that the heaviest losses in recent times among the membership were among Negroes. If so, as Haywood's defection suggested, this perceived retreat on the Negro Question was a factor. SAC–New York to FBI Director, 2 June 1958, 100-23825-5476, Patterson/FBI/FOIA File.

47. William Patterson, "On Self-Determination," n.d., 1950s, box 1, William Patterson Papers, New York University. See also SAC–New York to FBI Director, 31 July 1958, 100-80641, 100-23825-5835, Ben Davis/FBI/FOIA File. See also SAC–New York to FBI Director, 15 October 1958, 100-80641, 100-3-69-5926, 100-23825-6371, Ben Davis/FBI/FOIA File. See also *The Worker,* 10 August 1958. Patterson saw the mid-1958 arrival of Kwame Nkrumah, the leader of independent Ghana—and his rhapsodically euphoric reception in Harlem—as a reflection of his theory of the Negro Question. See also Cyril Briggs to Theodore Draper, 7 May 1958, box 31, Theodore Draper Papers, Stanford University: "I would not rule out the possibility that the trend toward integration may be reversed at some future time should the Negro people find it to be only a limited integration."

48. FBI Report, 29 May 1958, 100-25861, Patterson/FBI/FOIA File.

49. FBI Director to SAC, 5 August 1955, 100-3-75, 100-18956, Patterson/FBI/FOIA File.

50. Brief by William Patterson, 27 February 1956, box 24, folder 8, William Patterson Papers.

51. SAC-Chicago to FBI Director, 30 March 1960, 100-33741, Ben Davis/FBI/FOIA File.

52. *The Worker,* 27 July 1958.

53. Shirley Graham Du Bois to Ben Davis, 23 December 1957, 100-23825-3-414, Ben Davis/FBI/FOIA File.

54. J. Edgar Hoover to E. Tomlin Bailey, 6 December 1957, 100-3-31, Patterson/FBI/FOIA File.

55. William Patterson to W. E. B. Du Bois, 2 December 1957, Reel 72, No. 943, W. E. B. Du Bois Papers, Duke University.

56. J. Edgar Hoover to Robert Cutler, 6 December 1957, FBI Series, box 2, White House Office, Office of the Special Assistant for National Security Affairs, Records, 1952–61, Dwight D. Eisenhower Presidential Library, Abilene, Kans.

57. J. Edgar Hoover to Dillon Anderson, 9 January 1956, FBI Series, box 2, White House Office, Office of the Special Assistant for National Security Affairs, Records, 1952–61, Dwight D. Eisenhower Presidential Library, Abilene, Kans.

58. Report to SAC–New York, 15 August 1958, 100-23825-5927, Ben Davis/FBI/FOIA File.

59. SAC–New York to FBI Director, 12 February 1960, 100-23825-8654, Ben Davis/FBI/FOIA File.

60. Report to SAC–New York, 30 September 1958, 100-23825-6239, Ben Davis/FBI/FOIA File.

61. Special Agent to SAC, 15 December 1958, 100-17086, Ben Davis/FBI/FOIA File.

62. "The Dan Smoot Report," 30 September 1957, Right Wing Collection, University of Iowa, Iowa City.

63. Patterson influenced Hansberry, who matriculated at the Jefferson School, where he taught and wrote in her early years in New York for Robeson's short-lived newspaper. See SAC–New York to FBI Director, ca. April 1959, 100-23825-7199, Ben Davis/FBI/FOIA File. In the same collection, see also FBI Report, 14 April 1959, 100-23825-7260: Hansberry "tried to contact Ben Davis at his residence." Patterson saw her as a "woman of intelligence and courage" and asserted that her success suggested that "concessions are made to those yesterday it [ruling elite] exploited without relief"—"see the play," he urged. William Patterson, "*A Raisin in the Sun*: A Critique," box 12, folder 9, William Patterson Papers.

64. Rebecca Welch, "Black Art and Activism in Postwar New York, 1950–1965" (Ph.D. diss., New York University, 2002), 132, 167, 202.

65. William Patterson to Langston Hughes, 12 September 1949, box 127, f2379, Langston Hughes Papers, Yale University.

66. FBI Report, 9 February 1959, 100-23825-7003, 100-128814, Ben Davis/FBI/FOIA File.

67. FBI Report, 13 January 1959, 100-23825-6853, Ben Davis/FBI/FOIA File.

68. William Patterson to Langston Hughes, 7 June 1957, box 127, f2379, Langston Hughes Papers, Yale University.

69. Langston Hughes to "Dear Pat," 8 June 1957, box 127, f2379, Langston Hughes Papers, Yale University.

70. FBI Teletype, 18 September 1956, 100-3-81, Patterson/FBI/FOIA File. .

71. "Confidential" FBI Report, 19 September 1956, 100-340180, Patterson/FBI/FOIA File.

72. SAC–New York to FBI Director, 1 November 1956, 100-3-81-7546, Patterson/FBI/FOIA File.

73. SAC–New York to FBI Director, 1 November 1956, 100-3-81, Patterson/FBI/FOIA File.

74. SAC–New York to J. Edgar Hoover, 5 December 1956, 100-3-81, Patterson/FBI/FOIA File. See also *Daily Worker,* 10 October 1956.

75. J. Edgar Hoover to E. Tomlin Bailey, 25 November 1957, 100-39-313, Patterson/FBI/FOIA File.

76. FBI Memorandum, 29 September 1956, 100-39-294, Patterson/FBI/FOIA File.

77. FBI Teletype, 25 September 1956, 100-39-294, Patterson/FBI/FOIA File.

78. FBI Report, 31 October 1956, 100-39-299, Patterson/FBI/FOIA File.

79. William Patterson to Roger Baldwin, 12 March 1957, box 41, Frances Grant Papers, Rutgers University, New Brunswick, N.J.

80. Director, FBI, to SAC–New York, 9 January 1957, 100-3-81, Patterson/FBI/FOIA File.

81. "Secret." FBI Director to SAC-New York, 3 September 1957, 100-3-81, Patterson/FBI/FOIA File.

82. FBI Report, 1 March 1960, 100-80641, Ben Davis/FBI/FOIA File.

83. "Director, FBI to SAC-Chicago, 25 July 1957, 100-3-81, Ben Davis/FBI/FOIA File.

84. SAC–New York to FBI Director, 20 August 1958, 100-23725-6003, 100-3-69, 100-80641, Ben Davis/FBI/FOIA File.

85. SAC–New York to FBI Director, 22 January 1960, 100-23825-8529, Ben Davis/FBI/FOIA File.

86. SAC-Chicago to FBI Director, 3 September 1958, 100-23825-6066, Ben Davis/FBI/FOIA File.

87. SAC-Chicago to FBI Director, 18 December 1959, 100-23825-8324, Ben Davis/FBI/FOIA File.

88. SAC-Newark to SAC–New York, 11 January 1960, 100-23825-8440, Ben Davis/FBI/FOIA File.

89. SAC–New York to FBI Director, 22 February 1960, 100-23825-8707, Ben Davis/FBI/FOIA File.

90. SAC–New York to FBI Director, 2 October 1957, 100-39-311, Ben Davis/FBI/FOIA File.

91. *The Worker,* 17 August 1958.

92. *Cleveland Call and Post,* 27 December 1958.

93. FBI Report, 8 January 1959, 100-23825-6832, 100-80641, Ben Davis/FBI/FOIA File.

94. G. A. Nease to Clyde Tolson, 18 December 1958, 62-88217-2536, Patterson FBI/FOIA File.

95. U.S. Congress, House of Representatives, Committee on Un-American Activities, 86th Cong., 1st Sess., "Passport Security—Part 2," 22–24 April and 5 June 1959, Testimony of William Patterson (Washington, D.C.: Government Printing Office, 1959), University of North Carolina at Chapel Hill.

96. William Patterson to HUAC, ca. April 1959, box 53, George Murphy Papers, Howard University.

97. U.S. Congress, House of Representatives, Committee on Un-American Activities, 86th Cong., 1st Sess., "Communist Training Operations, Part 1," 21–22 July 1959 (Washington, D.C.: Government Printing Office, 1959). Patterson's role as an instructor and

member of the Board of Trustees at the Jefferson School for Social Science was derided as a "Communist front."

98. William Patterson remarks at HUAC, 16 November 1959, box 8, folder 40, William Patterson Papers.

99. U.S. Congress, House of Representatives, Committee on Un-American Activities, 86th Cong., 1st Sess., "Communist Activities among Puerto Ricans in New York and Puerto Rico," New York City, Part 1, 16–17 November 1959 (Washington, D.C.: Government Printing Office, 1960).

100. *New York Daily News,* 18 November 1959; *New York Times,* 18 November 1959.

101. William Patterson conversation with Ben Davis, 26 January 1958, 100-23825-3-450, Ben Davis/FBI/FOIA File.

102. FBI Report, 18 January 1960, 100-23825-8490, Ben Davis/FBI/FOIA File.

103. SAC–New York to FBI Director, 15 April 1960, 100-133884; FBI Report, 27 February 1960, 100-23825-8751, Ben Davis/FBI/FOIA File. Of the party leader Eugene Dennis, Childs said that he "does not work in the best manner at all times," though he "does know how to keep a secret."

104. FBI Report, 27 February 1960, 100-23825-8752, Ben Davis/FBI/FOIA File.

105. FBI Report, 25 April 1958, 100-23825-5260, Patterson/FBI/FOIA File.

106. SAC–New York to FBI Director, 22 March 1960, 100-80641. According to the FBI, Gus Hall "stated that he strongly suspected that Ben Davis Jr. . . . is an FBI informant." It was in this context that the CP hired a specialist to search leaders' homes and offices for electronic surveillance. See FBI Report, 23 October 1962, 100-23825-12109, Ben Davis/FBI/FOIA File. See also SAC–New York to FBI Director, 19 June 1962, 100-23825-11914, Ben Davis/FBI/FOIA File: "The Davis[es] have never been entertained by [Gus] Hall and have been in a tight bind financially for some time. Their financial situation has been a sore point in their marriage and the cause of frequent arguments. It is believed that the 'leaking' of certain information during an interview regarding Hall's luxurious spending habits would have considerable effect of Nina Davis," Ben Davis's spouse. "In addition the possibility of racial discrimination in the Halls ignoring the Davis[es] socially may be the result of such an interrogation."

Chapter 12. Fighting Back

1. SAC–New York to FBI Director, 13 August 1958, 100-39-331, 100-84275, 100-39, Patterson/FBI/FOIA File.

2. FBI Report, 5 January 1959, 100-123825-6807, 100-80641, Ben Davis/FBI/FOIA File.

3. SAC–New York to FBI Director, 15 April 1960, 100-133884, Ben Davis/FBI/FOIA File.

4. SAC-Chicago to FBI Director, 27 February 1960, 100-23825-8749; FBI Report, 27 January 1960, 100-23825-8546, Ben Davis/FBI/FOIA File.

5. FBI Report, 2 February 1959, 100-23825-6816, Ben Davis/FBI/FOIA File.

6. SAC–New York to FBI Director, 24 April 1959, 100-23825-7313, Ben Davis/FBI/FOIA File.

7. SAC-Chicago to FBI Director, 25 May 1959, 100-23825-7496, 100-33729, Ben Davis/FBI/FOIA File.

8. SAC-Chicago to FBI Director, 1 June 1959, 100-23825-7539, 100-3-81, 100-33729, Ben Davis/FBI/FOIA File.

9. SAC-Chicago to FBI Director, 21 January 1960, 100-84275, 100-39, Patterson/FBI/FOIA File.

10. FBI Report, 29 April 1960, 100-39-276, Patterson/FBI/FOIA File.

11. SAC-Chicago to FBI Director, 15 June 1959, 100-3-102, 100-23825-7624, Patterson/FBI/FOIA File.

12. SAC–New York to FBI Director, 8 June 1959, 100-23825-7575, 100-3-102, Patterson/FBI/FOIA File.

13. FBI Report, 24 June 1959, 100-39-352, Patterson/FBI/FOIA File.

14. SAC-New York to FBI Director, 17 May 1960, 100-23825-9156, 100-80641, Patterson/FBI/FOIA File.

15. Memorandum by William Patterson, ca. 1957, box 16, folder 28, William Patterson Papers.

16. SAC–New York to FBI Director, 2 October 1957, 100-84275-2999, Patterson/FBI/FOIA File.

17. SAC–New York to FBI Director, 18 February 1960, 100-39-364 (includes letter from Smith to Patterson, 19 January 1960 and Patterson's reply); FBI Report, 28 November 1958, 100-39-338, Patterson/FBI/FOIA File. On July 14, 1958, an informant asserted that Patterson told Moscow that payment for three thousand copies of the CPUSA newspaper would amount to $13,250.

18. SAC–New York to FBI Director, 23 September 1960, 100-23825-9554, 100-3-69-8004, Patterson/FBI/FOIA File.

19. SAC–New York to FBI Director, 22 September 1960, 100-23825-9544, 100-3-69, 100-80641, Patterson/FBI/FOIA File.

20. SAC–New York to SAC-Chicago, 16 October 1959, 100-23825-8067, Patterson/FBI/FOIA File.

21. William Patterson, "*A Raisin in the Sun*: A Critique," n.d. [ca. 1960], box 12, folder 18, William Patterson Papers.

22. SAC-Chicago to FBI Director, 20 September 1960, 105-87346, Patterson/FBI/FOIA File.

23. FBI Report, *Tass* [Moscow], 19 August 1960, 100-39-3835, Patterson/FBI/FOIA File. See also William Patterson to "Dear Friends," January 1961, box 2, folder 18, William Patterson Papers: "We attended the spy trial of the pilot shot down in American U-2 plane over Soviet territory. . . ."

24. *Baltimore Afro-American*, 10 September 1960.

25. "Top Secret" Report, 22 September 1958, 100-1203, 100-39, Patterson/FBI/FOIA File.

26. SAC–New York to FBI Director, 20 November 1961, 100-20789 ("original copy filed in 100-99729-188"), Patterson/FBI/FOIA File.

27. C. D. Jackson to "Dear Harry," 16 February 1962, box 69, C. D. Jackson Papers, Dwight D. Eisenhower Presidential Library, Abilene, Kans.

28. FBI Report, 7 November 1960, 100-23825-9680, 100-12485, Ben Davis FBI/FOIA File.

29. FBI Report, 10 October 1960, 100-23825-9663, Ben Davis/FBI/FOIA File.

30. FBI Report, 12 October 1960, 100-23825-9627, Ben Davis/FBI/FOIA File.

31. *L'Humanite*, 21 March 1960, FBI Report, 24 March 1960, 100-39-373, Patterson/FBI/FOIA File.

32. Article by William Patterson from Prague press, 18 May 1960, box 10, folder 19, William Patterson Papers. Patterson had long served as chairman of the committee to free Winston and his comrade, Gil Green. See Letter, November 1957, box 245, J. B. Matthews Papers, Duke University.

33. J. Edgar Hoover to Office of Security, Department of State, 20 July 1961, 100-39-400, Patterson/FBI/FOIA File.

34. SAC-Albany to FBI Director, 11 July 1961, 100-18478, 100-39-394, Patterson/FBI/FOIA File.

35. SAC–New York to J. Edgar Hoover, 9 October 1962, 100-372598, Patterson/FBI/FOIA File.

36. SAC to FBI Director, 21 February 1961, 100-39-394, Patterson/FBI/FOIA File.

37. FBI Report, 4 October 1960, 100-23825-9589, Ben Davis/FBI/FOIA File.

38. SAC–New York to FBI Director, 2 August 1961, 100-23825-10491, Ben Davis/FBI/FOIA File.

39. FBI Report, 25 April 1961, 101-23825-10174, Ben Davis/FBI/FOIA File.

40. Roy Wilkins, "Stalin's Greatest Defeat," *American Magazine* 152.6 (December 1951): 21, 107–10, 108, box II A68, Folder 6, NAACP Papers.

41. SAC–New York to SAC–Los Angeles, 26 August 1959, 100-23825-7868, Ben Davis/FBI/FOIA File.

42. FBI Report, 10 April 1959, 100-23825-7328, Ben Davis/FBI/FOIA File.

43. SAC-Chicago to FBI Director, 19 August 1962, 100-23825-11927, Ben Davis/FBI/FOIA File.

44. *Daily World,* 26 May 1973.

45. SAC–New York to SAC-Baltimore, 7 November 1960, 100-23825-9680, Ben Davis/FBI/FOIA File.

46. SAC-Albany to FBI Director, 28–29 August 1959, 100-28825-8004, Ben Davis/FBI/FOIA File.

47. FBI Report, 8 December 1959, 100-23825-8261, Ben Davis/FBI/FOIA File.

48. Lester Bailey to Roy Wilkins, Gloster Current, and Franklin Williams, 21 November 1956, carton 71, folder 31, NAACP Papers, University of California, Berkeley.

49. File on "Communist Suspects," 1960, carton 71, folder 31, NAACP Papers, University of California, Berkeley.

50. Report, n.d., carton 71, folder 31: "We the undersigned protest your candidacy [because] you either are or were one of the attorneys for the Civil Rights Congress."

51. Walter Kirschenbaum, director of public relations, Jewish Labor Committee, to Roy Wilkins, 7 March 1956, Group III, box A74, NAACP Papers. On Capitol Hill, in a session addressed by Senator Herbert Lehman, "The one and only person to approach us at the door without a badge was a reporter for *Jewish Life,* a magazine officially connected with the Communist Party. . . . [O]n Sunday afternoon at the Willard, I spotted Howard Johnson of the Communist Party Negro Commission. . . . [H]e was escorted from the hall. . . . [H]e later approached me in the lobby, as I told several of the union people later on, and threatened me in front of other people with political reprisals (which I took as the funniest thing I have heard in a long time) for keeping 'progressives from attending this great liberation movement of the Negro people.' We stopped a few other people, as you probably know, including Doxey Wilkerson, from entering the main hall on Monday and the church on Sunday." Ultimately, Wilkerson joined Patterson and others in helping Cheddi Jagan establish the University of Guyana. See William Patterson to George Murphy, 21 February 1963, box 53, George Murphy Papers, Howard University.

52. Press Release, 14 November 1957, Group III, box A76a, NAACP Papers.

53. Letter from unidentified correspondent, 7 November 1957, Group III, box A76a, NAACP Papers.

54. Testimony of J. B. Matthews on "Communism and the NAACP," 10 February 1958, Group III, Box A 76a, NAACP Papers.

55. William Patterson to Earl Dickerson, 25 March 1955, box 16, folder 25, William Patterson Papers. Dickerson also served on the board of the CRC in Illinois. See List of Board of Directors, 10 July 1946, box 8, folder 12, Matt Crawford Papers, Emory University.

56. SAC-Chicago to FBI Director, 5 May 1955, 100-3299, box 154, National Lawyers Guild Papers, New York University.

57. FBI Report, 20 July 1965, 100-45805-87, box 154, National Lawyers Guild Papers, New York University.

58. FBI Report, 16 March 1963, 100-23825-12520, Ben Davis/FBI/FOIA File.

59. *The Worker*, 3 January 1960.

60. *The Worker*, 25 October 1959. See also Report by William Patterson, 28 March 1959, 100-123825-7338, Ben Davis/FBI/FOIA File.

61. William Patterson to P. L. Prattis, 9 January 1958, box 11, folder 9, P. L. Prattis Papers, Howard University.

62. FBI Report, 28 November 1960, 100-23825-9746, Ben Davis/FBI/FOIA File.

63. FBI Report, 12 October 1960, 100-23825-9627, Ben Davis/FBI/FOIA File.

64. FBI Report, 23 February 1961, 100-23825-5, Ben Davis/FBI/FOIA File.

65. FBI Report, 25 September 1960, 100-23825-5, Ben Davis/FBI/FOIA File.

66. FBI Report, 4 November 1960, 100-23825-9693, Ben Davis/FBI/FOIA File.

67. FBI Report, 18 November 1963, 100-23825-13236, Ben Davis/FBI/FOIA File.

68. "A Documented Exposé of . . . Communist Agitation and Racial Turmoil: What Is Behind the 'Civil Rights' Revolution?" 1963, University of Kansas, Lawrence. For more on the ties between O'Dell, Davis, and King, see *Let's Quit Kidding Ourselves about "Civil Rights"! The "Civil Rights" Movement Is Basically a Communist-Inspired Program for Communizing the United States* (Anderson, Ind.: American Opinion Library, n.d.), University of Kansas, Lawrence.

69. William Patterson to Nina Popova, Friendship House, Moscow, n.d., box 3, folder 14, William Patterson Papers.

70. SAC–New York to J. Edgar Hoover, 9 October 1962, 100-102320, 100-372598. See also Frank S. Meyer, *The Moulding of Communists: The Training of the Communist Cadre* (New York: Harcourt Brace, 1961); W. Cleon Skousen, *The Politics of Struggle: The Communist Front and Political Warfare* (Chicago: Regnery, 1966).

71. Robert F. Kennedy and SACB v. William Patterson, 1962, Docket No. I-4-62, box 4, folder 18, William Patterson Papers.

72. Testimony of William Patterson, 25 January and 14 February 1962, Part II, Reel 27, Records of the Subversive Activities Control Board, NARA-CP.

73. Report of the Attorney General to the President and the Congress of the United States with respect to the Subversive Activities Control Act of 1950, as amended, 1 June 1963, box 5, Robert F. Kennedy Senate Papers, 1964 Campaign, John F. Kennedy Presidential Library and Museum, Boston.

74. *Baltimore Afro-American*, 30 December 1961.

75. Statement by William Patterson, ca. 1963, box 20, folder 1, William Patterson Papers.

76. FBI Report, 15 January 1963, 100-23825-12403, Ben Davis/FBI/FOIA File.

77. FBI Report, 17 January 1963, 100-23825-12298, Ben Davis/FBI/FOIA File.

78. FBI Report, 9 December 1962, 100-23825-12236, Ben Davis/FBI/FOIA File.

79. Messages on seventieth birthday, August 1961, box 1, folder 1, William Patterson Papers.

80. "Langston" to "Pat," n.d., box 1, folder 1, William Patterson Papers. In the same folder, see also William Patterson to "Dear Lang," 28 September 1961.

81. FBI Report, 22 January 1963, 100-23825-12290, Ben Davis/FBI/FOIA File.

82. Lawrence F. O'Brien to Congressman James A. Haley, 22 February 19, box 695, Subject File, White House Central Files, John F. Kennedy Presidential Library and Museum, Boston.

83. *Philadelphia Bulletin,* 16 November 1965.

84. FBI Report, "Communism and the Negro Movement—A Critical Analysis," 27 November 1965, Office Files of Mildred Stegall, Lyndon Baines Johnson Presidential Library, Austin, Tex.

85. *New York Journal American,* 18 June 1964.

86. *Los Angeles Times,* 1 September 1964.

87. *New York Times,* 26 September 1964.

88. *New York Amsterdam News,* 2 March 1964.

89. William Patterson to Louise Patterson, 4 December 1954, box 5, folder 3, William Patterson Papers.

90. Mary Lou Patterson, "Black and Red All Over," in *Red Diapers: Growing Up in the Communist Left,* ed. Judy Kaplan and Linn Shapiro (Urbana: University of Illinois Press, 1998), 110–15, 111–13. See also Kim Chernin, *In My Mother's House: A Daughter's Story* (New York: Harper and Row, 1984).

91. William Patterson to "Dear Rockwell," 5 September 1961, box 2, folder 18, William Patterson Papers.

92. William Patterson to George Murphy, 25 November 1969, box 53, George Murphy Papers, Howard University.

93. Wedding announcement, 12 October 1961, box 53, George Murphy Papers, Howard University.

94. SAC–New York to FBI Director, 16 April 1964 ("Original filed in 100-3-104-34-688," Patterson/FBI/FOIA File.

95. *Baltimore Afro-American,* 17 October 1964.

96. *New York Amsterdam News,* 5 September 1964.

97. FBI Report, 20 October 1964, 100-3-81-101-6, Patterson/FBI/FOIA File.

98. FBI Report, 5 November 1964, 100-39, Patterson/FBI/FOIA File.

99. FBI Report, 11 February 1965, 100-84275, Patterson/FBI/FOIA File.

100. William Patterson to George Murphy, 3 February 1967, box 53, George Murphy Papers, Howard University.

101. FBI Report, 13 August 1965, 100-39-480, Patterson/FBI/FOIA File.

102. FBI Report, 13 August 1965, 100-84275, 100-39, Patterson/FBI/FOIA File.

103. Gerald Horne, *Race Woman: The Lives of Shirley Graham Du Bois* (New York: New York University Press, 2000), 187; *Ghanaian Times,* 30 December 1964.

104. Bert Klesing to William Patterson, 5 May 1967, box 1, folder 2, William Patterson Papers.

Chapter 13. Patterson and Black Power

1. Statement by William Patterson and Claude Lightfoot, June 1961, Reel 75, No. 88, W. E. B. Du Bois Papers, Duke University.

2. William Patterson to Hermie Huiswood, 2 January 1962, box 1, Hermina Huiswood Papers, New York University.

3. William Patterson Speech, 26 February 1967, box 8, folder 34, William Patterson Papers.

4. William Patterson Response, n.d. [ca. 1960s], box 11, folder 9, William Patterson Papers.

5. Sid Resnick to "Brother Patterson," 27 August 1961, box 2, folder 3, William Patterson Papers.

6. Review of Patterson autobiography, 12 February 1972, box 3, folder 25, William Patterson Papers.

7. Benjamin Gitlow, "'The Negro Question': Communist Civil War Policy," ca. 1960s, Right Wing Collection, University of Iowa, Iowa City. See also "Communism and the Negro Revolution," Richmond, 1964, box 10, folder 9, Civil Rights Documentation Project, Howard University.

8. John A. Morsel, "The Meaning of Black Nationalism," *Crisis* (February 1962), carton 57, folder 61, NAACP Papers, University of California, Berkeley.

9. Statement by Roy Wilkins, 5 August 1959, carton 57, folder 61, NAACP Papers, University of California, Berkeley.

10. See "Hate Mail," carton 69 and carton 70, folder 8, 1950s and 1960s, NAACP Papers, University of California, Berkeley.

11. William Patterson to Lloyd Brown, 31 May 1973, box 4, folder 10, William Patterson Papers.

12. William Patterson, "Anti-Semitism and the Negro Ghetto," n.d., box 8, folder 58, William Patterson Papers.

13. "Negroes with Guns: An Exchange," *Mainstream* 16.2 (February 1963): 37–47. See Statement by William Patterson, n.d., box 10, folder 15, William Patterson Papers.

14. See, for example, Gerald Horne, *Fire This Time: The Watts Uprising and the 1960s* (Charlottesville: University of Virginia Press, 1995).

15. William Patterson to the Editor, 28 April 1972, box 4, folder 10; William Patterson to the Editor, 1 January 1969, box 4, folder 29, William Patterson Papers.

16. Speech by William Patterson, ca. 1972, box 7, folder 37, William Patterson Papers.

17. Article by William Patterson, 15 May 1966, box 10, folder 36, William Patterson Papers.

18. Article by William Patterson, 25 September 1971, box 11, folder 24, William Patterson Papers.

19. Joseph Hayden to Isabelle Auerbach, 16 October 1972, box 3, folder 25, William Patterson Papers.

20. William Patterson to P. L. Prattis, 8 October 1963, box 11, folder 9, P. L. Prattis Papers, Howard University.

21. Robeson, *Undiscovered Paul Robeson*, 349.

22. *New York Amsterdam News*, 1 May 1965.

23. Phillip Abbott Luce, *Road to Revolution: Communist Guerilla Warfare in the USA* (San Diego: Viewpoint, 1967), 105.

24. U.S. Congress, House of Representatives, Committee on Un-American Activities, "Guerilla Warfare Advocates in the United States," 90th Cong., 2d Sess. (Washington, D.C.: Government Printing Office, 1968).

25. *New York Daily News*, 20 July 1964.

26. FBI Report, 25 August 1964, 100-84275, 100-39, Patterson/FBI/FOIA File.

27. William Patterson to the Editor, 15 November 1966, box 4, folder 34, William Patterson Papers.

28. Article by William Patterson, 15 May 1966, box 10, folder 36, William Patterson Papers. For Patterson's further comments on Watts, see *Daily Worker,* 3 April 1966.

29. Alan Stang, *It's Very Simple: The True Story of Civil Rights* (Belmont, Mass.: Western Islands, 1965), 85, 88. See also James D. Atkinson, *The Politics of Struggle: The Communist Front and Political Warfare* (Chicago: Regnery, 1966); John H. Rousselot, *The Third Color: A Look at "Civil Rights"* (Belmont, Mass.: American Opinion, [ca. 1963]), University of Kansas, Lawrence.

30. Alan Stang, *New York: Communist Terror in the Streets* (Belmont, Mass.: American Opinion, n.d.), University of Kansas, Lawrence. Stang focused also on the reputed ties between Ben Davis and Dr. King. For a similar focus to Stang's, see John H. Rousselot, *Civil Rights: Communist Betrayal of a Good Cause* (Belmont, Mass.: American Opinion, n.d.).

31. Gary Allen, *Communist Revolution in the Streets* (Boston: Western Islands, 1967), 13.

32. *Muhammad Speaks,* 6 June 1969.

33. *Muhammad Speaks,* 29 August 1973.

34. Sarah Gibson, "African Revolution/Revolution Africaine," to William Patterson, 28 June 1963, box 19, James Jackson Papers, New York University: "I am enclosing a copy of the galley proofs of part of an article by Harold Cruse, which we are reprinting from *Studies on the Left*. . . . [P]lease do give my kindest regard to Louise (I still remember very well a pleasant 'Cuba Libre' evening we spent at your home)."

35. Elizabeth Sutherland to "Mr. Patterson," 16 June 1967, box 2, folder 4, William Patterson Papers.

36. James Forman, *The Making of Black Revolutionaries* (Washington, D.C.: Open Hand, 1985), 491.

37. Tribute to William Patterson, ca. 1966, box 1, folder 2, William Patterson Papers. See also George Crockett to George Murphy, 9 December 1966, box 1, folder 2, William Patterson Papers: "Since he is a former client of mine, I am personally aware not only of the magnitude of his contributions, but the extent of personal sacrifice he has made."

38. Statement by William Patterson, ca. December 1965, box 11, folder 43, William Patterson Papers.

39. Julian E. Williams, *The Black Panthers Are Not Black . . . They are Red!* (Tulsa: Christian Publications, 1970), 20.

40. "The Sky's the Limit: Documentary Proof of How the Black Panthers Plan to Plunge America into a Communist Revolution," ca. 1970, Wilcox Collection, University of Kansas, Lawrence.

41. David Emerson Gumaer, *The Panthers: Communist Guerillas in the Streets* (Belmont, Mass.: American Opinion, n.d. [ca. 1970]), University of Kansas, Lawrence.

42. Norman Hill, ed., *The Black Panther Menace: America's Neo Nazis* (New York: Popular Library, 1971), 125.

43. U.S. Congress, House of Representatives, Committee on Internal Security, "Gun Barrel Politics: The Black Panther Party, 1966–1971," 92d Cong., 1st Sess. (Washington, D.C.: Government Printing Office, 1971), University of Kansas, Lawrence.

44. Robert L. Allen, *Black Awakening in Capitalist America: An Analytic History* (Garden City, N.Y.: Doubleday, 1969), 87, 88.

45. Charles Garry to "Dear Bill," 5 August 1968, box 2, folder 4, William Patterson Papers.

46. Civil Rights Congress–San Francisco v. Earl Warren, 5 May 1950, box 5, CRC-Michigan Papers (Garry was the attorney of record in this matter).

47. U.S. Congress, House of Representatives, Committee on Internal Security, "The Black Panther Party, Its Origins and Development as Reflected in its Official Weekly Newspaper *The Black Panther*, Black Community News Service . . . Staff Study by the Committee on Internal Security," 91st Cong., 2d Sess. (Washington, D.C.: Government Printing Office, 1970), University of Kansas, Lawrence. See, for example, the *Black Panther,* 4 May 1969: a lengthy article on Patterson; 5 July 1969: an interview of Patterson and Charles Garry by David Hilliard and Bobby Seale; 28 February 1970: Patterson hails Newton; 13 June 1970: analysis of genocide petition.

48. Bill Beeny, "The Attack has Begun!," ca. 1973, Wilcox Collection, University of Kansas, Lawrence.

49. G. Louis Heath, ed., *The Black Panther Leaders Speak: Huey Newton, Bobby Seale, Eldridge Cleaver, and Company Speak Out through the Black Panther Party's Official Newspaper* (Metuchen, N.J.: Scarecrow Press, 1976).

50. *Black Panther,* 21 March 1970.

51. David Hillaird and Lewis Cole, *This Side of Glory: The Autobiography of David Hilliard and the Story of the Black Panther Party* (Boston: Little, Brown, 1993), 145. See also David Hilliard, *Huey: Spirit of the Panther* (New York: Thunder's Mouth, 2006).

52. William Patterson to William Mandel, 25 February 1969, box 3, folder 29, William Patterson Papers.

53. William Patterson on Huey Newton, ca. 1969, box 8, folder 12, William Patterson Papers.

54. William Patterson Speech, n.d., box 8, folder 30, William Patterson Papers.

55. *Berkeley Barb,* 20–26 December 1968.

56. *Daily World,* 2 October 1971.

57. Bobby Seale to William Patterson, box 2, folder 17, William Patterson Papers.

58. *Daily World,* 5 November 1969.

59. William Patterson on Eldridge Cleaver, n.d., box 9, folder 37, William Patterson Papers.

60. Donald Cox to William Patterson, 1 April 1972, box 2, folder 14, William Patterson Papers.

61. Reginald Major, *A Panther is a Black Cat* (New York: Morrow, 1971), 214.

62. William Patterson to Dr. Carlton Goodlett, 2 June 1970, box 3, folder 19, William Patterson Papers.

63. FBI Report, 15 July 1969, 100-39, Patterson/FBI/FOIA File. See also Gilbert Moore, *A Special Rage* (New York: Harper and Row, 1971).

64. Material on Conference, ca. 1969, box 15, folder 40, William Patterson Papers.

65. David Emerson Gumaer, *The Panthers: Communist Guerillas in the Streets* (Belmont, Mass.: American Opinion, n.d. [ca. 1970]), University of Kansas, Lawrence.

66. Fay Stender to H. V. Field, 19 June 1969, box 2, folder 5, William Patterson Papers.

67. Earl Anthony to William Patterson, 9 January 1968, box 2, folder 4, William Patterson Papers.

68. Bettina Aptheker to William Patterson, 24 December 1969, box 2, folder 5, William Patterson Papers: "Can you get Ruby Dee, Ossie Davis, Rev. [Ralph David] Abernathy, Susan Sontag, and possibly someone from Local 1199?"

69. William Patterson to Dr. Carlton Goodlett, 2 June 1970, box 3, folder 19, William Patterson Papers.

70. William Patterson to Robert Trujillo, 14 June 1969, box 2, folder 20, William Patterson Papers.

71. *New York Amsterdam News,* 14 February 1970.

72. Conference Material, March 1970, box 15, folder 43, William Patterson Papers.

73. Conference Material, March 1970, box 15, folder 45, William Patterson Papers.

74. Petition, 1970, box 16, folder 9, William Patterson Papers.

75. Ann Fagan Ginger, ed., *Minimizing Racism in Jury Trials: The Voir Dire Conducted by Charles R. Garry in* People of California v. Huey P. Newton (Berkeley, Calif.: National Lawyers Guild, n.d. [ca. 1969]), box 24, folder 7, William Patterson Papers.

76. William Patterson to Matt Crawford, 4 June 1968, box 17, folder 3, Matt Crawford Papers, Emory University.

77. William Patterson to Matt Crawford, 22 December 1967, box 8, folder 3, Matt Crawford Papers, Emory University.

78. William Patterson to Matt Crawford, 9 July 1968, box 8, folder 3, Matt Crawford Papers, Emory University.

79. John J. Abt with Michael Myerson, *Advocate and Activist: Memoirs of an American Communist Lawyer* (Urbana: University of Illinois Press, 1993), 272.

80. William Patterson to John Abt Dinner Committee, 19 February 1968, box 3, folder 2, William Patterson Papers.

81. George Murphy to Louise Thompson Patterson, 9 January 1970, box 53, George Murphy Papers, Howard University.

82. William Patterson, "Report on San Francisco Trip," 1969, box 15, folder 39, William Patterson Papers.

83. See Horne, *Fighting in Paradise.*

84. William Patterson, "Report on San Francisco Trip," 1969, box 15, folder 39, William Patterson Papers.

85. Harry Bridges and Louis Goldblatt to George Murphy, 16 January 1967, box 1, folder 6, William Patterson Papers.

86. Kay Boyle, *The Long Walk at San Francisco State* (New York: Grove, 1970).

87. Lecture by Claude Lightfoot, 15 October 1969, box 21, folder 3, Louise Thompson Patterson Papers.

88. Judson L. Jeffries, *Huey P. Newton: The Radical Theorist* (Jackson: University Press of Mississippi, 2002), 126.

89. Patterson Book Review, n.d., box 12, folder 7, William Patterson Papers.

90. *Baltimore Afro-American,* 17 February 1934.

91. Donna Jean Murch, *Living for the City: Migration, Education and the Rise of the Black Panther Party in Oakland, California* (Chapel Hill: University of North Carolina Press, 2010), 193.

92. Statement by William Patterson, n.d., box 17, folder 28, William Patterson Papers.

93. William Patterson's notes on Eldridge Cleaver and the "Ideology of the Black Panther Party," n.d., box 15, folder 25, William Patterson Papers.

94. William Patterson on the BPP, n.d., box 15, folder 32, William Patterson Papers.

95. William Patterson, "The Black Panther Party and the Black Liberation Struggle," *Political Affairs* 49.9 (September 1970): 26–36, 27, 35.

96. William Patterson, Attack on Cleaver and Newton, box 17, folder 46, William Patterson Papers.

97. William Patterson on *Revolutionary Suicide,* n.d., box 17, Matt Crawford Papers, Emory University.

98. Huey P. Newton, *To Die for the People: The Writings of Huey P. Newton* (New York: Random House, 1972), 167.

99. *Black Panther,* 19 September 1970.,

100. Newton, *To Die for the People,* 172, 174, 176, 177.

101. William Patterson to Toni Morrison, ca. 1972, box 4, folder 3, William Patterson Papers.

102. Toni Morrison to William Patterson, 17 May 1972, 23 May 1972, box 4, folder 3, William Patterson Papers.

103. William Patterson, Co-Chair Black Liberation Commission, to "All District Organizers," 2 December 1970, box 2, CPUSA Papers.

104. Speech by Louise Thompson Patterson, ca. early 1970s, box 8, folder 42, William Patterson Papers.

105. Memorandum from London, 9 February 1971, 100-407934-101, 100-39, Patterson/FBI/FOIA File.

106. "Proposed Agenda, Angela Davis Legal Defense Fund," 4 August 1972, box 20, folder 14, William Patterson Papers.

107. William Patterson to George Murphy, 22 July 1971, box 53, George Murphy Papers, Howard University.

108. Statement by William Patterson, n.d. [ca. 1971], box 20, folder 6, William Patterson Papers.

109. Material on Patterson birthday celebration, 25 November 1971, FBI Files on Earl Dickerson, box 154, National Lawyers Guild Papers, New York University.

110. William Patterson to Editor of *Afro-American,* 10 November 1970, box 53, George Murphy Papers, Howard University.

111. Marvel Cooke, Oral History, 1989, Columbia University.

112. P. D. R. Davies to D. R. Martin, 16 March 1971, FCO28/1414, National Archives of the United Kingdom.

113. Remarks by William Patterson, 1971, box 29, folder 10, William Patterson Papers.

114. *Baltimore Afro-American,* 22 May 1971.

115. Nathaniel Jones to Roy Wilkins, 22 October 1970, box VIII: 171, folder 4, NAACP Papers.

116. U.S. Congress, House of Representatives, Committee on Un-American Activities, 90th Congress, 1st Sess., "Subversive Influence in Riots, Looting and Burning, Part I," 22, 25–26, 31 October and 28 November 1967 (Washington, D.C.: Government Printing Office, 1968).

117. Margaret Bush Wilson to Roy Wilkins, 31 December 1970, box VIII: 171, folder 4, NAACP Papers.

118. Roy Wilkins to Margaret Bush Wilson, 7 January 1971, box VIII: 171, folder 4, NAACP Papers.

119. Gloster Current to Roy Wilkins, 7 January 1971, box VIII: 171, folder 4, NAACP Papers.

120. *Chicago Daily Defender,* 18 January 1971.

121. George Murphy to William Patterson, 30 July 1971, box 53, George Murphy Papers, Howard University.
122. George Murphy to "Dear Pat," 22 December 1970, box 4, folder 4, George Murphy Papers, Howard University.
123. William Patterson, "Trip to the West Coast of Winston and Patterson," box 18, folder 32, William Patterson Papers.

Chapter 14. Death of a Revolutionary

1. Carlton Goodlett to William Patterson, 31 July 1970, box 3, folder 18, William Patterson Papers.
2. Holland Roberts to Dr. Carlton Goodlett, 2 July 1947, Reel 2, Carlton Goodlett Papers, State Historical Society of Wisconsin, Madison.
3. "Delegate's Report on the National Civil Rights Mobilization," 1–17 January 1950, Reel 3, Carlton Goodlett Papers, State Historical Society of Wisconsin, Madison.
4. Memo from Roy Wilkins, 5 December 1949, Reel 2, Carlton Goodlett Papers, State Historical Society of Wisconsin, Madison.
5. William Patterson to "Dear Doctor," 22 August 1962, Reel 2, Carlton Goodlett Papers, State Historical Society of Wisconsin, Madison.
6. Earl Dickerson to Louise Thompson Patterson, n.d. [ca. 1980], box 24, folder 2, Louise Thompson Patterson Papers.
7. William Patterson to Matt Crawford, 4 June 1968, box 8, folder 12, Matt Crawford Papers, Emory University.
8. Carlton Goodlett to "Dear Bill," 2 April 1968, box 3, folder 18, William Patterson Papers.
9. Herbert Aptheker to William Paatterson, 8 October 1957, box 5, folder 19, Herbert Aptheker Papers, Stanford University.
10. Dr. Martin Luther King Jr. to "Dear Carlton," 1 July 1964, Reel 3, Carlton Goodlett Papers, State Historical Society of Wisconsin, Madison: "I do hope that our paths will cross again in the near future." In the same collection, see also Dr. Carlton Goodlett to "Dear Martin," 9 November 1965: The World Peace Council "is preparing a list of personalities whose outstanding work in behalf of peace should receive recognition. . . . I have been asked to ascertain from you whether you would accept being honored in this manner."
11. Dr. Carlton Goodlett to William Patterson, 19 May 1968, box 3, folder 18, William Patterson Papers.
12. Louise Thompson Patterson to George Murphy, 2 April 1977, box 53, George Murphy Papers, Howard University.
13. Ruth Reese to "Dear Pat," 24 April 1968, box 4, folder 8, William Patterson Papers.
14. William Patterson to Ruth Reese, 30 November 1972, box 4, folder 8, William Patterson Papers.
15. Speech by Carlton Goodlett, 11 December 1977, box 19, James Jackson Papers, New York University.
16. Dr. Carlton Goodlett to Louise Patterson, 25 March 1980, box 24, folder 3, Louise Thompson Patterson Papers.
17. Gus Hall and Henry Winston to William Patterson, 4 March 1971, box 4, folder 24, William Patterson Papers.
18. Lawrence P. Jackson, *The Indignant Generation: A Narrative History of African American Writers and Critics, 1934–1960* (Princeton, N.J.: Princeton University Press, 2011), 214.

19. George Murphy to Louise Thompson Patterson, 23 July 1973, box 53, George Murphy Papers, Howard University.

20. Patterson review of George Murphy, *A Journey to the Soviet Union,* box 12, folder 15, William Patterson Papers. See also his review in the *Washington Afro-American,* 11 November 1975.

21. *Baltimore Afro-American,* 16 February 1974.

22. Smith, *Black Man in Red Russia,* 172.

23. FBI Report, 23 May 1962, 100-23825-11633, Patterson/FBI/FOIA File.

24. Murch, *Living for the City,* 149.

25. George Murphy to William Patterson, 6 September 1978, box 4, folder 4, William Patterson Papers.

26. Dr. Carlton Goodlett to William Patterson, 5 September 1968, box 3, folder 18, William Patterson Papers: "I, for one, do not believe that Mother Russia can do no wrong. This to me is a serious disease from which many dedicated Communists suffer.... [O]ver the years you have been extremely kind to me. I have admired you, Du Bois, and Robeson."

27. Dr. Carlton Goodlett to William Patterson, 29 August 1968, box 3, folder 18, William Patterson Papers: "Eventually the Soviets must get out of Czechoslovakia—the sooner the better."

28. Dr. Carlton Goodlett to June Shagaloff, 2 October 1963, Reel 2, Carlton Goodlett Papers, State Historical Society of Wisconsin, Madison.

29. Conference Brochure, 10–11 November 1972, box 9, folder 31, William Patterson Papers.

30. John Sutton to George Murphy, 1 January 1977, box 1, John Sutton Papers, Howard University: "Pat is one of the finest human beings of all times.... [I]t is wonderful to have a friend like Pat. We met in Moscow some forty years ago.... [O]ne of the most touching messages I have ever received was the letter he wrote me just after the death of my mother."

31. Betty Sutton to "Dear Louise and Pat," n.d., box 2, folder 17, William Patterson Papers.

32. Rebecca Welch, "Black Art and Activism in Postwar New York, 1950–1965" (Ph.D. diss., New York University, 2002), 190.

33. Ossie Davis to William Patterson, 23 December 1969, box 3, folder 11, William Patterson Papers.

34. Ossie Davis to Roy Wilkins, 23 December 1969, box VI, A35, folder 4, NAACP Papers: Davis's spouse, the actor Ruby Dee, "and I are delighted—but not surprised—that you raise your voice in defense of equal justice under law for the Panthers."

35. Ossie Davis to "Dear Pat," 7 February 1976, box 3, folder 11, William Patterson Papers.

36. Ossie Davis to Alexei Kosygin, 18 May 1972, box 3, folder 11, William Patterson Papers.

37. Cyril Philip to "Dear Friend," 5 August 1971, box 20, folder 10, William Patterson Papers.

38. William Patterson to Ossie Davis, 7 April 1972, box 20, folder 13; see also William Patterson to Ossie Davis, 18 April 1975, box 23, folder 14, William Patterson Papers.

39. Interview with Anthony Montiero, 3 March 2011, in possession of the author.

40. William Patterson to Dr. Goodlett, 2 June 1970, box 3, folder 19, William Patterson Papers.

41. Poem by Beah Richards, n.d., box 29, folder 5, William Patterson Papers.

42. "Beulah" to "Dear Mr. P," 13 January 1978, box 2, folder 14, William Patterson Papers.

43. William Patterson to Louise Thompson Patterson, 16 July 1954, box 5, folder 2, William Patterson Papers.

44. William Patterson to Louise Thompson Patterson, 6 January 1955, box 5, folder 2, William Patterson Papers.

45. William Patterson to Beulah Richardson, 12 February 1955, box 16, folder 24, William Patterson Papers.

46. Josephine Baker to William Patterson, 17 January 1961, box 1, folder 6, William Patterson Papers.

47. Theodore Ward to "Dear Pat and Louise," 29 January 1976, box 2, folder 12, William Patterson Papers.

48. "Mele Kakikimaka and a Hauoli Makahiki Hou" from "the Davises: Beth, Mark, Lyon, Helen and Frank Marshall," 13 December 1954, box 5, folder 11, William Patterson Papers. See also Horne, *Fighting in Paradise*.

49. List of Patterson Tribute Committee, ca. 1967, box 1, folder 1, William Patterson Papers. See Frank Marshall Davis, *47th Street: Poems by Frank Marshall Davis* (Prairie City, Ill.: Decker Press, 1948) at Emory University (on the inside cover, Patterson's name is written in his hand; this is apparently from the collection of Louise T. Patterson at that archive).

50. CRC Board of Directors, 1946, box 8, folder 12, Matt Crawford Papers, Emory University.

51. Note from John Howard Lawson, n.d., box 7, folder 4, William Patterson Papers.

52. Patterson review, n.d., box 17, folder 43, William Patterson Papers: On *All in the Family* and *Sanford and Son*, he said: "Neither presents a character involved in today's struggle.... Dominant in the first is racist filth.... In the other Black men draw an image of a new immature, naïve and childlike Black."

53. Jessica Mitford to "Darling Muv," 25 October 1954, in *Decca: The Letters of Jessica Mitford*, ed. Peter Y. Sussman (New York: Knopf, 2006), 149. See also Jessica Mitford to William Patterson, 9 August 1977: "I'm fairly sure you'll have a lot criticisms" of her recent book, a memoir of her years in the CPUSA. "I know if I was French or Italian I'd be a Communist today; it was mainly what I saw as the ineffectiveness of the CP that made me leave" (502). William and Louise Thompson Patterson to Jessica Mitford, ca. 1977: in "one of the most difficult letters I have ever written," Patterson noted, "You write that the CPUSA and even more, the world-wide movement led by the CPSU has failed. I, an avowed representative of the CPUSA, feel the future of mankind lies in socialism." (503).

54. William Patterson to Jessica Mitford, 9 September 1977, box 4, folder 18, William Patterson Papers.

55. Jessica Mitford to William and Louise Thompson Patterson, 17 May 1975, box 4, folder 20, William Patterson Papers.

56. Catherine Fosl, *Subversive Southerner: Anne Braden and the Struggle for Racial Justice in the Cold War South* (New York: Palgrave, 2002), 125.

57. Sir Patrick Dean to Mr. Stewart, 10 January 1966, FO371/185052, National Archives of the United Kingdom.

58. Report from U.K. Embassy, Liberia, 29 November 1963, FO371/167416, National Archives of the United Kingdom.

59. President Lyndon B. Johnson to Prime Minister, 24 March 1965, PREM 13/680, National Archives of the United Kingdom.

60. William Patterson to Editor, 28 April 1972, box 4, folder 11, William Patterson Papers.

61. *Baltimore Afro-American*, 21 September 1971.
62. *Baltimore Afro-American*, 25 September 1971.
63. *New York Amsterdam News*, 13 May 1967.
64. George Murphy to "Dear Pat," 2 February 1974, box 53, George Murphy Papers, Howard University.
65. *Baltimore Afro-American*, 30 November 1971.
66. *Baltimore Afro-American*, 6 November 1971.
67. William Patterson, "The Significance of the Split in the Southern Christian Leadership Conference," n.d., box 11, folder 23, William Patterson Papers. See also *Baltimore Afro-American*, 5 February 1972.
68. William Patterson to Matt Crawford, 9 July 1968, box 8, folder 3, Matt Crawford Papers, Emory University.
69. William Patterson to Betty Murphy Moss, 24 October 1968, box 4, folder 27, William Patterson Papers.
70. Analysis of 1968 presidential election by Patterson, ca. 1968, box 11, folder 3, William Patterson Papers.
71. *San Francisco Sun-Reporter*, 24 August 1974. See also *Baltimore Afro-American*, 28 August 1973.
72. Article by Patterson, 15 September 1976, box 11, folder 22, William Patterson Papers.
73. Patterson review, 3 December 1975, box 12, folder 16, William Patterson Papers.
74. Statement by Patterson, n.d., box 11, folder 36, William Patterson Papers.
75. Book Review by Patterson, n.d., box 12, folder 6, William Patterson Papers.
76. *Baltimore Afro-American*, 2 May 1970.
77. Speech by Patterson, n.d., box 8, folder 34, William Patterson Papers.
78. William Patterson to Henry Winston, 22 August 1975, box 17, folder 28, William Patterson Papers.
79. *Black Panther*, 2 May 1970.
80. *Baltimore Afro-American*, 26 January 1974.
81. *Baltimore Afro-American*, 23 November 1974.
82. Article by Patterson, n.d., box 11, folder 30, William Patterson Papers.
83. Remarks by William Patterson on Luis Carlos Prestes, n.d., box 10, folder 45, William Patterson Papers: "That section of Negroes in the United States who are thinking seriously in terms of national liberation herald the 43rd birthday anniversary" of Luis Carlos Prestes, the leader of Brazil's Communist party. "Hundreds of Negroes marched with Prestes.... They are somewhat freer than in our own United States.... Freedom of [Prestes] will be a blow for the freedom of black men in every section of the Americas."
84. Article by Patterson, 21 November 1975, box 11, folder 42, William Patterson Papers: "The United Nations attacks racists.....The conclusion drawn against Zionism nor the verdict is anti-Semitic. That is why reaction in the USA is so greatly annoyed by it.... Zionism is anti-Semitic.... Blacks should, of historical necessity, be foes to Zionists."
85. George Murphy to William Patterson, 2 February 1974, box 53, George Murphy Papers, Howard University: "Since Zionists keep close tabs on the *Afro's* letter-writers when they deal with Israel and since Parren Mitchell, the Black Representative from Maryland, has been receiving some Zionist slings and arrows because of his honest and objective treatment of the matter in re: Israel, something on this would be in order"—i.e., a letter or article by Patterson.
86. FBI Report, 19 August 1970, 100-39-501, Patterson/FBI/FOIA File.

87. *Baltimore Afro-American,* 30 April 1974.

88. *Baltimore Afro-American,* 1 June 1974.

89. Louise Patterson to George Murphy, 5 May 1974, box 53, George Murphy Papers, Howard University.

90. Holographic Diary, box 1, folder 15, William Patterson Papers.

91. FBI Report, 12 January 1972, 100-84275, Patterson/FBI/FOIA File.

92. William Patterson to John and Bessie Sutton, 19 November 1972, box 2, folder 23, William Patterson Papers.

93. Louise Thompson Patterson to Alice Childress, 20 December 1979, box 9, Alice Childress Papers, Schomburg Center, New York Public Library.

94. William Patterson to Louise Thompson Patterson, 4 December 1954, box 5, folder 2, William Patterson Papers.

95. William Patterson to Louise Thompson Patterson, 2 September 1954, box 5, folder 2, William Patterson Papers.

96. William Patterson to Frank Spector, 14 September 1955, box 16, folder 26, William Patterson Papers.

97. Diagnosis of Dr. William H. Shlaes, 22 May 1950, box 2, folder 1, William Patterson Papers.

98. Helen Winter to William Patterson, 20 July 1971, box 17, folder 27, William Patterson Papers.

99. William Patterson to George Murphy, 22 July 1971, box 53, George Murphy Papers, Howard University.

100. Remarks by William Patterson, ca. 1966, box 8, folder 31, William Patterson Papers.

101. Remarks by William Patterson, 22 October 1971, box 8, folder 8, William Patterson Papers.

102. Mary Louise Patterson-Gilmer to Dear Friends of Pat, 14 February 1980, box 24, folder 1, Louise Thompson Patterson Papers.

103. "Certificate of Death," 5 March 1980, box 24, folder 17, Louise Thompson Patterson Papers.

104. *New York Times,* 7 March 1980.

105. *Daily World,* 13 March 1980, 17 April 1980. See Pamphlet, *Four Score Years in Freedom's Fight,* 22 October 1971, box 84, Reference Center for Marxist Studies Collection, New York University. Patterson, speaking in Chicago, said: "I am 80 years old plus a few days since the date of my birthday passed by."

106. *Cleveland Call and Post,* 13 November 1954.

107. Herbert Aptheker to "Dearest Louise," 12 March 1980, box 24, folder 2, Louise Thompson Patterson Papers.

108. Carlton Goodlett to Louise T. Patterson, 25 March 1980, box 24, folder 3, William Patterson Papers.

109. *Daily Worker,* 28 December 1955.

110. Cheddi Jagan to Helen Winter, n.d., box 24, folder 2, Louise Thompson Patterson Papers.

111. Y. H. Dadoo, Chairman, Central Committee, South African Communist Party to CPUSA, 17 March 1980, Louise Thompson Patterson Papers.

112. Remarks of Johnny Makatini, Representative of African National Congress to the United Nations, 13 March 1980, box 19, James Jackson Papers, New York University.

113. Statement by Congressman Ronald V. Dellums, box 24, folder 3, Louise Thompson Patterson Papers.

114. Statement by Central Committee of Communist Party of Vietnam, box 24, folder 3, Louise Thompson Patterson Papers. In the same site and in folder 2, see some of the other Communist parties sending condolences, including those of France, Canada, Indonesia, Malta, and Israel.

115. Funeral Program, 10 May 1980, box 24, folder 4, Louise Thompson Patterson Papers.

116. "Memorial Service," 19 April 1980, box 24, folder 4, Louise Thompson Patterson Papers.

117. "Memorial Service" and Statement by Ossie Davis, box 24, folder 4, Louise Thompson Patterson Papers.

118. William Patterson to Loften Mitchell, 19 November 1972, box 4, folder 1, William Patterson Papers.

119. Patterson Remarks, n.d., box 14, folder 20, William Patterson Papers.

120. William Patterson to Matt Crawford, 22 December 1967, box 17, folder 3, Matt Crawford Papers, Emory University.

121. William Patterson to Herbert Aptheker, 6 July 1977, box 111, folder 8, Herbert Aptheker Papers, Stanford University.

INDEX

Abernathy, Ralph David, 155, 198, 208
Abraham Lincoln School (Chicago), 88–89, 98
Abt, John, 13, 199
Abzug, Bella, 106, 115–16
Acheson, Dean, 129, 133
African Americans: black Communists, 4–5, 6, 8, 20, 31, 33–34; black nationalism, 190–91; Cold War, 29, 176–77; Comintern, 43; Communist Party, USA, 25, 31, 39, 69, 96, 182–83, 184, 265n46; concessions to, 11, 50, 91, 99, 104, 136, 148, 152, 159, 217; Genocide Convention, 129; ideological split, 2–3, 68; integration, 163; prison population, 119, 136, 147, 148; pro-Japanese opinions, 86; pro-Soviet opinions, 71; radicalism, 25, 39–40, 50, 68, 91, 110; Red Scare, 208; ruling class and, 183; seafarers, 70; self-determinations for, 32, 34, 93, 162, 228n38; socialism, 31, 39; Southern juries, 60, 69, 81; in Tsarist Russia, 222n71; union-organizing drives, 69; white allies, 4, 160; white partners, leaders', 245n49; WLP's opinion of, 8–9; working-class, 2
African Blood Brotherhood, 34
African Council, 150
African National Congress, 14, 216
Afro-American (newspaper). See *Baltimore Afro-American*
Afro-American Liberation Army, 197
Alexander, Kendra, 206
Alexander, Raymond Pace, 50–51, 60, 61, 111
Allen, Robert L., 195
American Civil Liberties Union (ACLU), 56, 100, 117
American Federation of Labor, 76
American Jewish Committee, 106
American Labor Party, 104
American Nationalist Negro movement, 6
American Negro Labor Congress (ANLC), 25, 31, 47
American Rangers, 85
A.M.E. Zion church, 126

Anderson, Marian, 76–77, 165, 243n94
Angela Davis Legal Defense Fund, 210
Angelou, Maya, 216
Anglo-American Communist Party of the Communist International, 68
ANLC. *See* American Negro Labor Congress
anticolonialism: anti-Jim Crow activism, 159, 163–64, 181; Black Liberation movement, 213; Soviet Union, 67; Stalin, Josef, 71; WLP, 133, 187
anticommunism: anti-Jim Crow activism, 160; anti-Negro practices, 57; concessions to Negroes to forestall leftward shift, 50; diminished reputations of Robeson and WLP, 192; Dixiecrats, 125; and Marshall, Thurgood, 252n8; NAACP, 2–4, 31, 113, 179–80, 205–6; racism, 3; and Randolph, A. Philip, 113; and White, Walter, 50; working-class blacks, 2; World War II, 91, 95, 98
Anti-Defamation League, 106
antifascism: anti-Jim Crow activism, 97; Comintern's "popular front" strategy, 72–73, 94; Communist Party, USA, 97; possibility of fascism in America, 103–4, 105, 144, 213
anti-Jim Crow activism: and Acheson, Dean, 129; anticolonialism, 159, 163–64, 181; anticommunism, 160; antifascism, 97; Black Belt thesis, 33; civil rights movement, effect on, 40; Cold War, 109–10, 129; collective guilt, principle of, 97; Communist Party, USA, 69, 94, 97; Communists and non-Communists, uniting of, 61–62; CRC (Civil Rights Congress), 100–101; and Davis, Ben, 178, 189; delusions, 180; domestic elites, 142; and Du Bois, W. E. B., 189; foreign support for, need for, 4, 11–12, 31, 107, 156, 190; and Graham, Shirley, 189; ILD (International Labor Defense), 56, 61–63, 69; India, 142; international support for, galvanization of, 56–57; and Jones, Claudia, 189; labor, 179; League of Struggle for Negro Rights (LSNR), 61, 89; Moscow gold, 4–5; NAACP, 48, 75, 179; racism, 159;

anti-Jim Crow activism (*continued*): and Robeson, Paul, 189; Scottsboro Nine case, 53, 69, 236n45; Soviet anti-Jim Crow film, 64, 246n56; Soviet participation, 5–6, 67; and Trotter, William Monroe, 129; and White, Walter, 5; "white allies" aligned with, 160; and WLP, 1–2, 4, 178, 180, 187, 189, 193; World War II, 98
antiracism: Comintern, 46; ILD (International Labor Defense), 44–45; Scottsboro Nine case, 47; Socialist Party, 63; Soviet Union, 64; trade unions, 113; World War II, 97
anti-Semitism: Chicago, 85; Negro ghettoes, 191; Peekskill mob action (1949), 106
Aptheker, Herbert, 155, 197, 208, 215
Armwood, Frances, E., 139
Associated Negro Press, 122

Baker, Ella, 209
Baker, Josephine, 211
Baldwin, Bereniece, 152
Baldwin, Roger, 39, 56, 167
Baltimore Afro-American (newspaper): blacks in the Soviet Union, 38; circulation, 208–9; CRC (Civil Rights Congress) advertisement, 134; Jim Crow and creation of Communists, 141; and Murphy, George, 159, 206, 208–9; and Patterson, Anna, 214; Peekskill mob action (1949), 105; and Powers, Francis Gary, 176; and WLP, 2, 38, 47–48, 75, 87, 122, 133, 161, 182, 212; WLP-Hillquit debate, 63–64
Bandung, Indonesia, 1955 meeting in, 149, 158–59, 167
Barbusse, Henri, 50
baseball, desegregation of, 9, 90–91, 113, 157
Bassett, Ted, 180
Bates, Daisy, 181
Bates, Ruby, 52, 58
Batista, Fulgencio, 167
Belafonte, Harry, 161
Berry, Abner, 245n49
Bill of Civil Rights for the Negro People, 59
Bill of Rights, 153
Birth of a Nation, The (film), 82
Bittelman, Alexander, 104
Black Arts Repertory, 192
Black Belt thesis: anti-Jim Crow activism, 33; confusion about, 98; global prominence of, 32; Muslim Movement, 193; NAACP, 228n38; Negro republic in Dixie, 32, 34–35; Pan-Africanism, 46; racial equality, 32–33; retreat from, 94; Scottsboro Nine case, 33; segregation, 34; self-determination for Blacks, 32, 34, 93, 162, 228n38
Black Dispatch (newspaper), 2, 133
Black Liberation movement, 56, 203, 213
black nationalism, 190–92, 202
Black Panther Party (BPP), 194–203; and Abernathy, Ralph David, 198; and Allen, Robert L., 195; armed struggle in the United States, advocacy of, 201; Black Liberation movement, 203; black nationalism, 202; and Bridges, Harry, 200; and Brown, Elaine, 201; and Carmichael, Stokely, 201; China, 201; and Clark, Mark, 198; Communist Party, USA, 199, 202; and Davis, Ossie, 197; decline, 203; Emergency Conference to Defend the Right of the Black Panther Party to Exist, 197–98; FBI surveillance, 199; founders, 194; genocide campaign, WLP's, 194, 198; and Goldblatt, Louis, 200; and Gregory, Dick, 198; and Hampton, Fred, 198; and Hill, Norman, 195; and Hilliard, David, 196, 200; and Kinoy, Arthur, 199; and Kunstler, William, 199; labor leaders, 200; "peaceful coexistence" between socialism and capitalism, renunciation of, 201; and Seale, Bobby, 200, 202; and Shakur, Afeni, 197; "United Front against Fascism" conference, 197; and WLP, 13, 187, 194, 195–96, 197–203
Black Panther Party Defense, 199
Black Power, 193
Bloch, Emmanuel, 120
Bloor, Ella Reeve (Mother), 26
Bond, Julian, 104
Bontemps, Arna, 8
Bowles, Chester, 114
BPP. *See* Black Panther Party
Braden, Anne, 211
Bridges, Harry, 200
Briggs, Cyril: African Blood Brotherhood, 23, 34; League of Struggle for Negro Rights, 61; Marxism, 24; *Negro Worker* (journal), 46; and WLP, 23, 24, 61
Broun, Heywood, 59
Browder, Earl: "class collaboration," 94; Communist Party, USA, 94–96, 98, 177, 239n16; and Davis, Ben, 96; and Ford, James, 96; ILD (International Labor Defense), 58; manner, 96; "popular front" strategy, 94; Tehran line, 94, 95; and WLP, 44, 96
Brown, David, 143–44, 146, 154
Brown, Elaine, 201
Brown, Lawrence, 23, 35, 70, 105
Brown, "Rap," 197

Brown v. Board of Education, 146
Brownell, Herbert, 149
Budenz, Louis, 68, 79–80, 95, 101, 133
Bukharin, Nikolai, 33–34
Bullard, Eugene (Jean), 105
Bunche, Ralph: political evolution, 219n1; and WLP, 36, 68, 129–30, 212, 219n1
Burnham, Margaret, 205, 206
Burns, Ben, 79, 81, 97–98

Calloway, Cab, 98
Camacho, Roberto (WLP's son-in-law), 185
Campbell, Grace, 24
Cannon, James P., 44
Capper, Arthur, 99
Carey, Archibald, 84
Carmichael, Stokely, 194, 201
Carver, George Washington, 37
Casspolis, Michigan, 82
Castro, Fidel, 167, 181
Catlett, Elizabeth, 214
Cayton, Horace, 97
Cayton, Revels, 93, 95
Central Intelligence Agency, 151
Chaplin, Charles, 43
Charney, George, 69, 137
chauvinism, 33–34
Chen, Sylvia, 70
Chiang Kai-shek, 7
Chicago, 75–91; Abraham Lincoln School, 88–89, 98; anti-Semitism, 85; black Communists, 8; black nationalism, 90; Childs, Morris, 79–80; Communist Party, USA, 75, 80, 89, 98–99; Davis, Frank Marshall, 79; gun sales, 90; NAACP, 74; Negro unemployment, 75; Negro working class, 75; Oakland-Kenwood Property Owners Association, 98; police brutality, 85; strikes, 98; as vanguard city, 79; Washington Park, 88; Workers' School, 80; WLP, 8, 64, 75–77, 88, 90, 98, 128, 136, 149, 204; Wright, Richard, 79
Chicago Defender (newspaper): black workers in the Soviet Union, 38; Burns, Ben, 79, 97–98; Communist Party, membership in, 9; Gomez, Juan, 65; NAACP support for Angela Davis, 206; Roosevelt, Franklin Delano, 94; WLP, 8, 38, 81–82, 84, 87, 89
Chicago Herald Examiner (newspaper), 81
Chicago Tribune (newspaper), 86
Childress, Alice, 8, 215
Childs, Morris: Chicago, 79–80; Communist Party, USA, 12–13, 158, 163, 167–68, 170–71, 173–76, 185, 201; and Davis, Ben, 170–71; as FBI informant, 12–13, 79–80, 158, 167–68; and Foster, William Z., 176; and Hall, Gus, 171, 174, 175; and Haywood, Harry, 168; and Lightfoot, Claude, 174; and Mao Zedong (Mao Tse-Tung), 176; and Meany, George, 171; and Randolph, A. Philip, 171; and Weinstone, William, 174; and WLP, 12–13, 79–80, 170–71, 183, 187
China: Black Panther Party (BPP), 201; Cuba showdown, 183; entente with United States, 201; Gorohovskaya, Vera, 32; Newton, Huey P., 201; "Nixon to China," 14; revolution (1949), 159; Sino-Soviet split, 175–76, 186, 201; WLP, 173, 175
Chisholm, Shirley, 198
civil rights: abandonment of black radicals as price of, 11, 50, 91, 99, 104, 136, 148, 152, 217; elite support for, 104; internationalism, 2; WLP, 2, 157
Civil Rights Congress. *See* CRC
civil rights movement: alternative route for, possible, 49; anti-Jim Crow activism, 40; CRC (Civil Rights Congress), 101; NAACP, 113; Red Scare, 49
Clark, Mark, 198
Clark, Tom, 100, 113
Cleaver, Eldridge, 107, 198–99, 202, 213
Cleaver, Kathleen, 197
Cold War: African Americans, 29, 176–77; anti-Jim Crow activism, 109–10, 129; concessions to African Americans, 159; Jim Crow, 141; racism, 159; Trenton Six, 117
Cole, Felix, 5
collective guilt, principle of, 97
Comintern: African Americans, 43; antifascism, 72–73, 94; antiracism, 46; Communist Party, USA, 33; and Engdahl, J. Louis, 44; Executive Committee, 44; and Foster, William Z., 44; and Gorky, Maxim, 45; International Red Aid (IRA), 68; Negro Question, 34; and Padmore, George, 71; Pan-Africanism, 42; Pan-American intervention, 42; "popular front" strategy, 72–73, 75, 77, 84–85, 87, 94; Second Congress of the Communist International (1920), 30; self-determination for African Americans, 34; Sixth World Congress, 34; "white chauvinism," 33–34; and WLP, 44
Committee for the Deliverance of the Victims of Scottsboro, 43
Committee of One Thousand White Trade Unionists to Fight Genocide, 135
Communist International. *See* Comintern
Communist Manifesto (Marx and Engels), 23

Communist Party, USA: 1945 meeting, 93–96; Abraham Lincoln School (Chicago), 89; activist activities, variety of, 245n45; African Americans, 25, 31, 39, 69, 96, 182–83, 184, 265n46; antifascism, 97; anti-Jim Crow activism, 69, 94, 97; Bassett, Ted, 180; black communists, 4–5, 6, 8, 20, 31, 33–34; Black Liberation movement, 203; Black Panther Party (BPP), 194–96, 199, 202; Browder, Earl, 94–96, 98, 177; charter members, 44; chauvinism in, 33; Chicago, 75, 80, 89, 98–99; Childs, Morris, 12–13, 158, 163, 167–68, 170–71, 173–76, 185, 201; "class collaboration," 94; COINTELPRO, 222n69; Comintern, 33; convention (1957), 158; CRC (Civil Rights Congress), 3, 100–101; Cvetic, Matt, 102; Davis, Angela, 204, 205; Davis, Ben, 11, 180, 183; Davis, Ossie, 210; Du Bois, W. E. B., 176; Evans, Timothy, 103; Fast, Howard, 12, 96; FBI infiltration, surveillance, 12–13, 80, 102–3, 151, 158, 168, 170, 173, 179, 183, 184, 185; Foreign Affairs Committee, 175; founders, 6; Gitlow, Benjamin, 6; Goodlett, Carlton, 209; government harassment, 161–62; Hacker, Carl, 44; Harlem, 69, 110, 183; Hartle, Barbara, 102; Haywood, Harry, 168; ideological rigidity, 209; ILD (International Labor Defense), 63; importance of, 12; internal struggle, 93–94, 156, 158, 161–62, 168; International Publishers, 95; International Workers Order (IWO), 245n48; Jones, Obidiah, 102; Kaufman, Bob, 11; labor movement, 109; Lightfoot, Claude, 180; March meeting (1963), 180; Markward, Mary Stalcup, 102; membership, black, 9, 33–34, 39, 40, 69, 83, 89, 95, 141, 259n2, 265n46; membership, Illinois, 75; membership, Jewish, 239n16; membership, national, 9, 11, 95, 96, 182, 184, 239n16; Montiero, Anthony, 210; Murphy, Carl, 39; NAACP, 110, 141, 165, 180, 191; Nation of Islam, 193; Negro Department, 44; Negro Question, 33, 93–94, 95, 142, 162–63, 168, 171, 261n49; "Negro work" by, 77; Newton, Huey P., 203; New York City, 40, 239n16; political association, reconstruction as a, 95; pro-Moscow (anti-anti-Moscow) faction, 162; Red Scare, 96; Robeson, Paul, 171; Scottsboro Nine case, 39, 43, 49–50, 64; Tehran line, 94, 95; Thompson, Louise, 8; Trenton Six, defense of, 101; Truehaft, Decca (later Jessica Mitford), 280n53; urban unrest (1960s), 192–93; Weinstone, William, 174; White, Walter, 49–50, 111–12; "white chauvinism," allegations of, 33–34, 96, 102, 103; WLP, 7, 11, 25–26, 27, 34, 93–96, 95, 156, 162–63, 173–76, 180, 182; Wright, Richard, 87

Congress of Industrial Organizations (CIO), 81, 82, 90

Congress of Racial Equality (CORE), 212

Cooke, Marvel, 204

Coughlan, Charles (Father), 89–90

Council on African Affairs, 138

Cox, Donald, 197

CP. *See* Communist Party, USA

Crawford, Matt, 93, 95, 217

CRC (Civil Rights Congress), 99–107; Abernathy, Ralph David, 155; Abzug, Bella, 106, 115; anticommunist prosecutions, 114–15; anti-Jim Crow activism, 100–101; Bail Fund, 137–38; *Baltimore Afro-American* (newspaper), 134; Braden, Anne, 211; Brown, David, 143–44, 154; Budenz, Louis, 101; chapters, number of, 154; civil rights movement, 101; Communist Party, USA, 3, 100–101; Communists, ties to, 34; Davis, Frank Marshall, 211; Detroit chapter, 138; Dickerson, Earl, 211; donors and members list, 126, 140, 145, 146; effectiveness, 10, 153; FBI infiltration, surveillance, 102–3, 110, 144, 152, 153; Field, Frederick Vanderbilt, 138; finances, 137; Ford, James, 150; formation of, 99, 101; Glatis, John, 102; global connections, 121, 125; Hammett, Dashiell, 137–38; Hunton, W. Alphaeus, 138; ILD (International Labor Defense), 9, 99, 101; Ingram, Rosa Lee, defense of, 118; Internal Revenue Service (IRS), 126, 161; Johnson, John H., 133; Lawrence, William, 101; Lightfoot, Claude, 153; liquidation of, 4, 11, 132, 150, 153, 155, 170; Los Angeles, 143, 153–54; Markward, Mary Stalcup, 102; Martinsville Seven, defense of, 117; McPhaul, Arthur, 138; membership, 121; Miami, 152; NAACP, 99–100, 111–12, 116, 179; National Negro Congress (NNC), 99; Peekskill mob action against (1949), 103–7, 142; rallies and meetings of, 120–21; Randolph, A. Philip, 106; Red Scare, 101–2; repression of, 101; Robeson, Paul, 154–55; Rosenberg, Julius and Ethel, defense of, 143; Rothstein, Ida, 138; Scales, Junius, 153; terror against, 152; Trenton Six, defense of, 117; Truehaft, Decca (later Jessica Mitford), 103; United Nations, 117, 131; *We Charge Genocide*, 125–26, 134, 142, 203; White, Walter, 3, 100; WLP, 3, 9, 10, 87, 88, 100–102, 139, 149, 152

Crockett, George, 110, 139, 194, 252n8

Cuba: Batista, ouster of, 167; Pickens, William, 66; Scottsboro Nine case, 65; showdown

over, 183; White, Walter, 66; Williams, Robert, 178; WLP, 6, 65–67, 68, 214
Cullen, Countee, 7, 35
Cunard, Nancy, 45, 70, 72
Current, Gloster, 100, 111, 205
Cvetic, Matt, 102–3

Daily Worker (British newspaper), 45
Daily Worker (New York newspaper), 49, 63, 156, 161
Damon, Anna, 96
Danbury Federal Prison, 141
Davis, Angela: and Abt, John, 13; and Alexander, Kendra, 206; Angela Davis Legal Defense Fund, 210; and Burnham, Margaret, 206; campaign to free, 203–5; codefendant, 206; Communist Party, USA, 204, 205; and Cooke, Marvel, 204; and Current, Gloster, 205–6; FBI, arrest by, 13; Marin County Jail, 206; NAACP, 205–6; overseas reactions, 204–5; and Thompson, Louise, 204; and Wilkins, Roy, 205, 212; and Winston, Henry, 206; and WLP, 13, 187, 203–5, 206, 216
Davis, Angela, mother of, 204
Davis, Ben: anti-Jim Crow activism, 178, 189; and Browder, Earl, 96; and Childs, Morris, 170–71; Communist Party, USA, 11, 180, 183; and Dickerson, Earl, 90; and Dodd, Bella V., 96; FBI surveillance, 12, 178, 181, 182, 268n106; and Franklin, C. L., 182; and Hall, Gus, 171, 268n106; harassment by government agencies, 182; and Herndon, Angelo, 56; and Houston, Charles Hamilton, 74; ideological purgatory, 217; and King, Martin Luther, Jr., 12; law school, 186; League of Struggle for Negro Rights, 61; "Meaning of Little Rock" symposium, 160; NAACP, 178–79, 180; New York City Council, 59; and Powell, Adam Clayton, Jr., 59, 164; Scottsboro Nine case, 56; wife, 268n106; and Wilkins, Roy, 178–79; and WLP, 56–57, 61, 93, 156, 158, 170, 178–79, 186
Davis, Ben, Sr., 5, 12
Davis, Frank Marshall, 79, 88, 211
Davis, Nina, 268n106
Davis, Ossie: Angela Davis Legal Defense Fund, 210; Black Panther Party (BPP), 197, 198; Communist Party, USA, 210; and Kosygin, Alexei, 210; Martinsville Seven, defense of, 210; and Robeson, Paul, 210; and Wilkins, Roy, 210; and Winston, Henry, 210; and WLP, 8, 197, 216
Dawson, William, 86, 123
Dean, Patrick, 211–12
Declaration of Independence, 153

Dee, Ruby, 216
Delaney, Bessie, 22
Delaney, Dr. "Hap," 22
Dellums, Ronald V., 216
Democratic Party, 85–86
Dennis, Eugene, 101, 162, 174
Dennis, Peggy, 162
De Priest, Oscar, 42, 59
Derrick, John, 18
Dewey, Thomas, 105
Dickerson, Earl: and Burns, Ben, 81; CRC (Civil Rights Congress), 211; and Davis, Ben, 90; FBI surveillance, 90, 180; and Goodlett, Carlton, 180; and Houston, Charles Hamilton, 76; and Johnson, John H., 90; Soviet Union, delegation to, 168; and WLP, 9, 76, 90, 140, 168
Dimitrov, Georgi, 58, 197
Dingaan, 47
Dissent (magazine), 4
Dixiecrats: anticommunism, 125; Democratic Party, 85–86; isolation and debilitation of radicals, 152; retreat, 135; WLP, 9, 85–86, 169
Dodd, Bella V., 96, 101
Dos Possos, John, 26
Douglas, Aaron, 8
Douglass, Frederick: abolitionism, 1; enslavement, 53; and Ford, James, 94; and Gomez, Juan, 65; isolation of Negro labor, 88; and WLP, 2, 215
Dreiser, Theodore, 58
Driscoll, Alfred, 117
Du Bois, Shirley Graham, 164, 186, 189, 217
Du Bois, W. E. B.: anti-Jim Crow activism, 189; Communist Party, USA, 176; and Hoover, J. Edgar, 182; ideological purgatory, 217; Ingram, Rosa Lee, defense of, 117–18; "Meaning of Little Rock" symposium, 160; Moscow, 176; *Muhammad Speaks* (journal), 194; NAACP, 39, 129; and Nkrhumah, Kwame, 186; passport, 170; Soviet attacks on Jim Crow, 5; Soviet Union, 25, 71; and Thompson, Louise, 83, 114; United Nations, 129; and WLP, 74, 114, 115, 118, 140, 163–64
Duclos, Jacques, 1, 177
Dunnigan, Alice, 122
Durham, Richard, 223n73
Dyett, Hall, and Patterson (law firm), 22
Dyett, Thomas, 22

Eastland, James, 169
Edwards, Thyra, 68–69, 70
Einstein, Albert, 43
Ellison, Ralph, 2

Emergency Conference to Defend the Right of the Black Panther Party to Exist, 197–98
Emeryville, California, 18, 22, 27
Engdahl, J. Louis, 43, 44–45
Engels, Friedrich, 23
Evans, Timothy, 103

Fair Employment Practices Committee, 90, 135
fascism in America, possibility of, 103–4, 105, 144, 213
fascism in Europe, rise of, 72, 109
Fast, Howard: Communist Party, USA, 12, 96; Croton, New York, 104; and Radosh, Ronald, 143; Rosenberg, Julius and Ethel, defense of, 143; and Stalin, Josef, 12; and WLP, 12, 118, 137, 140, 143
Faubus, Orval, 165
Faulkner, William, 160
FBI: COINTELPRO, 222n69; Davis, Angela, arrest of, 13; Mormon Church, use of, 154; Scottsboro Nine case, 43
FBI informants: Baldwin, Bereniece, 152; Brown, David, 143–44, 146, 154; Budenz, Louis, 68, 79; Childs, Morris, 12–13, 79–80, 158, 167–68; Clevelander, a, 127; Cvetic, Matt, 102; Evans, Timothy, 103; Glatis, John, 102; Harper, Clark, 102; Hartle, Barbara, 102, 152; Jones, Obidiah, 102; Markward, Mary Stalcup, 102; Marshall, Thurgood, 110; payoffs to, 102, 103, 153; summer camp, cook at, 185
FBI surveillance of: Black Panther Party (BPP), 199; Communist Party, USA, 12–13, 80, 102–3, 151, 158, 168, 170, 173, 179, 183, 184, 185; CRC (Civil Rights Congress), 102–3, 110, 144, 152, 153; Davis, Ben, 12, 178, 181, 182, 268n106; Dickerson, Earl, 90, 180; Flory, Ishmael, 82; King, Martin Luther, Jr., 184; NAACP, 180; Patterson, Mary Lou, 184; Robeson, Paul, 163; Williams, Robert, 178; WLP, 7, 10, 67–68, 69, 75, 80, 81, 89–90, 98, 127, 128, 137, 151, 157–58, 161, 162, 164–69, 173–77, 184, 185–86, 193, 197, 200, 209, 214, 223n77, 223n78
Field, Frederick Vanderbilt, 138
Field, Marshall, 88
First Amendment, 169
First International Conference on Negro Workers (1930), 46
First International Negro Workers' Congress (1930), 72
First International Trade Union Conference of Negro Workers (1930), 36, 68
Fisk University, 200
Flory, Ishmael, 82, 91, 97, 98

Flynn, Elizabeth Gurley, 173
Ford, James: American Negro Labor Congress (ANLC), 47; and Browder, Earl, 96; and Bukharin, Nikolai, 33; CRC (Civil Rights Congress), 150; and Douglass, Frederick, 94; First International Trade Union Conference of Negro Workers (1930), 36, 68; Hamburg, 36; ILD in Harlem, 55–56; and Jones, Claudia, 150–51; Kiswahili language, 36; League of Struggle for Negro Rights, 61; and Miller, Kelly, 76; NAACP, 74–75; Negro Question, 151; Paris, 68; revolutionary activity among Negroes, 68; and Schuyler, George, 72; Scottsboro Nine case, 58, 220n31; and Smith, Ferdinand, 150; Soviet Union, 67; vice-presidential campaign (1932), 65; and WLP, 34–35, 36, 61, 68, 93, 94, 145–46; World Congress of the Anti-Imperialist League (1927), 36
Forman, James, 104
Fort-Whiteman, Lovett, 24, 229n47, 245n49
Foster, William Z.: ailments, 162; and Childs, Morris, 176; Comintern, 44; and Dodd, Bella V., 101; and Mao Zedong (Mao Tse-Tung), 176; and WLP, 129, 145, 156
Fox, L. C., 9
France, 68
Frankfurter, Felix, 235n36
Franklin, Aretha, 182
Franklin, C. L., 182
Frazier, E. Franklin, 140
Friedman, Milton, 145–46, 154, 174
Froebel High School (Gary, Indiana), 90

Galt, Edith Rolling, 7
Galt, William (WLP's maternal grandfather), 16
Garner, John N., 235n36
Garry, Charles, 195, 198, 199
Garvey, Marcus, 34, 56, 76, 191
Gary, Indiana, 90
Gates, John, 153, 156, 162
Genocide Convention, 128, 129, 135
Gitlow, Benjamin, 6, 190–91
Glatis, John, 102
Gold, Ben, 135
Gold, Mike: Maryland's eastern shore, 53; Sacco and Vanzetti, defense of, 26, 27; WLP, 15, 26, 27, 44, 61, 65, 67
Goldblatt, Louis, 200
Golden State Mutual Life Insurance Company, 8
Goldsmith, Len, 100–101
Goldwater, Barry, 185

Goldwaterism, 185
Gomez, Juan, 65
Gone with the Wind (film), 82
Goode, Eslanda. *See* Robeson, Eslanda
Goodlett, Carlton, 207–10; and Abernathy, Ralph David, 208; and Baker, Ella, 209; Communist Party, USA, 209; and Dickerson, Earl, 180; influence, 207; international peace movement, 208; and King, Martin Luther, Jr., 278n10; NAACP, 113, 207; and Robeson, Paul, 209; Soviet Union, 209; State Department, 207; and White, Walter, 100; and WLP, 199, 207, 210, 215, 279n26
Gordon, Lottie, 168
Gorky, Maxim, 15, 45
Gorohovskaya, Vera (WLP's 2nd wife), 32
Graham, Shirley, 164, 186, 189, 217
Granger, Lester, 75–76, 113–14
Gray, Jesse, 193
Great Depression, 38
Green, Gil, 99
Gregory, Dick, 198, 213
Grimsby, England, 20, 22
Gropper, William, 104
Guess Who's Coming to Dinner (film), 8, 210

Hacker, Carl, 44
Hall, Gus: Childs, Morris, 171, 174, 175; Davis, Ben, 171, 268n106; unrest in Harlem, 193
Hall, Winston, 190
Hamburg: anticolonialism, 67; Ford, James, 36; WLP, 6, 7, 36, 43, 67
Hammett, Dashiell, 118, 137–38
Hampton, Fred, 198
Hansberry, Lorraine, 165, 212, 266n63
Harlem: Black Arts Repertory, 192; Castro, Fidel, 181; Communist Party, USA, 69, 110, 183; "Harlem Riot" of 1964, 192; ILD (International Labor Defense), 55–56; Thompson, Louise, 73; unrest, 73, 193; WLP, 8, 21–23, 27–28, 29, 47, 62, 67, 100, 132, 149
Harlem Renaissance, 84
Harlem Worker's School, 24, 59–60
Harper, Clark, 102
Harrington, Ollie, 130
Harris, Abram, 4–5, 25
Hartle, Barbara, 102, 152
Hayden, Joseph, 192
Hayden, Tom, 197
Hayes, Arthur Garfield, 26
Hayes, Roland, 35
Haywood, "Big Bill," 36, 44
Haywood, Harry: and Childs, Morris, 168; Communist Party, USA, 168; League of Struggle for Negro Rights, 61; Negro Question, 162–63; self-determination for African Americans, 34; and Stalin, Josef, 33; wife, 245n49; and WLP, 31–32, 67, 87, 111
Hennings, Thomas, 153
Herndon, Angelo, 56, 61
Herskovits, Melville, 60
Hewitt, Raymond "Masai," 199
Hill, Herbert, 113
Hill, Norman, 195
Hill, T. Arnold, 39
Hilliard, David, 196, 199
Hillquit, Morris, 63–64
Hitler, Adolf, 68, 84, 201
Hollai, Imre, 159
Holmes, John H., 74
Holt, Nora (later Nora Holt-Ray), 23, 24–25
Holtzoff, Alexander, 139
Hoover, Herbert, 5, 42
Hoover, J. Edgar: and Du Bois, W. E. B., 182; and Hopkins, Harry, 82; and Ingram, Rosa Lee, 151; and King, Martin Luther, Jr., 182; "Memorandum for the President," 141–42; and WLP, 80, 126, 127, 148, 164, 186
Hopkins, Harry, 82
Horne, Lena, 83
Houston, Charles Hamilton: Black Belt thesis, 74; and Davis, Ben, 74; death, 111; and Dickerson, Earl, 76; ILD (International Labor Defense), 3–4, 74, 100; and Marshall, Thurgood, 3, 111; NAACP, 3, 49, 62, 74, 99; Negroes and liberals, 100; and Pickens, William, 48–49; Scottsboro Nine, defense of, 48–49, 62; and Wallace, Henry A., 99; and WLP, 3, 48, 61–62, 74, 76, 114
Howe, Louise, 59
HUAC (House Committee on Un-American Activities), 113, 169–70
Huggins, Ericka, 196–97, 205
Hughes, Langston: Abraham Lincoln School (Chicago), 88; and Cunard, Nancy, 70; and Hansberry, Lorraine, 165; *I Wonder as I Wander*, 165; League of Struggle for Negro Rights (LSNR), 47, 58; Nazi book burnings, 7; Negro press, 81; *Not Without Laughter*, 36; Scottsboro Nine case, 61; and Senghor, Leopold, 183–84; *Simply Heavenly*, 165; Soviet Union, 36; and Thompson, Louise, 83, 84, 100; and WLP, 8, 25, 35, 46, 61, 88, 89, 100, 165–66, 183
Huiswood, Otto, 24
Humphrey, Hubert, 207, 213, 222n71
Hunton, W. Alphaeus, 138
Hurston, Zora Neale, 8, 83

I Wonder as I Wander (Hughes), 165
ILD (International Labor Defense), 43–51, 55–58; Alexander, Raymond Pace, 50–51; anti-Jim Crow activism, 56, 61–63, 69; antiracism, 44–45; budget, 73; Cannon, James P., 44; Communist Party, USA, 63; CRC (Civil Rights Congress), 9, 99, 101; Damon, Anna, 96; electoral politics, shaping of, 62–63; Engdahl, J. Louis, 43, 44; global connections, its, 6; Harlem, 55–56; Haywood, "Big Bill," 44; Houston, Charles Hamilton, 3–4, 74, 100; International Red Aid, 29; League of Struggle for Negro Rights (LSNR), 56; Marcantonio, Vito, 80; membership, 55–56; NAACP, 49, 50, 51, 56–58, 60, 74–75, 112; national convention (1932), 44; Negro liberation, route to, 56; Padmore, George, 74; Pickens, William, 49; "popular front" strategy, 77; Sacco and Vanzetti, defense of, 26–27; Scottsboro Nine case, 3–4, 25, 37, 41, 48–50, 57–58, 62, 69, 74–75; song about, 6; South Africa, 46; Southern juries, blacks on, 81; Stimson, Henry, 43; White, Walter, 49–50, 55; Wilkins, Roy, 74; WLP, 7, 25, 26, 37, 43–44, 55, 57, 69, 116
Immigration Service, WLP and, 67, 132
India, 142
Ingram, Rosa Lee: and Du Bois, W. E. B., 117–18; funds for defending, 137; and Hoover, J. Edgar, 151; prosecution of, 114; United Nations, 117–18; and WLP, 118, 164, 265n42
Internal Revenue Service (IRS), 126, 158, 161
International Convention on the Elimination of all Forms of Racial Discrimination, 194
International Court of Justice, 177
International Labor Defense. *See* ILD
International Longshoremen and Warehousemen's Union (ILWU), 113
International Publishers, 95
International Red Aid (IRA), 29, 68
International Workers Order (IWO), 82–83, 84, 137, 245n48
internationalism, 2, 214
interracial fraternity, 27
interracial marriage, 4, 46

Jackson, Andrew, 94
Jackson, George, 212
Jackson, James E., 208, 265n46
Jackson, Jesse, 212–13
Jagan, Cheddi, 175, 216, 270n51
Janken, Kenneth Robert, 49
Jet (magazine), 133
Jim Crow: advocates, 98, 100, 250n40; capitalism, 13; Cold War, 141; erosion/decline, 42, 182; global opposition, 10–11, 43; lynchings, 5; NAACP, 100; national security, 5–6, 109; opposition to (*see* anti-Jim Crow activism); restrictive covenants, 103; retreat from, 10; Roosevelt, Franklin Delano, 216; Scottsboro Nine case, 42; Soviet Union, 45; unconstitutionality, 10, 142; Wilson, Norman, 250n40; World War II, 98
Johnson, Jack, 83
Johnson, James Weldon, 7, 19, 25, 84
Johnson, John H.: and Burns, Ben, 97; CRC (Civil Rights Congress), 133; and Dickerson, Earl, 90; FBI agent, glorification of, 152; *Jet* (magazine), 133; and White, Walter, 114; and WLP, 9, 81
Johnson, Lyndon, 207, 212
Johnson, Manning, 34, 35
Johnson, Mordecai, 42
Johnston, Olin, 169
Joint Antifascist Refugee Committee, 152
Jones, Claudia: anti-Jim Crow activism, 189; and Ford, James, 150–51; husband, 245n49; ideological purgatory, 217; and Robeson, Paul, 177; and WLP, 140, 151, 177
Jones, LeRoi, 192
Jones, Nathaniel, 205
Jones, Obidiah, 102
Jones, Sydney, 84

Kaufman, Bob, 11
Kelley, William M., 39
Kennan, George, 71
Kennedy, John F., 183
Kennedy, Robert F., 182
Kenyatta, Jomo, 36, 46
Khruschev, Nikita, 222n71
Kilby Prison, Alabama, 51–52
Kime, Posey, 153
King, Coretta Scott, 208
King, Martin Luther, Jr.: and Davis, Ben, 12; FBI surveillance, 184; and Goodlett, Carlton, 278n10; and Hoover, J. Edgar, 182; march for integrated schools (1958), 161; NAACP, 56; National Baptist Convention, 155; Negro Baptists, 178; and O'Dell, Hunter Pitts (Jack), 174, 182; progressivism, 160; and Reese, Ruth, 208; stabbing of, 12; Western hemisphere Bandung-like conference, 159; and WLP, 159, 208, 223n73
Kinoy, Arthur, 199
Klesing, Bert, 187
Kosygin, Alexei, 210
Ku Klux Klan: anti-Catholicism, 104; armed resistance to, 127; Peekskill, New York, 104, 105; Scottsboro Nine case, 45; Subversive Activities Control Board (SACB), 151–52, 152–53; Thompson, Louise, 83; Wood, John, 151

Kunstler, William, 199
Kuusinen, Otto, 33, 34

Labour party, British, 19–20
La Guma, Alex, 205
Landis, Kenesaw Mountain, 91
Langer, William, 118, 139
Lanham, Henderson L.: outburst by, 122–23, 125; WLP, 9–10, 122–23, 138–39
Lansbury, George, 20–21, 23
Larkin, Edward, 154
Lawrence, William, 101
Lawson, James, 216
Lawson, John Howard, 26, 140, 211
League against Imperialism, 36
League of Struggle for Negro Rights (LSNR): anti-Jim Crow activism, 61; Hughes, Langston, 47, 58; ILD (International Labor Defense), 56; WLP, 47, 58
Lee, Euel, 53
Le Havre, France, 29
Lehman, Herbert, 270n51
Lenin, V. I., 23, 30, 31, 32
Leningrad, 29, 68
Lewis, Alfred Baker, 114, 212
L'Humanite (journal), 45, 163
Lie, Trygvie, 127
Life (magazine), 115
Lightfoot, Claude: and Childs, Morris, 174; Communist Party, USA, 180; CRC (Civil Rights Congress), 153; Fisk University speech, 200; "Open Letter to the Negro People" (with WLP), 189; Red Scare, 156; and WLP, 181, 208
Locke, Alain, 68
London: Robeson, Paul, 70; WLP, 29, 70, 126, 128, 131, 177, 186
London Daily Worker (newspaper), 163
Los Angeles Times (newspaper), 119–20, 184
Louis, Joe, 85, 246n70
Lovestone, Jay, 27–28
LSNR. *See* League of Struggle for Negro Rights
Luce, Phillip Abbott, 191, 192–93
Lumumba, Patrice, 185, 191
lynchings: Genocide Convention, applicability of, 135; Georgia, 122; Jim Crow, 5; Roosevelt, Franklin Delano, 86

Magee, Ruchell, 206
Magnusson, Warren, 139
Mann, Thomas, 43
Manuilsky, Dmitri, 33
Mao Zedong (Mao Tse-Tung), 176, 201, 202–3
Maran, Rene, 50
Marcantonio, Vito, 3, 80, 121–22, 138–39

Markward, Mary Stalcup, 102
Marshall, Thurgood, 110–12; anticommunist prosecutions, 252n8; and Clark, Tom, 113; and Crockett, George, 252n8; FBI informant, 110; and Houston, Charles Hamilton, 3, 111; Martinsville Seven, defense of, 111; McGee, Willie, defense of, 115; and Robeson, Paul, 149; Trenton Six, defense of, 117; and WLP, 110, 111, 112, 149
Marshall, William, 216
Martinsville Seven, 116–19; CRC (Civil Rights Congress), 117; Davis, Ossie, 210; global reaction, 10–11; Indian awareness of, 142; Marshall, Thurgood, 111; NAACP, 111; overseas protests, 116–17; play about, 210; prosecution of, 114; WLP, 4, 10–11, 111, 118–19, 144, 265n42; World Federation of Trade Unions, 116
Marx, Karl, 19, 23
Marxism-Leninism, 35
Matthews, Ralph, 11–12, 160
Mayfield, Julian, 8
McCarran, Pat, 113, 139
McCarthy, Joseph, 142
McClendon, Rose, 23
McGee, Willie, 114–16; and Abzug, Bella, 115; execution, 116; French protests supporting, 11; and Hansberry, Lorraine, 165; Indian awareness of, 142; International Workers Order (IWO), 137; *Life* (magazine), 115; Madison Square Garden rally, 119; and Marshall, Thurgood, 115; mass demonstrations, 119; overseas protests, 115–16; prosecution of, 114; State Department, 116; and WLP, 115, 119, 122, 144, 265n42; women's movement, 115
McGee, Willie, widow of, 152
McKay, Claude, 9, 29–30, 31, 35
McPhaul, Arthur, 138
Meany, George, 171
"Memorandum for the President" (Hoover), 141–42
Menon, Krishna, 130–31
Michelson, Clarina, 1, 26
Midwest Daily Record (newspaper), 79, 87, 97
Millay, Edna St. Vincent, 26
Miller, Arthur, 104
Miller, Kelly, 76
Miller, Loren, 39, 61, 84
Mills, Florence, 23
Mincey, S. S., 5
Minor, Lydia, 104
Minor, Robert, 104
Mitchell, Arthur, 76, 81
Mitchell, Broadus, 61
Mitchell, Charlene, 213

Mitchell, Clarence, 151, 212
Mitchell, Loften, 216
Mitchell, Parren, 281n85
Montiero, Anthony, 210
Moon, Henry, 7, 64
Moon, Molly, 7, 68
Mooney, Tom: and Derrick, John, 18; freedom for, 80; imprisonment, 18; Soviet Union, 46; and Whitney, Anita, 18; and WLP, 18, 24, 26, 55, 59, 235n36
Mooney, Tom, mother of, 58, 59
Moore, Howard, 205
Moore, Richard B.: African identity, 132–33; League of Struggle for Negro Rights, 61; Marxism, 24; Scottsboro Nine case, 58; and WLP, 23, 24, 61
Mora, Pancho, 214
Morley, Karen, 143
Morrison, Toni, 203
Morton, Ferdinand S., 24
Moscow: Du Bois, W. E. B., 176; Robeson, Paul, 70; WLP, 6, 7, 29, 31–32, 69–70, 72, 169, 176, 177, 178, 186, 187, 197
Moscow gold, 4–5
Mosell, Sadie, 51
Moynihan, Daniel Patrick, 213
Muhammad Speaks (journal), 194
Murphy, Carl, 39
Murphy, George: *Baltimore Afro-American* (newspaper), 206, 208–9; Black Panther Party Defense, 199; Scottsboro Nine case, 209; Soviet Union, 209; and Thompson, Louise, 209; Western hemisphere Bandung-like conference, 159; and WLP, 209, 212; Zionists monitoring of *Afro's* letter-writers, 281n85
Murphy, Rose, 18, 20
Muslim Movement, 189–90

NAACP, 110–19; affluent Negroes, 180; Alexander, Raymond Pace, 51; anticommunism, 2–4, 31, 113, 179–80, 205–6; anticommunist prosecutions, 110–19, 252n8; anti-Jim Crow activism, 48, 75, 179; Black Belt thesis, 228n38; black nationalism, 191; civil rights mobilization (1950), 113; Communist Party, USA, 110, 141, 165, 180, 191; convention (Chicago, 1933), 74; CRC (Civil Rights Congress), 99–100, 111–12, 116, 179; Davis, Angela, campaign to free, 205–6; Davis, Ben, 178–79, 180; Du Bois, W. E. B., 39, 129; Euro-American elites, alliances with, 191; FBI surveillance, 180; Ford, James, 74–75; genocide petition, 134–35; global connections, lack of, 6; Goodlett, Carlton, 113, 207; Houston, Charles Hamilton, 3, 49, 62, 74, 99; ILD (International Labor Defense), 49, 50, 51, 56–58, 60, 74–75, 112; Jim Crow advocates, 100; journal of, 39; King, Martin Luther, Jr., 56; Lewis, Alfred Baker, 212; Marcantonio, Vito, 3; Martinsville Seven, defense of, 111; membership, 55, 111; militancy, 25; National Negro Congress (NNC), 160; Padmore, George, 73; Red Scare, 109; right wing, surrender to, 110, 180, 264n25; Scottsboro Nine case, 42, 48–49, 56, 62–63, 74–75; Soviet Union, 71; Thompson, Louise, 74; Tobias, Channing, 1; trade unions, 113; Trenton Six, defense of, 111; Wilkerson, Doxey, 180; Williams, Robert, 178; WLP, 18–20, 23, 25, 49, 56, 62, 72–74, 85, 100, 109–15, 134, 140, 144, 149, 178–79; Workers' Defense League, 3
Naison, Mark, 110
Nation of Islam: Communist Party, USA, 193; as local manifestation of transnational phenomenon, 200; *Muhammad Speaks*, 194; pro-Nippon platform, 86; rise, 189; Temple of Islam, 89; WLP, 133
National Association for the Advancement of Colored People. *See* NAACP
National Association of Black Students, 206
National Bar Association (NBA), 50, 51
National Conference of Black Lawyers, 191
National Maritime Union (NMU), 150, 193
National Negro Congress (NNC): backlash against, 87; CRC (Civil Rights Congress), 99; Flory, Ishmael, 82; genocide petition, 129; NAACP, 160; "popular front" strategy, 75, 77, 87; Randolph, A. Philip, 87–88; WLP, 80, 87–88
national security, 5–6, 41, 109
National Urban League, 39, 77
NBA. *See* National Bar Association
Neal, Larry, 192
Negritude, 184
Negro American Labor Council, 178
Negro press: Associated Negro Press, 122; Hughes, Langston, 81; Marxism-Leninism, 35; Randolph, A. Philip, 81; Soviet Union, 71, 122; WLP, 148, 149
Negro Question: Comintern, 34; Communist Party, USA, 33, 93–94, 95, 142, 162–63, 168, 171, 261n49; conflation of plight of Africans and African Americans, 32; Ford, James, 151; Haywood, Harry, 162–63; international arena, 132; Lenin, V. I., 31; neglect of, 151; Pan-Africanism, 33; Stalin, Josef, 31; WLP, 34–35, 129
Negro Worker (journal), 46, 68
Negroes with Guns (Williams), 191
Nehru, Jawaharlal, 130

Nehru, Pandit, 7
Nelson, Steve, 144–45, 153
New Deal, 76, 85
New Dealers, 87
New Masses (journal), 76
New Negro, 35–36
New York Amsterdam News (newspaper), 24, 30, 39
New York Daily News (newspaper), 193
New York Times (newspaper): black racism, 190; "Free Huey" advertisement, 197; genocide petition, 133; Negro interest in Communists, 25; New York City mayoral race (1932), 63; Trenton Six, 117; WLP, 47, 147, 160, 184
New York World Telegram and Sun (newspaper), 134
Newton, Huey P., 194–203; Black Panther Party (BPP), 194; China, 201; Communist Party, USA, 203; drugs, 202, 203; and Garry, Charles, 195, 199; and Hilliard, David, 199; and Mao Zedong (Mao Tse-Tung), 201, 202–3; and Morrison, Toni, 203; *New York Times* advertisement, 197; *Revolutionary Suicide,* 202; and Seale, Bobby, 199; strong-arm tactics, 202; and WLP, 13, 195–96, 197, 199, 201–3
Newton, Huey P., mother of, 196
Nix, Robert, 60, 111
Nixon, Richard, 14, 210, 213
Nkhrumah, Kwame, 186, 200
Norris, Clarence, 41
Not Without Laughter (Hughes), 36

Oakland-Kenwood Property Owners Association (Chicago), 98
Obama, Barack, 211
O'Dell, Hunter Pitts (Jack), 174, 182, 184
"Open Letter to the Negro People" (WLP and Lightfoot), 189
Ottley, Roi, 97

Packinghouse Workers, 98
Padmore, George, 36, 46, 71–72
Pan-Africanism: Black Belt thesis, 46; Comintern, 42; Negro Question, 33; Soviet Union, 30
Paris: antiracist conference (1937), 83; Ford, James, 68; Robeson, Paul, 70; WLP, 1, 7, 67–69, 70, 83, 97, 106, 107, 126–27, 128, 129–31, 141
Parker, Dorothy, 26
Patterson, Anna (WLP's daughter), 32, 177, 214
Patterson, Eliza Laurent (WLP's paternal grandmother), 15
Patterson, Haywood, 111–12
Patterson, Jacob (WLP's paternal grandfather), 15
Patterson, James (WLP's father), 15–16, 17, 20, 61
Patterson, Lola (WLP's daughter), 32, 68, 95, 177
Patterson, Mary (WLP's mother), 16, 20, 22
Patterson, Mary Lou (WLP's daughter), 161, 184–85, 215
Patterson, Vera (WLP's daughter), 95
Patterson, Walter (WLP's brother), 17, 21–22
Patterson, William L. (WLP elsewhere): "American Negro as Revolutionist," 60; appearance, 52, 80; arrests, 18–19, 26–27, 38, 126, 132, 135, 141–49; *Baltimore Afro-American,* 2, 38, 47–48, 63–64, 75, 87, 122, 133, 161, 182, 212; birth, 7; *Black Dispatch,* 133; *Chicago Defender,* 38, 87; congressional interrogations, 9–10, 121–23; criminal contempt charges against, 81; *Daily Worker* (New York), 63; death, 2, 215–16; dress, 52; East Berlin, 205; education, 7, 17, 19, 20, 22, 23, 24, 29; FBI surveillance, 7, 10, 67–69, 75, 80, 81, 89–90, 98, 127, 128, 137, 151, 157–58, 161–69, 173–77, 184–86, 193, 197, 200, 209, 214, 223n77, 223n78; "Glorious Revolutionary Traditions of the Negro People," 47; Hamilton Hotel symposium (1944), 94; harassment by government agencies, 182; health, 19, 43, 66, 67, 73, 120–21, 128, 208, 214–15; HUAC (House Committee on Un-American Activities), 169–70; Immigration Service, 67, 132; income/finances, 21, 22, 23, 89, 157, 184, 186, 187, 200, 217; Internal Revenue Service, 158; life as a three-act play, 150; *Los Angeles Times,* 119–20; "Meaning of Little Rock" symposium, 160; "Negroes," references to in speeches/lectures, 132–33; *New York Times,* 47, 184; nickname, 24; passport issues, 29, 37, 125, 127, 135, 166, 173, 178; *Pittsburgh Courier,* 71, 155, 159; political training, 6, 7; pseudonyms, 81; public image/reputation, 2, 25, 44, 59, 192, 194; *San Francisco Chronicle,* 209; sister, 67, 70; song about, 6; State Department, 43, 65, 81, 127, 207; subpoenas, 170; Subversive Activities Control Board (SACB), 127, 144, 146, 178, 182;television appearances, 119, 176; threats against, 52–53, 152; *Time* magazine, 123; trials for contempt of Congress, 138–40, 145–46; University of Berlin, 7, 36; Western hemisphere Bandung-like conference, 159, 167, 174; wives (*see* Gorohovskaya, Vera; Sumner, Minnie; Thompson, Louise); writings, 45, 46, 81–82, 89, 127, 187, 189, 195, 212

Patterson, William L., political activism: African seafarers as couriers, 70; alliances with black business and black affluent, 8; anticolonialism, 133, 187; anticommunist prosecutions, opposition to, 110–19; antihunger marches, 37–38, 47; anti-Jim Crow activism, 1–2, 4, 178, 180, 187, 189, 193; anti-Nazi underground, 1, 7, 67; antiwar protests, 27, 28, 47; Batista of Cuba, ouster of, 167; Bill of Civil Rights for the Negro People, 59; black nationalism, 191–92; Bonus Expeditionary Force, expulsion of, 44; Chicago-area strikes, 98; civil rights, 2; Congressional campaign (1940), 81–82; criminal cases involving Negroes, transfer to federal courts, 60; Davis, campaign to free Angela, 187, 203–5; death house visits, 117, 118–19, 120; desegregation of baseball, 9, 90–91, 113; Dixiecrats, 169; electoral politics, shaping of, 62–63; fair employment practices, 207; "Free Huey" (Newton) campaign, 195–96, 199; genocide charge against Americans, 9, 119, 123, 125–37, 180, 194, 198; global connections, his, 6, 60; Herndon, Angelo, defense of, 56, 61; highlight of his political career, 187; high-powered law firms, appeals to, 153; hospital cutbacks, protests against, 59; Ingram, Rosa Lee, defense of, 118, 164, 265n42; internationalism, 2, 214; jury selection in politically charged cases, 198; labor struggles of miners and metal workers, 37; legal defense linked to mass pressure, 48; linking of local and global issues, 60, 115, 196; Lumumba's murder, protests of, 181; march for integrated schools (1958), 161; march on the White House, 41; march on Washington, 160–61; Martinsville Seven, defense of, 4, 10–11, 111, 118–19, 144, 265n42; McGee, Willie, defense of, 115, 119, 122, 144, 265n42; Montgomery bus boycott, 11; Mooney, Tom, defense of, 18, 24, 26, 55, 59, 235n36; multiracial alliances, preference for, 27; Negro business ties with Eastern Europe, 168, 173; Negro delegates to the United Nations, treatment of, 181; Nelson, Steve, defense of, 144–45, 153; New York City mayoral campaign (1932), 63–64; opposition to Tom Clark's appointment as attorney general, 113; organizing legal defense apparatus, 65; organizing protests as U.S. embassies, 68; organizing schools, 38; organizing Scottsboro defense meetings, 52; organizing workers, 36, 38; "party cleansing" by Communist Party, 31–32; "popular front" strategy, 84–85; postwar domestic policies, 93; Red Network, 60; "right of self-defense," 60; Rosenberg, Julius and Ethel, defense of, 142–43, 265n42; Sacco and Vanzetti, defense of, 1, 6, 23–24; Scottsboro Nine case, 1, 3, 5, 6, 10, 25, 41, 45, 48, 51–53, 55, 56, 160, 209; Soviet Union, solidarity with, 216; strike against *Chicago Herald Examiner*, 81; Trenton Six, defense of, 111, 117, 120, 153; unemployment insurance, 47; union activities, 82; United Nations, appeals to, 214; Wells, Robert Wesley, defense of, 120; Winston, Henry, defense of, 163, 177–78

Peekskill mob action (1949), 103–7, 142
Perry, Pettis, 96, 103
Pham Van Dong, 214
Philadelphia Tribune (newspaper), 39
Phillis Wheatley Association, 136
Pickens, William: Cuban denunciations of, 66; and Houston, Charles Hamilton, 48–49; ILD (International Labor Defense), 49; *New Masses* (journal), 76; Scottsboro Nine case, 49; and WLP, 36, 51, 76
Pittman, John, 98, 208
Pittsburgh Courier (newspaper): African American professor in Soviet Union, 71; editor, 159; publisher, 41; Vann, Robert, 98; WLP, 71, 155, 159
Pittsburgh Post Gazette (newspaper), 153
Pleasant, Mammy, 16
Poitier, Sidney, 210
Poston, Ted, 64
Powell, Adam Clayton, Jr.: and Davis, Ben, 59, 164; importance, 177; New York City Council, 59; Scottsboro Nine case, 73; and Wilkins, Roy, 74; and WLP, 59, 63, 123, 164–65
Powers, Francis Gary, 176
Powers, Hapgood, 26
Prattis, P. L., 159–60, 164
Prestes, Luis Carlos, 281n83
Price, Raymond, 46
Price, Victoria, 52
prisons: black population, 119, 136, 147, 148; Danbury Federal Prison, 141; Green Haven prison, 192; Kilby Prison, Alabama, 51–52; malnutrition, 147; Marin County Jail, 206; Sing Sing, 143; uprising in New York State (Attica), 196
Pritt, D. N., 131, 155
Proctor, Roscoe, 199
Prosser, Gabriel, 15
Pulitzer, Joseph, 151
Pushkin, Alexander, 71

racial equality, 32–33
racism: anticommunism, 3; anti-Jim Crow activism, 159; black racism, 190; Cold War,

159; erosion of, 182; interracial marriage, 4; Soviet Union, 30, 45–46; treatment of Communists, 10; WLP, 190, 192, 213, 214
Radosh, Ronald, 142–43
Randolph, A. Philip: anticommunism, 113; and Childs, Morris, 171; CRC (Civil Rights Congress), 106; and Hill, Norman, 195; isolation of Negro labor, 88; and Meany, George, 171; National Negro Congress (NNC), 87–88; Negro press, 81; Peekskill mob action (1949), 106; treatment abroad, 3; and WLP, 21, 87–88, 106, 179
Ray, Joseph, 24
Redding, Louis, 60
Redding, Saunders, 10, 61, 135, 142
Red Network, 60
Red Scare: African Americans, 208; black Communists during, influence of, 8; black rights, 217; civil rights movement, 49; Communist Party, USA, 96; CRC (Civil Rights Congress), 101–2; NAACP, 109; Peekskill mob action against CRC (1949), 103–7, 142; trade unions, 113; urban unrest (1960s), 193; WLP, 120
Reed, Ishmael, 192
Reed, John, 30
Reese, Ruth, 208
Rehnquist, William, 212
Resnick, Sid, 190, 192
Revolutionary People's Communication Network, 197
Revolutionary Suicide (Newton), 202
Reynolds, Hobson, 129
Rhodes, E. Washington, 39
Richards, Beah, 8, 149, 210–11, 216
Richardson, Beah, 8
Rickey, Branch, 114
Robeson, Eslanda (nee Goode): concert organizer, 104; New Year's Eve (1935), 70; WLP, 21, 22, 140
Robeson, Paul: anti-Jim Crow activism, 189; *Black Dispatch* (newspaper), 133; black nationalism, 191; and Brown, Lawrence, 23, 70; Communist Party, USA, 171; concert organizers, 104, 135; CRC (Civil Rights Congress), 154–55; and Davis, Ossie, 210; desegregation of baseball, 91; FBI surveillance, 163; and Friedman, Milton, 154; genocide petition, 125, 129, 131; and Goodlett, Carlton, 209; house arrest, 135; and Jones, Claudia, 177; law school, 186; London, 70; and Marshall, Thurgood, 149; "Meaning of Little Rock" symposium, 160; Moscow, 70; Negroes in possible future war against Soviet Union, 106; Packinghouse Workers strike, 98; Paris, 70; passport, 135, 142, 150, 151, 163, 170; Peekskill mob action against (1949), 104–5, 106; political commitments, 53; public image/reputation, 192; and Robinson, Jackie, 113; Soviet attacks on Jim Crow, 5; and Stalin, Josef, 114; symposium celebrating, 205; and Thompson, Louise, 135; and Truehaft, Decca (later Jessica Mitford), 162; United Nations, 129, 131; and White, Walter, 106, 114, 135; wife (*see* Robeson, Eslanda); and WLP, 2, 8, 21, 22, 23, 24, 35, 53, 61, 70, 83, 91, 98, 106, 114, 129, 132, 135, 159, 162, 163, 205, 210, 243n94
Robeson, Paul, Jr., 192
Robinson, Jackie, 113–14
Robinson, William "Bojangles," 60, 61
Roca, Blas, 4
Rockefeller, John D., 109
Rodney, Lester, 157
Rogers, J. A., 5, 145, 147
Rogge, John, 120
Rolland, Romain, 50
Roman, Meredith L., 46
Roosevelt, Archibald, 34
Roosevelt, Eleanor: genocide petition, 125–26, 133; Red Network, 60; WLP, 60, 127, 130, 134
Roosevelt, Franklin Delano: Germany, quarantine of, 85; Jim Crow, 216; lynchings, 86; Scottsboro Nine case, 58, 59; Truman, Harry, 94; Wallace, Henry A., 94; WLP, 58, 59, 76
Rosenberg, Julius and Ethel: Budapest street, 204–5; Fast, Howard, 143; WLP, 45, 142–43, 144, 145, 265n42
Rosenberg Defense Committee, 154
Ross, Nat, 52
Rothstein, Ida, 138
Rush, Bobby, 197
Rusk, Dean, 207
Russia, African Americans in Tsarist, 222n71

Sacco, Ferdinando, 26
Sacco and Vanzetti, defense of: Boston protests, 6, 26; and Gold, Mike, 26, 27; ILD (International Labor Defense), 26–27; Scottsboro Nine case, 42, 50; and WLP, 1, 6, 23–24
Sampson, Edith, 129–30
San Francisco Chronicle (newspaper), 120
San Francisco Sun-Reporter (newspaper), 209
Savage, Augusta, 8, 84
Scales, Junius, 10, 153
Schmeling, Max, 85
Schuyler, George, 72, 86, 97

Scottsboro Nine case, 41–65; anti-Jim Crow activism, 53, 69, 236n45; antiracism, 47; bias against defendants, 48; Black Belt thesis, 33; celebrity involvement, 43; Communist Party, USA, 39, 43, 49–50, 64; Cuban protests, 65; and Cunard, Nancy, 45; and Davis, Ben, 56; and Dreiser, Theodore, 58; FBI, 43; and Ford, James, 58, 220n31; and Gorky, Maxim, 45; and Houston, Charles Hamilton, 48–49, 62; and Hughes, Langston, 61; ILD (International Labor Defense), 3–4, 25, 37, 41, 48–50, 57–58, 69, 74–75; importance, 41; Jim Crow, 42; Ku Klux Klan, 45; march on the White House, 41; mobilization of public opinion, 48; and Moore, Richard B., 58; Mother's Day mobilization, 58, 59; and Murphy, George, 209; NAACP, 42, 48–49, 56, 62–63, 74–75; national security, 41; Negro bourgeoisie, 62; overseas reaction, 5–6, 42–44, 50, 160, 220n31; and Pickens, William, 49; and Powell, Adam Clayton, Jr., 73; public opinion, 48; race and gender connection, 236n45; rights, 48; and Roosevelt, Franklin Delano, 58, 59; Sacco and Vanzetti, defense of, 42, 50; sexuality, 236n45; socialism, 47; Southern juries, blacks on, 69; Soviet Union, 5–6, 46; State Department, 42, 45; and Thompson, Louise, 58, 209; and White, Walter, 49, 56, 57; white centrists, 50; and Wilkins, Roy, 6; and Wilson, J. Finley, 50; and WLP, 1, 3, 5, 6, 10, 25, 41, 45, 48, 51–53, 55, 56, 57, 160, 209

Seale, Bobby, 194–99; Black Panther Party (BPP), 194, 200, 202; campaign to free, 198; Communists, 195–96; and Newton, Huey P., 199; and Robeson, Paul, 205; whites, attitude toward, 198; and WLP, 196–97, 198–99, 202

Second Congress of the Anti-Imperialist League, 7

Second Congress of the Communist International (1920), 30

Seeger, Pete, 104, 118

segregation, Black Belt thesis and, 34

Senate Committee on Foreign Relations, 135

Senghor, Leopold, 183–84

Sengstacke, John, 164

Shakur, Afeni, 197

Shaw, George Bernard, 43

Shortridge, Samuel, 19

Sik, Endre, 32, 131

Simmons, Herbert, 179

Simply Heavenly (Hughes), 165

Sixth World Congress of the Communist International, 34

Smith, Al, 104

Smith, Asbury, 39

Smith, Ferdinand: and Ford, James, 150; ideological purgatory, 217; Red Scare, 156; WLP, 158, 166, 175

Smith, Homer, 70, 209

Smith Act, 137, 167

socialism: African Americans, 31, 39; Scottsboro Nine case, 47; WLP, 39

Socialist Party, 3, 63

Sojourners for Truth and Justice, 132

Soul on Ice (Cleaver), 199

Southern Negro Youth Congress, 82

Soviet Constitution, 265n42

Soviet Union: African Americans, 71; and Alexander, Raymond Pace, 51; American alliance with, 14; anticolonialism, 67; anti-Jim Crow activism, 5–6, 64, 67; antiracism, 64; blacks in, 38–39; Bolshevik Revolution, 23; and Carver, George Washington, 37; conflation of plight of African and African Americans, 30, 32; Cuba showdown, 183; dissolution of, 175; downfall of, 14; and Du Bois, W. E. B., 25, 71; and Ford, James, 67; and Goodlett, Carlton, 209; and Hughes, Langston, 36; international solidarity, spirit of, 38; interracial marriage, 46; Jews in, 162; Jim Crow, 45; leadership, crimes of, 11; leadership, power struggles, 70–71; living conditions, 31; and McKay, Claude, 29–30; and Mooney, Tom, 46; and Murphy, George, 209; NAACP, 71; Negro businessmen, 168; Negro press, 71, 122; nonaggression pact with Germany (1939), 86–87; Pan-Africanism, 30; "peaceful coexistence," 175, 201; pro-Negro attitude, 30; racism, 30, 45–46; recognition of, 109; Scottsboro Nine case, 5–6, 46; Sino-Soviet split, 175–76, 186, 201; Socialist Party, 3; travel to, promotion of, 71; U. S. nationals in, 71; and WLP, 24, 30, 42, 69–70, 173, 216

Sparks, Nemmy, 24

Stachel, Jack, 28

Stalin, Josef: anticolonialism, 71; black communists, 31; and Fast, Howard, 12; and Haywood, Harry, 33; Negro Question, 31; and Padmore, George, 71; revelations about (1956), 12, 31, 94, 155–56, 162, 175; and Robeson, Paul, 114; and WLP, 114, 169

Starobin, Joseph, 96, 137

State Department: Communist activities in Haiti, 65; and Goodlett, Carlton, 207; Haitian diplomats who pass for white, demand for, 81; McGee, Willie, defense of, 116;

Scottsboro Nine case, 42, 45; and WLP, 43, 65, 81, 127, 207
Stevens, Hope, 132
Stewart, Donald Ogden, 130
Stewart, Ella, 130
Stewart, McCants, 20–21
Stimson, Henry, 22, 43
Stone, I. F., 135
Student Non-Violent Coordinating Committee (SNCC), 194
Subversive Activities Control Board (SACB): Klansman on, 151–52; WLP, 127, 144, 146, 152–53, 178, 182; Wood, John, 151
Sumner, Minnie (WLP's 1st wife), 21, 22–23
Sutherland, Elizabeth, 194
Sutton, John, 36–37, 75, 209–10, 279n30
Sutton, Percy, 209
Sweets, Nathaniel, 164

Tagore, Rabindranath, 43
Talmadge, Eugene, 136
Terrell, Mary Church, 58
"Terror against the Negro Workers in America" (Gorky), 45
Thaelmann, Ernst, 43
Thomas, Parnell, 147
Thompson, Bob, 148
Thompson, Louise (WLP's 3rd wife): Birmingham, Alabama, 84; birth, 83; Catholicism, 83; and Childress, Alice, 215; Communist Party, USA, 8; Council on African Affairs, 138; Davis, campaign to free Angela, 204; and Du Bois, W. E. B., 83, 114; Harlem violence (1935), 73; hospital workers union, 157; and Hughes, Langston, 83, 84, 100; and Hurston, Zora Neale, 83; International Workers Order (IWO), 82–83, 84; and Johnson, Jack, 83; Ku Klux Klan, 83; League of Struggle for Negro Rights, 61; marriage, first, 246n56; marriage to WLP, 83–84; Marxism, study of, 84; and Murphy, George, 209; NAACP, 74; and Robeson, Paul, 135; and Savage, Augusta, 84; Scottsboro Nine case, 58, 209; Sojourners for Truth and Justice, 132; Soviet anti-Jim Crow film, 64, 246n56; Spain, 84; Spanish language, 83; as teacher, 83; University of California at Berkeley, 83; and Vishinsky, Andrei, 114
Thurman, Wallace, 246n56
Till, Emmett, 150–51
Time (magazine), 38–39, 123, 141
Tobias, Channing, 1–2, 129, 130
Todd, Oakley, 49

Toomer, Jean, 35
Touré, Sekou, 200
Townsend, Willard, 113
Trenton Six: American Civil Liberties Union (ACLU), 117; Cold War, 117; Communist Party, USA, 101; CRC (Civil Rights Congress), 117; funds for defending, 137; Indian awareness of, 142; and Marshall, Thurgood, 117; NAACP, 111; *New York Times* advertisement, 117; overseas protests, 117; prosecution of, 114; United Nations, 117; and WLP, 111, 117, 120, 153
Trotter, William Monroe, 2, 129
Truehaft, Decca (later Jessica Mitford), 103, 162, 211, 280n53
Truman, Harry S., 94, 99, 112
Truman Doctrine, 99
Tuck, William, 116
Turner, Elizabeth Mary (WLP's maternal grandmother), 16
Turner, Nat, 47
Twain, Mark, 19

U Nu, 159
Uncle Tom's Cabin (Stowe), 136
Unger, Abraham, 169
Uniontown, Pennsylvania, 37–38
United Auto Workers, 118
United Electrical, Radio, and Machine Workers, 89
United Electrical Radio and Machine Workers, 82
United Farm Equipment and Metal Workers, 82
United Nations: conference on racism and world peace, 209; CRC (Civil Rights Congress), 117, 131; and Du Bois, W. E. B., 129; genocide petition, 129, 131; Ingram, Rosa Lee, 117–18; Negro delegates to, 181; and Robeson, Paul, 129, 131; Trenton Six, defense of, 117; and WLP, 1–2, 128, 132, 181, 209, 214
United Nations Charter, 128
United Nations Declaration of Human Rights, 168
United Nations Declaration of the Rights of Children, 168
United Negro College Fund, 109
Urban League, 39, 77
urban unrest (1960s), 192–93

Vann, Robert, 41, 76, 98
Vanzetti, Bartolomeo, 26
Vishinsky, Andrei, 114

Voting Rights Act (1965), 189

Walker, Tee Walker, 182
Wallace, George, 209
Wallace, Henry A., 94, 99
Ward, Theodore, 8, 211
Washington, Freddie, 23
Washington Afro-American (newspaper), 160
We Charge Genocide (CRC), 125–26, 134, 142, 194, 203
Weinstone, William, 28, 32, 174
Welles, Orson, 89
Wells, H. G., 43
Wells, Robert Wesley, 120
West, Dorothy, 46, 246n56
Westchester County, New York, 22
White, Lulu, 100
White, Maude, 31
White, Walter: anticommunism, 50; anti-Jim Crow activism, 5; Communist Party, USA, 49–50, 111–12; CRC (Civil Rights Congress), 3; CRC (Civil Rights Congress) advertisement, 134; Cuban denunciations of, 66; and Current, Gloster, 100; genocide petition, 134–35; and Goodlett, Carlton, 100; and Hoover, Herbert, 5; ILD (International Labor Defense), 49–50, 55; and Johnson, John H., 114; and Robeson, Paul, 106, 114, 135; Scottsboro Nine case, 49, 56, 57; WLP, 140; and WLP, 50, 55, 56–57, 58, 62, 75, 114, 135, 140
Whitney, Anita, 17–18
Wilkerson, Doxey, 93, 180, 270n51
Wilkins, Roy: and Davis, Angela, 205, 212; and Davis, Ben, 178–79; and Davis, Ossie, 210; ILD (International Labor Defense), 74; and Jackson, George, 212; Muslim Movement, 191; and Powell, Adam Clayton, Jr., 74; Scottsboro Nine case, 6; Socialist Party, 3; Workers' Defense League, 3; and WLP, 56, 74, 112–13, 212
Williams, Eugene, 51
Williams, Frances, 216
Williams, Franklin, 110–11
Williams, Mrs. (Eugene's mother), 51, 52
Williams, Robert, 178, 191
Williamson, John, 159

Wilson, J. Finley, 50, 129
Wilson, Margaret Bush, 205
Wilson, Norman, 250n40
Wilson, Woodrow, 7, 129
Winchell, Walter, 133–34
Winston, Henry: and Davis, Angela, 206; and Davis, Ossie, 210; and Goldsmith, Len, 100; Harlem, unrest in, 193; overseas reaction, 177–78; and WLP, 8, 163, 177–78, 206, 208
Winter, Helen, 215
WLP. *See* Patterson, William L.
Women's International Democratic Federation (WIDF), 151, 174
women's movement, 115
Wood, John, 151
Woodson, Carter G., 208
Worker, The (newspaper), 157, 174–75
Workers' Defense League, 3, 113
Workers' School (Chicago), 80
World Congress of the Anti-Imperialist League (1927), 36
World Council of Peace, 155
World Federation of Trade Unions, 116, 155
World War I, 18
World War II: anticommunism, 91, 95, 98; anti-Jim Crow activism, 98; antiracism, 97; collective guilt, principle of, 97; ending of, 98; Jim Crow advocates, 98; as "white man's war," '86–87; WLP, 82, 86–87
Wright, Ada, 47
Wright, Bruce, 216
Wright, Richard: Communist Party, USA, 87; and Harrington, Ollie, 130; Washington Park, Chicago, 88; and WLP, 8, 130, 177
Wright, Roy, 52
Wrigley, William, 9, 91

X, Malcolm, 190, 193, 203

Yergan, Max, 68
Young, Charles (Colonel), 19, 20, 83
Young, Coleman, 194
Young, Whitney, 213
Young Communist League (YCL), 89

Zionism, 214

GERALD HORNE is the John and Rebecca Moores Professor of History at the University of Houston. His many books include *Negro Comrades of the Crown: African Americans and the British Empire Fight the U.S. Before Emancipation.*

The University of Illinois Press
is a founding member of the
Association of American University Presses.

University of Illinois Press
1325 South Oak Street
Champaign, IL 61820–6903
www.press.uillinois.edu